Girl Making

Fig 1: Ceci N'Est Pas Une Jeune Fille

After all, it is not only the writer of fiction who fuses reality with dreamlike states. This privilege also belongs, as Kafka taught, to the being-in-the-world of the modern state itself

Taussig 1997: preface.

GIRL MAKING

A Cross-Cultural Ethnography on the Processes of Growing up Female

Gerry Bloustien

Berghahn Books
New York • Oxford

First published in 2003 by

Berghahn Books

www.berghahnbooks.com

Library of Congress Cataloging-in-Publication Data

TK

British Library Cataloguing in Publication Data

A catalogue record for this book is available from the British Library

Printed in Australia
ISBN 1-57181-425-6 hardback
ISBN 1-57181-426-4 paperback

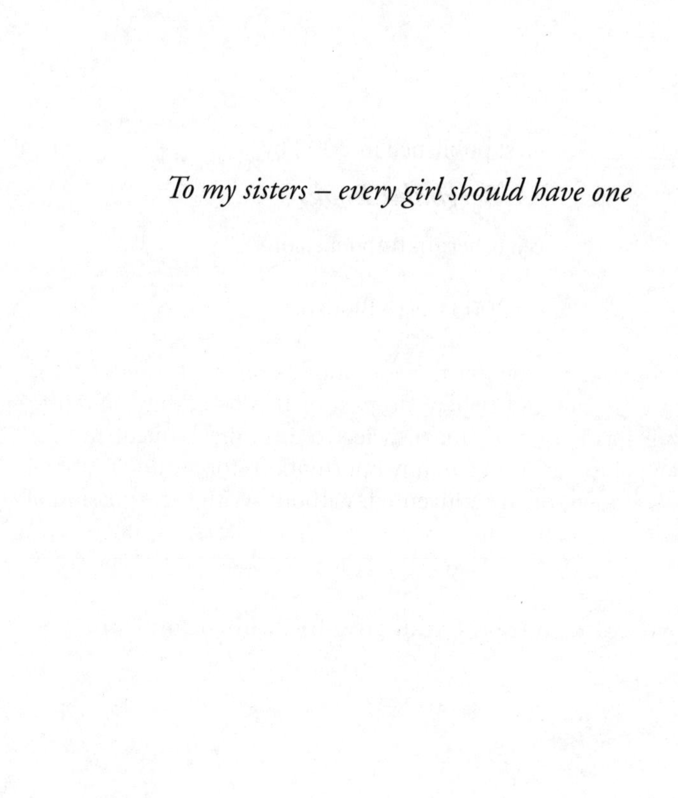

To my sisters – every girl should have one

Contents

Preface

In the wake of the moral panic which surrounded the shootings at Columbine High School in Littleton, Colorado, I made it a point to speak in as many different high schools as possible, trying to push past the media constructed stereotypes about American adolescence and engaged directly with teenagers who were coping with the heightened scrutiny that the shootings had brought. I always operated on the assumption that any school which would host me as a speaker was more progressive and open-minded than the norm, yet I was surprised how often students would chase me down as I was leaving, corner me in the bathroom or in a hallway, and tell me things that I am certain their teachers and administrators would prefer I never heard.

One day, I spoke in a progressive northeastern private school. As I was leaving, I was stopped by a bright-eyed young girl who wore glittery face paint, pastel clothing, and little pink flip-flops. "I am a goth," she said, before I could ask her name. The arch of my eyebrow must have communicated my surprise. Her bright and sparkly look was worlds removed from my own stereotypes about Goths. She explained that she used to come to school dressed all in black but that following Columbine, such attire produced too much fear and anxiety. The other kids wouldn't leave her alone until she conformed more closely to their expectations about ideal femininity. "I went under cover," she said, "I went into the closet." Looking furtively over her shoulder, she pulled a gothic-style necklace out from under her lavender and pink top to show me. "But I still wear this everyday, close to my heart," she continued, "so that I know who I am."

I don't operate on the assumption that I saw anything approaching the true or authentic self at that moment. She was acutely aware of the dramatic impact of her revelations. This was as much a performance of victimhood as the pink flip-flops were a masquerade of normality. Yet, there was a kind of emotional truth in that moment – we both recognized and acknowledged that she did not always show the world who she really thought she was; we both realized and acknowledged that some aspects of herself were at risk as the cultural climate of the school had shifted in response to very public anxieties about contemporary adolescent culture.

On another occasion, I received e-mail from a high school aged male Goth who told me that all of his life he had been treated like a 'monster' – by his parents, teachers, and classmates – and that becoming a Goth had at last allowed him to 'decide' what kind of monster he wanted to be. Dressing up in what many saw as ghoulish attire had allowed him to exert more control over how the world saw him and at the same time, had helped to identify him to others who felt the same way. Again, there is an awareness in these comments of adolescence as a performance, not simply an 'acting out,' in the sense that it is defined in opposition to adult rules and norms, but an 'acting in,' in the sense that playing roles brought one closer to self-awareness.

These glimpses of American Goth culture came back to my mind as I was reading Geraldine Bloustien's remarkable *Girl Making*. Her book explains much of what I observed, starting with her powerful consideration of adolescence as a period of 'dark play' through which identities are tried on for size, her recognition that this process involves a certain amount of risk taking and that there are real limits on who one can become and serious consequences for those who transgress those limits, her awareness of the differences and continuities between who we are in private and who we are in public. Her title says it all – adolescence is more of a process than a state.

I call the book remarkable because of the extraordinary level of intimacy Bloustien achieved with her young collaborators and the emotional honesty with which she writes about their experiences. Though Bloustien draws upon, engages with and significantly revises key theoretical formulations from cultural studies, performance studies, and anthropology, she never loses sight of the particularity of the social position and cultural identity of each of the girls included in this study. What strikes me most powerfully as I read this book is the mixture of ethical responsibility and empathic identification which allowed Bloustien to get this close to the girls, to learn things about them that they might not have shared with their friends or family, and to respect the boundaries they constructed around this knowledge. Such commitments show a level of respect for the culture of adolescence that is rare among even well-meaning researchers. Those commitments allow her to strip aside many of the myths and fantasies adults project onto teen bodies when we demonize or celebrate them within our own agendas.

Adolescence is so often depicted in terms of freedom or license – as unruly and out of control in reactionary writings about youth gone bad, as transgressive in cultural studies writings about subcultural resistance. Yet, Bloustien understands the constraints under which these teens operate -- barriers which effect them differently depending on their race, ethnicity, economic class, family situation, age, and gender. Limits are placed on who they can be, what they can say, who they can talk with, where they can go, and how they can act. She respects the choices they make as they seek ways to express themselves within and more rarely against those limitations. She shows us these young women as sometimes playing it safe, sometimes taking risks, but never fully escaping the influence of their larger social environment. She depicts certain fragile, transient moments in which they seem to assert themselves powerfully and unhesitatingly against their environments, where they command attention on their own terms, when they are able to enact their own fantasies onto otherwise institutionalized spaces. Yet she never lets us forget how short-lived these acts of resistance or self-affirmation may be, how little control they have over their immediate surroundings. In a powerful passage, for example, she shows us the gap between a young girl's sense of her room as her private domain and the observed reality of frequent family trespass into that space.

Other studies have tended to focus on one kind of youth experience, most often on members of spectacular youth cultures, and despite decades of feminist critique, more often than not on male rather than female adolescence. Bloustien's study offers us a cross-section of different kinds of adolescent female experiences, having found a methodology that allowed her to engage with girls from very different social spheres. It is striking how few of the girls in her study self-identify as members of a subculture. They see their worlds as divided into distinctive cliques and from the outside, they can identify others according to those stereotyped expectations, but as she notes, most of the girls see themselves as 'normal,' that is, as falling outside any predefined category. The word, 'normal,' suggest two seemingly competing impulses – the desire to see themselves as essentially like everyone else and the desire to define themselves on their own terms within the cracks of the social structure that surrounds them. Some of the girls have strong racial or religious identifications. Most find strong identification through their tastes for certain kinds of music or their participation in certain activities. But, they do not entirely define their identities through such affiliations, despite our tendency to place them into such categories for the purposes of analysis.

So often, writing about adolescence pathologizes fantasy and play, seeing it in terms of deception or confusion, as addiction or delusion, as rituals of resistance rather than as part of the normal process by which we come towards an understanding of ourselves and our place in the world. Bloustien respects fantasy, both in its narrowest sense (the teddy bears, elves and fairies which decorate the girl's bedrooms) and in its largest sense (the animating ideas and identities which shape their lives). Everything in our society works to hold in place fixed social identities, to define adolescents before they have a chance to explore for themselves who they are and who they want to be. Once a reputation solidifies at school, it is hard to escape. Yet, Bloustien sees adolescence as a period of becoming, offering us dynamic portraits of young women who change significantly in the course of this study.

This is in part because her methodology encourages the girls to collaborate with her in what turns out to be a highly self-reflexive process as they look at themselves and their world through the eyes of a camcorder. They highlight different aspects of themselves as they make decisions about what to film and what to edit out. Bloustien suggests that in the early stages of her research, she saw the camera as a means of accessing aspects of adolescent culture which she might not be able to experience directly and of getting the girls more actively involved and fully committed to her research process. Yet, as the girls embrace the camera, they turn it into their own tool for recording who they are at a particular moment and measuring how their sense of themselves changes over time. Bloustien doesn't see what the girls film as an authentic record but rather a careful staging of the self and thus traces not simply the finished document but the process of its making and remaking over time. The girl's selection process offers us enormous insight into the social production of meaning: they are not the victims of the camera's voyeuristic gaze but rather active collaborators "simultaneously participating within and observing their own transformation into something different."

She is sensitive to the differences between those moments they choose to keep private and those they choose to film for public consumption. Bloustien is aware of those moments where the camera seems to catch something they hadn't meant to share and those moments when the camera empowers them to behave in ways that they normally wouldn't be able to do. In this way, the camera gives her access to both private and public worlds, objective and subjective realities. Through the camera's eyes, Bloustien is able to help us see more clearly these girl's differing and evolving perceptions of themselves and their bodies, their relationships to their friends and their families, their engagement with popular culture, their interactions with both the private spaces of their bedrooms and the public spaces of their schools and the city streets. And she never looses sight of her own role in the process, the times when it matters that she is an adult and when it doesn't, the difference it makes that she comes to the project neither as a friend nor as a family member, but someone trying to understand them on their own terms. Bloustien is sensitive to the ways that others in the process see her, with parents sometimes fearing her presence as an invasion of their privacy or as a challenge to their relationships with their daughters, and other times seeking reassurance from her about the normality of their offspring. All of this is to say that the camera is anything but transparent here. The camera forces all involved to think more deeply about what happens in its presence and to reflect more fully about how they look through its lens.

Increasingly, we think of youth culture as occurring within a global context. The worldwide reach of corporate culture means that teens worldwide have access to the same songs, the same fantasies, and the same identities. They have also exploited the potential for networked computing to form virtual communities that cut across national and even regional borders. A teenager touring the world could visit almost any modern city, quickly locate where the Goths, the fly-girls, the skateboarders, or the anime fans hang out and find some shared set of references that enabled ready communication. Yet, Bloustien also wants to remind us of the very local and particularized experience of youth culture, the ways that these new fantasies get inserted into larger family and national histories, get staged in particular institutional contexts, get policed through specific governmental policies, and often serve fundamentally different needs. The closing chapters of the book pave the way for a consideration of the play between the global and the local in rethinking our understanding of youth culture.

I read this book from the perspective of a media scholar and find here enormous insights into the ways young people relate to new media technologies which enable them to actively 'author' their own experiences and reshape their identities for public consumption. Here, Bloustien gave these girls access to the cameras and allowed them to record their lives, yet increasingly, kids are taking the media in their own hands. We need more research to understand how the increased availability of such technologies in homes around the world alters the ways those teens think about themselves and the world around them. What does it mean that a teenager can produce a video record of key moments in her own life and share it with others via the Internet? What do we know about the autobiographical impulses shaping the design of their home pages? What does it mean to have a home page when, as she suggests, teens have so little space they can call their own and so little control over even those spaces that they do assert ownership over?

As one teenage girl explained to me, her homepage is "the only thing I have total control over and I like it." Another girl describes her home page as "a place where I can be free to express myself without fear of being torn down. It is a place where I can shine and be the star, and others will not be able to crush me." Here, the language speaks simultaneously to a utopian vision of the web as protected space and a dystopian vision of the threatening world she inhabits in her everyday life. Bloustien's book helps us to understand that tension – between the assertion of control and the fear of powerlessness, between the 'true self' which these teen promises we will find on her site and the performance she has constructed for others to view there. Teens speak of their home pages as microworlds, created according to their own specifications, allowing them to decide how much of themselves they choose to share with others and on what terms. As we investigate these phenomena, I hope we can find ways to discuss them with the emotional sensitivity and ethical responsibility Bloustien displays in this book.

I return to my own work having read *Girl Making* with new questions, new frameworks, and new appreciations of the challenges these youth have to overcome. She invites us to read such representations not as finished artifacts but as works in progress, constantly being remade and revised. Another teenage girl in my own research made this explicit: "Welcome to undecided. I don't know what I want in life and I am always changing my mind. Pink today may be black tomorrow." Here, the web, like the camcorder, operates as a tool for 'girl making.'

HENRY JENKINS
Centre for Comparative Media
Massachusetts Institute of Technology, 2003

Acknowledgements

It is impossible to thank individually the many people who have contributed directly and indirectly in so many ways to this project. This study would not have possible without the support, encouragement and assistance of a great many people but I want to mention some in particular.

For support, encouragement and critical insights, I want to thank Deane Fergie, Charmaine McEachern, Kingsley Garbett, Margaret Peters, David Buckingham, Anne Cranny-Francis, Henry Jenkins, Graeme Turner, Don Handelman, Mandy Thomas, Julie Mcleod, Helen Nixon, Sue Howard, Karen Jennings and Beverley Skeggs - all of whom, at different times, read, discussed and offered insightful comments on this work and gave me confidence.

I am indebted to Marion Berghahn, at Berghahn Books, as my editor and friend, for her enthusiasm for the project and her perception and insights along the production process. Together with the superbly efficient production team at Berghahn, Marion and Vivian Berghahn made the process of publishing this book suprisingly easy and indeed enjoyable. At the different stages of production, I am immensely grateful to the considerable experience, research and technical skills of Michael Bollen, Phil Gibson, Elaine Maloney, Michelle Wauchope, Stuart Dinmore, Pauline Ackland and Penelope Curtin.

The most fascinating and exciting moments of my research, of course, were due to the generosity, patience and tolerance of the ten young women, their families and friends upon whom the initial case studies are based. Their openness and acceptance of an (adult) stranger into their worlds and their willingness to intimately share so much of their everyday lives, both the moments of hilarity and quiet reflection, will be appreciated always. I learnt so much far beyond the scope of this study – although I never did learn to juggle effectively, to my intense embarrassment, chagrin and everyone else's amusement!

Thanks too to the staff and other participants at Cirkidz, Port Adelaide Girls School and the Youth Groups of Unley and Burnside Council, South Australia. Over the part two years, I have been privileged to gain the friendship of several more young people, from further afield in the US and UK, whose stories are told here. Again, the generosity of time and confidences cannot be overestimated and I am certainly humbled by all talents and the openness of all the young people I spent time with.

Clearly, the biggest dept of gratitude has to go to my family who lived this work along side of me for so many years. My wonderful children, David and Jacki, were both the inspiration and the challenge of this particular field of research. They frequently offered valuable and insightful criticism of my interpretations of so much of their teenage worlds, putting it all into a much-needed, everyday perspective.

Finally, I can never repay all I owe to my best friend and partner, Mark. He spent over ten years of his life, vicariously experiencing this project in all its various metamorphoses, sharing all the problems, the anxieties and the fun! He sometimes attended raves and often walked the streets with me in the early hours of the morning during the fieldwork; he came to many discos and rock concerts; he offered unflagging support and practical help, all with unfailing good humour, even when I was close to despair. He was my most demanding critic and always my greatest ally. For any insights and sensitivity in this book, I dedicate it to him.

Certain parts of this work have been published in other collections. Material from the Introduction appears in "Ceci N'Est Pas Une Jeune Fille", in 2002, Jenkins, H., McPherson, T. & Shattuc, J. (eds) *Hop On Pop : The Pleasures and Politics of Popular Culture,* Duke University Press. Material drawn from Chapter 1 and 3 appears in "Striking Poses: Teenage Girls, Video Cams and the Exploration of Cultural Space" *Youth Studies Australia*, 15, 3, 1996: 26-32; "It's Different To a Mirror 'Cos It Talks to You', in Howard, S. (ed.) *Wired Up: Young People and The Electronic Media,* London: Falmer Press, 1998; "The Consequence of being a Gift", *The Australian Journal of Anthropology,* Vol 10, April 1999. Material drawn from chapter 2 and 3 and 6 has appeared in "Far From Sugar and Spice", in Baron, B. & Kotthoff, H. (eds) *Gender In Interaction,* The Hague: Mouton Press, 2001; "Teddy Bear Chains and Violent Femmes", in McLeod, J. & Malone, K. (eds) *Representing Youth,* Youth Studies Australia; "On Not Dancing Like A Try Hard", in Bloustien, G. (ed.) *Musical Visions: Music as Sound Image and Movement*, Adelaide: Wakefield Press, 1999. All published with kind permission of the respective publishers. The illustrations listed overleaf are reproduced with the kind permission of their respective creators.

List of Illustrations

Introduction

Ceci n'est pas une jeune fille

> With good reason postmodernism has relentlessly instructed us that reality is artifice yet, so it seems to me, not enough surprise has been expressed as to how we nevertheless get on with living, pretending—thanks to the mimetic faculty—that we live facts not fictions. (Michael Taussig 1993: xv)

> This is not I. I had no body once—
> Only what served my need to laugh and run
> and stare at stars and tentatively dance
> on the fringe of foam and wave and sand and sun ...
> Can I be trapped at last in that soft face?
> (Judith Wright: *Naked girl and mirror*)

> *The most important thing for me is to retain my childhood for as long as possible.* (Hilary, at age 17)

An example of "dark play"

I see Hilary's face every week, as she, now as a young adult and law student, writes a regular column for a national newspaper. Callie died from a heroin overdose in 1998, when she was 19. I can only see her face again if I look at my fieldwork photographs or at her friends' videos. Two very different young women who, in their mid-teens, were participants in my research project and whose stories are presented in these pages. The last time I saw Callie was in 1996 at the private screening of our collaborative video, *Striking poses*, surrounded by fellow participants, friends and family, looking excited and thoughtful. She also looked that way when I first met her at the beginning of my fieldwork; she was a regular participant of Cirkidz, Bowden Brompton Youth Circus, a community-based youth arts organization that would play a central role in my study of young women and identity. On my first visit, the staff pointed her out as one of their most talented trapeze artists. She would have stood out in any case, I suspect, as she was also exceptionally attractive, talkative, popular and seemingly brimming with self-confidence. It was not until quite some time later that I was to realize just how vulnerable she was.

Yet the tragedy of Callie's death cannot be entirely dismissed as completely unexpected: all of the young people in my study were vulnerable to a lesser or greater degree – even Hilary who, even then, seemed so self-assured and self-contained. They were all desperately engaged in a delicate balancing act of discovering who they were – within a limited range of possibilities. I use the word "limited" advisedly for, despite shelf after shelf of self-help books and magazines all claiming that life's possibilities are many and endless, these teenagers knew instinctively, as do most of us, that their worlds were symbolically constrained. Every move, every expression of taste, every thought was an articulation of the social and cultural mores in which their lives were embedded, and in which they themselves had huge emotional investments. The tension and the difficulty of "growing up" emerges from this struggle of testing out those values and "emotional investments" while anxiously trying to remain safely within familiar boundaries.

This book is an integrated collection of the stories and voices of ten young women living in late modernity doing just that. Within their narratives, this anxiety of selfhood emerges as a recurring thread and an everyday occurrence, highlighting the way identity is a process, and demonstrating the roles that play and self-representation take in its ongoing constitution. The anxiety of selfhood was not, however, one that the young women necessarily tackled headon; rather, it was a tension explored through a continual process of embodied play and fantasy, an exploration of image and possibilities. Furthermore, this process of "self-making" through play (Batagglia 1995), was used by every girl, in spite of apparently clear differences in ethnicity, class and material circumstance. Play in this conception is understood to be a fundamental human activity, a process of representation and identification. In popular discourse, "play" has become synonymous with childish behavior, trivial actions we (should) outgrow as we reach maturity and adulthood. Yet the play described here is deadly earnest and is not limited to this particular set of young women. It is integral to all human activity throughout life; it is one of the fundamental ways in which all of us deal with uncertainty (Handelman 1990). When we trivialize the process, we call it "play"; when it becomes part of our more formal public institutions, we call it "ritual" (Schechner 1993). In Western cultural traditions, play has become separated from "the real" work of life. It has come to mean escapism, an expression of freedom from institutional obligations and structural constraints. With the huge shift in ideas characterizing late modernity, belief in certainties and notions of universal truths have increasingly wavered and fractured. Correspondingly, our understandings of the self and reality have splintered into incoherence and anxiety. Our reliance on play to deal with these complexities has become even clearer and more urgent.

The following chapters will describe how each young person struggled to explore the limits of her world, to negotiate these contradictions, pushing out the boundaries through her play. Most of the time, each girl's explorations could be likened to the deliberate stretching of a rubber band testing the limits of its tension – but being careful not to allow it to snap. Part of the pleasure and the thrill of such testing, however, is the knowledge that such play is potentially dangerous, that the metaphorical band can break and the game is over. The narratives of the young women described here illustrate this phenomenon, with Callie's tragedy representing the most extreme consequences. Such incidents are what Taussig has called "mimetic excess" (1993) – the potential danger and threat of mimesis. Schechner (1993), and Handelman and Schulman (1997) have referred to the same phenomenon as "dark play." Most of the time, however, the young people in my research project avoided such dangers, establishing careful strategies of containment, using humor, fantasy and parody to control the boundary-checking processes and to prevent potentially dangerous situations.

Bourdieu refers in his work to this personal investment and strategy as "a sense of the game" (1993; see also Bourdieu & Wacquant 1992). The game analogy is apt because we all understand that the "rules" or regulations we adhere to or impose upon ourselves are arbitrary but necessary if we want to be considered "serious players" in the various social fields, domains and arenas of life. Observance of these "rules," which apply to clothing, mannerisms, argot, food tastes, and music, demonstrate both to ourselves and to others that we are legitimate members of the particular segment of society, club, or grouping to which we aspire. But the rules are not fixed – they only appear to be – they are constantly being contested such that we spend our lives trying to make sense of our allegiances and our sense of self – challenging, representing and (re)creating as we go – striving to establish that elusive sense of selfness, "the real me," struggling, in the journey through adolescence towards maturity, to know exactly what to believe and who to trust. No wonder Hilary, in the epigraph to this chapter, "wants to retain her childhood for as long as possible."

The role of representation

Photographic images are crucial to this struggle, for they underpin the ways in which we learn to understand our worlds and our own places within them, enabling us to see ourselves as others see us. They are certainly central to the ways in which the young women in this story viewed their worlds and negotiated their own places within them. Take, for example, the photograph overleaf. It belongs to Kate, one of the young women in my project, and was taken several years ago at the beginning of my fieldwork.[1] It is a self-portrait, although taken by a third party under Kate's direction. Kate and her friend are wearing cosmetic masks and are gazing intently in a mirror observing the transformation. The photograph immediately high-lighted two important issues to me: firstly, I was aware that these two teenagers were simultaneously participating in and observing their own transformation into something different, something "other," while we, the spectators, voyeuristically looked on. Secondly, the teenage girls seemed acutely aware of the power of the camera, the image being taken under their direction and not mine.[2] It seemed that, through their rhetorical question – "Aren't we beautiful?" – and most of all, through their play, they were demonstrating their awareness that learning to be female and "performing" femininity is "hard work".[3]

Kate comes from a home where it might be assumed that such "performing" or learning was easier than for most. Her parents are highly educated, articulate people, both university lecturers, who sought to give Kate a sense of her own personhood. She is bright, and adventurous, attends a single-sex high school founded on feminist principles. The choice of school was hers, in contrast to many other students there, whose parents, she told me, had made the choice. Her surname, different from that of her parents, was deliberately selected for her and taken from a pioneering female ancestor – a symbolic gesture to give Kate a sense of her own identity and opportunities in life.[4] Yet even for Kate, particular gender regimes (Connell 1987) are entrenched and inscribed into the institutions of her life – ways in which she has learned to see herself as a developing woman, not simply a developing adult. If she seems to be gazing at the mirror quizzically and reflexively in this photograph, she was nonetheless adapting and playing with her image in an attempt to suit or contest the perceived hegemonic demands of her world. Because her world, like most people's, is constituted by not one but many intermeshing and often contradictory "domains" or "fields" (Bourdieu 1993), her attempts are carried out through endless strategies and readjustments.

My own strategies and adjustments

Through my own early experience as an (immigrant) woman, a teacher, and a mother of a teenage son and daughter, I too employed many strategies and readjustments. One of my strongest memories of my immigration and integration into Australian society was my sudden awareness of my physical difference. I was not tall, blonde and blue-eyed, but rather, dark-skinned, shorter than average and had a body shape far more "at home" in Central Europe. I was continually asked where I had come from, the implication being that it had to have been from somewhere else! It was an unexpected lesson in seeing myself as different, as "other," in ways that I had not before.

Twenty years later, I found I relived this sense of otherness, identifying as I do with my teenage daughter's difficulties with self-image. Having raised both of my children according to my interpretation of feminist principles and assertiveness, I noticed with concern their different levels of self-esteem as they both reached adolescence. From being a confident and very assertive child, my daughter, as she grew older, became insecure, obsessed with her body image and (as she saw it) her inadequate intellectual abilities. It seemed to me that she and many of her female friends struggled with a difficult balancing act. The discourse integral to their school and their social circles suggested a very particular, narrow way that she and her peers felt they could acceptably identify as both female and successful. She did not feel she fit the desired *mold*, a particularly apt metaphor because notions of physicality, body shape and image predominated.

At her school her physical appearance immediately seemed to mark her as different and distinctive, but with negative connotations – despite the school being characterized by a range of children from diverse ethnic backgrounds. Furthermore, success at school for my daughter and her friends seemed to depend heavily on relationships – same-sex friendships and boyfriend–girlfriend alliances – rather than on academic achievements. Without being perceived and acknowledged as popular and at ease with one's body, it seemed one could not be seen as successful intellectually. While this rule appeared to apply to both sexes, girls appeared to experience the phenomenon more acutely. I soon realized that my daughter's experience was not an isolated one. In our media-saturated society, "it is women who more often than not are the 'imaged' in our culture" (Walters 1995: 22). Women have a particular relationship with cultural texts and cultural icons and the contradictory representations of women are particularly significant in the shaping and constructing of commonsense understandings of femininity: women's bodies and lives not only are central in the most obvious visual forms of pornography but are in more subtle ways also – through the advertisement, the melodrama, the soap opera, the music clip.[5]

Having taught over the years in three high schools – one coeducational and two single-sex institutions – I found the same story repeated and amplified. While boys also seemed to face problems of socialization, the difficulties of "gender relations" (Connell 1987) seemed to have particularly long-term implications for young women.[6] The problem is not so much why certain "myths" about femininity, or even adolescence, persist and exist side by side, but as Ortner and Whitehead point out, "precisely one of understanding why certain 'realities' emerge in cultural thought in distorted forms, forms which in turn feed back and shape those realities" (1986: 10).[7]

I began the research underpinning this study for my doctorate in Anthropology at Adelaide University in the early 1990s. This was to be a longitudinal study, with at least 15 months of intensive participant observation. In fact, as the research project expanded and developed, it covered a span of nearly ten years, long after the original doctoral project was completed. The final stage was an exploration of "global girlhood," complementing the earlier study with work undertaken overseas and online, as I detail in the final chapter. The overall focus remains, however, on the ways in which young women from diverse social groupings and cultural backgrounds come to negotiate the difficulties and contradictions of growing up gendered within their own worlds and from their own perspectives. The age group of most interest to me was that of 15 to 18-year-olds. Research in this age group interested me significantly since, in Western cultures, it is during these years that an individual is popularly recognized as moving from childhood to maturity and thus adulthood. With that transition come new expectations, new responsibilities, new demands. Several social and legal infrastructures underpin these stages; for example, in Australia at 16 a young person can gain a driver's license and at 18 can legally enter a licensed premises and purchase alcohol. Sixteen also marks the entry into senior high school, and although legally a minor until 18, a youth can engage in heterosexual intercourse and can be legally married without parental consent – but cannot vote.

In the lived everyday experiences of the young women in my own study, it quickly became apparent to me that their respective personas could not be reduced or attributed to one particular element of cultural or social identity; rather, the various strands of class, gender and ethnicity were not only inextricably intertwined, but even more importantly, each also constantly jostled for importance and dominance, depending on the particular situation and circumstance. It is the exposure and discussion of these moments of slippage, of the fissions occurring between the attempts of cultural closure that makes this study innovative and unique. As I demonstrate throughout this work, "social classes do not exist . . . What exists is a social space, a space of differences, in which classes exist in some sense of virtuality, not as something given but as *something to be done*" (Bourdieu 1998: 12, emphasis in the original).

Because of the difficulty of entering into teenage groupings on anything other than a superficial level, most previous researchers have relied on observation, interviews and questionnaires for their information and based their research site on easily accessible public spaces, such as schools, youth clubs and dance halls. The study of teenage girls presents an extra dimension of difficulty for the researcher. For a long time the assumption has been that for girls, the domestic sphere, and particularly the bedroom space within the home, is highly significant as a rich symbolic space, being less threatening than the public sphere (McRobbie 1994). Yet what became clear in my fieldwork, in the transaction between private and public social space through the eyes and representations of the young women themselves, was that every geographical place is actually experienced as a space of power relations (Duncan 1996). Space is implicitly gendered, exclusive and contradictory, having therefore significant, concomitant implications for how an individual uses and believes she can use her surroundings. While the bedroom spaces were indeed arenas of great personal significance, they still reflected the wider underlying power relations already integral to the life of the teenager. Furthermore, even within each girl's circumstance, what constituted public and private spaces was not uniform: for some girls, the notion of private or personal space was a right. For others, the concept simply did not exist.

Research process—the eye ('I') of the camera

The ten young women whose voices and stories constitute this work were deliberately drawn from diverse ethnic and socioeconomic backgrounds. To enable me to explore and discover the unique lived worlds of these girls, I invited them, over a period of fifteen months, to document on video any aspect of their lives that they wished, selecting, filming and editing whatever they chose. The invitation in essence was to "play" with the camera, using it to explore their worlds freely. The original methodological aim was to provide a way for me, as a middle-aged academic, to get to know the girls and their worlds from their own perspectives. The camera I selected was the smallest but most advanced technologically available—a Hi 8, compact video-cam. Later, as the technology became more readily available and affordable, I used, in the investigations of the worlds of other girls in Indiana (United States) and in London, an even smaller digital camera. The reason for the choice of technologically advanced cameras was their capacity to be used without lights and external microphones, therefore intruding as little on the girls' lives as possible. Subsequently several of the girls confirmed that it was the compact nature of the camera that gave them a sense of confidence and freedom to experiment.

As I had assumed, the camera was able to enter into the girls' normally closed domestic or exclusive social spheres – places I was unlikely to be invited. I did not require that the girls show me their footage, only requesting they discuss it with me. In fact all of the participants were happy to share what they had captured on camera and often I was invited to be present at particular times and places, as I detail in the following chapters.

Moreover, I had envisaged that the incorporation of the camera into my fieldwork, under the control of the young participants themselves, would allow an element of reciprocity – I was not simply plundering the cultural world of my participants: I also had something to offer. For many of the girls it was their first opportunity to experiment with expensive technology, using it as they wished. The range of stylistic approaches adopted by individuals on various occasions was broad, from the ways that reflected their knowledge of music video to parodies of David Attenborough–style documentaries or mock current affair formats investigating this strange breed of the human species – "the teenage girl." At other times there were more serious attempts to document the fun or the more reflective moments on camera, the movement and often the excitement of particular social events being captured through hand-held camera techniques – the camera became the focus of the activity rather than being a voyeur. Toward the end of the first fieldwork period, I suggested to the participants that, if they wished, they could select a small amount of their footage that could be edited into a collaborative documentary for public viewing. It was an offer they all accepted in spite of the difficulty of the task. Selecting one minute from hours and hours of footage taken over a period of three years was no mean feat. The task also meant that I had access to another layer of analysis I had not originally anticipated.

What did I hope to learn from the girls' videos of themselves and their lifeworlds? Firstly, there was the broader social context of their video production. Underpinning the representations were the domestic and public worlds of the girls that I gradually came to know well as a regular visitor and a recipient of the generous hospitality and friendship gained over the long fieldwork period. It is important to realize that, in an attempt to understand their "realities," their perceptions of their worlds as they articulated, or failed to articulate them, the everyday lived experiences of ten teenage girls were explored through their own eyes.[8] In each case the key participants were centers of their worlds; their stories were told from their perspectives but circling around them were their close friends and acquaintances, their families, their caregivers, and for some, particularly significant authority figures–representatives of youth social services, the juvenile justice system and the law courts. As I took the camera to each girl's home, viewed footage, chatted with family and friends over coffee, or took up invitations to join them at particular social events, I learned a great deal about how they, their families and their friends viewed their worlds within their wider social networks. In addition, where possible, I accompanied the young people outside their homes. When Janine and her friends had rock band practices, I offered my services as an official photographer and a "gofer," running to purchase snacks and drinks in between sets. In Cirkidz, I would join the teenage groups for rehearsals and exercise, and attempt, totally unsuccessfully, to juggle. Pat was heavily into the "rave" scene, and at her invitation, I accompanied her to raves. On occasion I wandered the city streets at night with either Mary or Grace. As I describe in chapter 2, as an adult woman entering into the teenage world, I repeatedly had to confront the extreme physicality of this world. I had forgotten in my own adult socialization how much I had learned to control and contain bodily action. As I engaged more intimately with the teenage world I realized that I had to "unlearn" my adult body; I had to learn again to be more relaxed, to be "silly." On such occasions as I entered into the spirit of the events, I found I would forget my age and felt as though I fitted in with the young people (my own moment of mimesis?). My age only became an issue when my presence was noticed and drawn attention to by other outside figures, usually other adults.

The second significant aspect of the use of the camera in this process concerned the way in which the camera interpreted and redefined the girls' worlds. Because the girls were directly involved in telling their own stories on video – selecting, framing, filming and editing the footage themselves – an examination of the way they chose to interpret, negotiate, and challenge their perceptions and explore their developing sense of self, as well as their relationships with the various social institutions, thus became possible. How the girls acknowledged their social and cultural constraints was clearly demonstrated through the perceptual frames and boundaries they adopted in the task of videoing their worlds. Not everything in their world, it seemed, was for public viewing; not everything was selected for recording in the first place. The selection, the filming and the editing processes highlighted their struggles to represent themselves in ways that cohered with their already established social and cultural frameworks. On the surface such attempts at representation, such as Kate's, seemed like "just play" but with closer scrutiny we can identify specific strategies, "the human seriousness of play" (Levi-Strauss 1972; Goffman 1970; Turner 1982; Handelman 1990) providing insights into the ways gendered subjectivity are negotiated and performed. A brief explanation of these theoretical frameworks is useful here.

Theoretical frameworks

For the young women in my research project, as for most people, cultural identity has, since the onset of the information technology age, become something that is constantly in flux, a project continually and impossibly in the process of completion. The camera, the video, the computer, and all their related technologies have increasingly demonstrated that what we understood as reality and capable of being "objectively" represented is in fact constituted through its representations. From this perspective, as the usual economically determined model of class and gender become inadequate, related notions of subjectivity have to be reevaluated. Most useful for this purpose is Pierre Bourdieu's conception of "field" and "habitus" (1977; 1993), in which he uses an extended metaphor of a game to explain his theory of social reproduction. "Field" is the term he applies to the social spaces we live in that are not simply physical, but more importantly, symbolic arenas continually open to potential and active change. Rather than the impoverished notion of "society," he suggests the concept of an amalgam of relatively autonomous, but overlapping spheres of "play" or "fields." As in any game, each field, constituted by its own values and principles, possesses two main properties. Firstly, there is a pattern of objective forces, which resembles the *structure* or *rules* of a game: "a relational configuration endowed with a specific gravity which it imposes on all the objects and agents that enter into it" (Bourdieu & Wacquant 1992: 17). The dynamics of the actual game itself occupy a place alongside – a site of conflict, a relational (not irreducible to a physical) arena where participants struggle to establish control over the specific forms of economic, cultural and symbolic capital that function within it. This perpetual struggle and competition exists not only *between* but also *within* fields yet, to the participants themselves, everyday social life usually seems ordered and structured. This is partly because every individual possesses an embodied structuring mechanism, or "habitus" that is "neither strictly individual nor in itself fully determinate of conduct" (Wacquant, in Bourdieu & Wacquant 1992: 18). It designates "a way of being, *a habitual state* (especially of the body) and in particular, a *disposition, tendency, propensity*, or *inclination*" (Bourdieu 1977: 214, emphasis in the original). Through the internalization of external structures, each person's habitus responds, within a relatively coherent and systemized pattern, to the various demands of each social field in which the individual is engaged. This result is both structured and dynamic, a manner of behaving which is a "historically constituted, institutionally grounded, and thus socially variable, generative matrix" (Bourdieu & Wacquant 1992: 19).

In these ways the notions of "field" and "habitus" cannot be understood as separate from each other but are as closely related as two sides of one coin. It is important to realize that a field is not analogous to an empty geographical place, but is always a space of play that exists only to the extent to which players who enter into it have the emotional investment and the determination, the propensity and the ability to continue to pursue its goals (Bourdieu 1989). The notion of habitus in turn depends upon the structure that permits such agency. The relation between the social agent and the world is one of mutual "possession" (Bourdieu 1989: 10) or, expressed another way, "the body is in the social world but the social world is in the body" (Bourdieu 1982a: 38).

The sense of order we all experience within our lives, despite our anxieties about self and meaning, comes also from the way the structure of any field is determined by the current state of the power relations among those individuals and the institutions engaged within it. On occasion the power relations are relatively stable over a long period of time. In these instances, structural and power relationships appear to be more stable and less arbitrary than they really are, symbolic and cultural capital (Bourdieu 1993) manifesting themselves as the legitimate and the "authentic." In the following chapters, I will demonstrate how capital and notions of "authenticity" are legitimized in the everyday social practices of the young women; for example, when they use the notion of "coolness" as a form of symbolic capital. In this context I will also show how the word has differently refracted connotations according to the particular fields in which the girls are engaged.

Finally, social fields should be understood as systems of power relations independent of the people whom these relations define (Bourdieu & Wacquant 1992: 106). This means (returning to the original metaphor of game) that undoubtedly an individual will be engaged in playing several "games" at the same time, although the particular position in the field will change according to their particular investment in that specific state of play. For example, the Aboriginal girls in my fieldwork saw themselves variously as young *women* as opposed to young *men;* as young *Aboriginal* women as opposed to *Anglo–Australian* young women; as young Aboriginal *rock musicians* as opposed to Aboriginal *young women;* as Aboriginal *youth* as opposed to Aboriginal young *women.* These concepts of nuanced distinction (Bourdieu 1984) and "différance" (Derrida 1973, 1978) with their manifestation as "serious play" (Handelman 1990) and their application to my research project will be elaborated through the ethnographic detail and analysis constituting my fieldwork.

Play as strategy

The concept of play used here is closely tied to identity and notions of self, and is a means for dealing with uncertainty. As noted earlier, contemporary concepts of play are aligned to notions of the unreal, the invalid, the false. Thus play is often conceived of as "light," "trivial," "free" activity in contrast to notions of "heavy," "obligatory," "necessary" "work."[9] Before industrialization, however, while a distinction was made between the sacred and the profane, work itself was not separated from leisure and had, in all its senses, elements of "play" (Handelman 1990). In Western cultural traditions, as we began to believe more rigidly in certainty and in fixed and maintainable (symbolic) boundaries, play has become trivialized through rationalist understandings of the world. Play from this perspective is synonymous with leisure; it has come to mean the freedom from institutional obligations and also the freedom to transcend structural constraints, "to play with ideas, words, with fantasies, with words . . . and with social relationships" (Turner 1982: 7). Yet late modernity has awakened greater possibilities for play because those former boundaries are now perceived as less solid and fixed.

In this context therefore, I am arguing for a concept of embodied play as strategy, one that equates with pleasure but not with triviality. I am utilizing the concept of "strategy" in a very particular way, not to indicate any clear intentionality or "resistance" to hegemonic forces, but rather to indicate attempts to work within perceived or internalized structural constraints, which are used "to designate the objectively orientated lines of action which social agents continually construct in and through practice" (Bourdieu & Wacquant 1992: 129). From this perspective, play involves uncertainty, something that can be threatening and disturbing, which makes it a very powerful medium indeed.[10] It has "the potential to meddle with, to disturb . . . Subversive, it can rock the foundations of a given phenomenal reality by making their presumptions uncertain and unpredictable" (Handelman 1990: 70). Furthermore, a close affinity exists between play and terror, which also underlies Taussig's concept of mimesis, explicated in later chapters. Eugene Fink argues that: "Play can contain within itself not only the clear apollonian moment of free self-determination but also the dark dionysian moment of panic self-abandon" (1968: 25, cited in Handelman 1990: 767). It is precisely because play is so powerful and unsettling that it requires licence, a freedom to be able to state or imply that "this is play," "this is not real" (Bateson 1972; Handelman 1990).[11]

The power of play and mimesis

Drawing inspiration and insights from Handelman (1990), Bourdieu (1977, 1993), Bourdieu and Wacquant (1992), and Taussig (1993), I am using the concept of play here to describe a particular process of representation: strategies that incorporate, reflect on, and depict the individual everyday experiences and perspectives of growing up female in Adelaide, South Australia, in the mid-1990s. I am fascinated by the creative power of representation and play, and particularly concerned with the role that self-conscious representation, reflexivity, or posing played in the search for and portrayal of (self) identity for the teenage girls in my project, and how their own representations become "fact" for them. While the form of such searching can appear deceptively light, seemingly a playing with roles and images, in late twentieth century post-industrial society – especially as young people experience it – it can be an earnest endeavor. Wearing several hats and adopting a number of different poses is a matter of serious "work, even desperate work in their play" (Willis 1990: 2). The introduction of the camera in my fieldwork offered this symbolic space to play (Schechner 1993), to experiment. Simultaneously, as I shall detail throughout the following chapters, it highlighted the difficulties and constraints the girls experienced in their everyday world in their search for different strategies to "strike poses."

Participants as "filmmakers"?

The ten "key" participants in my fieldwork; that is, the ten young women who were directly involved in telling their stories on video, came from different areas of Adelaide, from a variety of socioeconomic backgrounds and from different familial situations and expectations. While they by no means represented the diversity of adolescent young women, each one of them engaged in the same kinds of strategies, comparable processes and ways in which they "re-presented" themselves through play both on and off the camera, thereby constituting their sense of realities. There were many ethnic groups that were not represented in my small diverse group of participants; however, I was looking at process and discovered that all the young women in my research engaged in the same processes, the same "strategies" of play.

Each individual struggled to establish a vitally important sense of uniqueness and difference while simultaneously grounding her view of the world within her already established social milieu. Conformity continually jostled with distinction, involvement with distanciation. Each girl needs to be seen not as a free-floating individual but as one who, in her own perception, is at the center of her own social network. It is this crucial nexus, this relationship between the elusive "real me" she strives to realize through play, and the "me" embedded within a web of social and cultural understandings and constraints, which I explored in my research.

The key participants were Sara, Fran, Kate, Hilary, Janine, Grace, Mary, Pat, Diane and Claire (not their real names), their ages ranging from 13 to 16 years at the beginning of the fieldwork period. Of these ten, six were from Anglo–Celtic[12] backgrounds; Janine identified as *Nunga*, South Australian Aboriginal; Mary was from Papua New Guinea; Fran had an Indian background, and Sara was born in Nepal. Only Kate, whom we met at the beginning of this chapter, came from what "traditionally" would be described as a highly educated, middle-class home. The others came from homes where the education levels and class positions were not nearly as clear-cut. The definition of what constituted a "family" for these girls revealed a complexity belied by the relative simplicity of government census forms. Four of the homes consisted of single-parent families, although there were frequently several adults living in the same household; two of the girls were officially under the care of the state, residing in foster homes; another two were living with one biological parent and a stepparent, some with additional siblings, who came and went at different times, from blended families, while two others were living with both biological parents. At the beginning of the fieldwork one girl was living independently but during the period of the fieldwork another of the girls moved out of her home and into a house with several other friends. Also over this time several household situations changed – exacerbated by unemployment or changes in relationships, reflecting the fluidity of social relatedness in many of the girls' lives.

In all cases, the participants' friendship groups, acquaintances and household members constituted other networks that directly and indirectly informed the study, adding an essential depth and richness. For example, Mary's friendship network was extremely wide because much of her day was taken up in the city itself. Her cohorts were often young people who spent most of their time on the streets, their activities involving alcohol and drug abuse, theft and property damage. Several had been in the juvenile detention center before I met them or were arrested during the time of my fieldwork. Mary herself was arrested for robbery with violence during this time. Another participant spent a great deal of her spare time involved with Cirkidz, a youth arts organization originally formed to teach circus skills to disadvantaged young people in Adelaide. Her social life completely centered on the young people she knew through the circus school and their friends. Thus, through her and through her video, I met and developed friendships with another group of diverse young men and women.

The centrality of these familial and social contexts to the way the participants viewed and negotiated their sense of personal gendered identity within their wider cultural milieu – that is, the influence of their familial and social networks on the quality and effectiveness of their play – is the key theoretical framework of this study. It was the very specific ethnographic methodology itself, the incorporation of the camera within the wider participant-observation process, which both allowed access to this "core context" and, through the videos, demonstrated its significance as the research developed. The girls' completed films were thus a foreground to a much wider, more complex background, two interconnected parts of one whole. Wagner notes that from out of every experience of the world there emerges a particular clarifying, interpretative framing perspective, the foreground that rises out of the chaotic background of everyday "sticky" existence (Wagner 1975). Similarly, my participants placed specific conceptual frames around their own understandings of their own lives in their self-conscious reflexivity, and in their attempts to make their videos. It was an interpretative perspective from which emerged differences and pluralities of attitude and behavior. The resultant insights, highlighting the particular and the local, emphasize the inappropriateness of talking about "youth culture" or even "teenage girl culture" as though it were uniform and global. In a similar way, Bourdieu points out the inappropriateness of assuming homogeneity across what are in fact, facets of different social fields. In terms of the category of youth and youth subcultures, he argues "that age is a biological datum, socially manipulated and manipulable; and that merely talking about 'the young' as a social unit, a constituted group, with common interests, relating these interests to a biologically defined age, is in itself an obvious manipulation" (Bourdieu 1993: 95).

The unusual methodology of incorporating a deliberately self-reflexive camera within participant-observation and other fieldwork strategies, allowed me to move beyond the traditional ways that young people, and particularly female adolescents, have been previously studied within their various cultural contexts. Rather than assuming a similarity based on class, ethnicity or gender, or focusing on what has been termed a particular "youth subculture," I have explored difference and related that difference to the way identity itself, refracted through gender and ethnicity, is considered and subsequently constituted. It is the concealed – the differences within what at first sight, seem to be socially or symbolically bounded groups – that should demand our attention. Essential to this project was an examination of what it means for young people from different cultural backgrounds to grow up in the same society and how this impacts on their own perspectives. An analysis such as this requires contextualization by a simultaneous examination of the material living experiences that the young people face (including the effects of class, gender and ethnicity) and an equally rigorous reflexive concern with the research process itself, since the researcher also is a historically constituted subject. In this way the taken-for-granted constraints and values, "that which cannot be said," as well as the more obvious concerns and issues that are discussed and challenged can be revealed. The result is a dialectic, an understanding of "the double reality of the social world which weaves together a 'structuralist' and a 'constructivist' approach" (Bourdieu & Wacquant 1992: 11). The two moments of analysis should not be seen as equal, for greater weighting must be accorded to the material conditions over the agent's subjective perceptions of them since "the viewpoints of agents will vary systematically with the point they occupy in objective social space" (Bourdieu & Wacquant p.11; see also Bourdieu 1984, 1989). Such a complex analysis clearly requires a move away from the usual methodologies as well as calling for more complex theoretical frameworks.[13]

Problems with texts

This study is unique in that it also reassesses the meaning of popular culture in the lives of the young people. Everyday lived experiences are often analytically reduced to the way individuals "interact" with media and cultural products, a practice highlighting a persistent difficulty in social science research projects generally, particularly prevalent in cultural studies, and not simply in those which focus on youth. This is the tendency to see everything as "text." Although there is an ethnographic concern in understanding culture as it is lived, there is a concomitant belief that everything can be discursively rendered and thereby easily understood. In contrast, I use the term "cultural text" more narrowly than many others researching in the field of youth studies. In particular, I am making a distinction between text and lived experience. The tendency in a great deal of the literature recently has been to conflate the two terms while simultaneously, and I believe, paradoxically, acknowledging that they are separate analytical concepts. Pam Gilbert and Sandra Taylor (1991) explicitly utilized the term in this way to highlight the way young people create their own cultural texts from commodities:

> *Following Leslie Roman and Linda Christian-Smith (1988), our definition of cultural text includes both representational forms (for example a video clip, or a teen magazine) and lived social relations . . . Although these two types of cultural text are separable analytically, they are closely interrelated in everyday social practice.* (Gilbert & Taylor 1991: 8)

As the focus of cultural studies until relatively recently has centered more on the way texts are "read" and enjoyed, most studies have tended to emphasize the role of the consumer as producer of new meanings. The emphasis in these studies then becomes the way the individual "makes meaning" out of the text and develops her sense of identity through the commodity in spite of social and material constraints. However, the empirical evidence in these projects is relatively short-term and extremely thin on the ground, supported by very little intensive ethnographic data. Enjoyment, in itself, as William Seaman argued, has been read as evidence of resistance: "the self assessments of viewers, while certainly relevant cannot stand alone as the basis for judging the success in overriding the incorporating devices of a television program" (1992: 304). Indeed, he then goes on to contest the popular implication that the greater the apparent pleasure taken by audiences "the greater the override." Virginia Nightingale also has critiqued the inappropriate use of the term "ethnographic research" as used so often in cultural studies. She has argued that when rigorous ethnographic description and observation are missing from such projects, there is often "a co-opting of interviewees' experience of the text by researchers who then use this as authority for the researchers' point of view" (Nightingale 1993: 163). Thus in these kinds of research projects, the lines between text and lived experience have become increasingly blurred. I would argue that too much power and influence are afforded to the cultural product with insufficient analytical consideration of the much wider cultural context and exploration of the ways texts *emerge* from everyday life.

Furthermore, I believe a critical distinction has to be made between lived experience and cultural texts, giving analytical priority to the former over cultural texts. Indeed to define "social relations" also as a "text" implies that everything can be easily read and interpreted, that everything is "sayable" and indeed "privileges the conscious, easily articulated response" (Morley 1992: 179. Also cited in McEachern 1998: 259). Such an approach obfuscates rather than clarifies the relationship between the text and the lived reality. The question rather should be: How do texts emerge from everyday life to become so meaningful? What exactly is the relationship between texts and lived reality? And in what ways can cultural texts, such as music, sometimes bridge the gap between the "sayable" and the "unsayable"?

In this study, then, I draw the distinction between text and lived experience and demonstrate how subjectivity is negotiated, reflected upon and constituted through everyday social practices. Texts become a way of testing out limits, and through play ultimately enable the representation and the simultaneous constituting of the self, an essential part of the "rhetorics of self making" (Battaglia 1995).

Youth culture: Questions of agency and structure

An alternative model for the study of young people, especially an anthropology of childhood and youth, is recognized as being well overdue (Hardman 1973; Suransky 1982; Wulff 1995; Caputo 1995) and needs to address several important topics at the same time. Firstly, it requires a rethinking of the concept of culture itself, for there has to be an awareness that "culture" is far more dynamic and shifting than traditional conceptions have allowed for. In this conceptualization, culture becomes an amalgam of signifying practices, or in Bourdieu's terminology, a "space of conflict and competition . . . in which participants vie to establish monopoly over the species of capital effective in it" (Bourdieu & Wacquant 1992: 17) rather than something that is fixed and bounded. Inevitably, from this perspective the notion of agency becomes vitally important. Young people need to be seen both as agents in their own right, cultural producers (not simply reproducers of adult cultures) and yet simultaneously *not* totally independent individuals, divorced from social structures and emotional investments. This in turn leads to a closer look at the complex relationship between personal agency and social structure, an exploration of the social and cultural constraints in the young people's perceptions of their developing sense of self. The second and related issue is that the study, through its methodology and concepts, has to enable the young person's perspective to be articulated, to address the ethical issue of "voice." This, in turn, means that the myth of the objective researcher has to be critiqued.

This question implies the extent to which individuals are understood as free-acting agents in their own world, and in the context of the young participants in this research project, involves an awareness of the "immediacy" of a teenager's social reality. While the young person is obviously enmeshed in the process of socialization, as she becomes an adult she is also actively involved in that process. From the teenager's perspective the "now" of her world is more important than that of the future. To conceptualize the teenage world any other way is to render the child as passive, "as standing idly by awaiting to be filled with adult knowledge" (Caputo 1995: 290).[14] In my fieldwork, the selection of young women from a variety of different socioeconomic, ethnic and "racial" backgrounds was a deliberate policy to avoid potentially essentializing notions of groupings such as gender or class, which indeed could conceptually render the young person passive or a victim of circumstance. Instead, I have sought to explore their interactions and differences and not assume homogeneity. The common threads binding the participants were age and gender: the girls were, on average, aged 15 at the beginning of my fieldwork. However, I demonstrate that the particular strategies adopted by each girl for dealing with her experiences of growing up female were not these factors but rather were inextricably linked to her personal familial and cultural experiences and understandings. As I noted previously, the young people could be seen as actively engaging and making meanings from within their own perspectives.

I have also raised and crystallized the issue of voice and reflexivity for myself and the teenagers themselves through the use of a camera as well as requiring the young women to be active participants in the study on several levels and not simply "informants," the latter connoting passivity not agency. Finally, the fact that the young people's culture was also at least partially my own – in terms of gender and location – leads me to revisit several controversial and interrelated issues in terms of analytical frameworks: the thorny issues of distance, "objectivity" and reflexivity.

A question of distance or sitting too close?

All ethnographers are historically positioned and what they observe in the field and what they take note of depends on their own lived experience which will enable or hinder their own observations. Furthermore, the perceived need to "scientifically" objectify the focus of the inquiry can lead to an obfuscation of the studied. If, at first sight, it seems easier to study a culture close to one's own – language at least seems to be less of a difficulty – there are other distinctive problems which emerge for the "auto-anthropologist" or "native" anthropologist that need to be addressed.[15] Strathern has asked "how one knows when one is at home" (Strathern 1987: 16). She unpacks some of the issues of reflexivity and authorship, arguing that "auto-anthropology" is not a question of "heightened self-consciousness" but one "where the anthropological processing of 'knowledge' draws on concepts which also belong to the society and culture under study" (18).

In my fieldwork, where I was researching in my home city, this certainly was an issue for me, although perhaps in an even more complex way than Strathern would have visualized it. The ten young women participating in the project came from the same geographical city boundaries, but simultaneously from different social backgrounds, different social networks. All shared English as a first language (all except three were born in Australia) but not all shared the same value systems and not all shared the same cultural and social practices as I, a middle-class female academic. The differences arose mainly through refractions of class and ethnicity, but even this is too simple an interpretation. Kate, Hilary, Fran and Claire could all be considered middle-class in terms of their educational opportunities and aspirations and their relatively affluent backgrounds – yet in practice, their everyday life experiences were extremely different, partly due to their parents' expressed values and lifestyles. Kate was raised to be extremely independent and questioning, as indicated at the beginning of this chapter, an upbringing reflected in the kinds of material goods she had around her, the expectations, social responsibilities and obligations she had about possessions and space. Claire's home life was far more controlled and contained, so that her explorations and expressions as a young adult were curtailed. Fran, Sara and Hilary were extremely spiritual, but their spirituality was expressed in quite distinct forms. Fran consciously acknowledged the influence of her mother's former hippie days and the attraction of New Age spiritualism; Hilary was attracted to a very traditional form of Christianity; Sara's home life was governed by Buddhist beliefs and values. However trivial such distinctions may seem, they had repercussions on each young person's sense of self and on her sense of her own representations in her video and in my ethnography. How much more so for the other young women in my research whose backgrounds were fundamentally different from mine – through class and ethnicity – and through *these* refractions, their personal experience of gender.

Janine's *Nunga*, South Australian Aboriginal background and Mary's Papua New Guinean heritage, and the fact that both of these young women were under the care of the state and therefore had spent a great deal of their lives in institutions, meant that I, as a researcher, could not assume a shared cultural practice. Apart from different language usage at times and different conceptions of social relatedness, both of these girls and their families had experienced confrontations with authority figures, and legal, medical and educational institutions that were far more complex and fraught than I could ever conceive of. The potential for exploitation by me as a researcher seemed very real and I experienced a great deal of anxiety and concern working out strategies to deal with this, as I recount throughout the following chapters.

For Diane, of British migrant background, living in a geographical area where high (youth) unemployment and material disadvantage was the norm, her family's relationship with government institutions was not so much confrontational but essentially one of powerlessness and dependency, a question of "them" and "us." Far more conservative in outlook than any of the middle-class girls and their families, the discourse that emerged in Diane's home environment was continually one of suspicion of outsiders and of difference, be it racial, ethnic or sexual. In fact, the first question that I was asked by her stepfather was, "Why are you studying only girls?" It was only after a great deal of contact with Diane and her family that I realized that homosexuality and alternative sexual preferences were constantly stated fears and concerns in her social environment. Furthermore, teenage violence in terms of break-ins, and mugging "rollings"[16] was a very real experience in her life, not something experienced at a distance through the tabloid press or electronic media, and therefore constantly discussed among her friends and family. In Strathern's terms, where I positioned myself, or believed that I was situating myself, as "researcher," "author," or "writer," clearly needed to be addressed and constantly negotiated. If not intrusion in their lives, how these different girls and their various social networks therefore conceived of my presence, my research project and my representations of their experiences, were also issues to be constantly considered, explored and indeed agonized over. Marilyn Strathern's observations (1987) together with Bourdieu's insights (Bourdieu & Wacquant 1992: 11) concerning "social praxeology" constantly resonated with me.[17] It was my concern for a less exploitative methodology and for an experimentation with the ethnographic representational text that led to my use of the video camera, outlined below and detailed in the next chapter.[18]

Using a camera: Unsettling the subjective/objective divide

Issues that I felt needed to be addressed were all aspects of reflexivity, issues of the ethnographic authority of the anthropologist at home, the ethical issues of representation of those studied by the ethnographer and the effect of ethnographic style and rhetoric on issues of authorship. I felt that assumptions of perceived homogeneity underlaid the methodologies traditionally used, despite the recent critiques and attempts to enter into a dialogue with those being studied or to make explicit the process of ethnography in the text. This seemed to be so whether it was a written or a visual text (as, for example, in the works of Crapanzano 1986; Dwyer 1982; Rabinow 1988; Said 1989; Ginsberg 1995; Marcus & Fisher 1986). In other words, I felt that a great deal of the research undertaken in urban Australian communities still assumed a homogeneity of culture, be it based on class, ethnicity, race or gender and did not provide a way of exploring contrasting distinctions between the participants' views of themselves against or within another more structural framework. Paradoxes and contradictions were not accommodated. I was resolved to explore at least part of this particular analytical problem, and to highlight the problems with some of what I saw as a number of anthropology's key premises.

I knew that rather than explore the social and cultural dynamics of one group – however defined – I preferred to start from the micro-perspective of several individuals, moving to an exploration of each person's relationship with the varying significant groups and institutions. In other words, I was moving from the inside core out rather than the outside social world in, as is usual practice. That meant I had to define my own field since I couldn't justify my research by claiming that I was, for example, studying working-class, teenage girls in Bowden Brompton or middle-class girls in Burnside. The traditional categories of such studies usually obscure the fact that within these groups lie many differences. I hoped to focus on this insight.

My focus therefore was on girls from across Adelaide's metropolitan area, not one small easily containable field site. I deliberately sought participants from a range of socioeconomic groups, location and ethnic and educational backgrounds. Originally I had hoped to work with only young women aged 15 at the beginning of my fieldwork. I believed that, in Australian culture, the transition from 15 to 16 was, for the young people themselves, a vitally significant time, a time when the young often develop a new sense of autonomy, real or perceived, from their parents or caregivers. However, several of the girls who expressed keen interest in taking part in my research were younger or older than this key age, so I included them in the study.

Although I began my fieldwork with no particular number of teenagers in mind, I soon realized that I was restricted to choosing a relatively small number. It was clearly going to be far too difficult to work intensively with too large a cohort, since I would be developing close relationships with my ten participants and their families, visiting them regularly at home and in their friendship groups, and on many occasions joining them in their social activities. Moreover, I had to take account of the physical demands of this research: my field site encompassed Adelaide's metropolitan area, so I was visiting different suburbs daily. The advantage of restricting the number of participants was that I was able to learn a great deal about ten girls, their families, their friendship groups and their wider social networks in ways that would not have been possible with a much larger group. In several cases the relationships developed into "friendships," as is often the experience of a fieldworker, despite the huge gap between my teenage participants and myself in terms of age and education. Three of the girls actually referred to me as a "friend" when talking to other people in my presence. Others were more distant at different times, but several girls used me as a confidante as though testing out their own ideas against my more adult viewpoint. All of the girls knew that I had a teenage daughter of my own and often asked about her health, or progress at school or asked about our relationship.

I firmly believe that the camera and my status as a researcher and a filmmaker and my past experience as a teacher, allowed me to form a relationship with the teenagers which otherwise would have been regarded as suspect or even nefarious. I also believe that I was permitted a special relationship with the families because everyone knew that I was working with a number of girls across Adelaide. The girls, and sometimes their parents, often wanted to hear about what everyone else was doing – reassurance, perhaps, that their experience of adolescence was within a popular conception of the norm. My experiences and observations were used therefore as a yardstick of "normality." Nevertheless, as I indicated above, I felt extremely privileged by the fact that sometimes the age gap seemed to disappear and I was treated as a friend, although I was ever-aware of the ethical dilemmas that this inevitably brought in its wake.[19]

Notwithstanding, it is important to remember that there were actually far more participants than ten in my fieldwork. The central players in this narrative were the ten young people who held or directed the cameras and told their own stories from their perspectives. Because they came from a variety of backgrounds, their assumptions and taken-for-granted worldviews were reflected in these perspectives. To gain a coherent understanding of their worlds, I also made many visits and talked at length with their friends and families. I met and talked to young people and adults in their homes; in youth clubs, police stations, youth remand centers, and their schools and in other social institutions, as the following chapters will illustrate.

Structure of the book

The structure of the rest of the book accords with the notion of exploration, from the intensely personal and intimate into widening circles of family, social networks and public institutions. Indeed, the developing pattern of inquiry could be likened to a spiral, as I observe, record and interrogate the process of each girl's struggle to represent and constitute her sense of self. Each chapter returns to the same questions, but each time from a layer of more knowledge and deeper comprehension of the influences that impact on the complex process of self-making.

The following chapter examines the methodological frameworks and research paradigms informing the use of the camera in my fieldwork. It begins with an account of my attempts to situate myself as an ethnographer in a cultural field very different from my own and the difficulties that inevitably arose. As noted previously, the problems of being an anthropologist at home had to be confronted and thoughtfully overcome. This section of the book also describes in detail the reflexivity that emerged from the methodology. It examines the ways the young participants began to use the camera for "serious play" in order to explore, reflect upon and create a viable and "fixed" sense of self. The concepts of "serious play," mimesis and mimetic excess are elaborated and applied to the contexts of my fieldwork.

Chapter two centers on the way this play and desire to become "other" in the girls' self-making, was underpinned by all aspects of their bodily praxis, from their clothing, adherence to fashion and style, to what they consumed and ingested. Here we observe again that what seems like an arbitrary choice of what to wear or what to eat is closely aligned to other familial and social cultural value systems – in other words, each girl's "sense of the game." This section draws upon Bourdieu's concept of *habitus* to explore this nexus between play and bodily praxis.

Self-making has to take place in physical contexts and relies on a sense of license or framing in order to occur at all. Chapters three and four investigate the relationship between place and play by exploring the way "private" space is created and negotiated in both private and public domains. Chapter three demonstrates the ways in which the girls used their bedrooms or other aspects of their domestic arenas as spaces to experiment with a developing gendered identity. In this context, dyadic friendships are paramount – the best friend who is the "me" who is "not me." The following chapter continues this exploration but focuses on arenas usually considered more public – the city streets, dance clubs and shopping malls. It particularly challenges the notion of public access and the myth of public spaces. Chapter four also focuses upon the closer links between the girls' sense of access outside the domestic arenas and their familial and social networks, leading to a consideration of polyadic friendship groupings, social networks consisting of several friends, and in particular, those which develop within schools.

Chapter five explores the relationship between these significant polyadic friendship groupings, their hierarchies and the girls' wider social networks. Here the art and importance of being "cool" is shown to be relative; what is ideal and desirable in one social grouping is unacceptable in another. In this chapter we also see that the various cultural groupings with which the teenagers are affiliated can be seen not as *sub*cultural but *micro*-cultural, very much in tune with each girl's parental values and affiliations. Moreover, the ways whereby the teenagers' engagement in serious play is contained constantly within their "sense of the game" is demonstrated: it is a testing of symbolic boundaries while remaining safely within the borders.

The sixth chapter continues from this ever-increasing spiral of influence to examine experiential communities, through the teenagers' affiliations with music, fandom, and dance. Music, I argue, is *the* social glue for young people. It is the ideal mimetic vehicle, the social magic that allows self-making to take place in a variety of forms and contexts. Like the camera itself, music encourages and enables an ideal self to emerge through a fantastic play at being other. Like the camera, too, music's power lies in its overwhelming phenomenological facility for play and mimesis. Yet here too, we see that the desire and engagement for otherness is not unlimited but very much constrained by each girl's habitus, her tacit sense of "the rules of the game." I argue here that musical taste is not arbitrary nor, in the case of young people, is it necessarily oppositional, often relying for its power and significance on its micro-cultural "authenticity." In this way we can see why Mary loves reggae music while Grace adores Violent Femmes.

The final chapter demonstrates the global significance of this form of play and self-making: we see the same forms of identity-in-process in six case studies of teenage girls in America and in Britain. This chapter also tightens the connection between the specific ethnographic method and the documentary project that emerged from the girls' collective film. In the act of selecting, analyzing, and re-presenting the ethnographic material, a parallel clearly emerged between this process and what the young participants were doing in their documentaries and self-making. Just as the young participants ignored some aspects of their lives, taking them for granted, or highlighted other areas, deliberately choosing to foreground these scenes in their narratives, so too I made choices. I also drew attention to certain images while overlooking or playing down the importance of others, through my own, often unconscious perspectives, my theoretical frameworks or through my own intellectual limitations. The resulting portraits, mine as academic and ethnographer and those of my young participants, as auto-ethnographers, reveal the complexity and richness of cultural experience. The choices also highlight that ethnography, like filmmaking and like identity itself, is a process. As soon as one attempts to capture the narrative in any fixed paradigm, it slips from one's grasp and reveals itself for what it can only ever be – partial and incomplete. In the ongoing process and struggle of their self-making, the young women in the research project were undoubtedly well aware that they were "striking poses." They were attempting to pin down the ephemeral, the elusive, the fiction that became "fact" only in the process of their fantasy.

The thematic thread that links this spiral of observation is the concept of identity as process, and it is play that enabled this process to occur. It is "space to play" that allowed the young women in my research project to explore aspects of their personhood, to experiment with "otherness" and try on other "selves" for size. Here we see the process of self-making in action, through bodily praxis, a process that is symbolically bounded by each girl's understanding of her world. This reflexivity, the simultaneous recording and constituting of the self, is particularly evident in the ways the teenagers engaged with the camera and the way they struggled to represent the elusive and remarkable phenomenon of self-making in the next chapter.

Notes

1 See figure 1. The names used here are pseudonyms. In their documentary, the girls themselves use their own given names but, as I explain below in the main text, this is because what my participants chose to reveal in their videos was selective – what they had decided was appropriate or important to be revealed.

2 I am using the term "girl" interchangeably with "young women" to refer to the teenage participants in my fieldwork, despite my original reservations concerning the appropriateness of the term in terms of non-sexist language. The young women themselves used the word to refer to themselves not in any derogatory sense unless they used the additional attribute "little" before it.

3 The photograph also immediately brought to my mind the now famous photograph of Joan Crawford, by Eve Arnold and featured on the cover of Richard Dyer's *Stars, heavenly bodies*. As with the photo of these two adolescents, Crawford's image revealed the various layers of constituted "reality" – that we construct and are constituted by our representations. Secondly, she too demonstrated the power of the camera. In Arnold's original collection of photographs, the accompanying information indicated that Crawford wanted the photograph to reveal the hard work entailed in being a star.

4 It was also a practical decision as her parents are in a de facto relationship and believed that it should not be assumed that their daughter should receive either or both of their surnames. Kate now appreciates the fortuitous choice as a matter of aesthetics – her given name "did not go well" with either of their surnames, she felt.

5 I am not of course denying that in recent years certain representations of men have also become more objectified and subjected to the gaze. There is still, however, a qualitative and quantitative difference in the way the genders are represented and portrayed visually.

6 In an article in a quality Australian newspaper, Margaret Le Roy explored "Why women will always hate their bodies" (1993). It is through the body that gender is primarily constructed by others; that is, how one perceives that one is observed by others; it defines one's femininity and masculinity. But even from early childhood the "common sense" way in which boys are discussed is through their behavior, what they do. For little girls the discussion primarily focuses on how they look. Admittedly, little boys are conventionally expected to portray toughness in their stance and dress and little girls are meant to demonstrate more conventional feminine traits through their gestures and behavior as well as their appearance. However, I contend that from very young ages most girls develop a sense of being "naturally" the object of other people's gaze, of being rather than doing, whereas boys develop a sense of "naturally" being the subject – all this in spite of the advances of feminism and the growing awareness in individual families. If we understand this inevitability as "normality" then, as did Connell, I want to ask, "where did this 'normality' come from? How is it produced? And isn't there a little too much of it?" (Connell, 1987: 2).

7 It is through the body that girls accept, challenge and experiment with their future roles and statuses as women. It can be seen in the adoption of physical stance, the development of a particular style, the particular "look" one struggles to acquire. This can also be seen in the forms of ritual which incorporate image, body movement and dance. In its extreme form, it is manifested in the phenomena of eating disorders which can be read as the ultimate attempt to gain control of one's life through the self-destructive control of one's body. See also Smith 1988 and Skeggs 1997 on related issues of gender and representation.

8 What a complex notion "everyday lives" has come to be (Elias 1978; De Certeau 1988; Drotner 1994)! Here I use the term to describe the way individuals perceive and engage in their worlds. It is a perception of the world rather than just a sphere of existence. Drotner summarizes it thus: "Everyday life is a means to create some certainty in a world of ambivalence" (1994: 352).

9 For the etymologies of "play" and "work" and some of their current applications see Webster's Dictionary, The Oxford Dictionary or the Macquarie Dictionary. Also, for a concise and extremely accessible overview of the development of the concept of play see Turner 1982: 33–5.

10 See Handelman (1977, 1990) for a fuller explanation of the paradoxical implications of play that I cannot do justice to here in this limited space.

11 "The profundity of the play medium lies with its uncertain changeability and in its capacities for commentary" (Handelman 1990: 70).

12 The term Anglo–Celtic is used throughout this work to indicate young people from white British backgrounds as opposed to Asian, African, African–Caribbean or European. The term intends to provide a way of talking about ethnicity that indicates the parent cultures and traditions that are clearly so much part of the young people's understandings of their worlds.

13 In order to explore all facets of such a quest I found I had to blur disciplinary boundaries, drawing upon insights and perspectives from Anthropology, Cultural Studies, Feminism, Psychology and Film Studies.

14 Caputo draws an analogy between this limited conception of youth with earlier conceptions of certain world cultures as "remnants of previous time." This view, she argues, conceives of some cultures as exotic and fixed, "frozen in a conceptualisation of time that negates the present." I found this a particularly compelling argument in the light of debates about Australian Aboriginal culture and practices. See Fergie 1995, 1998; Weiner 1996.

15 Of course the language which exists in one's own culture is not necessarily the language of the researcher for there can be differences in education, dialect, slang or even the first language itself. When I taught high school children several years ago I was often struck by the other languages spoken at home away from the school environment – Greek, Italian, German, Korean, Cantonese and so on. The children learned to slip between these languages effortlessly. In this current fieldwork several of the girls spoke another language in different environments: Mary frequently spoke in Papua New Guinean "Pidgin"; Janine would dot her speech with Pitjantjatjara terminology when she was with her family and friends; and all of the girls would use terms in English that were unfamiliar to me generationally. "Teenage slang" changes constantly and deliberately–that is part of the nature of the beast. The meaning of the word would change if I dared to use it – even the innocuous and ubiquitous word: "cool." As one girl said, "It sounds really strange when you use it."

16 Attacks by teenage gangs to obtain fashionable clothes or money from others.

17 Strathern's insightful argument about epistemologies and representation raises the same interesting moral questions outlined above and prevents a simplistic claim to anthropological authority. She reminds the academic researcher that the kind of ethnographic text that is produced is not a matter of "authorial choice but of cultural and social practice" (p. 23).

18 It also inspired the determination not to use the term "informants" but rather to adapt the more engaging, less implicitly power-ridden term, "participants."

19 When I was given information about illegal activities or drug taking, either their own activity or that of friends, I was required as any person working with young people to be nonjudgmental and discreet while simultaneously making my own views clear on the topic. Only one parent asked me for information about her child. I reassured the parent that no dangerous or risk-taking behavior was occurring but I also indicated that my conversations with her child had to be regarded as private. Several times I did find that I was the confidante of the parent as well.

Chapter 1

Camera Power

> Photography implies instant access to the real. But the results of this instant access are another way of creating distance. To possess the world in the form of images is, precisely, to re-experience the unreality and remoteness of the real. (Susan Sontag 1977: 164)

> *The most important thing I have got from making this video is the chance to analyse myself a bit . . . and that means to see myself the way others see me. It is also a chance to look at myself and my morals and see whether that is how I really want to be portrayed.* (Fran)

Introduction

Fran's words above were spoken in direct address to the camera as she contemplated her filmmaking and the role of editing in her self-representation. Unknowingly and through her own experience, she echoes Susan Sontag's observations. Her words hint at both the conscious and unconscious processes, the simultaneous acknowledgment of engagement and distance involved in such a task. There is both "the chance to analyse myself a bit" (an opportunity to see herself as she *is*, the belief that her identity is "fixed" or already established, in some way) and the "chance to . . . see how I really want to be portrayed" (the means to *recreate* the image, the belief that her identity can be *reinvented*). What already is and what can be, representation and referent merge at that moment. On another occasion in my fieldwork, 15-year-old Hilary also captured this paradox in a striking visual image. She held a small mirror up to her face in her left hand while her right hand held the small video camera.

The effect in the video frame was an image of Hilary's face, complete with camera lens turned upon herself and symbolically enclosed within her own hand. In the background of the frame, distinct although in less-sharp focus, was a television set.[1]

In the previous chapter, I described how the power and transformative quality of play was essential to the process whereby young people reflect upon and constitute their (gendered, self) identities. Here I introduce two aspects of play, the concept of "serious play" for that which could *conceivably* be real and the concept of "fantasy" or "unreal play" for that which could not be real – moments of exaggeration or mimetic excess. For the young women in my fieldwork, *serious play* and *fantasy* both constituted self-making. They were the essential ingredients in reflexivity, in experimenting with and exploring gendered personhood.

Fig 2: "My goodness, this is me!"

Further, I argue that the role that popular culture played in the production of that self-identity was salient – television, music, film and magazines were the sites of the production of such play and fantasy, not simply the means of consumption. In other words, the production through play of "the possibly real" and fantasy (the "could-not-be-real") and, thereby the constitution of identity itself, was a very active exploratory process. Both activities frequently utilize and find expression in popular culture. In this chapter I focus on one aspect of that process, the effect of self-recognition and self-creation through the mechanism and power of the camera lens. I am exploring how the attempt at image-making – the recording process – and the final product – the result of the recording process – blur the lines between representation and what is being represented; signifier and signified integrate and mesh within the everyday experience. The central concept underlying this process is that of mimesis, the blurring of self and "other."

In this section I am concerned with the camera both as a methodological tool and also as a significant cultural symbol – the different meanings that are potentially evoked by its presence and the significance of that presence. The first aspect, the discussion of the camera as methodological tool, requires an account of the *process* of my placement in the field. I detail the difficulties of my initial contact with the ten young women in my research and their social worlds, underscoring the problems for an adult researcher of becoming accepted as an "insider" in female teenage friendship groupings. I then illustrate the efficacy of the particular strategies I undertook to remedy the situation. As an aspect of detailing the process of fieldwork, I introduce the notion of the different friendship "clusters" or "groupings" that the girls occupied. It was through these small friendship groups that I initially got to know the girls. It was only after my greater personal involvement with each individual that I was able to untangle the social networks more specifically and discover how and why they were connected and where these webs overlapped.

I am therefore using the concept of "cluster" in a very specific way, for these friendship groups were very much part of adult and parental social networks. Nevertheless, the ten participants still need to be considered from their own perspective as ten "nuclei" at the center of ten wider, sometimes integrated and sometimes overlapping social networks. While it would be tempting to see these wider networks in terms of class or ethnicity, this would suggest a simplistic hegemonic sense of identity (Harré 1981) which I did not find in my fieldwork. These social networks were certainly symbolically bounded (Cohen 1986) in that each network was constituted by particular characteristics that were emphasized as being central to its sense of identity. Yet at different times, certain characteristics and components of that identity were emphasized by the network members while other aspects were played down.

For example, as I noted in the previous chapter, the Aboriginal girls all shared aspects of a common social network in that they all identified as *Nunga* (many were biologically related in some way), they were all inhabitants of the same industrial working-class area of the city and went to the same school. There were times when these girls clearly articulated their sense of Aboriginality through their speech, their actions, their dress. Yet on other occasions this aspect of their identity was pushed into the background as they placed greater emphasis on their membership of a rock band, seeing themselves more importantly, at that moment and place, as musicians, not primarily Aboriginal musicians. In another setting, they identified as members of *their* female school community as opposed to another school group, a school group that included many non-Aboriginal members. These were not separate identities, of course, but like the ephemeral and varied patterns in a kaleidoscope that "gel" at a particular moment, possible coherent patterns within a larger whole framework. A more appropriate extended metaphor for my purposes would be the camera frame. Within the camera frame we attempt to capture representations of ourselves or the "selves" of others, seemingly "frozen" in time.[2] The still photographic images we decide to keep and approve of, retained in an album or drawer, do not capture the whole self but represent an ephemeral syntagma within a larger paradigm of potentialities.

The second section of this chapter leads inevitably into a fuller account of mimesis and consideration of the related role (and gendering) of technology within and outside domestic spaces. Although the girls used a video camera most of the time rather than a single reflex camera (although they did employ both in the telling of their stories), the same essential apparatus and symbolism underlie both types of technology. In both, a framing device is used to select and separate specific images from the surrounding cacophony of people, scenery and "things." This leads us to consider the narrative forms the girls employed in their use of the camera, for these generic styles are not separate from ways of seeing and of knowing. Selection and narrative are ways of making sense, interpreting and giving cohesion to something that inherently seems without order.

Secondly, the camera, whether it reproduces still or moving images, is an instrument of control.

The nuclear family that refuses to be ideal and whole in spite of the advertisements to the contrary seemingly becomes unitary and linked again through the narrative of our photos and photograph album. Photographic frames allow us to create ourselves; they "facilitate a ready reflexivity" (Peace 1991: 12). This last point emphasizes the linking theme of this chapter and the wider book, that of identity as *process*. Identity refuses to be static so we attempt to contain something that is continually in the process of *becoming*, continually in flux. It is carefully "managed" within a larger comfortable psychic "fit" whether that psychic fit is how we *imagine* ourselves to be, or whether it is how we represent ourselves to others and ourselves in *material* form – in the photograph album, in the picture frame above the television set (Peace 1991) or in the home video. It is this social and cultural fit which Bourdieu (Bourdieu & Wacquant 1992) calls "the sense of the game." In describing one aspect of that process, the simultaneous effect of self-recognition and self-creation through the mechanism and power of the camera lens, I am looking at how that process integrates, interweaves and in some cases, blurs the lines between fantasy and everyday experiences while simultaneously holding them in a tension of difference.

To begin then, I elaborate on the concept of mimesis, its application to my area of research and an incident that took place at the beginning of my fieldwork that rather poignantly illustrated for me the complex power of fantasy and play.

Mimesis and methodology: An alternative view of the city

Janine, Wanda and Janelle, members of an Aboriginal all-female teenage rock band, had been videoing themselves in the park. In the Botanic Gardens, where they began their film, they had practised interviewing each other and experimented with the camera. We had been there all day in forty-degree heat and now, hot and tired, we were wandering back to the train station to go home. We set off down North Terrace, Adelaide's aesthetically fine main boulevard, lined with museums, galleries and marble statues – reminders of the city's rich and formal colonial past. Suddenly the seriousness of their earlier videoing changed. Wanda gave us an alternative view of the city, directly addressing the camera which was still held by Janelle:

> *"Here," she said to the camera, sotto voce and beckoning with her finger, "I'll show you something!" She led the camera over to the war memorial fountain, an impressive monument with its solemn stone angels and its martyred immortal soldier. "'Ere is where you come when you're a bit stuck for the fare home after a night out and you've been experiencing too much alcohol." She led the camera around the back of the fountain to the small wishing well. "See?" Wanda winked knowingly at the camera and still in a slightly hushed voice, as though she were sharing a secret between friends. "You come 'ere, lift up the wire and take enough to get 'ome." She shrugs exaggeratedly. "It's easy!" She then led the camera further down the street, serious purposeful demeanor – investigative journalism perfected – while Janelle continued to film. She stopped before some young women at a bus stop. "Excuse me. Would you like to be in a documentary?" The camera caught their nervous expressions. "What is it on?" they asked. "Women and sex," replied Wanda, before sweeping onward majestically toward the station.*

Theoretical frameworks

The anecdote about Janine and her friends encapsulates, for me, the basis of my intentions for this chapter. Before my eyes, these young women subverted what had been a serious attempt to capture themselves "authentically" on video, by turning it into a very funny parody of the whole difficult exercise. In speaking (with winks and nods to the camera) of "experiencing alcohol," of being at the railway station at night or stealing money from the war veterans' fountain, the girls were deliberately overturning at least two discourses: firstly, the documentary mode itself and secondly, a racist/sexist discourse. Articulating the very stereotypes that would normally be used against them as young Aboriginal women – underage drinking, petty crime and vandalism ("'Ere's where you get your fare home") and overt sexual activity ("women and sex") – the girls appeared to be taking control of these negative images. Yet, what is more significant was that none of these depictions appeared on their final footage, neatly edited for public consumption. There, we only saw a group of young Aboriginal women practising in their rock band with friends or being with a large extended family at home. What is happening here? Why the gap? In what ways does the camera allow a play with image and identity to occur, a play that is both unsettling and liberating at the same time?

Identity as process: Play and mimesis

Engagement with popular culture, especially in relation to young people, is a complex dialectic activity, one that oscillates repeatedly between total engagement and a balancing, knowing distanciation. From my own observations and understandings of the young women in this study, I perceived their involvement with popular culture to be a deeply engrossing, *embodied* play – a "deep play" (Geertz 1973, 1975), an experimentation with aesthetics, form and image that was experienced through the body and infused with meaning. There was no total unthinking abandonment to pleasure, although there were moments of disengagement with the everyday; indeed, sometimes their play bordered on the perilous where they took serious risks.[3] This was not the play of people who believe that their actions could be, in some way, ultimately politically subversive. A legitimate skepticism was intrinsic to this play – the skepticism of those who know that they too can create images and knowledge, can subvert socially sanctioned conventions, but that ultimately such a stance as proactive was illusory; it was, after all, in popular discourse "just play." The concept of play being used here is not so much about changing the rules, or calculatedly implementing strategies, but rather, a deliberate extending of the constraints and symbolic boundaries, like the pulling of an elastic band to the limits of its tension. Such play is indeed "a feel for the game" (Bourdieu 1977, 1990; Bourdieu & Wacquant 1992). Seen in this light, play has a very serious function indeed.

Here, then, I am using the concept of play to describe everyday experiences and perspectives of the young South Australian women who were the subjects of my fieldwork. The introduction of the camera during the fieldwork offered a "symbolic" space to play, to experiment, a step into the subjunctive. Simultaneously, it highlighted the usual difficulties and constraints the girls experienced in their search for "alternative selves" (Schechner 1993: 39).

Play in action

The use of the video camera as a methodological tool only occurred to me after I realized the extreme difficulty of "entering" or at least having comfortable and regular access to teenage groups that, almost by definition, would be closed to me as an adult researcher. I had assumed that my previous experiences as a teacher, and a parent of teenage children and, to some extent, my status as a university researcher would somehow open up doors, and reveal confidences. In some ways, I had also believed that being of the same gender and sharing the same broad Australian culture would be a bonus to my acceptance. My initial clumsy contact with potential participants was through Bowden Brompton Youth Circus, affectionately nicknamed by the group itself and known through the wider community as Cirkidz.[4]

Cirkidz was a community youth arts group initiated in 1985 by Tony Hannan and Michael Vesta, who "first pulled kids off the street to teach them circus skills."[5] Both young men had worked with quite a variety of young people with problems and difficulties. Their particular insight was to use their own background training in, and knowledge of, circus skills to help young people who were socially and materially disadvantaged. In other words, the skills gained through circus training were perceived by the staff to be socially and emotionally empowering in more ways than just physical attainment.[6]

The empowerment operated on four levels. Firstly, it was based on the body. In Cirkidz young people learned to take risks and experiment with their bodies in safe ways that they could not do outside the circus. Risk-taking with the body in adolescence is not unusual. Experiments with legal and illegal drug-taking, body-piercing and extreme physical states have been widely documented over a long period of time (Young 1971; Brake 1985; Dorn & South 1989; Redhead 1993, 1995; Kozicki 1986; Iso-Aholas & Crowley 1991; Rojek 1989). Cirkidz enabled the desire to experience these risks to be channelled into useful, socially acceptable skills with young people learning to regard their bodies in more positive and desirable ways. For example, the new skills that the girls learned were often more dependent on strength than aesthetics. Both young men and women learned that being strong and in control of their bodies was a positive attribute. Several young women, including one of the staff members, told me on different occasions how excited they were to discover through Cirkidz that they were *strong*.

Secondly, children at Cirkidz learned to be part of a team that was built on mutual trust, not competition. If the participants were performing acrobatic or tumbling tasks, one child's awareness of the placement of her own body guaranteed the safety of another child. Thirdly, pedagogy was tackled differently at Cirkidz from the way it would usually be encountered at other, more formal educational institutions. Each participant was encouraged to learn at her own pace. The classes were not formally structured at that time but functioned on a mentor basis. Each child was free to approach a tutor in order to learn how to acquire specific skills. Fourthly, the circus school was proactive in advocating social skills and social justice. It emphasized healthy lifestyle practices and attempted, through open discussion and the distribution of posters, and pamphlets and through example, to combat ethnic and sexual prejudice. All these aspects of the circus were acknowledged, and seen by the staff and parents as positive learning experiences for the children and teenagers.

I had learned of the organization some years earlier when my own children had been members there. I also knew that the school attracted a range of young people from different socioeconomic backgrounds. I first learned about Cirkidz through word of mouth, not through formal advertising or promotion. My son had decided to try a session because one of his friends had joined. Because *he* enjoyed the activities, my daughter also wanted to attend.

At the time of my fieldwork Cirkidz was based in an industrial inner-city area, one of the first parts of the city to be established with its narrow streets and factories flanking the main arterial road heading out of the city. It was therefore a very old part of the city, patently a materially impoverished and working-class district with very little of the trendy refurbishments apparent in other inner-city areas. There was, however, a sense of "community" that perhaps was not so readily found in the newer suburbs.

Fig 3, 4: Cirkidz sheds 1993–1994

Many local children still attended the circus school, sometimes through recommendations from their school or simply because it was in their area and it gave them, in their own words, "something to do" and in the adults' view "kept them off the streets." The fees for the classes for these participants were minimal or waived. Over the years, however, the circus had begun to attract children from different socioeconomic backgrounds right across metropolitan Adelaide. By 1993, in some circus classes, relatively affluent middle-class children, often from highly educated backgrounds, rubbed shoulders and shared activities with others from very different economic and material circumstances and from different ethnic groups. The significance of this and the connections between the families will be detailed throughout the book.

As a unique organization, Cirkidz seemed the ideal basis for a particularly rich case study. It was to be my first point of access to a range of young people and their social networks. Having recently been a parent of children at the school, I was already a familiar face. An additional bonus for my particular research project was that, at that time, there were quite a few girls enrolled. The focus of my research was not on the organization itself, but on some of the participants who regularly attended and their regular locales, *including* the circus. Having sought permission from the director of Cirkidz and explained my purpose, I approached some of the teenage girls after a class and naively asked if anyone would be interested in taking part in a research project outside Cirkidz. The immediate reaction from the teenagers was negative and suspicious. One girl viewed me guardedly through a screen of hair and asked astutely: "What do you want to know?" Taken aback by her frankness, I answered lamely and stupidly, "About you."

A different strategy!

Taken aback and disheartened, I realized I needed a different strategy. I had to be able to offer something that would break down the barriers, the obvious and the invisible, between me as an adult researcher and the girls as teenage subjects. On my next visit to Cirkidz I determined not to arrive "empty-handed" but rather to offer some means of reciprocity. I had already formulated the notion of using the camera to provide a means for the girls to construct representations of themselves since I could see that the technology had the potential to offer a number of positive dimensions to my research. Firstly, I believed the girls could be interested in learning how to operate a camera and subsequently produce a visual record for themselves. In this way, I reasoned, I would not simply be learning from the participants of the study, I would be able to teach and offer something in return. This, I felt, was a particularly important ethical consideration because of the inevitable power-relationship involved, due to the relatively young age and education level of my potential participants, noted in the previous chapter.

Secondly, the camera could justify my presence in the girls' familial and social groups and could offer a viable incentive for their wanting to be involved in my research. It could provide me with an acceptable role within their groups. Finally, it could enable a close contact and ongoing relationship with the girls not only in a public setting but in a more private domestic setting. Even at this early stage I hoped that the camera would venture where it would be inappropriate or impossible for me as an outsider and an adult. Perhaps it would then provide a vicarious understanding of these more private spaces through the girls' discussions or even viewings of their videos. The video camera might even facilitate a close contact with their families and friends, significant others in their lives.

Subsequently, I also realized that the camera had the capacity to offer the participants an authoritative voice distinct from mine and from any official voice. This is not to say that the girls might not *deliberately* have chosen a way of representing themselves that echoed an official or adult voice, perhaps responding to what they felt was expected of them, or even subconsciously responding in this way. That was of course a consideration and even a probability, but the possibilities of alternative interpretations and expressions were still there. Furthermore, I am not naively suggesting that the products of their videos would somehow speak for themselves – that what the girls filmed and produced would somehow be a more authentic version of how they saw their worlds than my interpretation of events. I did not believe that the product of the video camera was ever simply a reflection of what *was*, of actuality somehow raw and unprocessed just waiting to be discovered. Rather, I perceived that the utilization of the camera was a way of making clearer the *process* of mutual discovery and creativity of both the researcher and subjects. The camera offered insights into the "layering" of ethnography, the different ways understanding and knowledge are negotiated and realized as part of everyday transactions in the world. As Wagner observed, "The ethics and methodologies of fieldwork should become 'transparent' to the creativity being studied" (Wagner 1975: 159).

I believed this transparency could be made more explicit by the methodology I had chosen. Just as the teenagers' involvement with the *process* of the documentary-making solved the potentially exploitative power relations, so also did this provision enable participants to "speak" in their own voice and to edit from their footage, resulting in a more "authentic" voice. Their selection would reflect how they interpreted their experiences, from both their initial "framing" of their worlds and subsequent decisions to exhibit only partial views of that material. My interest would lie in those aspects of their lives they took for granted, the images they regarded as indexical and those they regarded as iconic – in the aspects recorded, ignored or edited from the final footage. What would *not* be filmed would be as interesting to consider as what was selected for the camera. The methodology was inevitably creating an ethnography that highlighted a great deal about the ethnographic process.

Because I wanted the camera to be as unobtrusive in the girls' lives as possible, I obtained the most compact Hi 8 camera available at that time. The quality of the footage obtained through the small domestic Hi 8 camera in my fieldwork was broadcast quality and the camera had the capacity to perform in very low-light conditions. Further-more, the camera itself was light and easily operated with one hand. Unlike the size of usual professional Hi 8 cameras, this one was small enough to be considered as very domestic, comfortable within the home environment as well as being unobtrusive in more public places.[7] I did not offer the girls the use of any external microphones or lights in order to keep the use of the camera as simple and as "casual" as possible. The emphasis was on their being able to experiment and play with the camera rather than their producing high aesthetic quality footage.

There was an additional and unexpected effect of using this domestic format that I had not originally appreciated. In the final edited version of the documentary, the girls' original Hi 8 footage was framed within a more polished studio Betacam production, where the girls spoke directly to the camera. This distinction between home-shot video and more polished footage inevitably emphasized the difference between "rehearsal" and "performance," a very concrete demonstration of Goffman's (1959, 1967) notion of "back stage" and "front stage." On the most obvious level, the juxtaposition of the two formats stressed the distinction between the footage taken "then" (filmed three years earlier), and the "now" footage (videoed when the girls were looking back at their younger "selves"). On a more theoretically exciting level, the contrast also made *visible* the different layerings usually obfuscated in the gap between any research project and the final polished product; the interpretive gulf between the "messy" open fieldwork and the more closed, narrowly focused, ethnographic text.

I deliberately chose *not* to teach the girls the usual standard ways of producing a documentary from a developed, written script to the film; that is, the traditional and admittedly, the most established, efficient and economic (Western) way of telling a story through film or video. Instead, I suggested that the girls approached their "stories" in a more experimental, open-ended manner. They did not need to create a script. They could employ the camera exactly as they liked; they could film alone, with friends, with family or with strangers. Each participant could hold the camera or direct others to video for her. She could choose anything at all for her subject matter, although I hoped that she would be able to indicate, in discussion with me afterwards, or demonstrate, how and why it was meaningful to her in some way. What that "meaning" would be and how they would interpret this brief, was another layer I hoped to discover as I observed the process of the video-making.[8]

Unlike the single reflex camera where the unacceptable images are never photographed and therefore never reviewed, or if they *are* captured on film, they are discarded to sit in a drawer or are thrown in the bin, this method revealed what was frequently invisible, what was unacceptable or even unknowable by the girls themselves. It appeared in the raw footage they took but subsequently rejected from their final film or it was noticeable through its absence – the material not filmed either because it was too obvious to them to be noteworthy (we select "events" from our lives to memorialize on film, as suggested Peace 1991) or because it was too threatening to record on camera. I believed that I would learn through the camera, and through the process of representation would discover what the girls believed they could articulate and what was probably unsayable by them because it was unknowable – the unquestioned and taken-for-granted aspects of their lives.

Cluster 1: Meeting Sara, Kate, Wendy, and Cindy

When I returned to Cirkidz the following week and offered the use of the camera to different teenage girls, I received, in marked contrast to my initial request for participants, a very positive excited response. Four girls, Sara, Kate, Wendy and Cindy, immediately expressed interest in participating in the project. As we sat in a circle on the floor at the end of their session to discuss the details, we were surrounded by several other interested younger boys and girls, also wishing to be involved.[9] At that first meeting at Cirkidz I told the eager participants that the potential audience for their final products could be a public one – through the forum of the Young Film Makers' Festival or ACE TV (community television), if they wished – but they did not have to work toward this goal. I suggested that they should film first, unrestricted by a closed-ended script and select sections for editing afterwards. This method, as I said, would not usually be one that a filmmaker would choose because it would be uneconomical, in terms of both time and money.

Had the girls adopted the traditional method of filming, they would undoubtedly have been constrained by the ideas of "correct material" and been overly concerned with getting their final film "just right." I did not want them to edit "in camera" – I did not want them to film over their mistakes or unwanted material. I wanted to be part of their discussions about the footage they wanted to keep and that they would ultimately reject. I knew I would be as interested in the material they decided to leave out of the final editing process as that they included; in the material they would regard as suitable for exposure to a wider audience. Furthermore, as I developed closer relationships with the girls and spent time with them in the different social contexts of their lives, it was in this very *process* of negotiation and discussion that I learned about the aspects of the girls' lives they chose *not* to film. In other words, the camera also indicated the invisible, the unstated as well as the highly visible.

More girls

This group of four volunteer girls was the first social network or "cluster" I encountered. The girls who were keenest to control the camera at this stage were Sara, Kate and Wendy. These girls did not socialize with one another outside Cirkidz and, as I was to discover quite quickly, came from very different family backgrounds and expectations. Sara was originally from Nepal, living at that time with her adoptive parents and her biological brother in a relatively isolated area in the hills backing the city. Her father was a skilled laborer and her mother an ESL teacher although neither parent was consistently employed full-time. Kate is the girl we met in chapter 1, an only child of two highly educated middle-class parents, both university lecturers. She too lived in the hills but in a far more suburban area. Wendy lived with her father, a retail salesman, his partner and their blended families in an inner city section of the city. The home was a small, sparsely furnished weatherboard house. The immediate link between the three girls was attendance at Cirkidz. Four other girls showed interest in the project but were less keen to hold the camera. They wanted to see what the first three did and perhaps to take part in *their* films. These four were Fran, Grace, Callie and Helen. It was several months down the track before Fran and Grace offered to participate fully and Wendy decided to drop out of the project.

The other key teenage participants in my research were obtained through "professional" networking and fortuitous meetings. I realized that Cirkidz alone was not going to provide access to enough groups of young people from diverse backgrounds. I needed a greater number of participants from a wider variety of backgrounds if I were to achieve the aims I had set myself. My original training and experience in secondary education meant that I had many contacts in various areas of youth education and social work. Through these networks, I visited different schools in a variety of metropolitan areas, ensuring a range of ethnic and socioeconomic domains.

At one of these schools I met Diane and her friends. The school was in one of the northern suburbs of the city. The teachers themselves, in staffroom discussion and in the official discourse of the school, talked about the school as a successful, highly academic institution, although relatively few children went on to tertiary education. Most of the children were from Anglo–Celtic backgrounds, by far the majority being first generation Australians with British parents.

The school also had an unofficial reputation, amongst pupils and their families from surrounding areas, for drugs and violence. When I talked to some of the teachers and youth workers about the local area, several of them said they felt the central problem of the school, and they *did* see the school as having problems, was "new money." Their view was that this was an area where the parents had immigrated from working-class, overcrowded cities in the UK. Their background did not appear to value education, only making money as quickly as possible. What money they did earn here parents wanted to use and display. The architecture in the area seemed to reflect these values: the nearby residential houses were often large and ostentatious – rather like a film set. Huge, grandiose houses were frequently being erected almost overnight.

Both inside and outside the school discussions took place relating to youth unemployment and boredom and a perceived youth "problem." The local shopping mall was patrolled regularly by police, security guards and youth workers on watch for young people in trouble, as victims or perpetrators of petty crime or other antisocial behavior. Illegal drug-taking was known to be rife in and out of school. I spent a few days with several of the youth workers, accompanying them as they "cruised" this area on foot and chatted to the young people there. Close by the mall was a heavily used drop-in support center for young people, designed to provide help for victims and abusers of violence, drugs and other social problems. The youth workers in the area talked at length about the particular problems of the locale: high youth unemployment, drug abuse and alcoholism, child abuse and domestic violence. The teachers, school counsellors and youth workers argued that the children grew up respecting material goods, but other values in their lives, including seeing the need for education, seemed lacking. Although Diane's home and particular familial situation was far from affluent, I was to discover that the values in her home and social networks were in keeping with those of the area.

In contrast to Diane's world, I came into contact with that of Claire, Hilary and Pat in *their* corner of Adelaide. These girls all attended the same eastern suburbs high school where many of the parents were professional and tertiary-educated. However, I did not make my initial contact with these girls in their school but at a special youth organization called *Tangent*, run by the local council. Most of the local government councils in South Australia during 1993–1994, in the metropolitan area and beyond, were attempting to respond to a recurring moral panic about youth unemployment and youth crime. Several councils had undertaken extensive research to learn more about the extent of "the youth problem" in their area. A number of councils were particularly successful and innovative, combining forces in hosting a huge youth forum to obtain direct access and information from the young people themselves. After the forum, *Tangent* was created, its brief to empower the young people in the area to articulate and meet their own needs.

It was during my attendance at one of these meetings that I met Claire, Hilary, Pat, Kylie and Sally. Of these, the first three decided they wanted to participate in my research project. These three girls inhabited a relatively prosperous area of the city although their actual familial situations were not particularly affluent. None of their parents was a professional but several were involved in small businesses. Hilary was in a single-parent family. What *was* apparent here from the first meeting was the girls' own sense of positive possibilities. Of their own volition they had joined a local government organization in order to have a voice and gain control over their own affairs. Hilary and Claire particularly believed in the power of youth representation. They decided to join my research project because they believed that it would be another means to express their views and to make a difference.

I met Mary through a different government agency, the Family and Community Services, also known as FACS. I had spent some time discussing different aspects of youth issues with one of the social workers there, when she suddenly asked if I would like to "work with Mary" and a number of other girls in her care, most of whom were Aboriginal. Mary, from Papua New Guinea, had been in foster care but was now in her own house under an independent living scheme. That meant she was financially and emotionally supported by the state, directly though various youth workers, so that she could learn the skills to be self-sufficient and self-confident. The social worker obviously felt that Mary's joining my project would be therapeutic for her young client and illuminating for me. So Mary and some other girls were offered the opportunity to be involved and tell their own stories on video. The other girls were Aboriginal teenagers who were currently living in the residential juvenile detention center. The Aboriginal girls were not interested in either talking to me at any length or filming aspects of their lives. This I found hardly surprising considering their curtailed life experiences at that stage! However, I found an immediate positive and excited response from Mary. For my part, I was gaining very different youth perspectives through Mary's world. Most of Mary's friends and acquaintances were young male offenders. Mary herself was arrested during my fieldwork, as noted in the Introduction.

The last "cluster" of girls to participate in the project comprised Janine and her friendship group. Through my teacher contacts and also through the youth workers at FACS I had learned about an Aboriginal female rock group based in a girls' school at Port Adelaide. I went to the school, attended a rehearsal and after the rehearsal spoke to the girls involved. Three of the eight girls in the band – Janine, Wanda and Janelle, whom we met at the beginning of this chapter – said that they would like to take part. Initially these girls interpreted their part in the project as making a film about their band and did not talk about using the camera individually at all. It was only after Wanda and Janelle disappeared from the project that Janine began to video her world more personally.[10]

With each of the ten "key" girls in the project I began my investigation with their personal perspectives, moving outwards to learn about their homes, their families, their social institutions and wider social networks. In this way my fieldwork took me into schools, youth clubs, raves, juvenile detention center's and the courts. I became physically involved in Cirkidz as a "spare adult" offering to help out, and as is the way with Cirkidz, ultimately participating in the classes themselves. I took part in the rehearsals of Black Image, the Aboriginal rock band, playing an instrument or singing to the best of my poor ability when they needed an extra person. I became their official photographer when they were performing in public. I helped out in rehearsals for the Rock and Roll Eisteddfod at two different schools. It was these overlapping, frequently conflicting views that inform this book. It was a move to understand ethnographically the ways in which the girls were enmeshed in their social worlds and how they themselves perceived and interpreted these enmeshments. The camera allowed me to make these comparisons, using a "jeweler's eye" (Marcus & Fischer 1986) between these different, often highly personal, always subjective perspectives and those adult viewpoints that were then framed in official discourses.

"It's different to a mirror 'cos it talks to you"

The question of why the camera was so successful, and so efficacious an entry point into the field across different social domains and locales so far remains unanswered. The most obvious explanation for their enthusiastic acceptance of the project was that the girls saw the task of representing themselves on video as exciting. Unlike questionnaires or interviews, which may be perceived as dull and time-consuming, leaving little room for personal involvement and experimentation, here they were active participants. They also seemed to understand immediately that with the camera they would have far more control over the final product.

Notwithstanding, the alacrity with which the participants took on the task undoubtedly suggests another, more complex aspect of the role of representation in everyday life and particularly the camera's pivotal place and acceptance in Western culture. Photographs and film have become significant cultural symbols; they epitomize particular ways in which real life experiences are framed, interpreted and re-presented. Their very indexical quality creates an immediate paradox, for although the camera seems to blur the distinction between the represented and the representation, we also know it can be used creatively to *construct* new images.

As a recording instrument, the camera is always used with an audience in mind. Inevitably, it is the means of surveillance, a means to objectify whereby the representation of a particular cultural space or context can be created, one that is different from the real life experiences it focuses upon. It can also be used for personal reflexivity – a way of seeing ourselves both as we think others see us – or re-inventing ourselves the way we would like to be seen. Because we can continually re-invent ourselves in this way, the resulting image is not necessarily reified or static (Barthes 1981: 12–14).

Thus, to fully understand photography and the camera is to realize that as a technical device it has gone way beyond being a simple recorder of actual events. It now occupies a fascinating and contradictory role. It can be, and frequently is, a voyeuristic tool for surveillance and a means of control. It is frequently employed now in shopping malls, banks, domestic dwellings and for various other forms of law enforcement. The camera also lends itself to being a tool both for *understanding* others and for being reflexive about oneself – a "surveillance" or monitoring of the *self*. It symbolizes a particular way in which real life experiences are framed, interpreted, and re-presented. Crystallized in the form of memory, photographic images allow us to recreate ourselves. Old selves can be wiped out as though they had never been and new selves creatively reborn. Even on a simplistic level, the very act of keeping a photograph album entails the selection of some images and rejection of others; we represent ourselves to ourselves the way we want to be remembered (Peace 1991).

Horkheimer and Adorno in their work understood the role of mimesis to be vital in the civilizing process of human beings and the development of the subject (see Gebauer & Wulf 1992). In their understanding, human self-preservation from earliest times meant adaptation to the terrors of nature by mimicry. As the individuals copied the actions and appearance of that which they feared, the distance between "self" and "other" disappeared. Fear of nature, the authors argued, was fear of dissolution of the self. This adaptive process had a two-edged aspect to it. It was both effective in its subordination of the human being to the overwhelming power of nature and yet also represented a way of *overcoming* the power of nature. It is effectually an early sign of human consciousness. In attempting to return to nature, the self is indicating separation and distinctiveness. The instinct to sink back into, to become one with nature, was, Horkheimer and Adorno argued, an internalized tendency of all human beings. It was referred to as "the death instinct" by Freud (1961). Roger Caillois (1959) called it *le mimetisme*.

Michael Taussig (1987, 1993), drawing on Walter Benjamin's insights concerning photography and other manifestations of "the art of mechanical reproduction," developed further the concept of *mimesis*, the embodied ways of becoming "other." This is, arguably, the fundamentally human way of attempting to gain mastery over that which we do not understand. He describes the way colonized or subjugated groups appropriate for themselves the representations of the dominant culture of their societies. In this way, accepting for themselves the stereotypes laid upon them, they "become 'other'." With the introduction of highly technologized means of representing self and "other," Taussig argues that the fusion between the two has become greater. *Mimesis*, or embodied mimicry, becomes a way of *becoming* "other," "wherein the replication, the copy, acquires the power from the represented" and "the capacity of the imagination [can be] lifted through representational media . . . into other worlds" (Taussig 1993: 16). In this way uncertainty and fear seem to be overcome and the very *means* of domination can be reappropriated. The dominated can take on board the method of subordination, reproducing this "otherness." In so doing they often inadvertently reaffirm the process of domination through their attempts to understand, to resist, to self-empower. It is a way of attempting to appropriate the power of the dominant and has been seen by many as a (perhaps misplaced) strategy of "resistance."

Paul Willis (1977), John Fiske (1989), Lisa Lewis (1990, 1992) and Angela McRobbie (1978, 1984, 1991) have all explored similar aspects of this phenomenon, especially the way young women have created their cultural identities through forms of popular culture and cultural commodities. Such research has tended to assert in various ways that: "the everyday culture of the oppressed takes the signs of that which oppresses them and uses them for its own purposes" (Fiske 1992). While certainly these authors have more recently and quite rightly questioned the romantic notion of "pleasure equals resistance," it is still true that underlying their arguments lies the implicit tendency to see an intentional, politically motivated expression of frustration, anger and rebellion behind young people's behavior. These works reveal their underlying links to the classics of subcultural theory and the belief that values attached to "youth subcultures," "contain the possibilities for social change" (Taylor 1993: 25).

Not everyone agrees that such manifestations indicate resistance. Marshall Sahlins exclaimed ruefully that in anthropology recently there had been a tendency of "translating the apparently trivial into the fatefully political" (1993: 17. Also cited in Brown 1996: 729–49). Discovery of resistance in all facets of social life often indicates nostalgic yearning on behalf of the analysts themselves for earlier, now faded (perhaps jaded) revolutionary ideals.

In a recent article Michael Brown points to the connection between the frequency of *use* of concepts of resistance and the perceived *need* for anthropologists to use these notions as an important rhetorical tool. He cites the example of feminist projects particularly, in their pioneering focus on the manifestations of power in the micro-politics of everyday life, claiming to have discovered resistance in the everyday survival strategies of the powerless (Brown 1996: 729). He argues that one aspect of the postmodern critique of ethnographic representation has left lingering uncertainty about the validity of analytical claims. In this intellectual climate notions of resistance become an important rhetorical tool to "convince others of the correctness of one's position and oneself of one's own moral rectitude" (Jackall 1994: 191; Brown 1996: 729). Perhaps more importantly, the indiscriminate attribution of resistance weakens its value as an analytical tool; everything becomes seen in terms of conflict and binary opposition, domination and resistance, with none of the subtleties that attention to ethnographic detail usually affords.

Rather than seeing aspects of "othering" or mimesis as resistance, I contend it is more important to understand such activity as part of the everyday play with identity, the constant development of the "protean self" (Lifton 1993). The contemporary era is a time when traditional certainties have been removed, when the constant re-inventing of the self is part of the everyday discourse clearly manifest in advertising and all forms of media, including self-help books. It is a time of "the New Age disorder" (Castells 1996).

Technology, gender and identity

A major factor in societal changes has been the rapid development over the past 20 years of new technologies. It is not simply that technological change is a component of society, but that the origin and trajectory of all technological changes are always social (Castells 1996). That is, while technological change is not the single determining factor of social change, it is a major influence on many interwoven aspects of social life, not least of which is the understanding of the self. The relatively recent widespread use of the Internet points to a seemingly liberating aspect of this development. Through discussion groups, websites and other encounters across time and space one can re-invent the self as necessary, time and time again (Turkle 1995). How liberating this elusive self, but yet how dangerous in its capacity for constant reinvention! Recent popular television programs such as *The X Files* and *GP* hint at the dangers that lurk behind this constant reinventing of "the self," where identity is ephemeral (Nixon 1996). I will return to this important nexus between technology, identity and gender in more detail in the following chapters. For now, I simply raise the following points.

Firstly, the way the girls used the camera and understood themselves to be simultaneously both object and subject points to a wider social issue. The development of the informational society, which is the world in which the girls in my fieldwork grew up, has greatly influenced our concepts of self in a number of key areas. Technology can be understood as a vehicle or indeed "a language" for action (Benston 1988: 15). The experience for most men and women in relation to technology is very different. Men and boys grow up ideally expecting to know a great deal about technology, about how machines and tools work. The worldview that grows up along with this perspective emphasizes rationality, objectivity and control over nature. On the other hand, women are not socialized into understanding technical matters. Instead they are expected to be good with people rather than things, to value interpersonal skills, to focus on emotion. This is not to say, of course, that women do not use tools or machines. Inevitably more and more everyday interactions are through and with machines and devices of all descriptions, in and out of the home, in and out of the workplace. Relevant here is the gendered nature of technology, in terms of its use and the knowledge about its functioning.

Mimesis and agency

The person operating a camera potentially has more control over the resultant representation than the person in the sight of the lens. Yet if the subject and object of the camera is the same person, the technology can also be used for personal reflexivity. For such a moment of awareness leads not just to a knowing of the self but also to what Homi Bhabha has termed an "interrogation" of the self. Alluding to Richard Rorty's discussions of the self, Bhabha writes:

> *Pre-eminent amongst these representations has been the reflection of the self that develops in the symbolic consciousness of the sign, and marks out the discursive space from which The Real Me emerges initially as an assertion of the authenticity of the person and then lingers on to reverberate—The real me?—as a questioning of identity.* (1987: 6)

Similarly, John Forrester (1987) points out the irony and central problem that now seems to face the present day search for and understanding of the self, when he writes:

> *The experience of perceiving oneself is now taken to be the most alienating experience of objectness possible. And most importantly, an experience one deceives oneself about in the search for the unified self.* (1987: 15)

So with the representation of the self comes perception, insight, and simultaneously, delusion – empowerment and alienation. We seem to capture the historical specificity of the moment but are left wondering about the concept of an "essentialist" self, the "authentic self" – is it there? Who am I? Do I exist? Again Hilary's visual image with the video referred to at the beginning of this chapter was striking because at that moment she captured that uncertainty and incredulity within the camera frame, underlining it powerfully with the words in voice-over, "My goodness, that is *me*!"

Power through representation: The mimetic faculty

With the development of techniques of mechanical reproduction and the technology of visual recording, Western culture has become obsessed with looking and recording images of what is seen (Coward 1984: 75). As I demonstrate throughout this book, the girls in my study *played* with representation, *played* with image.[11] Often this play involved their taking upon themselves different expressions of femininity, refracted through their identifications with particular aspects of ethnicity and class. Sometimes this occurred in ways that reinforced traditional stereotypes. Sometimes their exaggerated expressions of femininity seemed to suggest a form of "mimetic excess" (Taussig 1993), a way of exploring the possibilities and simultaneously rejecting them through play. However, as I shall demonstrate through analysis of the girls' use of video, I did not come to see these strategies as resulting from any clear intentionality, from any clearly perceived goals, or even any sense of "resistance." In fact, their behavior renders many of the usual polarizations, such as notions of agency or structure or of submission or resistance, as relatively impoverished.

The strategies or play displayed by these girls reveal an ambivalent and contradictory agency, an attempt to "create a fit" between the structural constraints of their internalized, embodied values and belief systems and the particular demands and expectations of the current social relational world within which they are engaged – the spaces of objective relations (Bourdieu & Wacquant 1992: 97) or having "a sense of the game" (Bourdieu 1977, 1990; 1993). The ways these young women perceived, reflected on and represented their worlds in their everyday activities demonstrated a particular, but often tacit, response to the various constraints surrounding them, including their own sense of place within their familial and social contexts. Their play, their image-making, their use of fantasy highlighted a simultaneous testing, stretching and affirming of the symbolic and structural boundaries circumscribing and constraining them.

Taussig asks rhetorically, "Is it conceivable that a person could break boundaries like this, slipping into Otherness, trying it on for size?" (1993: 33). Perhaps the answer lies in our limited conception of identity. Although we have rejected for the most part the concept of identity as a "unified essence," we haven't yet fully understood the notion of identity as a *process*, "who one is to become" (Hall 1995: 65). Ultimately identities are narratives – stories we tell about ourselves – and they are fictional. But identity cannot be looked at in isolation. I would argue that the way each girl used the camera to interrogate and construct her sense of self revealed a questioning of the concept of a unified self and a great deal about how she saw herself through several different possible engendered subject positions (Moore 1994). It pinpointed the sense of uncertainty that the girls experienced as they struggled to manage this elusive sense of self. The point is that there is no one single subject position offered to these young women growing up, but many. The fact that they were aware of these multiple conflicting discursive sites can be illustrated by a close look at the ways these girls constituted themselves, "experimented" with a variety of images and poses. As my research progressed I found that *my* analytic focus sharpened on the *ways* the girls used the camera to deal with these tensions, to represent and constitute themselves through a variety of possible frameworks.

Other ways of seeing

There seemed to be an awareness by all of the girls that the camera was an exciting way of simultaneously exploring and constructing themselves, discovering and constituting "the real me" and emphasizing difference. Hilary, for example, wanted to show how "*other* girls acted and behaved" and that "not everyone is the same. We are all individuals." She was aware of the power of media representation and was annoyed that, as she perceived it, teenagers were so often depicted in a negative light, especially in the tabloid press. In this way, then, she and some of the others saw the potential of the camera as a "political tool," a vehicle for presenting alternative points of view to a wider audience. This did not mean, however, that the girls always approached their films with any obvious generic formula in mind; rather they seemed to experiment with form as well as content in their footage.

Initially, there was a tendency to stage formal interviews and to generalize for the audience about teenage behavior. The narrative form was drawn straight from those television programs that best seem to "capture reality" – news and current affairs. Many of the girls were eager to be the "television host," the mediating authority figure, keen to interview *others* on what *other* teenage girls like and feel, rather than be the focus of attention themselves. Several went around their schoolyards like investigative journalists, armed with microphones and camera to ask their friends and acquaintances "significant questions":

> *"Do you think boys should tell their girlfriends how to dress?"*
> *"How do you feel about smoking and alcohol?"*
> *"Do you think boys are only after one thing?"*

It was an interesting distancing of themselves as "subject," and initially my frustration was intense as I realized that the girls saw themselves as investigators of others, not the object of scrutiny themselves. I then began to understand that this was the initial testing-out of space and possibilities – to see what was "permissible" in their own eyes and in their own worlds – to explore what their world would look like through the more seemingly "objective" lens of the camera.

Apart from this "straight" interview form, where the questions were deliberately open-ended, such play with the camera also provided an opportunity to encourage others to articulate what the investigator already knew or suspected.

> Pointing the camera and microphone at her friend Marika, Janine asked "*What do you do in your spare time?*" Marika looked a bit incredulous at the question. "*Hang around. Run away from the cops.*" "*What were you doing?*" asked Janine sternly. Marika looked uncertain, laughed nervously, looked at the camera and then back again at Janine. "*Mucking around. Drinking beer,*" she said. "*Oh, so you drink do you?*" asked Janine. "*Nah not me!*" replied Marika quickly – one eye on the camera again – "*it's the other fellas.*"

Experienced journalists would recognize this as entrapment! So, on one level the girls were using the interview and related documentary style to find out things for themselves – to discover what other young people their age did and didn't do. The camera and microphone could either provide a license to confirm what they already suspected of their friends and acquaintances or it could provide a forum for such discussion. Again, we need to see such activity as a form of "strategized" play.

After this more hesitant beginning, the mimetic activity, this attempt to see themselves as *other*, developed more noticeably. A greater experimentation occurred in the mode of documentary itself. In an attempt to articulate and test their own feelings and the constraints of their world, the girls turned the camera on themselves by making *themselves* the overt, acknowledged subjects of the investigation in two related ways. Either the technique that I came to call "ask me questions" was used, or the girls used "the fly on the wall" mode of address, pretending the camera did not exist. The "fly on the wall" is the concept of "the fourth wall" in the theatre or cinema.[12] It was the view for the spectator or voyeur usually unacknowledged by the (social) actor. Sometimes both techniques, "ask me questions" and "fly on the wall," were used by the same person at different times. Both were modes of distancing or *othering* in attempts to gain some kind of mastery over both the situation and the representation.

Ask me questions!

Several of the girls asked me to film a section of their video by acting as camera person and interviewer. Grace, for example, asked me to come to her house on particular afternoons or early evenings when she knew her mother and her younger brother would not be at home. This, she informed me, was to ensure privacy. After we had set up the camera in her room, she would sit in front of it and say, "Ask me questions!" In situations like this I often found that the period when I asked the questions – "What is your name? Tell me about yourself? What kind of a person are you?" – didn't last very long. The questions seemed to be used as starting points to enable the young person to describe significant aspects of her life. Perhaps to be "asked questions" in this way offers license to be personal. So much of our culture, especially for women, emphasizes the inappropriateness of talking about oneself so that a space has to be created in order for one to "objectify" oneself, in order to be "other."

Although these conversations were recorded, I emphasize again that it was always understood that the resulting raw footage was under the control of the subject. In other words, whatever the person said and did in front of the video could be removed or, if it were retained, could be used for the final edited video, or left aside. This strategy seemed to provide the freedom to "play" with confidences and important information, a license to "unsettle" and "unravel" conventionally controlled behavior, to create and constitute reality at the same time. In this way, aspects of the girls' lives that perhaps would not have been revealed to an adult researcher were talked about relatively openly on the video.

Although all of the girls talked about illicit drug use – either their own use or the difficulties they faced when with friends – I did not expect anyone to commit themselves to discussing their own involvement on camera. *Off* camera, as they talked about their various social activities and mused about friendships, parties or other events, they were all quite candid, specific and detailed in their discussions with me. Yet, one afternoon, Grace spent several hours chatting in front of the camera about her own and her friends' experimentations with illegal drugs. She told me where and how they obtained the substances, the cost, which ones she had tried and which ones she was too afraid to try. She told me about the large cross-section of friends she had and how they would meet up often in the city. The main activity they had in common was their shared use of a combination of alcohol and amphetamines – "I can't imagine a world without drugs. It'd be so boring." She told me that her group regularly took "Dope, acid trips (LSD) and Rohypnol." I met many of these friends during my fieldwork, several of them repeating this information in their casual conversations with each other. Although *off* camera she had chatted about these activities before, *on* video Grace was very careful "not to name names" of those friends who had actually taken some of the harder drugs and she announced that she certainly would not select those sections of her video for public viewing. However, she made no attempt to wipe the material completely off the tape by recording over it.[13]

The "ask me questions" mode thus seemed to provide an opportunity for the young people to talk about very personal, often difficult problems through this method of distanciation. This was "serious play," an opportunity to simultaneously explore and portray themselves as "other." In this mode, Sara talked about her unpleasant experiences of racism at school; Fran talked about her difficult and antagonistic relationship with her father; and nearly all of the girls talked about the difficult balancing act of being simultaneously both child and (female) young adult.

The fact that the girls talked about these "risky" things is less interesting than the fact that they chose to reveal them on videotape as part of their documentary footage. It seemed as though actions and thoughts performed on tape, but not in front of a *visible* audience, could create a space for experimentation. Something recorded can be watched, examined, understood as though it were someone else's experience. As Fran at the end of film-production time confirmed, the camera was a means to constructing the desired image:

> *Since I started making this film . . . I'm seeing myself through other people's eyes, how other people see me. It's been good though, because if you see something you don't like, you can change it. It's different to a mirror 'cos it talks to you.*

The reference to the "talking mirror" highlights again the difficulty of maintaining a secure sense of self, an awareness that the self can be changed and that change is part of its constitution. The gap between the "performing me" and the "inner me" becomes blurred.

Maintaining "the fourth wall"

Another blurring of spheres resulting from the utilization of a documentary style occurred when the camera was used to record day-to-day events but its existence was not acknowledged during the filming. Mary was quite specific about this. She wanted the camera to show her normal activities of collecting her social security check, going shopping and so on, while pretending that the camera "was invisible." She led the imaginary camera audience through the mall, chatting to acquaintances as she went to window-shop at her favorite sports clothing store. The clothes there were way out of her price range but she directed the camera to show her judiciously scrutinizing the items of clothing, feeling the quality, checking the prices and chatting to the staff as though she were a regular purchaser. She certainly was a regular visitor to the sports store, but she was not able to afford the prices of these expensive brand-name clothes. At no stage did Mary attempt to talk to the camera. She behaved as though the camera were invisible; she was merely capturing her usual activities on film.

As was the case with several of the girls, there were events and aspects of Mary's life that she decided to portray very differently. For example, some things were not recorded or talked about *on* camera at all. Away from the camera Mary had talked about her experiments with drugs including "magic mushrooms" – fungi with hallucinogenic properties that grow wild in the local hills. On another occasion, she had given me a detailed account of shoplifting and car theft and chases in the city. These activities were repeated to me later by several of her friends, through their conversations with each other in my presence, and later by Mary's social worker.[14] As indicated above, most of Mary's friends were boys and some were known offenders, frequently appearing before the courts or spending time in the detention center, yet these details of petty crime or "offending" did not appear in Mary's footage. In front of the camera, it seemed that Mary was anxious to portray a respectable, socially responsible self for others to see and understand. It was also, as I realized later, a way of constructing a portrait of herself that she could feel good about.

> *I felt through making this film I could acknowledge myself. I can see some very good parts of me.* (Mary)

Frequently the "fourth wall" technique was temporarily abandoned so that the individual could alternate between objective and subjective mode. Initially the event may have been recorded without acknowledging the camera and then suddenly the video and assumed audience were acknowledged and included in the diegesis. In this manner, several of the girls filmed their own or other people's parties. On these occasions other guests experimented with the camera. Sometimes it caught self-conscious conversations or physical jokes that highlighted the usual concerns of young people. Grace and her best friend chatted resignedly about sexual double standards as they cooked together in Grace's kitchen. At Fran's party, one of the boys planted a deliberately noisy kiss on another boy for the benefit of the camera, while another put on lipstick and then in close-up shot pouted and kissed at the camera lens. Amid the resulting hilarity one of the boys asked, "Will you respect me in the morning?"

Fig 5: Mary in the sports store

Pat was very involved with "techno rave" culture and so filmed quite a number of dances. Her material detailed the crowds, the ritualized performances of the DJs and the MCs and, using a strobe facility on the camera, she managed to express most expressionistically the mood of the dances and the effect of the lights and the music. The strobe basically meant that the dancers were shown moving slowly and rhythmically like automatons while the music and the background chat of the dancers continued at their normal pace. Again, there was no direct gaze to the camera during these scenes – the operator was effectively invisible and ignored as she recorded the event. However, when she filmed scenes at a techno community radio station where she helped out occasionally, or when she filmed the preparations behind the scenes for a number of techno raves, the people she was filming responded to the camera's presence by laughing, chatting and showing a self-conscious awareness of the camera lens. Publicly, Pat seemed to be portraying herself as very much part of the "scene," describing herself as a "raver" and distinguishing between the "real thing" and the many Try Hards, those who attempted to be authentic but failed. It was only *off* camera that she talked angrily about the sexism and double standards she perceived in the ravers' scene.

So these were moments of gaining distance, of "seeing myself as others see me, of analyzing myself a bit" (Fran), of attempting to grasp "the real me." Yet, simultaneously, the camera provided an awareness that "the real me" was not ready-made but available to be constructed – the self and identity are not simply reflected upon and represented but constituted in the very act of representation, in the very act of play. In some cases, direct address to the camera, as a kind of confessional, was used as a way to pin down this elusive self.

"Authority" and "authenticity" through direct address

Of all the girls, Diane used the camera most personally as a form of diary. Several times after an important evening, a special party or event, alone in her room, Diane would record her feelings, excitements and anxieties on the video. The self she portrayed and projected on these occasions was primarily someone who, in her own words, "enjoyed partying totally" but simultaneously was concerned about difficulties of friendships, the pressures from peers and parents concerning appropriate social behavior, and the difficulties of negotiating relationships with the opposite sex without incurring the reputation of a "slut." Her monologue was punctuated every now and again with qualifications in case the camera should think she were being too forward, obsessed with boys, or even too self-absorbed. "Have I bored you yet?" she would ask of her imagined audience. Toward the end of my period of field research, she was to articulate the pleasure of using the camera as a diary because "It became like my best friend. I knew if it got bored or didn't like what I said, it wouldn't get huffy or run away."[15]

Such use of the camera again points to an awareness of the elusiveness of an "authentic self" and a need to manage and control the uncertainty (Goffman 1959, 1970). It was a way in which the girls created boundaries of certitude, signalling what was private and what could be considered as constituting "the real me." As the friend of one of the girls told me:

> *That's why some people keep diaries. A diary can be more important than a best friend. Sometimes, you can't tell a friend what you are thinking because you may not know whether you really believe it. How can you tell someone something when you don't know whether you know it yourself yet?* (Belinda)

Earlier I described Mary's video footage as she went about her normal business behaving as though the camera were invisible. On a separate occasion, however, but clearly not intended for a wider audience, she gave a detailed verbal account on video – totally unsolicited – of the physical abuse she had undergone as a child when she was first brought into the country by her adoptive parents. This account was subsequently repeated to me by her social worker. Before she began to speak, Mary dressed herself in her best clothes and created on the kitchen bench a display of photographs of herself as a small child with her biological parents. Then as she spoke in direct address to the camera, "the fourth wall" completely dissolved. This aspect of her life she appeared to be recording entirely for herself – a way of *othering* or distancing the events, of enabling her to gain a new perspective on them. These were not to be shown to others, she said. As a companion and a friend in her actual world, which was obviously more than that which was portrayed on video, I was permitted to be privy to the less conventionally acceptable aspects of her life. On the parts of the video that were to be selected for showing to a public audience, however, the representation of her life and her identity was more carefully and, in some ways, "creatively" drawn.

What is clear here, then, is that both Diane's and Mary's public performances were drawn with far more certitude and confidence than their more "private" selves. It is the slippage that appears between the shifting subjectivities, the possible and the enacted selves, that becomes the problem, the aspect of everyday life and representation that has to be "managed." Identity is as much about exclusion as inclusion: who we are requires a delicate and continual drawing-up of shifting boundaries. Perhaps an appropriate metaphor would be a kaleidoscope. In contemporary Western culture, perceptions and interpretations of social reality are potentially endless. With each twist of the cylinder another pattern clicks into focus. Out of these random patterns we impose order, but our hold on what is order and what makes sense can be very shaky indeed. We have to hold tenuously onto quite contradictory notions of reality, switching from one to another as we feel appropriate. Play enables us to do this for "playing . . . [is] . . . the underlying continuum of experience" (Schechner 1993: 42).

Locating "the real me"?

Not only did the camera provide a reflection of the participants' sense of identity but its use enabled that identity to be constituted. Shaviro, drawing on Walter Benjamin's understanding of the experience of film, referred to the tactile cinematic image and the effect on the observer. The blurring of what is observed and the observer become, he argues, a moment of mimesis. How much more so is this when the subject of that depiction is also the object – for example, when the girls turned the cameras on themselves, on their own sense and portrayal of self? The resultant "real me" is hard to grasp, impossible to pin down.

> *Following Benjamin and Taussig, we must radically redefine the very notion of identification, and say rather that the subject is captivated and "distracted," made more fluid and indeterminate, in the process of sympathetic participation. Mimesis and contagion tend to efface fixed identities and to blur the boundaries between inside and outside* (Shaviro 1993: 53).

My observation of Fran's attempt to capture herself on camera provides an interesting example of this. As was often the case with the other girls, I felt there was an interesting gap between the ways I frequently saw her *off* camera and the way she tailored her portraits to experiment, to play with her camera image, to experiment with different identities.

I had arranged that Fran should have the camera to video some quieter sections for her film in her home. I knew her as "Fran" in full swing at Cirkidz, energetically taking part in the workshops or in performance at shows. I had been present when, in Sara's film, Fran had been part of her friendship group and I had also viewed Sara's video of her party where Fran had been a guest. I saw her as ebullient. Her verbal and body language were extravagant and totally unrestrained, irrespective of whether there was a camera present to catch her moods and behavior or not. At Cirkidz workshops she dominated the conversation with loud comments, bawdy or insulting jokes and raucous laughter. The most agile of the members, she performed backflips and bodily contortions with ease and with superb skill and dexterity, as figure 6 shows. She carried her body with an unrestrained ease and was extremely physical with her close friends, both male and female, on occasion raising comment. Certainly her physical intimacy with most of the boys in the group had disturbed some of the girls from time to time. On Sara's video, where she had taken film of her friends in the city, there were several shots of Fran doing multiple somersaults on the lawn outside the Adelaide Museum, totally oblivious to the stares of passersby; at Sara's party, she was shown on camera dancing wildly while calling attention to another girl's dancing movements by yelling, "Hey look everyone, M.'s fucking a pole!"

So this was the girl I knew. This was the first time, though, that Fran had suggested that she would like to video her own world, be director of her own film, as it were. I was totally unprepared for the Fran I met at her house on this occasion. She arrived at home about ten minutes after I arrived, entering relatively quietly and immediately apologizing for being late. She was dressed in a short skirt with black leggings and a large black felt hat – a far cry from her usual casual outfit of shapeless T-shirts and baggy shorts or patchwork pants. She kept the hat on the entire time I was there and throughout the videoing session; she was obviously proud of it and liked the way she looked in it.

Fig 6: Fran in performance

Fig 7: Fran in sophisticated mode

In her room, in front of the camera, she sat upright and quietly poised on her bed asking me if I had had a good week and generally making "polite conversation" for a few minutes. After she adjusted the bedside lights so that a dull blue light shone on her face, she talked about who she felt she was, her ambitions, her likes and dislikes. It was in this context that she told me that she particularly enjoyed her quality of childishness and her ability to play, a comment highlighting, for me, the very self-consciousness of her pose and the awareness that her more mature serious stance was just as much a play with image and style as her earlier expressions of frivolity and fun.

Actions and thoughts performed on tape, but not in front of a visible audience create a space for experimentation, a moment of blurring of what are designated private and public worlds. A fascinating moment illustrating this occurred when Grace suddenly told me that she wanted to dance. She had been filming and talking about her bedroom in my presence and then she suddenly asked me to leave the room. Alone, she played her favorite tapes and danced by herself in front of the video for about ten minutes. Then I was allowed back into the room and she continued her more mundane filming. It seemed as though here was an instance of music enabling the "saying" of what was perhaps usually unsayable, something that could only be articulated silently through the body. This anecdote leads on to another rich area of speculation – the symbolic roles and utilization of music.

Music and mimesis

Music played a central role in footage taken by all of the girls, a point that will be discussed later in the book. I will use this section to comment on some of the ways in which music was combined with the girls' camera use through dance and other aspects of performance. Several girls recorded their own dancing to their favorite musicians, but when it was "serious play" it was recorded as either "fly on the wall" (as in Pat's depictions of the rave scene) or as a secret activity (as in the case of Grace). In any other recording, the girls tended to exaggerate their movements – using humor to stress their ironic stance. So, for example, when Diane filmed her two friends Helen and Jane dancing in front of her TV to one of Peter André's songs, their movements echoed exactly those of the dancers on the television screen in the pop clip. The girls swept in front of the screen, shoulders raised, gazing with sophisticated disdain over their shoulders, back at the camera.

Helen: *This is how sluttish models walk.*
Diane: (from behind the camera lens as she filmed) *Oh very sluttish! Remember to smile. You'll be famous.*[16]

This kind of exaggeration, or mimetic excess, always hinted at the moments when "contradictory realities coexist, each seemingly capable of cancelling the other out" (Schechner 1993: 36).

Fig 8: Dancing to Peter André

Playing with (self) identity

The different uses of the documentary form allowed the girls to record themselves as investigators, seekers of "truth" and to create themselves in their own images of socially acceptable, mature young adults. But play – to return to my premise at the beginning of the chapter – can be exciting and dangerous because it is unpredictable. Play can expose the lack of containment – the inability to maintain a fixed, carefully controlled self. The carefully drawn mask can slip.

Such moments of slippage, moments of heightened awareness of the (lack of) management of identity, were often accommodated on video through mimetic excess and humor.[17] In this instance the more serious recording of experience was abandoned in favor of exaggeration, a very clear excessive posing or ironic stance. The example of Diane with her friends, above, is one such moment. Perhaps a less immediately obvious example of mimetic excess, but a poignant one, nevertheless, was revealed in Kate's video. She and a friend began to question each other about leisure time and school. After a while, they began to stage the interviews, deliberately placing the interviewee in deep shadow to "conceal" her identity while asking emotive questions about school, parental and peer group expectations and so on. The interviewee would pretend to cry and the interview would finish with the interviewer enquiring quietly and with a great show of concern, "Would you like to end the interview now?"

Because the girls attended different schools and because Kate's school was perceived as more academic, their video personae differed accordingly. So, in the first scenario, Kate pretended to suffer distressing teasing by her peers because her B grade average was not high enough. When they swapped roles, her friend pretended to be distressed because *her* friends teased her for her *high* academic achievements. This portion of the video was an extremely elaborate parody of a current affairs program but it also resonated with their own concerns and awareness of class differences and familial expectations. After a while, they returned to the interview topic but adopting a more serious vein. However, they soon switched off the camera, perhaps aware that the scenario was too unsettling to discuss or portray without humor or intense role play.

Cleaning up the image

In this chapter, I have explored the use of the camera by the girls as a means to "play with" and "explore" possible identities through particular generic styles and televisual forms. In the process I have considered the particular efficacy of the photographic frame and small domestic video camera to enable this reflexivity. When the participants came to edit and condense their footage in the edit suite, the exercise proved even more liberating because sound and image could be separated and new selves could clearly be created in the final video product. Images could be removed as though they had never been. Old "selves" could be revisited and scrutinized for their "authenticity" at representing "the real me" or "the me as I am now." Sara expressed the difficulty of the exercise in the following way, grinning ironically:

> *I've changed a lot over the three years which made editing hard. Sometimes looking at myself was like looking in a mirror at a great big zit.*[18]

The normal way of analyzing film texts – even such home-produced artifacts – would be through film theory which draws on semiotic and psychoanalytic concepts as, for example, in the work of Modleski (1988), Penley (1989), Williams (1983, 1989) and many others. However, while these approaches are valuable and insightful, here I am drawing on what may be described as concepts of identity that have emerged in late modernity, specifically the concepts of play and mimesis.[19] I seek to emphasize the phenomenological and physiological factors that underlie filmmaking and viewing. The cinematic apparatus in this paradigm is not creating "an impression of reality" (Baudry 1986) but a palpable and disturbing power.

Childhood and adolescence usually allow space to play, and play, as we have seen, is a very serious, often desperate, venture – a testing and stretching of boundaries to harness a sense of certainty. For the teenage participants in this study, their engagement with narrative style, genre and form in their own filmmaking indicated their searching for and struggle with their sense of shifting possible identities. At the end of the filming process, Hilary stated: "The film has shown me change is the only certainty in life."

Of course in any stage in life, but perhaps most dramatically during adolescence, change is most clearly manifested through the body – changes that are experienced phenomenologically and that are remarked on by others. In the next chapter I examine the relationship between technology and the body, how the camera was specifically used by the girls to understand these changes and to "play" with the usual perceptions of the feminized body. This inevitably leads us back to the question of play, of serious play or, in Schechner's terminology, "dark play" (1993). Is part of the danger of the protean self that it can be ungendered, that in its very constitution it opens up more spaces for uncertainty rather than providing a sense of cohesion or closure?

Notes

1 See figure 2 on page 30.
2 Sontag talks of the photographic image as being like a "neat slice of time" (17). She is in fact distinguishing here between still photography and film or video. However, I would argue that the difference is not so significant and in fact that her insights concerning photography are particularly applicable to my observations of video usage.
3 Here I am particularly referring to drug taking, sexual promiscuity without appropriate concern for birth control or sexually transmitted diseases, but other more casual risk-taking took place that involved experimentation with the body in various forms.
4 In 1994 the name was officially changed from Bowden Brompton Youth Circus to Cirkidz Inc. because it was realized that the circus was unlikely to be staying in its current location in Bowden Brompton.
5 Information obtained from Bowden Brompton Community Youth Circus, Marketing Action Plan, Interim Report, ABK Marketing and Communication Consultants, 11 September 1993: 3.
6 Information given in private conversation.
7 My instinct in this regard proved to be right as the following anecdote suggests. Claire had "reserved" the camera through me for an important event she wanted to film. However, when the time came for her to have the camera it was discovered to be faulty. Because the event was important and obviously of limited duration, I hired another Hi 8 camera for her to use while ours was being repaired. She took the new camera but returned it unused after the weekend. "It was too large," she said. Not only was it too cumbersome for her but it looked too obvious and too obtrusive to be just present and eventually ignored in a social situation.
8 Although many homes do possess this technology, the cameras are not often seen as something the younger members of the house can "play" or "experiment with." Just as use of the television and video recorders in the home are frequently strictly controlled (Morley 1981), so I discovered are the video cameras!
9 At that stage I was attempting to limit the age of participants to as close to 15 years of age as I could so I only offered the camera to the first group.
10 I am using the term "disappeared" because, unlike the other girls, the Aboriginal girls made no formal declaration to me that they didn't want to remain in the project. They just simply didn't turn up at the arranged times. It was an aspect of the fieldwork I had to learn to deal with.
11 They were of course not the only ones to do this. The book postulates that such play is a human trait, and certainly not restricted to female adolescents in Australia. See chapters 6 and 7.
12 This concept was first identified and crystallized into theories of theater by Stanislavski (1980). In Brechtian theater, of course, "the fourth wall" is removed, the space between actor and spectator torn down to reveal the artifice, to expose the suspended belief cf. Willett "The Chinese artist never acts as if there were a fourth wall besides the three surrounding him. *He expresses his awareness of being watched . . . The audience can no longer have the illusion of being the unseen spectator at an event which is really taking place* . . . A further means is that *the artist observes himself*" (1964: 92, emphasis added).
13 Grace was also quite adamant whenever I brought her video footage into her house that I hand it directly to her and not leave it with her mother. She obviously had more concerns than the other girls, but all the girls treated their "raw" or "wild" footage (untreated material) as private and confidential, showing it only to very trusted others.

14 I heard these accounts again through conversations with the authority figures and legal representatives involved, such as the police, social workers and the magistrate when, later, Mary herself was brought before the court.

15 Whom did Diane and the others believe they were addressing? Diane once answered in a response to this question "whoever is going to watch." Yet one must also assume that there is an element of the internalized camera, the understanding that one is always the object of a gaze (see Walters 1995).

16 I discussed this section with Diane several years later after she had edited her final footage. We had attended a radio interview for the ABC March 1997 about the completed film *Striking poses* where I had talked about language and I had explained how the word *slut* was regarded as a heavy word by most of the young women in my research. Embarrassed and rather incredulous, Diane asked me after the interview, "Did you mean to say that word *on air*?" I suddenly realized that Diane's removal of the word from her final footage was deliberate. She had included this visual section but had dubbed a different sound track over the top. The comment about "sluttish models" had been erased and now only Peter André's music was present.

17 Schechner (1993) refers to these moments as "dark play" and indeed some of these moments can be entirely without humor.

18 Obviously one of the worst scenarios for a teenager is discovering the face in the mirror has a blemish that she hadn't noticed before ("a zit"). It is another aspect of the body seen as "out of control." This issue is explored more fully in the following chapter. However, highly significantly in the context of *this* discussion, it is worth noting that "zits" can be covered up and eventually they disappear as though they had never been.

19 While the original ideas of mimesis (and certainly from Walter Benjamin's perspective) obviously could not have been interpreted as "postmodern," the way that such "othering" and playing with shifting subjectivities reflects a blurring of symbolic boundaries can suitably be regarded in this way.

Chapter 2

My Body, Myself

> What after all, is more personal than the life of the body? And for women, associated with the body and largely confined to life centred on the body (both the beautification of one's own body and the reproduction, care and maintenance of the bodies of others), culture's grip on the body is a constant, intimate fact of everyday life. (Susan Bordo 1993: 17)

> *It's pretty funny looking at old photos. I got them out today because well I'm kind of looking to see who I am . . . and I think that who you are is made up of our past . . . It's really funny seeing me on the outside 'cos all I know is me on the inside.* (Hilary, direct address to camera)

Introduction: The 'withness' of the body

The body is an inescapable and paradoxical presence! In the previous chapter I discussed how Grace, during a session where she was filming her room, suddenly asked me to "go outside. I want to dance." She then continued to video, but this time recording herself as she moved rhythmically to the music. Subsequently she indicated that I could view the tape later; however, at that moment, it seemed, she wanted to experience and record the moment alone. It was a poignant example of the intensity and anxiety of when the embodied self reflects upon and constitutes itself as "other." Grace wasn't simply dancing alone. She was dancing in a new dress she had just bought and had put on to show me.[2] She was watching herself dancing, watching the movement, watching the impression and recording that moment. It was undoubtedly a moment of surveillance, a manifestation of attempted control. All bodies, as Foucault (1979, 1981) has argued, are subject to surveillance, from both overt external sources and internalized control. In this very process of "watching," Grace was carrying out an objectification of herself, a chance to survey, to alter, to become something and someone else. It was above all a surveillance of herself as "body in action."[3]

In this chapter, by focusing my analytic lens on the significance of this kind of self-surveillance, I am extending the earlier discussion of the way the girls reflected upon and constituted their sense of self. Specifically, I am investigating the intersection of embodied subjectivity, gender and representation. In describing the ways in which the girls in my fieldwork negotiated their worlds through their bodily action and the ways they talked about embodiment, I am looking at how they sought to explore and "represent" themselves through their bodily practices. The girls' "rhetorics of self-making" (Battaglia 1995) were enacted through their bodies, their explorations involving negotiation of both similarity and difference, the marking of boundaries between self and other (Harraway 1990, 1991; Feher et al. 1989). As in the previous chapters, I again draw on notions of "play as work"; in this case it is body work, "the most immediate and most important form of labour that humans engage in" (Schilling 1993: 118). In other words, this was "serious play" indeed.

Following the framework already established earlier in the book, and indeed taking a lead from Hilary's words at the beginning of the chapter, I will explore the significance of bodily expression and bodily experience from the "outside" to the "inside," from the public realm of experience to the more subjective and personal. Such a journey also takes us through a consideration of the senses, conceived of in their own hierarchy of significance, from the distant and extrinsic (sight and hearing) through to the more "basic" and tactile (touch and taste).

The incident concerning Grace serves to remind us of the essential paradox and difficulty of any discussion of the body in the constitution of subjectivity, for the body is both "contained and container at once" (Stewart 1984: 104), both biological organism and cultural representation (Falk 1994). Hilary articulates in a different way what Grace is enacting. She talks about knowing herself "only from the inside" and wanting to learn more about herself from representation, from photos, from her past. But in order for both girls to conceive of their bodies in this way, in terms of "inside" and "outside," they are also drawing on an historically and culturally specific mental process. It is a process that defines "me" in relation to "not-me." It is Derrida's concept of *différance* (Derrida 1976, 1981), being a separate "individual," who requires an "otherness" for its emergence. It stands theoretically separate from society like a painted relief but emerges as "naturalized," the way things are. In other words, one can only see and "know" oneself through a cultural prism.

One of the consequences of such a cultural conception of the self and the body lies in the notion of control: who owns the body? Who is responsible for this body and its actions? In contemporary Western society, including Australia, the dominant cultural belief is that personal control of the body is the responsibility of the individual alone; that is, that the individual subject owns her body. In this way, the individual's concern and management of her body is dependent upon the primary cultural belief in individuality and independence (Becker 1994).[4] It is one of the major defining attributes of mature personhood. Deutsch calls this "the body as achievement concept," arguing that it is through the body that the distinction between identity and personhood lies:

> *My body is only as it is articulated within my being as a person. To appropriate the physical means to acknowledge the given conditions – the physical structures, drives, powers, capacities – and to bring them firmly into the fabric of my achieved identity. A body, then, always belongs to someone. The primary meaning of the concept is its achievement sense . . . A person is his/her achieved identity.* (Deutsch 1993: 8–9)

This does not mean that this primary belief is never contested nor that, in fact, enormous paradoxical "conflicts of interest" do not arise within this premise, for individuals belong to several cultural fields of influence at the same time, as I shall demonstrate below. In fact, one of the main issues of contention that arise between parents or adult authority figures and adolescents centers on exactly this question – who has the right to control this body? For young people, and especially female adolescents, that is where a great deal of the sense of struggle and concern about the body resides.

For teenage girls – because women are far more often acutely subject to the scrutinizing gaze of others – such discourses lead to a despising of, and a distancing from, their own healthy pubescent bodies as they attempt to survey and critically monitor, and affect their own corporeality (Walters 1995). For teenagers, especially around the age of 13 to 16, the gap between the idealized images of the body, the "appropriate" limiting and constricting ways of behaving and their real life experiences, is particularly glaring.

This is mainly because the pubescent body is changing and developing at a rapid rate and these changes are not usually under the control of the individual. There are physiological changes to height, weight, skin, and fat distribution in ways that can be rapid and therefore frequently distressing. They occur just at a time when the young person is starting to feel perhaps more independent and in control of her world. There is also usually a move at this time from the more protected atmosphere of primary school to the larger, more competitive world of high school. Hormonal changes taking place inside the body manifest themselves mainly on the outside but also in the way the teenager feels about herself, her peers and her relationships with others.[5] There is a general feeling of being out of control and out of step with herself because it is a time when the body and the conscious "self" seem particularly out of kilter. She becomes particularly self-conscious about her body. The teenager also becomes especially aware of, and internalizes, the cultural significance of these physiological changes as others, both adults and peers, comment on these developments and as the young people compare themselves with others (Simmons et al. 1973). Again, as recent research suggests, this seems to be particularly so for girls.

In adolescence, girls show an increased tendency to value body image and same-sex popularity. Thus girls might be placed in increased jeopardy both because they value peer opinion more ("the reflected self"), especially at the point of transition to secondary school, and also because they value body image more at a time when their body is changing dramatically and social comparisons along this dimension become more problematic (Hendry et al. 1993).

A further consequence of the notion of individual ownership of the body is one that is central to this whole book, that the public portrayal of the self relies on a paradox, the tension and blurring between sameness and difference, between being and becoming, between referent and representation. The paradox occurs primarily because there is an understanding that, as the body is perceived as the responsibility of the individual person, so, it is believed, in its representations lies the essence of the self. The way cultural symbols are manipulated and expressed through the body in dress, gesture, deportment and adornment is a key strategy towards this end (Goffman 1959). It is a way of expressing the self as different, or in deconstructionist terms a marking-out of différance (Derrida 1973, 1978, 1981); in the case of the young women in my research, for example, a way of "constituting" themselves as female as opposed to male or as adolescent as opposed to adult.[6] At the same time (for one cannot be a "self" in isolation) such cultural symbolism also indicates distinction (Bourdieu 1984). That is, each person struggles to express a certain kind of femininity, a certain kind of adolescence, a certain kind of individual.

Dress, adornment, stance, a "pose" – all cultural symbols manipulated to express the self – indicate to others that this person belongs to a certain group, and is a certain type of person. In other words, they signal group identity. The adoption of particular types of cultural symbols facilitates a way of distinguishing and promoting oneself through association with others; the "disciplined" body becomes seen as a cultural symbol of success. These two terms, *différance* and distinction, are not actually discrete but depend upon each other for meaning; like the two sides of a sheet of paper, separated only theoretically. Individuation, in this conception, depends on distinction.

In this way, the body itself can be seen as a paradox. It is the "site of enormous symbolic work and symbolic production" (Turner 1984: 190). Bodies become the way personal value is demonstrated both to the self and to others, but only through continuous effort. They are sites where a great deal of work is required to perfect these images; the body becomes a project, a "work in progress" (Rodin 1992: 58; Smith 1988). Perfection of the body does not become the end goal in itself but a sign of the quality of investment, the symbol of the determination and commitment to "self-making."[7]

Furthermore, in this conception, successful body work as an indication of the ability and self-discipline of individuals elides to reflect their moral fiber; the disciplined body is one that one ought to possess, ought to be. Self-surveillance of the body indicates moral surveillance and responsibility. This is particularly and intensely so for the female body – because the body itself in Western tradition has been seen as the basis of epistemological and moral error, women are (still) culturally perceived as more closely associated with their bodies than men (Bordo 1993). In this way, the female body, along with other complementary derivative distinctions, becomes the epitome of moral ambivalence.[8] If the body is the basis of "un-reason," that is instinct and appetite rather than thought, the female body consequently is seen as the source of moral abjection.[9]

In this context, we can see that "serious play" is a way of testing out rather delicate territory. It is a way of exploring and establishing issues of ownership – who owns this body? Who has rights to this body? It is a way of establishing personal status and group identity. It is a way of simultaneously investigating, constituting and representing what kind of self is deemed appropriate, what kind is possible and, by implication, what kind is totally unthinkable. It is a way of establishing a moral body. To untangle the implications of these conceptions, I will analyze a range of incidents of "fantasy" and "serious play," from those where the girls explored embodied experience in social contexts they deemed public, to other areas they constructed as private.[10] Sometimes the exploration of the self became too threatening, "too close to the bone," as it were. It evolved, then, as we have seen before, into mimetic excess. This was either expressed by adoption of an extreme parodic or ironic stance or emerged as "dark play" where no humor was possible.

To serve as an entry point into this discussion of the relationship between body and self and of how that nexus intersects with each girl's sense of psychic "fit" within her world, I will introduce two bodies "in action" to see the ways two young people "watched themselves."[11] It is also an introduction to clear indicators of simultaneous sameness and difference, highlighting many of the issues outlined above. The occasion was my first dramatic encounter with Bekk.

Watching the watchers

It was my second visit to Diane's media studies class at her school. The previous week I had been struck by the small size of this class (consisting of only about sixteen students) and by its gross gender imbalance. Of the sixteen, the only girl attending at that time had been Diane. The students were working in pairs to complete various projects. Diane and her partner had been investigating "heavy metal" music, which in this case specifically meant loud, electric guitar music where the emphasis was on the aggressive, often discordant sounds rather than the lyrics. The lyrics, understood by the initiated but not so easily by the casual listener, were often extremely sexist and antisocial. During the time of my visit an extremely graphic and lurid cover of a popular heavy metal CD was being passed around the classroom. Diane preferred "techno pop," she told me, giving examples of commercial dance music, songs by Michael Jackson, Peter André and New Kids on the Block. However, "heavy metal" was the only music her partner was interested in so they were studying that. This deference to male music "taste" and the way gender could influence and affect the style and form of the music and its context, was one I was to meet continually in my fieldwork.

On that first occasion, I had become aware of a marked difference in bodily deportment and appearance between the boys and Diane. The boys had openly lounged in their chairs, sprawled over the desks, talked and laughed loudly and seemed quite relaxed. In comparison, she sat upright, absolutely controlled in the way she positioned and presented herself. Her bodily "restraint" was expressed in other ways, apart from deportment. Her hair, obviously freshly washed, was immaculately groomed. Her school uniform was neat and orderly, in marked contrast to those of the students around her, in fact in contrast even to the physical conditions of the classroom! At this early stage in my fieldwork and our acquaintance, I assumed her patent lack of ease was due to her being the only girl in the classroom.

When I arrived in the same room the following week, I discovered there was another female student in the class – Bekk!!! In contrast to

Diane's quiet entry, Bekk entered the room like a tornado. She was bubbly, flirtatious and garrulous, wearing her blond shoulder-length hair in what was a popular scraggly "messy look" style. She wore a white T-shirt printed with a lurid design, indicating it was very obviously not an official school uniform. She was loud and, ostensibly, supremely self-confident. She immediately mingled with the boys, chatting about her weekend and her time away from school. She had been away for a week and a half. On spotting me, she yelled across the room to the teacher: "Mr B., have we got a new teacher? Who is that?" Then a few minutes later she asked me directly: "Are you a new teacher?"

She wandered restlessly around the classroom, toward the heater at the back of the room and then over to the chairs and desks where Diane was sitting. As she meandered, Bekk loudly delivered a stream of diverse personal anecdotes: that she had had food poisoning from drinking mint sauce the week before; that the boys must have learned how to put the classroom heater on since she had been away; that her mother didn't like Les (Bekk's current boyfriend), who had been living with them for the past three weeks; that she wanted someone to "put on some music. I want to dance!" Then, apparently feeling that more dramatic activity was needed, she grabbed a tie from one of the boys, tied it around her own neck, and exclaimed, "I love wearing ties. They suit me."

The teacher intervened, attempting to bring back some semblance of order into the classroom. The students, in some show of settling down, obligingly split into groups, with about six moving to adjoining rooms that had video and sound-mixing facilities. However, six other students stayed in the classroom, chatting to each other and to me. Diane sat near me to talk about my film and research project. As I showed Diane the video camera, one of the boys asked if he could look through the lens. He immediately trained the camera toward Bekk, who lay full length across the desks. Far from retreating from the camera's gaze, she stretched out her body in an exaggerated pose of a fashion model and enquired: "Do you want to see my legs?"

After a while she moved again, until she was by me. She repeated the story of her food poisoning, explaining that it was from drinking an entire bottle of mint sauce, a dare from her mother "for ten bucks. So I did it," said Bekk, "and I was ill." Her mother hadn't given her the money but she had bought her two packets of cigarettes, so "that was the same thing." Bekk gave all this information totally unsolicited, obviously aware that it won her attention.

Finally the conversation returned to the topic of music again, and specifically about Madonna since her concert was forthcoming. Bekk admired Madonna tremendously because "she stands up for what she believes in." One boy in the class quickly and crudely chipped in: "She makes other things stand up." Bekk told him to "shut up." The teacher who had been working on a computer in the classroom, but apparently simultaneously listening to the interchange, intervened:

Teacher	*What do you think Madonna believes in?*
Bekk	*She believes in standing up for what she wants. She believes in doing what she wants.*
Teacher	*Yes but why does she do that?*
Bekk	*She believes in it.*
Teacher	*But what do you think she does it for?*
Bekk	(quieter) *Money, I suppose.*

The teacher's assumption that Madonna's convictions (and therefore her attractiveness to young women) were merely part of her marketing strategy was presented as though to counteract Bekk's obvious admiration for Madonna. However, as I had already begun to suspect, Bekk couldn't be suppressed for long. She launched into a counterattack:

Bekk	*She has a great body. If you look at her arms they are really muscly because she works out all the time. I can say that. I notice girls' bodies but I'm not being a lesbian or anything. I can go up and say to Diane "Diane, you have got a good body." Boys can't say about another boy, he's got a good body, because they are scared of people thinking that they are . . .*
Diane	(interrupting) . . . *Some boys say that other boys have got "cute butts" but they are just fooling around. They are just pretending to be . . .*
Bekk	*I tell my boyfriend, "you look at her. She's got a good body."* (laughs) *He says "You're weird."*

Bekk decided she wanted to hear some louder music so she left us abruptly and went into the room next door to return a few moments later wearing a baseball cap backwards. She said she had borrowed a cap from one of the boys whom she said thought she looked like the lead singer from the Divinyls.[12] Then she added: "and he just kissed me. Everyone tries to kiss me."

Bodily praxis as modes of knowledge

This extended introduction to Diane and Bekk "in action" serves as an entry point to the discussion of "bodily praxis as a mode of knowledge" (Moore 1994). It is also a mode of "capital" (Bourdieu 1984, 1993). We not only witnessed Bekk and Diane physically interacting with others but also heard their comments on their understandings of different aspects of embodiment. Their understandings were nonverbal, expressed primarily through their own bodies and also through their articulated interpretations of bodily practices of others. This included the significance of bodily appearance and the perceived status of the bodies of some popular cultural icons, such as Madonna and The Divinyls. In general, through their dress, stance and language, the girls indicated clearly the importance of the body as "physical and symbolic capital" (Bourdieu 1984; Schilling 1993) – although in some aspects their understanding of its "currency" seemed very different.

For Bekk, her self-value came from being able to compete with the boys in terms of space, language and an assertive sexuality, to "stand up for what she believes in" like Madonna. For Diane, with her self-contained, quiet demeanor and acquiescence, it seemed to derive from marking herself out as different from the boys. Both girls, in their own quite different ways, were appropriating a particular exaggerated representation of femininity. Both representations seemed to be extreme. Furthermore, in their sympathetic discussions of Madonna, both girls indicated an ambivalent struggle to contest the usual confining images of women as passive recipients of the gaze of (male) others. There was an awareness that such assertiveness, whether it was Madonna's or their own, comes with risk. Bekk could declare herself the subject of the gaze, "I can say that. I notice girls' bodies" but only while quickly asserting "I'm not being a lesbian or anything."[13] She also asserts herself to be clearly heterosexual in her allusions to her boyfriend Les and in her supreme confidence that she is attractive to boys ("Everyone tries to kiss me!").

In the conscious and unconscious ways both girls present themselves in their world, they draw our attention to other important aspects of "bodily" management or body work. Their different presentations of dress, hair, voice and deportment suggest that these are richly complex areas for more detailed consideration. In Bekk's anecdote about her food poisoning, notions of bodily control and maintenance are subverted in two ways: firstly, ordinary food (mint sauce) has been used in-appropriately and to excess. Secondly, rather than express anger at her daughter for the behavior, Bekk's mother (usually mothers are considered the providers of nurturing food) initiated the behavior ("It was a bet so I did it") and rewarded it with cigarettes – another harmful substance.[14]

So how do we untangle all the complexities of embodiment hinted at here? In the first instance, taken together, these aspects of exploring socially acceptable boundaries and bodily behavior can be seen as "play" in order to gain knowledge.[15] The body is the locus and primary symbol of simultaneously acquiring, articulating and negotiating particular understandings of the world. Bodies, as Bourdieu reminds us, "take metaphors seriously." Wexler (1983) argued for awareness of the primary role of body image, gesture and style as symbol in research into young people's cultural expression:

> *The new social movements are movements of identity and not traditional economic or political movements . . . they are the movements of the body, of personal freedom in daily life.* (cited in Lesko 1988: 127)

Bodily expression in this conception is firmly linked to identity. But what remains unproblematic in so much of the research into Western youth's social groupings and culture, is the question of whose identity is being talked about? In what ways is distinction as important as similarity in youth perceptions of style and social performance? How and why are symbolic boundaries marked out between one body and the next even within the same social groupings?

Taking metaphors seriously: Exploring difference

What I am exploring here is not simply the way young people make themselves similar to each other, by demonstrating allegiance to social groupings, for example, but the way bodies allow and sometimes enforce expression of difference. Why is there such a difference in the way Diane and Bekk felt that they could and should engage in the world? The two teenagers described above shared the same geographic locale and had similar social, ethnic, and class backgrounds.[16] Yet even from the relatively short instance above, we obviously cannot assume that Diane and Bekk, both "working-class" girls, perceived and negotiated their worlds in exactly the same way. They had differently nuanced ideas about representations of themselves as female, different ways of "playing" with gendered identity, different ways of expressing these understandings through their bodies. But exploration of that difference is far from simple.

To understand articulations of difference, we need to turn again to look at other bodies in action, to understand the differing ways in which all the girls in my fieldwork negotiated the ubiquitous gaze; firstly, there is consideration of the relationship between embodiment, (gendered) subjectivity and (micro) culture, consideration, in other words, of the ways bodily behavior and the verbalized attitudes of these girls reflected and were attempts to negotiate their particular taken-for-granted cultural understandings of their realities. The second related consideration is how the macro culture and pervasive dominant discourses of femininity, including its expressions through the media, coalesce with those particular understandings; how they complement and where they appear to contest or be contradicted by everyday experiences. Where is the "lack of fit" most apparent? The third issue necessary for consideration is the way morality pervades both sorts of discourses, the meta and micro narratives, the different but interlocking ways of understanding and being in the world. I will return to all of these issues as we consider the ways particular girls explored their sense of self and their worlds, through their bodies.

Taking metaphors seriously: The joy of physicality

What struck me at the outset of my field research were the very different ways that the young people I came into contact with, and got to know, used their bodies – differently from me and often differently from each other. The overarching culture shock for me, entering as an adult woman, was the sheer physicality of the teenage world. The girls on the whole were still at the age when delight in freedom of movement was taken for granted, and I had almost forgotten in my own adult socialization how much I had learned to control and constrain bodily action. So, for example, any conversation I had with Kate was undertaken without any semblance of "formality" in spite of our age and education differences. There was no deference to me as an adult even from the first time we met. On one particular occasion Kate conducted almost the entire conversation with me either standing on her head or practising other yoga positions. Another time, when I arrived at her house, the first thing I saw was Kate lying on her stomach outside the house on the driveway doing her homework. At first I wondered if this was part of a science project (studying ants or something), but she said no, she just felt like doing her homework on the path. Other notes in my fieldwork remind me that she would greet me in her driveway at home hanging from an old tire or jumping on her trampoline. It was rather like arranging meetings with the Cheshire Cat in *Alice in Wonderland;* I was never quite sure where she would be next.

As noted earlier, during my fieldwork I began to use my body in ways that as an adult I have become unaccustomed to, attending rave parties and discos and participating in the teenage workshops at Cirkidz. The latter particularly involved learning many different kinds of bodily skills: attempting to juggle (acquiring new hand-eye coordination skills); learning to clown (acquiring the ability to be relaxed, to be "silly" and "unlearn" the appearance of control); or learning to be the base of a human pyramid (acquiring the necessary skills to be strong and share personal space and indeed parts of my body with others). On a much simpler level it meant doing what my teenage participants did, such as being prepared to squeeze under the staircase at school because that was where a conversation was taking place away from the eyes and out of hearing of the teacher on duty.

It wasn't simply the lack of physical inhibition or having greater physical freedom of movement that I often noticed; it was also paradoxically the overt concern with scrutinizing aspects of appearance and body parts. Perhaps because one was freer with the body, one was aware that it was more "in the limelight," more under the possible gaze of others. Even without that awareness, however, girls learn early that they have to "watch themselves" (Berger 1977). They learn, in other words, that learning to be female is hard work and that it requires a constant self-surveillance of the body to meet a ubiquitous female ideal.

Taking metaphors seriously: Femininity as discourse

To analyze the ways in which the ideal female body is understood and represented is to immediately engage in a myriad of paradoxes. The ideal female in dominant Western discourse is young but sexually provocative; she is childlike but expected to be morally responsible; she is passive but manipulative, full of "feminine wiles." In this discourse, her paradoxes simply confirm her enigmatic status.

The primary discourse encountered by the girls in my research in their everyday lives was the dominant Western discourse of femininity, widely circulated in electronic and print media representations. It was embedded in the discourses of their homes, their schools and places of leisure even if it were also contested or negotiated there. An extremely narrow, limiting set of codes that circumscribe the ideal female body characterizes this albeit fluid discourse.[17] In the context of the dominant Australian culture (and indeed in most of the Western world) that ideal – the sum of its codes – currently has four major components. Firstly, it is of a slender young woman. Indeed, the body should appear to be without obvious muscle, or, as Rosalind Coward notes, a body that is "firm but bulgeless":

> *The shape is slim, lacking in "excess fat" which is defined as any flesh which appears not to be muscled and firm, any flesh where you can "pinch an inch" . . . The only area where flesh is tolerated is around the breasts . . . but even with breasts, the emphasis is on the "well-rounded" and "firm" in keeping with the bulgeless body.* (Coward 1984: 40–41)

Secondly, although looking physically active, this body is passive, more done to rather than doing. Although perhaps expected to be more assertive than in the past twenty years, the female body is never allowed to be aggressive in this discourse. It takes up minimum space in public arenas and creates little noise.[18] The third component is that paradoxically, despite the sexualized or even eroticized context, this body is not in fact sexually mature, for it is the prepubescent underdeveloped shape that is currently ideal in magazines, television, film and print advertisements.[19] Because it is ideally prepubescent, the body actually lacks other secondary sex characteristics such as bodily fat and hair. Margaret Le Roy notes that "What more than anything else arouses (self) repulsion is our secondary sex characteristics – body hair and fat . . . signs of sexual maturity; they are about being a woman rather than a girl" (1993: 10). The final aspect of this ideal feminine bodily aesthetic is that it is always nonblack and light-skinned. It was an aesthetic I discovered that was well and truly internalized in the young women in my research, as I detail below.

Early in my fieldwork I found there were several occasions when this awareness and surveillance of the body became quite explicit, as for example, during my early visits to Cirkidz. There I was struck by the openness with which the girls discussed and talked about their bodies: one of my first sights was seeing Callie and Fran standing at the back of the room gently feeling each other's faces. When I came up to them they said they were trying to decide whose skin was the softest, and invited me to feel too! Although less overt elsewhere, I found that this scrutiny and commentary on physical appearance, amongst all the girls during my fieldwork was commonplace and frequent, friends drawing attention immediately to any slight change in the girls' weight, hairstyle and clothes. Although Bekk considered she was unusual "noticing girls bodies," in fact every girl in my fieldwork seemed acutely aware of and commented on others' appearance and behavior.

On one occasion, as described previously, Diane was videoing in her bedroom with her two friends Jane and Helen. At one point, Jane took the camera and filmed her sister Helen, while Diane asked the latter questions from a magazine romance quiz. As the others responded aloud to the quiz with great hilarity, Jane made a simultaneous commentary sotto voce, giggling as she filmed.

> *"Here we have the world's most famous model being filmed with the world's most famous interviewer."*
> She zoomed in with the camera for a close-up.
> *"Hmm! Nice skin!"*

Sometimes the comments were far from complimentary, as when Jane then zoomed the camera in onto her sister's body: "Look at that belly! Look at that belly!" Such comments were made with affection and in a spirit of fun. Humor such as this often allowed a girl to express admiration or make a disparaging remark about another girl. Certain girls felt they had license to comment adversely or to genuinely voice their admiration for another girl's physical attractive-ness or behavior. But as I indicated in the anecdote about Bekk, this was not without risk. There was a fine line between what was appropriate scrutiny and what was not; who could touch whom and who could not.

A question of touch

Best friends could often be in extremely close proximity, sharing clothes, space and bodies, activities normally carried out in the private spaces of bedrooms or at least in areas where the girls could feel free to gossip, laugh, role-play and be intimate with each other and not feel embarrassed. Stuart Hall (Hall et al. 1976) and Angela McRobbie (McRobbie & Garber 1976) dubbed such behavior as "bedroom culture," meaning peculiarly feminine activity enjoyed by teenage girls in the privacy of their bedrooms as opposed to public arenas. In its original 1970s conception, researchers interpreted this as a kind of gendered resistance, noting it was young women carrying out activity that was particularly pleasurable to them. I agree that the pleasure is there but I do not agree that there is also necessarily an element of resistance. Rather, it was, as I noted earlier, play – different forms of exploration with the body, with space, with relationships. I argue that play is far more about "learning the game"; in other words, more about learning about accommodation and incorporation than resistance.

Fig 9: Grace and her best friend

Several parts of Grace's video were executed in the company of her best friend Katie, the two girls sitting huddled up on a couch together chatting directly to the camera. Their bodies were so close together, with arms and legs resting on the other's, that it was sometimes hard to determine whose body belonged to whom.

In their discussions on camera they talked about their friendship and the importance of sharing everything – clothes, music, accessories. The video also had several segments where they were obviously sharing food, cooking and chatting together as they cooked. Boyfriends, however, could not be shared. When I asked what would happen if they liked the same boy they answered that they had a rule to protect their relationship – "neither of us would touch him!"

Other female friends who behaved similarly were Fran and Callie. On one occasion at lunchtime when I went to Fran's house to discuss her filming, she and her best friend were both still in their pajamas ("We couldn't be bothered to get dressed yet"). They conducted the entire conversation with me in Fran's bedroom, they lounging on Fran's bed – lying across each other without inhibition or embarrassment – while I, sitting in a chair opposite, tried to look as though I always had discussions with young people in this way![20]

Mutual grooming between friends was another activity that often took place when a friend "stayed over" for the night. This often included experimenting with hairstyles, makeup, or dress-ups. Kate explained in great detail the elaborate routine that she and Amy undertook to make Kate's hair curly. It involved painstakingly twisting Kate's usually straight hair into about forty tiny "rags." Such intimacy involved trust. A best friend here becomes a "*doppelganger*," an extension of the self, the me who is not me. She can see and reach parts of the body that the other can't – like the back of the head – and in many ways personifies the concept of the alter ego. This is why "best friends" are so valuable especially in early female adolescence.

This does not mean that such intimacy always went unnoticed by other people or was acceptable in all female groups. Grace and Katie commented with a dismissive laugh that often people asked them if they were lesbians "because we are so close." They were obviously aware that their physical affection caused comment but seemed to consider themselves, at that stage, as completely heterosexual in orientation.

All of the girls in my research, including the many beyond the ten key participants, indicated that intimacy or affection between women in public attracted comment and derision. Fran told me about walking down the main shopping mall in Adelaide arm in arm with her mother and receiving catcalls, again about supposed sexual orientation, suggesting their behavior was inappropriate. While the girls who attended Cirkidz learned on the whole to take such comments in their stride, for other girls in my research, the concern about attracting negative comment or being thought to have a homosexual orientation led many of them to internalize these restraints and negative attitudes. Quite ordinary activities could arouse gossip, create suspicion. I noted earlier Bekk's speedy caveat that she was "not a lesbian or anything." On a quite different occasion, Anne took over the camera and was filming Diane, her best friend, at school. In a voice-over while she was videoing, she eulogized about her friend's qualities as well as her physical attractiveness. Suddenly she seemed to pull herself up sharply, saying, while still on camera, to her prospective audience, "I don't want you to think I'm like that. I have a boyfriend and everything."

It was not simply affectionate behavior to another woman that could bring upon one the "accusation" of being a lesbian. Hair cut too short or wearing an outfit deemed too masculine could also create unwanted attention for the individual. Even Martine, a young successful female executive in a major music company, told me the same story. After speaking for some time about the importance of female empowerment, she then added she felt she could not go to venues alone or even with a female friend because "if you are not with a male partner you are considered a 'dyke' or there is something wrong with you. You have to be in a heterosexual relationship – you cannot be considered being single by choice."

I shall return to this point, the internalization of surveillance and constraint, in more detail below because it frequently carried with it a sense of moral guardianship. It is an important aspect of the "naturalizing" of heterosexuality and the required gendered relations that emerged with it. For the moment though, I just make the obvious point that as girls in my research began to video themselves and their friends, turning the camera on each other and themselves, the "objective" scrutiny intensified. The first place that such scrutiny fell upon was on "the body's body" or the importance of clothes as manifestation of the "self."

Clothing the body

During the course of my research several of the girls made a point of talking about their favorite clothes or proudly displaying their new items to me, commenting, on and off the camera, on the importance of the garments to their sense of self-image. It was noticeable that the girls who could least afford the expensive fashionable labels wanted them and bought or attained them in some way.[21] These were girls from lower socioeconomic backgrounds – including the girls from

Aboriginal homes – where a combination of single parenthood and unemployment was the norm. This was not simply a blind slavish following of fashion but a selection that was meant to indicate acquired prestige and membership of a discriminating group. Diane articulated it clearly. She had just "modelled" her new fashionable and expensive birthday clothes to me with great delight and pride. I asked her why she had particularly asked her parents for Adidas Equipment tops and Nike shoes, recognizing that money was particularly restricted in the family (her stepfather had recently been made redundant from his only employment).[22] She answered thoughtfully, "I can hold myself up when I wear them. People look at me and think, she knows the latest fashion. She cares enough to wear them. It boosts my confidence."

Jasmine's mother, an Aboriginal single parent, told me resignedly that she felt that "the problem with kids today is that parents (like her) try to make up for what they didn't have in their own childhood and give them lots of things. Now the children expect it. They want Nikes, Adidas T-shirts. They are all spoilt." At the same time she indicated that she was trying to save up for new linoleum for the kitchen floor because her present floor was shabby. She didn't want her children to feel ashamed, she said, when their friends came.

Clothes and appearance were important, then, for group membership and acceptance and for knowing that one's body could be portrayed with confidence. The parents recognized that even when it was impractical to buy their teenagers the clothes they desired. There can of course be just as much an adoption of a style and stance when the individual assumes a "nonconformist" look as an "antfashion," antimaterialist statement. A grunge or retro look where the teenager deliberately wears shabby, torn, and mismatched clothes provides a look or style that is meant to portray a casual, non-fashion look.

In a totally different setting, I noticed the importance of clothes at the Blue Light discos that I attended during my fieldwork. These are dances held and organized by the police in an attempt to counter youth "antisocial" behavior. There I was surprised at how young some of the dancers were, approximately only about eight or nine years old, but also at how they deliberately presented themselves as much older. Although they were tiny in stature and obviously physically underdeveloped compared with their older counterparts, many of these eight-year-old girls were dressed in ways that made them look like mini-parodies of sixteen-year-olds – tight short skirts, panty hose, high heels, makeup and tight crop tops. I was used to eight-year-olds dressing up in older clothes for fun or play, experimentally as it were. I was not used to seeing tiny pre-pubescent girls dressing up as "serious play" in this way. And it was serious play, femininity as decidedly hard work!

Toward the end of one of the evenings, at about ten-thirty, a couple of slow romantic numbers were played and several of these younger boys and girls were dancing romantically together. I noticed on this occasion – as I did on subsequent occasions – how one of the young couples, again probably about eight years old, was approached by an older group of children – most of these children being about twelve years old – who apparently didn't feel the young couple was being romantic enough. They instructed the boy how he should be holding the girl and told them how to kiss each other. The little boy (who was quite a bit smaller than the girl) and his partner smiled and giggled with embarrassment but accepted the instruction!

I discovered a parallel monitoring of clothes and behavior in the many raves that I attended. At first I noticed only the unisex baggy outfits, the oversized T-shirts and wide short pants or long trousers the boys and girls seemed to wear. I thought it was an aspect of the almost sexless dance rhythms and the way the electronic music, lights and dance movements emphasized the machinelike, robotic qualities of the dancers. However, after attending several dances myself and talking to Pat and her friends, I realized that the implicit dress code was in fact far more restrictive for girls. Often the girls would come with their hair in little bunches or tiny plaits reminiscent of small children. Rather than the large loose tops, many of the girls would wear short cropped tops and close-fitting pants or short skirts; less suitable for dancing but marking them out as female and therefore more conventionally feminine.

Other significant aspects of dress and image emerged when a number of girls dressed specifically for the camera. Many of these were noted in earlier chapters, for example, Fran's deliberate choice of more sophisticated "feminine" clothing for her direct address to the camera. Mary too, in her poignant "confessional" use of the camera when she discussed her childhood experience of abuse, deliberately selected clothes that portrayed her as mature and controlled.

Clothes in some situations can confer (adult) authority and status. During the time of my fieldwork, several of the girls attended end-of-school formal dances where they wore very expensive evening dresses, many of which looked extremely anachronistic to my eyes. An even more bizarre example of anachronism to me was when Janine showed me with great pride her evening dress acquired for the yearly *Nunga* Ball that she attended with other family and friends. The rich, colorful "satins" that she and her sisters wore on these glamorous occasions, with the compulsory accessories of long white gloves, reminded me with a shock of old photographs of missionary days and colonial encounters.[23]

Clothes also serve a further purpose, imparting a great deal of symbolic significance in various social groupings and institutions, acting iconically as direct pointers of social closure (Gerth & Wright-Mills 1974), a role that entails "the singling out of certain social or physical attributes as the justificatory basis of exclusion" (Parkin 1979: 44. Also cited in Nilan 1992). Pam Nilan's study of female groups in a Sydney Catholic school points to the way the girls used styles of dress and comportment to categorize fellow students into social groupings.[24] I found the same in my research.

The *Nunga* girls, for example, indicated their allegiance to their social groupings by choosing the fashionable and popular Adidas track suits, T-shirts and tops in a particular color range – those of the Aboriginal flag – and combining them with images and icons of black celebrities. Thus they almost always wore clothes of black or Aboriginal colors (red, black and yellow) or clothes with particular symbols on them representing a black identity. Bob Marley was a favorite. On the other hand, several of the girls from Cirkidz, despite their diverse socioeconomic backgrounds, favored secondhand retro-clothes, implying an alternative, rather nostalgic antimaterialistic image. They were scathing in their comments about people who wore Adidas clothes, calling them "Townies." To the initiated, clothes and style indicated whether the wearer had "got it (the look) right," really belonged, or was inauthentic, simply a "Try Hard" (Nilan 1992), that is, one who attempts to indicate affiliation with a particular group but fails miserably to impress.[25]

Clothing style is also the first, easily identifiable way that young people indicate allegiance to a particular social grouping or experiential community (Hebdige 1979). Sometimes the layering of significance of this could be extremely complex. Kate, for example, loved to "dress up." Wearing unusual outfits and makeup at home, she and her friends would often deliberately experiment with different images and styles. With money from her weekly allowance and baby-sitting, Kate had purchased a secondhand wedding dress. While she enjoyed playing and dancing in the dress, her actions should not be construed as an indication of a desire for traditional romance. In fact, I believe that Kate would see this play with the dress as a kind of sophisticated ironic stance. As I noted in chapter 1, Kate was encouraged at birth to consider herself as strong and independent. Her parents, who were not married, brought her up in an open and feminist manner striving to give their daughter a sense of her own personhood. Kate herself liked to believe she was "an individual."[26] She showed me her wardrobe, half of which was filled with garments she called her "hippy clothes," many of which, like the wedding dress, she purchased herself from markets and opportunity shops. They made her "feel like an individual," she said, an interesting echo of Diane's reasons for choosing quite different types of clothes.

This is not to argue, of course, that the ideal styles and "fashionable looks" do not change. The fashionable today is not necessarily so tomorrow. At the lower end of the market, in strategic contrast to the fashion statement of the elite, classic image, the emphasis is on a plethora of styles. Yet, there is still an overall conformity of appearance – the length of the skirt, the style of the outfit; which parts of the anatomy can be exposed and emphasized and which not. Fashion, in all its forms, is concerned with sexuality and each era's fashionable image is about a particular connotation and interpretation of sexuality and therefore about which aspects of the body are considered particularly sexually provocative – the waist, the ankle, the buttocks, the breasts, etc.

Today's fashionable image, undoubtedly influenced by the ideology of rapid material progress, physical speed and the technological advances of film, video and computers, not only is concerned with adornment but involves sexual daring, status and knowledge (Berger 1977; Coward 1984; Williamson 1986). Even in the photographic still this is expressed in terms of change, movement, posture and gesture. The modern girl is knowledgable, physically active, on the move, "going places." She is photographed, framed in the public sphere rather than the domestic – frequently the image captures and freezes the active moment – a jump frozen in the air, a group of friends laughing animatedly. Or if she is pictured in the domestic scene, she is preparing herself to go out, to "party," be adventurous.[27]

All of these aspects of embodiment, the importance of belonging (or being seen to belong) to a particular group, the impact of popular culture and a significant nexus of clothing, style and behavior were clearly demonstrated by an incident in Sara's video. Sara, along with several friends, took the camera for a day and the girls videoed trying on hats at a city fancy dress hat shop, until they were thrown out of the shop by the management. This session inspired them to seek special permission from a major department store in the city to film themselves inside the teenage section trying on clothes. The resultant episode revealed some very interesting aspects of the girls' play, whereby they experimented with image, clothing and bodily style and the effect of the camera in a group and in a more public place. I was invited to attend also, so I came with another video camera to film the filming – in true anthropological style!

On our arrival at the changing rooms, which were sectioned off for our exclusive use, Sara, Fran, and Callie immediately selected a number of garments for trying on. They were in such a hurry to dress up that Cathy and Grace hardly had time to set up the cameras. It seemed as though they were not dressing up for the cameras but rather for themselves.[28] There had been no previous discussion about who was dressing up first; the significance lay in who did not dress up initially. Firstly, there was Grace, who was unsure of her "social standing" and acceptance in the group; her recent experimentation with drugs and attachment to a wider, risk-taking group had caused some distance from these friends. And then there was Cathy, who was physically the largest of the group. The clothes that the girls were trying on at this stage, were designed for slight skinny figures with flat chests.

Initially the process seemed very chaotic because the girls did not wait for the camera to be focused. They dived into the changing rooms and then reemerged wearing the dresses, looking at themselves critically in the mirror and asking of the others, usually quite seriously, "What do you think?" The cameras were strategically located in the changing room space, but outside the individual cubicles, so that each appearance of a "model" was captured on camera as were their comments heard from behind the cubicle curtains.

Sara offered to film the others as they gleefully selected several other items of clothing. Armed with the camera, she recorded their discussions about, and their trying on, accessories like belts, hats and beaded jewelry and then their return to the changing room armed with their various choices. This section was filmed subjectively and evocatively, Sara following the others around the shop floor as though the camera were another member of the group. Fran, in particular, consciously "performed" to the camera. She smiled, beckoned and gestured to the camera along the way, holding up clothes or putting them against her for its approval. Serendipitously, as the girls explored the shop floor, the pop music being played over the public address system and screened on the large television monitors was Madonna's pop music clip Vogue, exhorting the listener to "strike a pose!" At one point, Sara filmed these large video screens because "They're an important part of shopping now, aren't they?"[29]

The second selection of clothes for trying on was markedly different from the first – judging by their raucous laughter and scathing comments, these clothes were at the end of the fashion continuum.

The girls now demonstrated an interesting contrast in their play with the clothes themselves – trying them on, swirling in front of the mirrors and making derogatory comments about the garments. There were screams of laughter as they came out of the changing rooms (even when such a reaction was unwarranted in my eyes). Now the "serious play" had turned into parody.

What was important was the image that these clothes seemed to suggest: when Sara appeared in the tight shorts and matching top, the others screamed "What you need is a smoke." Sara obligingly pretended to smoke, assumed a sophisticated jaunty stance and, spare hand hooked into the top of her shorts, she swaggered in an exaggerated model walk along the length of the fitting room. Similarly, when Fran tried on a slinky black dress, Callie, who was behind the video camera at that time, called out "Act like a model. You have to waggle your butt," so Fran exaggerated her walk.

At the end of the session when they all sat in an exhausted heap on the floor of the changing room, I asked them how "real" the exercise had been. They replied that it wasn't.

> *"Oh,"* I questioned, *"well, why did you want to come here and film this?"*
> *"Because this is what we would like to do but can never do,"* they answered.

They did it because it wasn't real? This comment cries out for close analytical scrutiny.

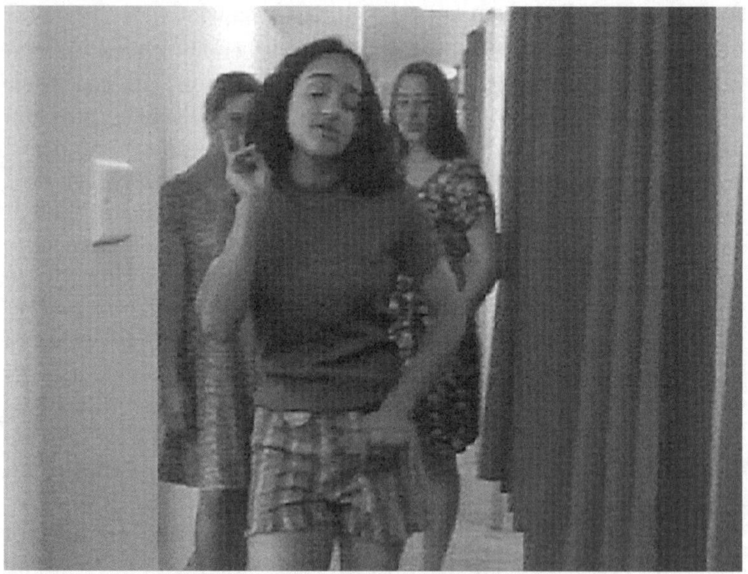

Fig 10: "You need a smoke!"

The body and mimetic excess

In what sense could they mean that this wasn't a real experience? What was happening here? As Taussig has observed: "Once the mimetic has sprung into being, a terrifically ambiguous power is established; there is born the power to represent the world, yet that same power to falsify, mask, and pose. The two powers are inseparable" (Taussig 1993: 43).

The girls' comment: "Can never do" implies that public experimenting involves money and adult authority. Without the camera and the formal request to the store, the girls would not have been so free to try on the clothes and not buy. Unlike the situation in *The Mad Hatter*, the young women were treated with respect in this shop and not thrown out.

It also suggests far more than this. What seemed to be occurring here was a publicly articulated play with (what was for these girls) an alternative expression of femininity through clothes and style. As a group, as we saw with Kate, this collection of girls prided themselves on being "alternative." To be "cool" for them meant to be anti-traditional in terms of femininity. It meant to be unsophisticated (although still greatly interested in and aware of the opposite sex). It meant being able to talk freely and openly about sex and sexual encounters. It also meant being scathing about what they perceived as the usual female preoccupations with fashion and weight. Their usual forms of clothing were shapeless, oversized T-shirts, baggy pants or shorts. They scorned the expensive "designer label" clothes that were so important to other girls in my research group.

But a different scenario was emerging. This "trying on of image and style" was very much concerned with embodiment, with actually seeing and representing themselves, through the full-length changing-room mirrors, through the eyes and comments of each other and through the lens of the camera. Immediately there was an intensification of scrutiny. While the girls were trying on the clothes, in spite of their eclectic selection, there appeared to be an outright rejection of anything that closely fitted their bodies – although this was not given as the reason. Rather, they would just say they hated the clothes and would disappear quickly into the changing rooms. This was so, even for Sara and Grace who were both slight enough to look exactly as the designer had intended them to look.

Yet that rejection was turned on its head at the exhortation of the girls' friends, to "act like a model!" It was an invitation to convert what might usually take place in total privacy as "serious fantasy" or "serious play," into a public carnivalesque performance, an excess of mimesis, if you like. This phenomenon has been noted by Willis (1990). Goodman (1992) also makes interesting observations about the role of comedy as subversion, "opening up the debate around the subject of the representation of women's bodies" (284).

With the camera in a semiofficial capacity the young women had license to experiment and play with the clothes and accessories in a public arena, to do what is normally only done in the private spaces of bedrooms or similarly sanctioned areas. However, because this was a public space, and because they were with other members of their group, the seriousness of the experimentation was transposed into aspects of parody, marked out much more clearly as "exaggerated play." We saw similar manifestations with Kate's cavorting in her wedding dress, Bekk's exaggerated femininity based on Madonna's assertiveness, or even Fran's adoption of a sophisticated "feminine" look described in the previous chapter. These, in many ways, are examples of mimetic excess.

Their use of clothes is *not* the same as that of the children at the Blue Light discos, the young women at the raves, Diane in her desire for fashionable garments, Hilary's more classically sophisticated appearance, or even Janine and her family's outfits for the *Nunga* balls. There was no intended humor or attempt at distance in these incidents. Here instead we have the equivalence of the papal robe, the nun's habit, the military uniform. Taussig, in discussion of the Cuna Indians' use of clothing, elaborates on the power of the mimetic and the power of dress:

> *Not only is the healer copying the look of the West (imitation); he is also putting it on (contact). In putting it on he is establishing physical contact with the West, the touch, the feel, like putting on a skin . . . the healer's very body becomes the vehicle onto which mimetic appearance becomes three-dimensioned, becomes optics in depth.* (Taussig 1993: 191)

I suggest that a similar transformation is occurring here. The girls' identities are represented through their clothing, however inappropriate or anachronistic it may seem to an outsider. In these examples, clothing indeed enables the mimetic, indeed the "magical" transformation into something other. Mimesis is the technique employed to create certainty, to capture the elusive "real" – "the sensuous moment of knowing includes a yielding and mirroring of the knower in the unknown, of thought in its object . . . a yielding that is, be it noted, despite apparent passivity, an act both of imitation and of contact" (Taussig 1993: 45–46).

Yet again Taussig's insights remind us that the transformation and constitution of the self into and through the "other," "despite apparent passivity" requires work. The whole body is implicated in this work or "serious play," for the whole body is a project. It is a project that has at its underlying core a paradox; for this project is in itself a problem. It cannot be completed, it cannot be finished yet it strives to reach perfection, to be perfected, to be achieved.

Femininity as work!

In my fieldwork I quickly learned that clothes and the deportment of one's body together indicated "authenticity" and some kind of allegiance to a social grouping, to an ideal. The most important aspect of the look, whichever it was, was that it had to appear effortless, intrinsic to one's personality. It was a manifestation of the "real self" and because part of the romantic discourse was that this "real self" is authentic, naturally springing from inside the individual, it had to appear unconstructed.[30] It was this effortlessness, the naturalization of an extremely constructed image that required diligent and constant skill and work.

In this way the discourse of femininity ties the image of the ideal "other" in the *consumption* to the *production* of that ideal. The magazines such as *Dolly, Girlfriend, Seventeen, Cleo* and *Cosmopolitan* that specifically target (young) women, rely on the assumption of the knowledgeable consumer, on the reader's understanding that her body can be constructed and changed through commodities. "You are what you wear" announces an article in *Dolly* (March 1993: 85). Clothes can be used to portray personality: "Blue is the perfect colour to reflect your sunny spirits, with its peaceful yet cheery overtones" (*Dolly* Special Edition, 1994). They can be used to disguise the "problem areas" of the figure, camouflaging "pear shaped" or "top heavy" bodies with special cuts or specific fabrics. The overall message is clear. Rather than a whole self expressed through a whole body, girls become used to envisioning themselves as parts of body in the same way they believe others see them. Diet regimes and advice columns in women's magazines also suggest "targeting problem areas of the body," further encouraging and promoting the perception of the body as fragments. They critically assess and work on their own skin, body shape and weight as discrete aspects of their bodies that need controlling and changing in order for the "self" to approach perfection.

Just as Coward found:

> *Female desire is courted with the promise of future perfection, by the lure of achieving ideals – ideal legs, ideal hair, ideal homes, ideal sponge cakes, ideal relationships.* (Coward 1984: 13)

Women learn to see themselves as "other" through a pervasive discourse of femininity, one that gains its authority and power from its ubiquity, especially in media images and through Western concepts of self being "frameable," bounded and knowable. But real life embodied experiences cannot help but explode the myths. Despite women having internalized aspects of this idealized "other," they are simultaneously aware of the implicit contradictions. They cannot but be aware of the fact that they are "pretending to believe," that there are yawning gaps between the self-images in the photographic frame, the mirror and the bodily experience.[31] The tenuous congruity of these different contradictory knowledges is possible because a fundamental premise of the myth is that it requires work to realize; in other words this "other" is deemed possible through agency. The fact that the woman does not become the perfect ideal is not because the task is impossible, but because she hasn't been assiduous enough. In mimetic terms, she hasn't learned to "create the magic" to its greatest effect. Clothes are a relatively easy means to create the ideal image. They can be put on and taken off at will. However, the transformation of the material body itself is harder to realize.

Skin

Apart from clothes, skin seemed to be the next most important aspect of self-scrutiny by the young women in my fieldwork. Skin blemishes such as pimples are indicators of lack of maturity and therefore lack of control. Skin was "nice" when it was soft, light and clear of pimples or "zits" and facial hair. Pimples and facial hair could be removed but not the color of the skin. For the three groups of girls whose skin color was darker than the others it was an immediate way in which they obviously did not fit the feminine ideal. Mary dealt with her lack of fit by deliberately calling attention to her difference. She called herself BB to her friends, explaining to everyone that it stood for Black Bessy. When I and some of the youth workers pointed out that such a name had racist overtones – in fact none of us, I discovered, could bring ourselves to call her by this name – Mary just shrugged and smiled. It was her way of being distinctive. Sara, as I noted earlier, was also extremely aware of her skin color and often expressed a belief that she was the victim of racism, especially at her high school. She saw her dark skin as an impediment to a full realization of her personhood. As she noted resignedly, "In this day and age it would be easier if I were white. I've got a lot of things to say and I don't get much of a chance to say them."

However, it was an incident that occurred when I was with Janine and her friends that really highlighted for me the issue of skin color and identity. As I noted earlier, Janine and her friends belonged to an all-female Aboriginal rock band. The band was called Black Image, originally created and named by their school as a way of encouraging the *Nunga* students to stay on at school longer and to give them a means of developing their skills, talents and self-esteem. The band practised during school time and after school and had external tutors who were musicians in their own right, as opposed to teachers. The tutors were also selected by the school because of their skin color – one was *Nunga* and two were Torres Strait Islanders. It was assumed that the girls would identify more closely with black musicians and see them as positive role models. It was on the occasion described earlier of the filming in the botanical gardens, that I was to learn that the girls' enjoyment and pride in their Aboriginality was ambivalent.

> Wanda was sitting on a bench ready to be interviewed while Janine and Janelle were setting up the equipment. It was in the middle of a 40-degree day so we were all starting to feel extremely hot and damp. Suddenly Wanda shrieked: *"Hurry up, I'm getting tanned."* She slid over to a less sunny part of the bench. She was by far the darkest of the girls and extremely attractive and so I thought she was making a joke. As the filming proceeded, every time she got anywhere near the sun she'd would lament loudly, *"Oh I'm getting tanned!"*
>
> At last I realized she was not attempting to be funny. This was a serious concern to her. Finally I said: *"Are you serious?"*
>
> *"Yeah"* she answered. *"I hate getting tanned. I'm dark enough already. I go black in the sun."*
>
> The others didn't laugh or protest. They knew what she meant.

The poignancy of their sense of otherness was also encapsulated for me in the way they talked about themselves as *Nunga,* while non-Aboriginal people, friends or relatives, were referred to as *Australian.*

Consideration of skin also brings us back to the question of touch and intimacy. I noted earlier the way best friends could and often did touch each other freely in some groups. However, because of its associated contact sense, the skin is a highly charged aspect of selfhood.[32] Not everyone has license to touch and in some groups, concern about imputation of the "wrong" sexual orientation led to considerable discussion about appropriate behavior. A more dramatic concern about touch and possible implications surfaced one day when I was talking to Janine at her home. We were viewing a section of her video so that she could decide which parts she wanted to keep for the final documentary. Suddenly we came to a section that I had particularly enjoyed. Janine and some of her school friends had filmed themselves practising dancing in the school hall at lunch time. I recognized one of the Asian girls in the friendship group but I hadn't seen her in Janine's company recently. I asked if they were still friends. Janine answered vehemently. She hated Kena now, she said. Everyone hated her because she was a slut. On being asked for further elaboration, Janine explained, head tilted away from me in obvious embarrassment, that Kena and another girl had had a shower together.

Taken back at the condemnation for something I assumed often happened at school camps, I tried for a further explanation. I pointed out that maybe in Kena's culture it was acceptable to have a shower with someone else. Janine didn't answer so I tried another tack.

"Maybe it's not true," I finally offered, lamely. At that Janine looked at me, this time asserting even more strongly, "Oh yes it's true. I know her friend and she said it's true. Kena's a slut."

The ultimate scrutiny: "Slut" is the heaviest word!

The power of the word "slut" is awesome. Apart from its constant and casual use among the girls when they wanted to insult another, there were several occasions when its power as a word was discussed. For example, during an informal talk one day with Janine and her friends, the word was raised and analyzed. The girls had been in trouble with the headmistress because, on a school trip, they had approached some girls from another school and called them sluts. I felt as we sat and talked the word seemed to assume an almost material presence amongst us. One of the girls sighed. "Slut is the heaviest word!" she was moved to say.

It was "the heaviest word" because firstly it carried with it all the connotations of the body/mind and the "damned whores and God's police" split (Summers 1994). A term exclusively used for women or girls, it is part of a vast vocabulary of abuse, all referring in some way to a girl's/woman's sexual reputation.[33] As Grace and Katie, talking casually on one occasion about friends and relationships, suddenly noted, boys were not called "sluts" they were called "gigolos" ("a proper slut word for boys," confirmed Grace). But they also noted that the word "gigolo" carried a quite different connotation.

> Katie: *When a boy is called a gigolo he is pleased. But when a girl is called a slut – well, she cries.*

Generally speaking the word "slut" implied promiscuity although, as we have seen already, the word could readily be appropriated to other situations that had nothing to do with actual sexual behavior. What is significant is that it was a sexist term of abuse that both the boys and the girls adopted to label and curtail girls' behavior and movement. Girls were far more likely to be called a slut in any situation by boys or by girls if they were "unattached" or in the current terminology "single," since a girl's name or reputation was "protected" if she was understood to "belong" to a particular boy. The word therefore also carried with it the assumption of assumed heterosexuality. Gossip and innuendo were of course the easiest way for a reputation to be lost rather than evidence of actual offending behavior. A good reputation was a delicate thing, easily lost and difficult to regain.

> Grace: *You can get a bad reputation in a week. But to lose it* [that is, to get rid of it] – (shrugs with a resigned laugh) *well, it can take about a year!*

My fieldwork notes are replete with tales from teenage girls and adult women talking about the difficulty of negotiating public space without losing one's good reputation. All anecdotes involved issues of bodily control, whether it was in terms of dress, general conduct or language. In other words, the issue of having one's body constantly in a "male gaze" of scrutiny was a very real experience for nearly all the (young) women in my research. This meant the girls first of all learned to see their bodies as potential sexual objects that needed to be hidden or controlled if they were not to be in danger – literal or metaphorical. Secondly, their bodies came to be seen as the rightful possession of their boyfriends.

"That's what you get for having nice legs!"

Young women learn early on that they are constantly the object of a scrutinizing, often judgmental gaze. This gaze is quickly internalized and constantly reinforced by comments from (usually female) peers. Scrutiny and comments from adults, however, have more serious implications. On one occasion, when I was filming at a Blue Light disco, one of the senior police officers supervising there, a middle-aged avuncular figure, asked if he could borrow the camera. He looked through the lens, marvelled at the small size of the camera, and then passed it back. About ten minutes later he was back by my side, "I should have borrowed it now, shouldn't I?" he said with a grin and a wink. I followed his gaze to a young girl aged about fourteen who had recently come into the dance hall. She was wearing a tight white sweater. "She's well-developed isn't she?" he said salaciously.

The tacit assumptions and often overt sexist attitudes toward young women that this comment revealed were faced daily by all of the girls in my project and which they articulated on several occasions. To grow up and become physically developed meant that in the public arena one was literally and metaphorically in the public gaze and spotlight. One was not only a young adult, one was a young woman! Here was the paradox and ambivalence of being the object of the gaze. It required vigilance – skill and work to attain the desired perfection, but simultaneously, it required a vigilance of a different kind – to be ever alert to the dangers lying in wait for young women exposed to public gaze.

To be the object of the gaze, to be a desirable female, was also then, to be potentially a victim of sexual or physical violence, and to be seen as "asking for trouble." For all of the girls in my research, potential or actual unsolicited sexual harassment or even sexual violence was part of their everyday experience. If sexual harassment did not occur in their homes, then it was present amongst their peer groups and in the street. All had tales to tell of incidents that had occurred to them or to someone close to them.

Fran told me of her 16-year-old friend Gina, who was walking down Rundle Street early one morning on her way to work experience. She suddenly was attacked from behind and a man grabbed her breasts. "That's what you get for having nice legs!" the man told her as he ran off. Gina was deeply distressed and Fran was angry and indignant "It's not fair!" she said several times. "They shouldn't be allowed to do that. No one has the right to do that!"

The moral discourse of feminine embodiment: "Rightful" possession

What this meant then was that the developing female saw herself reified as a sexually provocative *other.* To be female was to be dangerously, menacingly desired; on the other hand, she felt the need to ascribe to an ideal *other* – which included being responsively sexually attractive and desirable. These images were obviously contradictory and neither image was necessarily one of her own making. They were formed beyond her as it were, perhaps outside her realities and very much a function of the wider power relations in her culture.

> *The discourse of femininity articulates a moral order vested in appearances to a market and the production of commodities. Images change while fundamental features of doctrinal organisation, particularly those suppressing the active presence of women as subjects and agents vis-a-vis men, do not.* (Smith 1990: 171)

The moral dimension within the discourse of femininity is particularly powerful and circulates through the cultural texts that target young women. It places the responsibility of sexual control firmly on the young woman herself. She feels guilty if she is not presenting herself as sexually attractive – according to the prescribed codes. It is her fault if she is not being cheerful enough, friendly enough, alluring enough to attract the opposite sex and be popular. However, if too daring in self-presentation, then she runs the risk of social condemnation. To be acknowledged as attractive equates with being regarded as "sexy," but this immediately becomes an area of conflict in terms of a girl's appearance; if she is perceived to be dressed in a sexually provocative way or if she acts in a particularly aggressive manner she can immediately attract the epithet of "slut." If she is "traditionally" reserved or modest in appearance – according to the dominant codes of her day or her particular social milieu – then she can seem too conservative and therefore too childish in her manner and appearance.[34]

The most explicit and poignant expression of the difficult position in which young women constantly found themselves in the reification of their bodies as sexual objects, was imparted to me in the form of a song. The sense of self for the Aboriginal girls in my project was constituted by their *Nunga* identity and their gender positioning within their own cultural milieu. Primarily, they saw themselves through their heterosexual relationships, as girlfriends and future mothers, relationships where they often experienced violence. Another group of *Nunga* girls whom I met through their involvement with Port Youth (an Adelaide-based theater company), expressed the same ironic awareness of their subordinate positioning in society. Their "disco rap," created as part of an improvization on their social/sexual relationships, poignantly reflected an awareness and yet an acceptance of their powerlessness in gender relationships. I have reproduced the words in full:

Disco Rap

Verse 1:
As I pulled out my ID
The bouncer said there was no need[35]
As I walked into the toilet
This guy asked me to pull it[36]
You're nothing but a slut
Looking for a good fuck
So get on the dance floor
And I'll give you a lot more
As my friends were dancing
I was romancing.

Chorus:
What a scheme (x 3)[37]
What a mighty good scene
When I want a scheme
I wanna make you scream
I wanna take you boy
And use you as a toy.

Verse 2:
Drinking alcohol is so damn cool
And those who don't are such fools
When the bartender gave me a wink
I went to the toilet and spewed in the sink
If you want to have a buzz
Come on and take some drugs
Whilst listening to the latest CDs
I was tripping out and thought I was seeing 3D.

Chorus:

Verse 3:
DJ was his name
Playing music was his game
So get up and dance to the music
Take control and don't lose it
Violence was in the air
But I didn't really care
Underneath the lights
There was the biggest mob of fights
So if you want a lash[38]
You're gonna get smashed.

The song suggests these girls are a long way from any romantic notions of "sugar and spice." It could be argued that in their very articulation of the scenario, the girls are experiencing some sense of empowerment. The chorus for example suggests that the girls feel that they were in control ("I wanna take you boy/ and use you as a toy") but it was hard to believe that these girls were really in a powerful position in these situations. While the sentiments conveyed by the song may have been an exaggeration and a fantasy created in the context of a drama workshop, when talking and listening to the girls afterwards chatting to other girls whom they knew, I realized that their rap in fact reflected many of the usual social practices – sex, violence, excessive drinking and drugs – of their everyday lives.

This brings us to the final aspect of embodiment for consideration. To this point I have explored aspects of "self-making" through the surfaces of the body – clothes, hair, skin and bodily deportment. Now it is timely to turn to the parts of the body usually hidden from view, even from the self. To talk about knowing oneself from the inside involves a conception of the subjective experience of the body. Yet of course, as I stated earlier, such a dualistic conception is a cultural construction. All emotional sensations, whether pain, pleasure, hunger, desire, anger, love, hate or shame are essentially lived and experienced in and through the body. Inside and outside, mind and body are simply expressions of the phenomenological experience. Csordas reminds us that understanding embodiment "requires that the body as a methodological figure must itself be non dualistic, that is, not distinct from or in interaction with an opposed principle of mind" (Csordas 1990: 8). However, as we explore the "internal" aspects of the body, the ways the insides of the body are also controlled, there seems already to be a discursive split in the mind-body conception. That is, people often, deliberately and consciously decide to perpetrate some action in relation to their bodies – whether it is to eat healthily or moderately, overindulge, binge or purge themselves. When people are suffering extreme pain, they do indeed metaphorically separate the part of themselves they regard as the acorporeal "self" (a separation that necessitates the belief in the intact, unified, controlled "me") from the body that is out of control (Sacks 1984; Good 1992; Jackson 1992). What I argue in this section then, is that just as activities that involved the exterior of the body were manifestations of self-surveillance and control, so internal activities such as ingestion and emission of substances were also carefully monitored. They were also, in other words, an essential part of "serious play" and the rhetoric of self-making, because of their essential paradox and elusiveness. They are of course the most difficult aspects of the body to discuss.

Ingestion: You are what you eat

Bakhtin argues that, with the evolving of modern society "in which all the orifices of the body are closed" (Bakhtin 1968: 320), to be a complete and mature person in contemporary Western understanding is to be independent and to be in control of one's body functions. This means that individuals are in control of the flow of substances *in* and *out* of the body; the body, in other words, has become more "closed" to outside forces (Falk 1994). Food is an important aspect of this, in terms of the amount, the type and the manner in which one consumes it. Eating has become a far more individualized activity even though meals are still shared with families and friends at home or in restaurants or other public places. The role of the meal and food has changed, however, affected by the emphasis on the individual.

Mary Douglas reminds us that:

> *All margins are dangerous . . . Any structure of ideas is vulnerable at its margins. We should expect the orifices of the body to symbolise its specially vulnerable points.* (Douglas 1984: 121)

The modern body thus expresses its controls over boundaries at an individual level by controlling the "flows" between the inside and outside. For example, in our comparatively affluent society, to be considered a mature person one eats just enough for the body to be satisfied. To eat more than one needs indicates a poorly (self) disciplined body and denotes a child's lack of self-control. For a woman this is particularly so. As noted earlier, the aesthetic ideal is the slender woman with the contained appetite. As Bordo has argued, with the increased emphasis in magazines and other media texts on the glamorization of slenderness, exercise, diet and image problems, "almost all of us who can afford to be eating well are dieting – and hungry – almost all the time" (Bordo 1993: 103). While not a new phenomenon (medieval women were known to use the strategy of severe dieting as a form of empowerment, as described in the research of Caroline Walker Bynum 1987), the late-twentieth-century manifestation of concern about image and weight has reached epidemic proportions.

But the control over food flow has another related function, for it is not simply the amount of substance that is important as a register of the self but also the type of food or drink. Literally and metaphorically, food and drink selection and monitoring involve symbolic categories of taste or distinction (Bourdieu 1984; Lupton 1996). What I want to concentrate on here are three aspects of food consumption in its relation to personhood and "serious play" that were particularly significant in my fieldwork. Firstly, there is the aspect of food as fun; that is, the social importance of shared food. The second aspect covers food as a general manifestation of "taste," a marker of social distinction, along a vertical plane. The third area encompasses food as a marker of other identities, of *différance* (Derrida 1976, 1981), along a horizontal plane of difference, as it were.

Among the participants of my research project food was a common topic of discussion and eating together was a common activity amongst friends. When I first got to know them, all of the girls expressed a delight and an interest in food, several of them having occasional responsibility for preparing and cooking food for their families. At this time all of the girls had voracious "adolescent" appetites for cakes, candy, and other sweet things. At band practice I was often the "gofer" for Janine and her friends, sent to pick up the snack food for rehearsal breaks. Kate frequently had several bags of sweets in her possession obtained with her own money, and one day at my house when she came to view part of her film, she devoured a mountain of small cakes without reserve or inhibition. I found it amusing as well as fascinating not only to see her obvious pleasure in eating but also to note that she was not constrained by any adult notions of polite restraint.

Over the period of my fieldwork a number of cultural constraints relating to food began to evolve. For example, for many the desire for sweet things became a guilty secret delight rather than a childish pleasure. In Hilary's video she filmed her friend and herself shopping and "playing" in the city for a day. They filmed their huge bags of purchased sweets, in fact videoing the inside of the paper bag to emphasize its contents and then deliberately discussing their greed in terms of their childishness.

Sally: *"How old did you say you were, Hilary?"*

In this light, the sucking of lollipops can also be understood as a deliberate statement or "pose" of childishness for the young people who attended raves. Pat saw the sucking of Chupa chups (lollipops) as part of the overall effect of the baggy clothes, the short pants or the bunched hair of the girls. It was, she asserted, part of the need for young people to revisit their childhood but as adolescents. It was of course not simply a question of a regression to childishness – a fear of putting on weight led most of the girls to be far stricter in their intake of food as they grew older. I noticed a considerable and deliberate weight loss in many of the girls as they aged. While for some it was leaving behind teenage "puppy fat," for others it was an adoption of the feminine ideal of being slender.

For some of the girls, however, particularly those who attended Cirkidz, selection and consumption of particular food items meant a way of demonstrating their alternative lifestyles; these girls were all vegetarian, adamantly rejected alcohol and cigarettes ("they are so unnatural") and yet they frequently smoked marijuana. When this group of girls ate, they did so with great gusto and enjoyment; no anxieties about eating in public for most of these young women! It was, I felt, another public demonstration of their rejection of the traditional constraints of femininity.[39]

For Mary, food was also a way of reasserting her identity. She would go to the house of her friend Rana whenever she could. There under the guidance of Anna, Rana's mother, she would learn how to make traditional dishes from her homeland. Anna was a woman from Papua New Guinea, married to an Australian. Mary would "trade" cooking lessons, food and occasional overnight accommodation for baby-sitting and general help with Anna's eight small children. Once she had learned how to cook the dishes, she would practise them at her own house and cook for her many visitors, most of them boys off the street. In this way food for Mary was a major vehicle for her to constitute her dislocated identity, as a Papua New Guinean woman and as nurturing mother figure.

Food that is not food

If food was a way of marking out symbolic social boundaries of distinction and difference, so were other substances. All of the girls were aware of illicit drugs and several of them used drugs. But even the type and frequency of drugs taken was an indicator of self-making. Certain drugs cost more money than others, connoting more about the individual's social status than about their behavior.

The most common drug, because of easy accessibility and social acceptability, was alcohol. It was readily obtained at dance clubs and discos in the city and young women were the primary targets of the cheap sweet drinks. For example, champagne could be obtained regularly at one or two dollars a glass. Sometimes alcohol would be offered free to club members once they had paid their door entrance price for the night.

Cigarettes were the next most popular drug, with their connotations of "coolness" and sophistication. For girls they had an attraction of being associated with loss of weight as well. As noted above, cigarettes and alcohol were spurned by the Cirkidz group as they saw themselves as far too concerned with the body's health to take up such practices. They did not reject marijuana, however. They saw this substance as "natural," probably because it was a substance that they could grow easily themselves in small quantities. It had the other obvious attraction of being a drug that their parents, or the significant adult figures in their worlds, had taken in their youth (or were still taking). In other words, for many of this group, the drug had the same degree of social acceptability as cigarettes and alcohol did in other groups.

I noted earlier that, of all the girls, Grace was the most explicit about the role that harder drugs played in her world. When I first got to know her, illicit drugs were a vitally important part of her world. They were the central purpose of the social activity of her group. It seemed to me that her engagement with drugs was an activity of "dark play" (Schechner 1993).

> *Dark play subverts order, dissolves frames, breaks its own rules so that the playing itself is in danger of being destroyed.* (Schechner 1993: 36)

When the drugs are so dangerous as to involve serious risk, drug taking suggests a play that is excessive. It is a behavior that echoes that of the obsessive dieting of the anorexic; it gives the impression of control over the body. It breaks the social taboos about substances and substance control, what one should and should not put into the body. Falk (1994), referring to the work of Georges Bataille and Roger

Caillois, argues that such a transgression should not be seen as a denial of the taboo but an action that "transcends and completes it" (Bataille 1962: 63. Also cited in Falk 1994: 86). The act of transgression in relation to the atypical consumption of food or other substances involves pleasure in opposing what is to be feared. Yet also, in its very constitution, such action reaffirms the cultural boundary of what is and what is not appropriate behavior or substance. Perhaps this can be seen as the ultimate act of mimesis – the absorption into the other that threatens, in its transformative act, to completely consume the original. In so doing the protean self finds its center, is absorbed back into Nature, back into non-being:

> *In a sense the "forbidden food" – indexically the taste sensation – takes control of the eater. The eater is overwhelmed by the (taste of) the food – allowing himself to be consumed by the experience.* (Falk 1994: 88)

To be completely "taken over" by drugs, whether it is excessive alcohol or amphetamines or an hallucinatory drug, is to "go beyond" the body constraints. The expressions "stoned out of my mind" or "off my face" imply a pleasure in losing control, losing the "withness" of the body.

Keeping the insides in

The final aspect of play as bodily control that I want to look at, albeit briefly, is that of emission; how substances have to be contained within the body. If there is censorship concerning what may or may not be taken into the body, there is also monitoring of what may or may not come out. Foodstuffs, sneezing, excessive laughter, regurgitated matter are all substances that the mature person does not permit to occur in public. For young women there is also the difficulty of negotiating menstruation and menstrual blood.

Despite the current spate of television advertisements where young women seem to be able to talk easily and without inhibition about the effectiveness of their sanitary napkins, menstruation is still a secret and taboo subject even amongst most young women themselves. It is of course an important area where the containment of the whole mature person can come unstuck – for embarrassing leakages of blood, odor or stains all immediately destroy any semblance of self-control or self-possession.

> *One of the first skills a young woman has to develop is that of dealing with menstruation in mixed company without anybody guessing what they are about, slipping into the lavatory with a sanitary napkin up a sleeve,*

> *washing stained underwear on the sly in co-ed digs. It is arguable that young women would find menstruation less problematic if they did not have to behave as if they were ashamed of it.* (Greer 1991: 1. Also cited in Lees 1993: 208)

In my own fieldwork, sexuality and sexual experiences were more easily talked about than menstruation. The only two incidents that I am aware of where menstruation was a topic at all was where it was a topic of embarrassment. Significantly, both incidents occurred at coeducational secondary schools where the "norm" for bodily behavior often seems to be taken as male. In the first situation, two girls were discussing their disgust with a third, claiming that they would not share a tent with her again on school camp. It became apparent that the third girl's transgression was that she hadn't worked out a suitable strategy for disposing of her sanitary napkins and so had left them in a rubbish bag in the tent. The two girls were unable to talk to a teacher about it, or to the offending girl, and the problem remained unresolved and the source of great distress among the three young women for some time.

The second situation involved another school camp and a new pupil. The instruction had been that the students all bathe in the sea every day in their swimsuits (there were no showers at the camp – another assumption that all "normal" bodies are male and do not have particular needs for hygiene!) The new pupil was unsure of how to cope with this request on two levels. She was embarrassed to enter the water in her bathing costume as she felt it would be apparent she was menstruating and on the other hand she did not want to *not* bathe for a week. She approached a female teacher but could not bring herself to explain the problem. The teacher sent the girl to another child to see if the problem could be resolved. However, as neither girl could articulate the problem, it remained unsolved. As young women take on board the dominant cultural images and circulating discourses of themselves and their bodies, it is no wonder that menstruation is the unspoken topic even among girls themselves.

Notes

1 The term "withness of the body" is taken from Mary Beth Whitehead's epigraph and the accompanying poem "The Heavy Bear" by Delmore Schwartz (1959, *Selected poems*).

2 In fact it was her *only* informal dress at that time becauses she didn't usually like wearing dresses or skirts. Her usual outfit was jeans or other casual trousers. She did possess a bridesmaid dress that she showed me that she had worn at her father's remarriage.

3 Our bodies are inescapable! Not just in moments of physical distress or pain but in our everyday social encounters, the degree of our awareness of our bodies and the bodies of others facilitates or hinders our sense of relatedness; how at ease and how communicative we feel. The essence of that ease is our sense of (self) control. A crumb of food left on the teeth when we smile, an article of clothing slightly askew, bodily fluid escaping from any orifice, indicates to others – and to ourselves if we are made aware of the social slip – that we have less than perfect control of our appearance and our bodily functions. The body thus "is the locus of all that threatens our attempts at control. It overwhelms, it erupts and disrupts" (Bordo 1988: 92). Grace's behavior was also, in terms of the conceptual framework I have used so far, a moment of "serious play." This was not a moment of lighthearted self examination or the distancing of the self in a moment of humor. The very fact that Grace wanted to explore this moment alone, in "private" as it were, suggests that this was a very delicate and potentially disturbing moment for her, a moment of mimesis.

4 Not all cultures experience this understanding of personhood, of course. I will argue that in contemporary Australian culture the person is commonly understood "as an individuated being as opposed to the person as a relational or interdependent member of the community" (Becker 1994: 100–1). This has consequences for the way young people experience their bodies in a number of ways. Firstly, as in all cultures, cultivation of the body is the responsibility of those who are deemed to possess it. Thus, in some societies, the nurture and portrayal of the body clearly and unambiguously falls under the care of a kinship group, a mother, a father, or other clan member. This will be discussed in far more detail in chapters 4, 5 and 6 as I apply these concepts of personhood more closely to social networks.

5 I am using the female form as a generic term here for simplicity and because, although male adolescents also are affected by these processes, I believe it is still far more acute for girls. They are still the primary target of teenage advertising that focuses on look and image.

6 I am indicating here that "difference" does not have anything to do with biological facts as such but the manner in which cultural expression indicates one body female and one body male. All the girls in my research expressed their understanding of femininity in often extreme inscriptions.

7 In fact it is not simply in consumer capitalism that body work has added value to the body. See Douglas 1986; Blacking 1977; Lock 1993.

8 Such as nature/culture; male/female; appetite/reason. See Ortner 1974; Ortner & Whitehead 1986.

9 Early Christianity of course associated woman with physical lust, defining and describing her as the negative of man and reason. The mind associated with the male is extolled at the expense of physical matter connected with the female (Figes 1978; Cixous 1981; Cranny-Francis 1995). For some time, feminist theorists within and outside the discipline of anthropology have attempted to explain and critique the way women have been represented in terms of body, biology, nature,

and instinct (see Ortner 1974; Suleiman 1986; Jaggar & Bordo 1989; Grosz 1990; Bordo 1993; Csordas 1994). While anthropologists have been aware that such representations are not universal and that the explanatory force of the women/nature; male/culture divide has also been critiqued (Mathieu 1978; MacCormack & Strathern 1980), Western male bias still has been carried into the field by anthropologists trained in Western practices. Along with this bias are certain ways of thinking about and acting on constructions of the feminine. Henrietta Moore calls this "the three-tiered structure of male bias" in fieldwork (1988: 2). For my purposes I refer to this association of women's bodies with the need for surveillance and moral responsibility, as I argue in this chapter that these underlying myths remain in the everyday experiences and social practices of the young women in my research. The young woman who steps outside socially prescribed or "appropriate" behavior is in danger of being described (by other girls as well as boys or adult figures) as "a slut" or "a whore" – connecting her "aberrant" behavior with an excess of female sexuality. All of the young women in my research thus carried around with them a constant concern about how their bodies were viewed by others, particularly in terms of moral behavior. The worst thing any of the girls could be called was "a slut," as we shall see.

10 This path also takes us inevitably through consideration of the role of the senses, for they too are culturally hierarchized and differentiated; sight, hearing and smell, often conceived of as the most important senses, rely on distance. They are senses that require a gap between the body and the referent, the thing perceived, heard or smelled. Touch and taste are the two senses that require contact with the body. They are the most intimate of the senses; as such, I will argue they are most closely intertwined with notions of selfhood and therefore can be the most difficult and ambiguous to explore through play.

11 "A woman must continually watch herself. She is almost continually accompanied by her own image of herself ... from earliest childhood she has been taught and persuaded to survey herself continually" (Berger 1972: 46).

12 A popular music group with a female lead singer, Christine Amphlet, *The Divinyls* was formed in 1980 and is still rating highly today. Of their six albums, two are in the United States music charts. A relatively recent single called (significantly for my purposes) "I touch myself" reached no. 4 in the United States music charts (Scott 1997).

13 Boys, they both noted, were even far more afraid of being labelled "other." There was clearly an even stricter hegemonic code of behavior for young men in their world governing appropriate forms of masculinity. Girls, they seemed to agree, paradoxically have more flexibility and freedom in this regard which, of course, was part of their "definingly" feminine attribute.

14 This leads us into another important area of mother/daughter relationship which I will return to in chapter 3, when I explore the significance of domestic spaces for self-making.

15 This notion of bodily praxis being the core of self knowledge is not a new idea. It has been the focus of a great deal of research in Cultural Studies, especially concerning Youth (Hebdige 1979; Lesko 1988) and central also to understandings in Educational Psychology, Social and Cultural Anthropology, and Sociology (for example, Douglas 1973; Featherstone, Hepworth & Turner 1991; Turner 1992; Jagger & Bordo 1989; Sontag 1979; Bourdieu 1984; Taussig 1987, 1993, among many). It has been especially central to understandings of (young) women's identity construction and (self)representation (Ardener 1993; Smith 1988; Moore, 1994; Bordo 1993).

16 The concept of social class, as it occurs in most of the existing research on young people, fails to take account of the complexities of self-perception on "class" and

other social divisions. Class grouping in particular is often assumed to be homogeneous and frequently regarded as self-evident and unproblematic as a means of classification. The result is often then a circular explanation or analysis of behavior: working-class girls do this *because* they are working-class girls. This is developed further in chapters 4, 5 and 6.

17 It could be argued that over the past few years in Western culture the discourse of femininity has changed more rapidly through the voracious demands of consumer capitalism for novelty. However, a close look at those changes and at their manifestation in young women's and teenage girls' everyday lives, reveals in fact that little has changed in certain assumptions of women's gender relations. Some of the more dire consequences are, of course, the growing numbers of anorexics and victims of other eating disorders. Bordo observed that "the taking up of eating disorders on a mass scale is as unique to the culture of the 1980s as the epidemic of hysteria was to the Victorian era" (1993: 168).

18 A great deal of research has looked at the way women's "noise" is devalued and the way women's speech is rendered trivial. It becomes designated as "gossip," "chatter," or "natter," whereas men's speech is understood to have more importance or status as "talk." See Spender 1980; Ardener 1975; Gilligan 1982; Griffin 1978. Because such beliefs about the gendering of language and speech become naturalized, such understandings have great implications for the education and socialization of girls. In the classroom "boys are seen as lively, curious, boisterous and aggressive while girls are seen as docile, quiet and passive" (Poole 1986).

19 Two recent images from print media lend support to this argument. The first is a stark and disturbing photograph on the front page of the weekend edition of a quality national newspaper, accompanying an article about the young age of models and the extreme thinness demanded by the fashion industry. The photo depicts angular plastic mannequins designed with a protruding rib cage to emphasize their gaunt frames. The second article and photographs were featured in *Who*, a popular weekly magazine which, in providing photos of young teenage models and while purporting to express shock and disapproval, added to what amounts to "the eroticization of little girls" (Walkerdine 1997).

20 I actually used to wonder with Fran and Callie whether their expressions of affection were sexual explorations, as it was well known that Callie's mother was in a lesbian relationship. In other words, Callie had grown up with an open understanding of sexual orientation. However, as both Fran and Callie at this stage were very much into discussing particular boyfriends, any exploration on their parts in this way did not seem to be taken too seriously by either of them.

21 If one didn't have the monetary means one either "racked" the clothes (stole them from the stores) or "rolled" other people, that is, attacked other young people to obtain the clothes. Several of the girls in my fieldwork had either been victims, observers or perpetrators of these types of scenarios.

22 This was a family that talked to me about the possibility of having to sell the family car if Diane did manage to gain entry into a TAFE hospitality course. It was the only way they could conceive of paying for the fees.

23 I can only note again the appropriateness of Taussig's observations about mimetic transformation. The significance of this particular kind of clothing will be referred to later in the text.

24 See chapter 5 for more detail concerning the symbolic roles that clothing and styles play in the creation of inclusivity and exclusivity in friendship groups.

25 "Try Hard" was a derogatory term that was used to signify someone who was not "one of us." I heard the term repeatedly during my fieldwork to indicate "otherness."

26 I think part of Kate's physical behavior – the way she would meet and talk to me in different places – was an aspect of her desire to see herself as "different." For a similar reason my own daughter rejects any popular brand-named clothes such as *Sportsgirl* or *Esprit*. Her reasoning is "everyone else wears them I like to wear clothes that make me feel an individual." Thus like Kate she prefers to buy clothes from secondhand or "op-shops." I return to this phenomenon further later in this chapter and also in subsequent chapters.

27 Current advertisements for sanitary pads and tampons emphasize the new physically active, assertive female and are about one brand of tampon over another in the light of how unrestricted they allow her to be. This is not without its problems though – see below in the main text!

28 I think it is significant that the girls talked about "trying on" the clothes but I saw their activity as "dressing up," an activity that I would see as parallel to Kate's activity in the domestic sphere. See above in the main text.

29 As Western culture has become dominated by the visual image, it has also increasingly become one where new technologies have blurred the boundaries of what is popularly understood to be "real" and what is understood to be constructed. Baudrillard, of course, has long argued that we have incorporated the gaze into ourselves so that we internalize an "audience" in all that we do and say: "It is no longer a question of a false representation of reality (ideology) but of concealing the fact that the real is no longer real, and thus of saving the reality principle" (Baudrillard 1983: 25).

30 When the *Nunga* children wore the Adidas clothing they were seen by non-Aboriginal children as "Try Hards." The clothing was an indication of one's authenticity, one's legitimate right to be seen as a member of that group. The clothes alone could not confer that authenticity upon one.

31 I find it interesting in Taussig's observations and analysis of the mimetic faculty that he argues that it is different for women, as women have to learn to accept another's mimesis, "pretend to believe – to mime – on pain of death that what they are witness to are real gods and not their kinsmen acting as gods. In this way the public secret essential to mystical authority is preserved . . . In this vast scheme, women however become skilled . . . with the power not to simulate another, but instead to dissimulate, to pretend to believe in the Other's simulation" (1993: 85–86). It is precisely this ability to "withhold belief" that is so powerful and effective in making women want to become another not of their own making and that contradicts their own real life experiences.

32 As with all of the ways human beings organize their world, the senses too of course are ranked hierarchically. In Western culture sight and hearing are usually considered the first two senses; both are distant senses not requiring physical contact between person and referent. Smell occupies an ambiguous halfway mark as it is so closely associated with the body and the body's reactions. Smell is a particularly evocative sense that can bring sudden flashes of memories from the subconscious. It straddles the line between outer and inner senses. Touch and taste, the last two senses, at least in Western culture are intimate senses dependent on contact with the physical body for actualization. They are of course the two senses that babies learn to use first for their knowledge of the world and therefore are regarded as the least sophisticated of all the senses, aligned with appetite, instinct and the primitive. Yet, of course, taste and touch are also particularly tied to expressions of sexuality. Advertising explicitly links enjoyment of food and pleasure in touching with sexual desire. Conversely, denial of food for the body has often been seen as a way of purifying the soul of its gross bodily impurities. See Bordo 1993 for a fascinating discussion of the ideology of hunger and its application to consumer culture. Also Douglas 1978; Turner 1994;

Eckerman 1994; Elias 1978, 1982. This close alignment with the body itself rather than to the intellect leads to these senses having their ambiguous place in our negotiated self-making. They are closer to "unreason," to being out of control and therefore less reliable as a foundation for "authenticity" and "truth" about the self.

33 See Sue Lees (1993) for a detailed discussion of equivalent abusive terms in her British research.

34 Too childish because conservative style or behavior can be seen as appropriating too closely adult values. In this way, paradoxically, the teenager is perceived as childishly aping the adults and not asserting her own potential independence and difference from them. Diane told me that when Helen wanted to annoy her and to highlight what she saw as Diane's lack of independence from her parents she would call her "little girl."

35 The girls are underage so the fact that the bouncer allows them entry without the appropriate ID suggests that they have been to the dance many times before and that there is an "arrangement" between the bouncers and the girls. See chapters 4 and 6 for more details on this common practice.

36 Commit a sexual act/have sexual intercourse.

37 *Scheme* always has a sexual connotation. It means to arrange to have sexual intercourse with someone. In spite of the previous verse, there is little that is "romantic" about it!

38 A fight.

39 Obviously part of the girls' allegiances to "healthy lifestyles" and vegetarianism was a reflection of their own family values and belief systems, but as I have already pointed out, attendance at Cirkidz itself was also seen by most families as an appropriate aspect of their value system. Most of the teenagers who were attending Cirkidz during my fieldwork also went to schools known for their alternative or feminist ideologies.

Chapter 3

Whose Private Space?

> The wish to be "private" at times and the feeling that some actions are more appropriately performed in private than they are in public seem to be almost universal, yet the concept of privacy has no precise and uniform content; it is therefore very difficult to define, whether, indeed in ethical, psychological or simple linguistic terms (Lidia Sciama 1993: 87)

> *This is my room, where I spend all my time. It is my own private space where I can do literally what I want to.* (Diane, direct to camera)

Introduction: Spaces to play

In the previous chapter I recounted several incidents where the teenagers in my fieldwork were engaged in the serious task of "body work"; that is, negotiating both similarity to and difference from others through their bodies. I demonstrated that this exploration in behavior, style, dress and demeanor was a way of marking out and testing boundaries and an essential part of the rhetoric of self-making. In this context, we observed several teenagers "watching themselves" in different contexts – Diane and Bekk in school, Sara and friends in the department store, and Grace and Kate recording their conversations on video camera. In this way, the nexus between representation, embodiment and the constitution of selfhood was highlighted, particularly the ways in which it was enabled through the medium of a camera. In this way too, we began the journey into questions of material contexts and social groupings because, as stated earlier, "bodily praxis" (Moore 1994; Bourdieu

1977; 1990) does not occur separately from its physical contexts. It was *significant* that Bekk and Diane's self-representations occurred in the classroom and similarly, that the "striking of poses" by Sara and her friends, took place in front of the mirrors in the department store's changing room. Equally, the incident where Janine, Wanda and Janelle introduced us to their wonderfully dramatic alternative view of the city, only occurred the way that it did because of the crucial nexus between the specific geographical place, the time when the incident occurred and the girls' perception of that time-space.

Such a relationship of place, time and subjectivity highlights the importance of what is usually described as "private space," a space where one feels *able* to play or to test out boundaries. This chapter explores some of the ways in which a specific time and place seemed more "open" for play in the development of "self-making" in the experiences of the young women in my fieldwork. I begin this exploration by focusing on the concept of *body-space* (Duncan 1996) – that is, how *space* itself is created, enabled, hindered and negotiated through bodily praxis. To do so, I adjust the analytical lens again by arguing that, for the young women in my fieldwork, the perceptions of who they were, who they believed themselves to be and who they wanted to become, were acquired not only through their physical experience of being, but also through the interrelated and integrated aspects of "bodily praxis" – *place, space* and *play*. Here we discover that the conception of "private space" became crucial to the rhetoric of self-making in their videos, and particularly the ways in which their *bedroom* spaces were so central to their simultaneous constitution and representation of self. The bedroom is a particularly appropriate place to explore body-space since most of the teenagers indicated that these rooms signalled an arena of great significance and personal reflexivity. They represented "a place where you can really be yourself," (Belinda) or in Diane's words, her "own private space" where she could do "literally" what she wanted to.

Once the teenagers started to speak directly and more personally to the camera, their bedrooms seemed to be the most favored places for this to occur. Each girl's video included a photographic exploration of the bedroom itself, sometimes quite explicitly, and with a verbal commentary in voice-over and sometimes not, beyond the camera's gaze. Yet in spite of this shared acknowledgment of the importance of their own bedrooms, there seemed to me – as might be expected from such a diverse group of young women – important differences in the decor and style, the location within the house, and the use of their bedrooms. Furthermore, while most of the teenagers seemed to see their own rooms as some reflection of their individual personality and taste, it was clear on closer observation, that the choices that determined the "look" of the room, each girl's creation of "the real me" expressed through the ambience and style of the room itself, were very much in keeping with her wider social and familial values. To illustrate this contention, I need firstly to unpack some commonplace assumptions of the three concepts that underpin this notion of "private space" – that is, *place, space* and *play.*

Place as spaces of power relations

In terms of *place,* we can already see that to be embodied is always to be a "body in action," to move or be moved through and to negotiate different geographical and physical locations. More importantly perhaps, *particular* places seem to permit a greater freedom of movement than others, even though simultaneously we are aware that this perception of permission seems arbitrary. After all, Bekk and Diane were in the same classroom, presumably bound (at least, theoretically) by the same school rules and yet Bekk, and the male students, were able to behave in a far less inhibited way there than did Diane.

A second aspect, and one explanation for the difference between Bekk's and Diane's perception of that place, is that ultimately, every geographical *place* is actually experienced as a *space* of power relations and therefore, for individuals, not all places are deemed to be equal. As Nancy Duncan argues: "social relations, including importantly gender relations, are constructed and negotiated spatially and are embedded in the spatial organisation of places" (Duncan 1996: 4). Or again, as Bourdieu has pointed out, space cannot simply be understood as geographical or material boundaries, "realities that can be touched with the finger" (Bourdieu & Wacquant 1992: 228); rather, geographic space needs to be appreciated and deconstructed as "a space of relations," an arena of potential struggle for "symbolic power" (Bourdieu 1991). Inevitably, that means that space is never neutral; it is implicitly gendered, and exclusive and is frequently contradictory (Massey 1994; Lefebvre 1991; Gregory & Urry 1985; Soja 1989). Places and the way we conceive of them as *spaces,* are not only the *setting* for social interaction but they are also the *medium* of social processes (Gregory 1986: 451). Put another way, "behavior and space are mutually dependent" (Ardener 1993: 2). This can have far-reaching consequences in the way specific individuals experience their surroundings.

Frequently, this experience of space is envisioned in quite simplistic ways; for example, how women "collectively" and hegemonically might experience particular spaces, this particular coupling undoubtedly offered because both space and gender are ordering principles and therefore closely interrelated. As Massey has argued:

> *The limitation of women's mobility, in terms both of identity and space, has been in some cultural contexts, a crucial means of subordination. Moreover, the two things – limitations on mobility in space, the attempted consignment/confinement to particular places on the one hand, and the limitation on identity on the other – have been crucially related.* (Massey 1994: 179)

While such observations may seem undeniable, closer observation of how specific people actually create and negotiate space signals something far more complex and paradoxical. Personal experience and attention to ethnographic examples, should remind us that there is not a straightforward, deterministic relationship between "limitation of mobility" and "subjugation" and thus, between space and gender. Firstly, of course, such a reference to women's experience blurs over aspects of class, race and age; not all women are equally subject to particular limitations on mobility (Moore 1994; hooks 1991). For example, the middle-class Anglo–Celtic teenagers in my fieldwork usually expressed less awareness of being harassed by police or security guards than did the teenagers from Aboriginal backgrounds. The teenagers who had dark skins or who identified as non-Anglo–Celtic (or in their own words "not Australian") frequently talked about their experiences of feeling outsiders or negatively different in some way. Within the home, conceptions of private space were not uniform either. For example, the teenagers from less affluent families often had less physical domestic space at their disposal than the teenagers from homes that were materially more privileged. The teenagers from separated homes or blended families, where they occupied two or more dwelling places, thought of their bedroom spaces in different ways from the teenagers who had only one such space to call their own. Some teenagers shared their rooms with other members of their family or were expected to give up their rooms regularly for a visiting relative or family friend. Ideas of what constitutes private space even with the domestic realm are far from straightforward.

When Bourdieu reminds us that "bodies take metaphors seriously," he also is highlighting the way that bodily praxis takes place within structured time and space (Bourdieu 1977; Moore 1994). An essential aspect of that embodied experience is that each individual's interpretation of her material world is based on her gendered, social positioning within that culture: each person experiences and creates manifestations of power and distinction through her day-to-day negotiation of social relations and the dominant cultural discourses. In his famous analysis of the Kabyle house, Bourdieu describes the way power, privacy and privilege are formalized in the everyday experiences of the household members:

> *One or other of the two systems of oppositions which define the house . . . is brought to the foreground, depending on whether the house is considered from the male point of view or the female point of view: whereas for a man, the house is not so much a place he enters as a place he comes out of, movement inward properly befits a woman.* (1977: 91. Also cited in Moore 1994: 77)

This interpretation by Bourdieu also implicitly underlines the complexity of the concept of space and privacy when we consider bodily praxis in this light. Firstly, it is clear that the meaning of particular space never exists a priori – for example, a particular room such as a bedroom is not necessarily equally "private" for all people in the household. Furthermore, again it seems equally clear that the concept of "private space" itself is not a universal, understood notion across all cultures or even within one culture. An individual's social positioning within her wider society or within her micro-culture of family or immediate social networks affects her understanding of access or use of space. For some, the notion of personal or individual "private space" is a right. For others, as Sciama implies, the concept just does not exist (1993).

On a simple level, there are different understandings of personal space within and between cultures and thus people have varying degrees of tolerance toward being physically close to another person (Goffman 1956, 1959, 1967; Hall & Whyte 1960). For example, I have already referred to the way the Cirkidz teenagers hugged each other and me on each meeting, and yet for Janine and Diane, coming from very different backgrounds, such intimate physical contact between teenagers was an anathema or even a perversion. On a more complex level, control of space always means control of knowledge and exercise of power. It can mean both the actual physical and the emotional control over another person: this control can be manifested as directly constituted through force or surveillance or as an indirect power internalized, embodied, and "misrecognized" by the receiver (Foucault 1976; Bourdieu & Wacquant 1992: 194). Alternatively, as a form of symbolic violence, such control of space can be manifest in *both* ways simultaneously – experienced as an external force and internalized by the receiver. In other words, experience of space, and thus conceptions of *private* space, are never straightforward and are often paradoxical.

As indicated in the epigraph to this chapter, some of this complexity and paradox underlies the words of fifteen-year-old Diane. As we have already seen, she *seemed* quite restrained in her demeanor and in her activities, and yet we find that she *believed* that she was not constrained at all. In describing her bedroom as her "own private space" she seemed to believe that she possessed her own exclusive area, an arena where she felt she was *totally* free to experiment, to explore, to "play" – "I can do *literally* what I want to." Yet in many ways (or at least, to an outsider), Diane's room seemed far from an independent "free space." It was, for example, manifestly cluttered with very conventional icons, artifacts and consumables common to an Anglo–Australian 1990s girlhood: there were pink and white china ornaments, dolls, a teddy-bears' chain, and many posters of clean-cut male pop stars decorating the walls and surfaces of her room. This "private space," in other words, seemed to reflect a consumer-driven, romantically idealized, heterosexually oriented female childhood or early teenage-hood rather than represent an area in which to experiment or to test out any ideas or values that were different from her family's perspectives.

Furthermore, because of the small living area of her house, and because there was no physical means of barring entry to adults or uninvited guests (her room did not have a lock), Diane's bedroom seemed to be both physically and psychologically all too easily accessible to others to be truly "her own private space" or "room of her own" (Woolf 1977). Seemingly then, this was hardly an "adolescence of experimentation"; there were no rebellious images of teenage-hood here![1] So, in what sense could this possibly be understood as "private space," either literally or metaphorically? What did she mean when she spoke of "privacy"? In what ways did Diane believe this to be a "room of her own," reflecting her own constitution and representation of an independent self?

I will return to Diane's creation of her "private space" in more detail at the end of this chapter but, for now, I merely highlight the fact that her room, which she called her "private space," seemed paradoxically to represent and reflect a childlike self-image that, on the one hand, was full of nostalgic images of *childhood* and that, on the other, simultaneously cohered with the particular *adult* values in which she was enmeshed. Furthermore, I argue that she was not alone. If we look more closely at the way all of the teenagers in my fieldwork constructed their "private space," we will discover interesting parallels in the way they constituted their self-making through their material contexts, reflecting the established values of their family and immediate social networks rather than being rebelliously discrete.

Play as a negotiation of space

While human activity and thus social relations seem to be theoretically separable from the geographical spaces in which they occur, the material context impacts upon and inevitably frames, and is framed by, the behavior within its "contours"; in other words, "self-making" as an aspect of human embodiment, is intricately linked with *where* and *when* that experience occurs.[2] The link between bodily praxis and physical spaces then, becomes even more apparent when one recognizes that the more constrained the actual or *perceived* frameworks for material existence, the more internalized and appropriated become the constraints, and the more controlled the *imagination* for possible alternatives. In other words, I argue that there is a direct correlation between *perceived* restriction and the ability to "play" freely. This is not to suggest that all victims of oppressive regimes passively accept their fate, or that there is no struggle to negotiate perceived constraints. However, I believe that a far more complex phenomenon applies. I am interpreting "limitation of movement" not only to imply a physical boundary to freedom or restriction of access to certain locales imposed on the agent from powerful others. I am also suggesting that these constraints become naturalized so that effective symbolic boundaries are erected and internalized.[3]

A further dimension to this argument, as I suggested earlier, is the concept of *play* itself. Both serious play and fantasy are central to the constitution of self. Earlier I defined fantasy, not in the way it is usually represented as trivial and disengaged from reality, but rather as an aspect of reality where, in the form of *serious play,* it can represent activities where the "unspeakable" is "spoken." While taking place in physical spaces, play in effect, requires *a negotiation of* space. Goffman referred to a similar concept in his notion of perceived symbolic "frames" that modify behavior in different social contexts. Play is essential for the testing and pushing out of symbolic boundaries and play itself has to be understood to be socially *permitted* within a particular cultural context (Goffman 1959; Bateson 1972).

This understanding is very different from the conventional understanding of "play as resistance," for I am arguing, as I have elsewhere in this book, that play is more about *accommodation,* an embodied evaluation of where the individual feels she can comfortably "accept" or negotiate the "rules of the game" rather than *subverting* the ground rules.[4] Implicit in this understanding of play – this getting a "feel for the game" – is a tacit recognition and acknowledgment of these symbolic boundaries. Thus the link between play, space and place in this concept of self-making, is the perceived prerequisite of "*space* to play" (Bateson 1972; Handelman 1990). Actual or perceived limitations on mobility (Massey 1994) and the constraints on (self) identity (the *perception* of the "freedom" to move or even to *be* in certain spaces), are directly related to the (perceived) ability to explore other possible selves – "permission," as it were, to play. Many forms of play are mimetic and, as Bourdieu reminds us, mimesis includes both an *active* and a *cognitive* component.

This interpretation of play and space, and the role of mimetic activity, brings us back to the concept of *bodily praxis* as a mode of knowledge. While play may seem to occur anywhere and at any time, its emergence and thus its "political" and "strategic" power and efficacy are directly related to where and when the activity is interpreted as being *allowed* to take place.[5] So, far from being trivial, play is powerful precisely because it can enable the redefining of places. As Rubin argues: "The power to define is the power to control ... We create reality wherever we go by living our fantasies" (1970: 142–43). Indeed, play in such circumstances can be perceived by some as dangerous and potentially subversive for it "challenges official culture's claims to authority, stability, sobriety, immutability, and immortality" (Schechner 1993: 46).

But not everyone is equally able to "define" or to "control." Not everyone sees the necessity of challenging "official culture's claims to authority." As we have already witnessed, individuals experience their world and negotiate spaces differently. Individuals from similar social backgrounds can have quite different understandings of their *need* or their *ability* to play in this way and to explore other alternatives. They may have different understandings of what is meant by "personal," "private" and "public" space, different ways of using their bodies in various locales and arenas. Again, to return to the incident of Diane and Bekk, the former felt that appropriate behavior *for her* in that place was compliance and quiescence. The second felt that she could assert her own influence, her own voice and her own challenge to authorities, by loudly and disruptively "standing up for what she believes in." As I pointed out in the previous chapter, each girl's sense of *différance* (Derrida 1973, 1978; Kamuf 1991; Grosz 1990) was linked to her micro-cultural value systems, her particular *habitus* acquired over her lifetime in the home and in the familial community.

As I noted in chapter 1, the notion of *habitus* has significant implications for this study and therefore deserves consideration in greater detail. In the first instance I shall examine the ways in which the teenagers in my project negotiated and contested the space perceived as *available* to them as young women, *from the perspectives of their own micro-cultures.* Not all of them, as indicated above, had the same conception of what space *was* actually open and welcoming to them, both in the public and in the domestic sphere. Not all shared the same desire to engage in "serious play" in the same spaces. As a way into untangling the complexities of such conceptions of space, I will use an example from my fieldwork – Hilary's very unusual and special "Lost Forest."

Rediscovering "The Lost Forest"

> *This is my Lost Forest. It is not so much a place that is lost but a place where I can remember. This is where I can remember how to be a child.* (Hilary, voice-over to camera)

When I first got to know Hilary, then aged 15, she introduced me to her very "magical" Lost Forest. Later, it became a particularly important aspect of her video footage and was included in her final cut. About six months before the start of my fieldwork, she had moved into her current home with her mother and younger brother. The house was quite small but Hilary had her own room which, like her own physical appearance, she characteristically kept immaculately tidy and organized. A great deal of Hilary's footage portrayed her in her room studying or reading, her desk clearly representing scholarship, order, ambition and self-control in her life. Sometimes the raw footage included sections where she was apparently directing her mother as camera operator to capture some very deliberate contemplative shots – a teenage girl videoed (fly on the wall) as she sat quietly thinking, meditating, or reading. The off-screen comments in the raw footage revealed such dialogue as:

Mom	*Is this okay?*
Hilary	*Can you see the title of the book in the shot as well?*

Fig 11: Hilary in a contemplative mood

In another video shot, she had someone else (again, her mother perhaps) video her as she sat swinging pensively on a wicker hanging chair in the garden. She portrayed herself here as deep in thought, lost in a contemplative reverie and (apparently) oblivious to the presence of the camera.

She was certainly a conscientious, thoughtful and very academically able student and obviously wanted to portray these aspects of her persona publicly. When I first met her, she had been elected school captain (head prefect), indicating her widely acknowledged leadership qualities, her academic prowess and her determination to be successful in many areas in her life. Hilary's room, while reflecting all of these qualities, also contained a few hints of different, "alternative" spaces. I stress that these were not portrayals of some deep dark *secret* or previously unexplored space in the way "privacy" is often conceived as exclusive (for they still appeared in the raw and the edited footage), but certainly they were aspects of her life that were quite *differently* narrated and portrayed.

Firstly, around her room among the academic books and the more adult icons were hints of a childhood nostalgically idealized and "remembered." There were, for example, several romantic images of fairies and fantasy – a small picture of a fairy, an illustrated children's book cover portraying a wizard and a tiny porcelain statue of a pixie. As with many of the teenagers who had such artifacts in their rooms, these images were not just ignored or glossed over. Hilary's camera zoomed in (although without commentary) on these images of wizards, fairies or magic when she visually surveyed her room – brief glimpses of such images in between other more serious, "adult" shots. Significant in themselves, as I shall detail below, these little snippets of fantasy seemed to herald the greater importance of Hilary's other, larger alternative space, her Lost Forest.

After she had moved into her new home Hilary had discovered that under the built-in wardrobe in her bedroom were some loose floorboards ("Like in *The Lion, the Witch and the Wardrobe,*" she explained) revealing an empty space under the house, a sort of small, hidden, secluded cellar. Hilary had decorated this tiny space with rugs, cushions, candles and more romantic posters of fairies, spirits and magic. It became a dark, mysterious place, a chamber that she named the *Lost Forest* where fantasy and imagination prevailed.[6] She would take her friends down into the cellar or used it alone, to read, to listen to music, to think. In place of the loose floorboards she put a trapdoor to enable easier access but the entrance was still small and narrow so that it seemed, at least in my eyes – and to the rest of my body – to represent a barrier to more adult invasion.

Fig 12: Seek the magic

If outside the Lost Forest, even within her bedroom proper, was an adult world of certainty, responsibility, and order, then the inside space seemed richly dense with unspoken possibilities – a place still seemingly in the process of evolving into something *else.* Unlike her adult world of control and order, a world of the rational mind, *this* place was self-consciously rich and crowded with magic, emotion, romance and the senses. The rugs on the floor, the semidarkness of the candles and the pungent, exotic odors of incense made this place a space of the body. This was where the "civilized" body experienced the sensations it had been encouraged to distrust and disregard (Elias 1978). To reach the Lost Forest Hilary had to enter into a different *physical* space (through a trapdoor that was too small for adults to enter easily), perhaps reinforcing her self-awareness of her still young, physically immature body. It was a space that was clearly separate from her more controlled self and yet in its deliberately imaginative assembly, was still precisely and neatly contained and containable. In other words, while seemingly dramatic and alternative, a manifestation of some kind of Freudian repression of the subconscious, the "child" to Hilary's usual portrayal of the "adult," this seemed all too *consciously articulated* a contrast between this world and her "everyday" world. An alternative interpretation, one that doesn't signal a repressed psyche, is required.

Like Mary, in her videoed narration of herself as a rejected "Gift," or Kate in her love of dressing up, Hilary seemed able to hold the different aspects of her life together in a fully conscious, indeed a *theatrical*, tension.[7] Rather than its being a subconscious creation, I would argue that through the Lost Forest, Hilary was clearly performing a very deliberately dramatic example of mimetic excess. Firstly, the Lost Forest clearly was designed in a way that perfectly cohered with her already established familial values. The room itself was a very significant part of her self-representation. For example, she spent a considerable section of her final footage *introducing* this space to her viewers. The camera focused on the trapdoor, which appeared to open of its own volition (the gesture thus portrayed as a miraculous, magical moment of revelation) before the camera zoomed closer.[8] Once the camera entered the Lost Forest, a singularly distinctive room was revealed – a room lit like a magic cave or grotto, full of candles, wall hangings and soft cushions and a book entitled *Wizard's Spells.*

Fig 13: The lost forest

Obviously on a straightforward level, Hilary was re-creating a childhood context that was rich, exciting and distinct from her more adult world of responsibilities and ambition. She commented in her voice-over that the Lost Forest was a place where she could "remember how to be a child." This section underscored other aspects of her video footage where, while portraying herself "playing" on the floor with a tiny plastic toy collection, she claimed that it was important for her to "hold onto my childhood for as long as possible."

Yet it seemed to me that the Lost Forest was not so much about a specifically *remembered* childhood space at all; rather, it was a manifestation of the powerful, dramatic and creative quality of *play*. That is, it was a way of *creating* an *idealized* past in the middle of an uncertain and often scary future.[9]

The Lost Forest was significant in another way too. It seemed that this subterranean place represented a space that was, simultaneously, physical, mental and social (Lefebvre 1991: 11–12) or in the words of Soja, "all spaces (should be) seen as filled with the products of the imagination, with political projects and utopian dreams, with both sensory and symbolic realities" (Soja 1996: 62, parenthesis added). Soja calls such places a simultaneously *real-and-imagined* space; both a place of liminoid mimetic blurring (the imagined, the "*not*-real") and yet also one carefully marked out as a separate, discrete territory (the geographically "real" – that which *can* be touched with the finger!) In its very creation, indeed, it seemed to demand a redefining of space and thus an unsettling of some of the usual, simplistic ways in which space is categorized into private and public arenas.

Redefining space: Unsettling the private and public divide

One of the common expectations about social space in many cultures, including Australia, is that the domestic arena is not accessible to outsiders without an invitation.[10] Indeed, it is the different ways in which a family member and a non family member or a close friend and a stranger behave in the domestic realm that sharply differentiates the usually unarticulated categorizations (Ardener 1993; Hirschon, 1983; 1993; Dragadze 1993). For example, in most cases in Australian homes, a stranger who enters the domestic realm does so on the understanding that s/he will conform to a particular set of behaviors and expectations perceived as being different from familial or close friendship behaviors. Thus, a stranger does not enter a house without knocking or before asking for permission to enter. Once inside the house, s/he does not wander from room to room without invitation; a stranger does not look into other "private" areas of the home – places such as fridges, cupboards, correspondence. To relax too much by leaving *on* certain articles of clothing (for example, a hat, a coat) or removing certain articles of clothing (shoes, belt, top clothing) risks social censure.

In "mainstream" Australian social groups, certain behaviors – in this instance relating to domestic spaces – are usually regarded as implicit rules of protocol and apply mainly to middle-class adults. Yet it was immediately clear to me from my fieldwork experiences that not all of the groups and social networks into which I entered, shared these codes of behavior. Certainly, the young people themselves, often without these privileges of personally "marking off" territory of exclusion (they were not male nor adult and many were not white nor middle-class), frequently either ignored such protocols or took obvious delight in breaching such rules of etiquette.

Lefebvre referred to the *"illusion of transparency"* of space, pointing to the way in which space seems capable of being "taken in by a single glance from that mental eye which illuminates whatever it contemplates" (1991: 28 cited in Soja 1996: 63). Because the attributes of space seem self-evident, they are frequently categorized into private and public spheres as though these were neatly bounded areas that could be defined and understood objectively. Indeed, as we have seen, Hilary herself neatly separates her study/bedroom proper from her subterranean world of magic. Diane also seems to be assuming that there *is* a conceptual difference that can be utilized in particular geographical or material places, in speaking of "her own private space." She is also assuming that she *can* use particular space "privately" in this way, as something that is exclusively hers.

For example, her bedroom in this context is private and exclusive as opposed to the more open and inclusive living areas of her house, the school classroom, the street or any of the other spaces she enters and occupies as a young woman in her micro-world. Yet in one of the first parts of her video footage recorded in her bedroom, she and her friends are mimicking a *Peter André* music clip playing on the television set in front of them. They dance, laugh, and copy the dancers on the screen, perfectly replicating the gestures and movements. Later, with great hilarity, they read out a romantic quiz in a teenage magazine. Indeed it seems, then, that far from separate from the world around them, the values and pleasures of the outside world were in fact welcomed in. Occasionally they also intrude, uninvited; for example, at one point in this section of her video, Diane's father opened her bedroom door unannounced and told the teenagers to "keep their noise down." So in spite of her vision of "private space," it is hardly separate or even neatly separable from the more "public" areas of her life. Rather, it is closely associated with the more everyday values of her family and her wider social network.

Of course, the terms themselves, "private" and "safe," like the concept of space itself, although freely used in popular discourse, are never unproblematic nor uncontested. Firstly, like the concept of body ownership and management of the body, privacy also involves the ability and the affectivity of the agent to be in control. Yet, of course, not everyone experiences the same *right* or *means* to privacy. Similarly, not everyone even *shares* this same perceived concept of privacy. I noted earlier that the Aboriginal teenagers in my project did not seem to have the same contemporary Western (and many non-Western) cultural understandings of an independent body nor an independent self. Similarly, I discovered that they did not *expect* to have something they could call their "own private space" the way Diane did. Their bedrooms were often shared with their siblings or other relatives and even more importantly, were reallocated as needs arose within the family. So, in other words, conceptions of what "privacy" actually meant to the various teenagers in my research project were firmly embedded in the perspectives of their own micro-cultures, accepted and unquestioned through their own particular *habitus.*

Secondly, as suggested above, geographical places alone do not automatically *prescribe* which activities take place within their particular physical boundaries. There is no such thing as a space that is definitively to be used for public or private activity. Privacy, for example, can be interpreted as both a material boundary such as signs that say *Keep out, private property*, or a state of mind. One can be involved in "private" activities, such as very exclusive conversations or secret business deals or even daydreaming in a very public environment, for example, in a street, a cinema, or a shopping center. Privacy has several other contradictory con-notations too. It can indicate constraint (for one can be either inside or outside the symbolic or material boundary of exclusivity), but it can simultaneously imply shelter and protection from an outside "reality" that is perceived as dangerous or corrupting.[11] Furthermore, spaces that are understood as "private," such as the home, are not necessarily safe for all the people within their walls, as has been witnessed many times in cases of physical or sexual abuse. I have already briefly recorded Mary's account of her traumatic childhood. She also commented several times on how unsafe she felt in her childhood home and later in the various foster homes she occupied.

On the other hand, spaces that are often regarded as public and therefore assumed to be *inclusive,* such as shopping malls, are frequently *exclusive* for "marginalized" others – the young, the less affluent, the unemployed in the community who primarily want to congregate and socialize but do not have the monetary means to "consume." Other public places such as bars and dance clubs enable some very private activity to take place simply because of the sheer numbers of people who attend.[12] Indeed, in all places, relative anonymity can encourage some very "exclusive" activities. Conversely, places usually designated as private such as bedrooms, especially for teenagers seeking places to entertain their friends, can sometimes be used for very public activities. Fran's video footage includes a party at her house, most of which was held in her own bedroom.

What emerges from all of these contradictions, is the shared perception of privacy being a physical and a metaphysical state that is closely aligned to cultural understandings of power and status and, as such, it is also directly related to bodily praxis. The profound significance of the implicit relationship between privacy, power, and embodiment is demonstrated by the diverse ways in which each of the teenagers marked out their private spaces within their domestic spheres.

Domestic spheres: The problems of gaining access

From the first moments of fieldwork, I realized I was potentially entering a minefield in negotiating whose domestic sphere I could comfortably enter and whose I could not. I could not take for granted any thought of easy access or otherwise. At the start of the research, however, I did believe that the implicit protocol of access and acceptance into domestic spaces would apply even more rigidly to an adult researcher such as myself, working with teenagers. Indeed, during the initial stages of my research, I expected to meet the teenagers and talk with them only in open places that most people would designate as public. We talked in cafes, Cirkidz rooms, school classrooms and youth clubs. I did not expect to enter their domestic spheres until after a great deal of time and a great deal of trust had been established – and then, only if I were invited. This was firstly because unlike most researchers in this field, I was working primarily with the young people themselves rather than with their parents or adult caregivers and secondly, because I was using a less-structured methodology than is usually the case. My aim, to use such long-term, intensive participant observation rather than questionnaires or interviews with the young people themselves, meant that my presence in the family would be less time and function "bounded" and therefore it could be regarded as far more intrusive than the way a researcher's company might usually be considered.

And yet I was also aware that, for the young participants of my project, the domestic sphere was the place where the most important aspects of self-making were likely to occur. I assumed that their relatively young age and their gender, alone, would mean that a great deal of their social activities would take place in the home. As noted early in my fieldwork, the camera did seem to allow me a legitimate and nonexploitative access into these domestic arenas. It could go where I could not and it gave me the "authority" to work closely with the teenagers in a variety of social contexts. The key enabling factor, I discovered, to my acceptance and, indeed, the camera's presence in most cases, was the overall ambience and ethos of each individual household – the spaces within *that* micro-world considered open to particular others and to strangers, and those which were not.

It tended to be mothers who directly or indirectly facilitated my presence in those domestic spaces. In the case of Sara, for example, my presence in her home was by direct invitation from her mother. Indeed, hers was the first home I visited to discuss her video footage. Sara's mother, an older parent with a background in teaching, not only suggested my visit but also seemed to understand immediately why it would be important to my research. "You should come and see Sara in her home environment," she suggested one day over the telephone, "then you can probably learn more about why she is the way she is." Such insights and generosity always took me by surprise. I had expected to experience far more caution about the way I would be received into the girls' family environments and, indeed, I know that for many parents and caregivers there was actually considerable and understandable concern about my presence in these domestic spheres.

It was in anticipation of parental concerns in this regard that I had written a letter to the families of all the key participants explaining the purpose of my research and asking for permission to proceed. Yet only three families *overtly* expressed concern. Diane's parents, for example, asked me to come "for a talk" before their daughter was permitted to work with me. I went to their home very nervously, feeling as though I were about to be interviewed for a job. On their side, Diane's mother and father were clearly nervous about allowing access to someone representing a world to which they had no ordinary ingress – the university – and they saw me, at least at first, as someone who might introduce unwanted "different values" into their house or who might pry into their affairs. One of the first questions they asked me at that interview, as I noted earlier, was to explain why, according to my introductory letter to them, I was planning to study mainly *girls*. They obviously found this particular research interest into femininity unusual and suspicious.[13]

After the first occasion, I was permitted and welcomed into the family home by Diane's parents, but always with some degree of formality. I was always offered a cup of coffee and expected to sit down at the kitchen table to chat with her mother for some time before talking to Diane. Often there were other relatives, neighbors or close friends already seated at the table when I arrived. In these situations, I frequently felt I was useful to the family image, boosting their sense of "distinction" and importance – I was a researcher from the university "working" with their daughter. In many ways, this created a dilemma for me because I always felt that there was a danger that, for Diane, I would be seen as a parental figure rather than someone who could easily relate to the teenager. On the other hand, it was obviously necessary for parents and caregivers to feel comfortable with my presence in the household and find a reciprocal purpose for my presence for *them*, and so these long discussions at the kitchen table were important and necessary.

Because of the small amount of available physical space in the house, the more personal conversations with Diane relating to her film footage and other aspects of her social world always took place in her bedroom away from the rest of the family. There Diane would relax far more and treat me as *her* friend rather than her parents' acquaintance. But I always felt that I conducted a great deal of my fieldwork in this sort of psychological "schizophrenic" divide where the language and content of the discussions differed according to whether I was talking to daughter or to parent and according to where the conversation took place. A similar dilemma would occur in Sara's house, where her mother would also welcome me and want to spend long periods talking to me over cups of tea. In fact, it was undoubtedly also a strategy used by the parents of both families to get to know me in a similar way while I was trying to get to know *their* household and *their* daughters.

In the cases where I got to know the teenagers through youth workers or other representatives of the juvenile justice system or welfare departments, I sometimes felt the full force of the girls' and their families' ambivalence toward such officials. On some occasions, I would be invited into their homes as a friend while in other spaces, such as in the street or the court, I was ignored. In the case of some of the families of the Aboriginal teenagers, for example, I often felt I was *tolerated* rather than welcomed because so many officials/welfare agents had access a great deal of the time. Although I did not enter homes unless I was invited and was very cautious about making sure the teenagers and their families felt they had "choice" about when and where they saw me, I realized that, for several of the families, "choice" to ask me not to come or to leave, was not a familiar or comfortable concept in these scenarios. They sometimes dealt with this perceived lack of choice in indirect ways.

In relation to Janine's family, for example, I experienced a great deal of difficulty in organizing definite times when I could come to talk about the video footage. Janine and I would often arrange what I believed to be a mutually convenient time. I would telephone again, often just before leaving home, to check that the time and day were still okay. Janine would say "yes," but on several occasions after having driven the 45-minute journey to her house, I would find that she had suddenly "gone out" or "had to go and help Nana at work." I never saw this as her personal *teenage* attempt at avoidance. Rather, I wondered whether the family as a whole found it difficult to ask me to change the time or whether they thought it was more empowering to just pretend that I wasn't coming. All in all, I was being shown that I wasn't very important in their whole scheme of things. Occasionally Janine *would* remember (or decide) to call me and ask me to change the time or day of our meeting but more often, she didn't. On the other hand, if I did not contact *her* as soon as she expected me to, she would castigate me roundly on our next meeting. "Where've you been? I thought you'd been *murdered*!"[14]

In Diane's and Kate's homes, I felt I was regarded by the respective parents with suspicion, for very different reasons. As I indicated above, in Diane's white, working-class family, there was concern about "the authorities" and the way officialdom tended to override the family's own desires and concerns.[15] In contrast, Kate's parents, both middle-class academics, were anxious (perhaps quite understandably) about being potentially the subject of research themselves rather than being agents in such a scenario. I privately sympathized with their concerns and dilemma, as I could see that it would be difficult for them not to be concerned at having their privacy symbolically breached in this way. On the other hand, as they had brought their daughter up to be independent and self-confident, I could see that they felt it had to be *her* choice whether she wanted to stay in or leave the research project.

A quite different set of circumstances faced me when I entered Fran's and Hilary's micro-worlds and "private spaces." In Fran's economically middle-class, though unconventional home I was always treated as though I were a friend of her own age, welcomed in, but basically ignored by the rest of the family. Indeed, it was only after six months that Fran "formally" introduced me to her mother. Hilary, on the other hand, began our acquaintance by *inviting* me to meet her mother with whom she felt I would "have so much in common." I did meet her mother, although I found I still spent far more time talking to the daughter and very little speaking to the parent. Her mother understood this to be my aim and so tended to leave Hilary and me to talk about her film or about her current social experiences.

The section that follows explores some of the ways other teenagers made certain parts of their domestic spaces their own and further highlights the way such "private spaces" are deeply entrenched within each girl's own domestic sphere and familial values. It will also dispute many of the commonsense assumptions frequently held about teenagers and their rooms, such as the belief that teenagers desire to create spaces that deliberately subvert middle-class notions of control and domesticity (for example, McRobbie 1978, 1991. See also McRobbie & Garber 1976).

Domestic spheres: Rights of access

When I arrived at Sara's house on that first occasion, I immediately became aware of its isolation. Sara's home was forty-five minutes by car from the city. The nearest public bus stop, which was on the closest main road to her house, was more than another forty-five minute walk down a narrow country lane. This difficulty of access meant that many of Sara's social activities depended on having someone else taking her to the nearest public transport by car. While she could walk the long trek to the bus stop by day (and she frequently did), night time activities were severely curtailed.

The home itself was a large brick home reached at the end of a private dirt road and at the top of a narrow, winding, quite hazardous track. My car labored considerably getting up the hill and I grimly thought about making the same journey once winter set in. Even to reach that point was not straightforward. Sara had given me quite complex directions for finding her house, for it was not clearly shown in the metropolitan street maps. However, I received quite idiosyncratic directions such as: "Go past Black Stump Road. You'll see a building that used to be a post office. Straight after that you will see a small winding track. Watch out for the geese and the sheep as they wander across the road . . ."

Once at the top of the track, there was a view of trees, fields and vastness so that one indeed did feel a sense of achievement and separation on reaching the house. At first sight, the house, as I said, was a two-story, although only partially constructed, home made from brick. There were many pieces of equipment and building tools, such as wheelbarrows and small cement mixers, planks of wood, sand and more bricks lying around the outside of the house. Also around the home (there was no cultivated garden as far as I could tell, just natural "bush" and scrub) were several old cars clearly in the process of being repaired and reassembled.

I learned that the house was being built personally by Sara's father and that due to the sporadic nature of work and the necessary finances, the project had taken thirteen years so far. Sara jokingly, though poignantly, commented that by the time her father finished her *real* bedroom – a space allocated upstairs – she would have left home. In fact, that was exactly what happened. On my first visit to the home, Sara's temporary bedroom downstairs was still not complete. There was no ceiling above her bed, just the bare galvanized iron roof. That meant that in both summer and winter she would have experienced the extremes of the weather.

The family of four lived in the small finished section of the house downstairs. The main living area was used for cooking, eating, studying, talking, TV watching and working on various hobbies and assignments. When I first got to know the family, Sara's brother was already living away from home during the week, because he was attending a school quite some distance away. Sara's room also contained many of her brother's belongings. Nominally at least, the parents and each child had their own bedroom, although in this household, "private space" was something that the family members were expected to share.[16] Furthermore, the limited amount of spare physical space available in Sara's house also indicated that all available rooms and surfaces were "shared" too – books, papers, clothes, tools, implements were stored on all possible surfaces in the living rooms, including the floor.[17] Even finding a spare seat was difficult. Because the main living area led straight into Sara's room, it inevitably meant that a great deal of the household clutter migrated into that room too.

Two questions emerge immediately from this initial introduction into Sara's family's domestic sphere. Firstly, if Sara's "private space" was very much a part of the family spaces, did she ever attempt to mark off territory of her own? Secondly, if she did, how did she do this? The two questions provide an important springboard for an examination of how Sara – and indeed all of the girls – tackled her own need or otherwise, for privacy.

Sara's room: Into the dragon's lair

Sara's bedroom was a smaller version of the comfortable clutter characterizing the larger living room, with clothes and other items strewn everywhere. On the first occasion, when I arrived, she seemed completely engrossed in transferring articles from one pile and placing them in another as though she were involved in a giant move or tidy-up. The rearrangement did not produce any more space – just a slightly different perspective. She had her tape recorder or radio playing loudly with the perfume of burning incense filling the room. Her bed was low to the floor and was covered with clothes, articles, and papers. There were several posters and photographs on her wall, many to do with Cirkidz. A large desk to the right of her bed was covered with a variety of objects, books, clothes, papers and quite a large television set. To the left of the desk along the left wall of the room was a chest of drawers and a wooden chair. Every conceivable square inch of the room, including the floor, was covered in something. During our talk that day, Sara's brother amicably came into the room without knocking to collect some of his belongings; his lack of formality suggested that this was a common occurrence.

Ostensibly, as indicated earlier, there was no clear demarcation of Sara's area from anyone else's space in the household, apart from the door leading into her room. Yet there were several ways in which Sara *did* attempt to carve out "space to play" for herself, metaphorically if not physically. Firstly, as did many of the teenagers, she appeared to make her room symbolically separate from the rest of the house through her *particular* choice of decorations on her wall, although, unlike many of the other teenagers in my fieldwork, there were no posters of pop or rock stars on Sara's bedroom walls. There were, however, several posters of Cirkidz events, small photographs of close friends, and a huge poster of the film *Chaplin*. She said she admired Charlie Chaplin greatly. There was also a collection of magazine photos of Gary Sweet, an older Australian actor, epitome of the taciturn outback hero. Above Sara's bed was another very colorful, exotically drawn poster of a dragon. Sara said the dragon picture, given to her by her mother, was Nepalese like herself. It also reminded her of herself when she was angry, she said. As was the case with Hilary's Lost Forest, it seemed that here was an alternative aspect of Sara's potential self that she wished to explore and portray. She usually presented herself to me as very amicable and rarely ruffled, so apart from this statement, it was not an aspect of her personality I ever experienced, on or off the camera, until right at the end of the three years of our friendship.[18]

Moving her bedroom furniture around was another way in which Sara marked out her "territory." Every time I visited I would find that the room looked different. Even in that small area, the bed or cupboard would be changed around so that the perspective of that whole space appeared to be completely new. Yet another way Sara defined her space was utilizing the actual physical space she *did* have to create a *mental* space for her imagination, specifically the use of her bed and the outside balcony surrounding the house. Through the video camera and through still photographs Sara drew attention to the importance of her bed. When I looked at these shots, I asked Sara why she had taken the photos:

Gerry	*Okay I can see what this is [the bed]. What is important about it for you?*
Sara	*I spend a great deal of time there.* (laughing)
Gerry	*Do you enjoy sleeping there or is it that you like dreaming – I mean daydreaming there?*
Sara	*Yes, I enjoy thinking here. I can be private here.*

The balcony was another area that allowed Sara more privacy and "space to think," as she called it. She would sit outside on a huge chair looking at the surrounding trees, bush land and sunsets. Sometimes she would eat or read out there. There were several still camera shots taken by her of the landscape, the sunsets and the chair itself.

An unusual and imaginative technique for carving out private space was one to which I have already alluded. In a location where physical space was at a premium, Sara seemed to have made an area her own by "demanding" a distinctive aural and scented arena. The loud music and unusual pungency of the incense filling the physical spaces of her room, were a far cry from domesticity and conventional adulthood. Yet at the same time, it is clear that Sara symbolically carved out her own "territory" within the domestic arena while guaranteeing that her "own space" did not differ greatly from that of the established familial pattern. Again, it was pushing the boundaries just so far but no further. Although Sara's parents were born in Australia they had long been attracted to and practised Buddhism. Their decision to adopt Sara and her brother from Nepal was part of their expression of love and attachment for that country and its values. Thus, the incense, and the images and photos on her walls were all perfectly in tune with her adoptive parents' outlook and Buddhist affiliations. Yet, at the same time, there was just enough "playing" at the borders of these values – the loud music, the shifting furniture, the freedom to daydream on her bed or on the balcony – to enable her to feel she had a room of her own, her own private space.

Fran's room: "Yeah! I enjoy being myself!"

Fran was a girl who liked to mark herself out as "different" from the "mainstream," resisting labelling and categorizations. She told her audience clearly in her video: "I don't fit into any category. I've got a bit of this, and a bit of this, and a bit of this!" – although in many ways, and certainly at first sight, Fran's domestic sphere and bedroom space echoed Sara's. There was more physical space, as her house had more rooms in use, but each room also had clutter that seemed to spill out into and often sit, almost inappropriately, in other rooms and spaces. In the hallway, for example, I always saw several bicycles, while on the front porch was an old tattered and ripped sofa and several packing boxes. Fran's home, a Victorian "villa," was located in an older inner-city suburb. The term "villa" does not refer to the size of the house but its design. In Australia it describes a particular type of building common at the beginning of the century. It had a central corridor that ran from the front of the house to the back with all of the rooms running off this hallway. She lived there with her mother, her younger brother and her mother's partner. The house was not particularly large but the back garden was spacious and was clearly being used by the family to cultivate plants and vegetables.

Fran entertained all of her visitors, including me, in her bedroom. We never stayed in the kitchen to talk, as I did occasionally at Sara's house. If I arrived early at her house, sometimes before she arrived home, I was invited inside and then left to my own devices. Her family ignored my presence and seemed, at least on the surface, uninterested in why I was there. No one made any attempt to engage me in "polite" conversation, unlike the situation in Diane's family where I was expected to have coffee and chat to the family for some time whenever I came to the house.

Fran's room itself was a double bedroom, approximately ten feet square. It contained a double bed, a desk, wardrobe, a smaller cupboard and chair and often another mattress on the floor for guests "sleeping over." Since this was a very old house built in the late 1800s, the ceilings were about fifteen feet high, lending another dimension of spaciousness to this crowded room. On occasion there was also an old-fashioned sewing machine set up in the middle of the room. It seemed that every piece of furniture in that crowded room was there for its function rather than for any aesthetic purpose. Indeed, the overall effect was one of eclectic "busyness" or the "organized clutter" of a *work* room. In other words, in spite of the clutter and perhaps because the room echoed the appearance of the rest of the house, this room did not feel like a teenager's attempt to move away from domestication but simply resembled a young person's attempt to use the room for a multitude of tasks. Both off camera and on, Fran portrayed her room being used for studying, sewing, drawing, talking alone to the camera, chatting with friends and partying. In other words, it was a place for both very quiet contemplation and rowdy fun with friends.

Fran's walls – like Sara's – also reflected her interests and her attempts to portray and constitute herself symbolically through icons and imagery. Photographs of family, friends and herself covered her walls, with her mother frequently taking center stage. Fran commented on these photographs several times in her raw footage: "This is my mum. She is my best friend." On a separate occasion she announced in voice-over: "This is my mum in her 'hippie' years," as the camera trained on a close-up shot of her mother taken some twenty years before. Then she added theatrically: "My mum is *brilliant!* If she was on sale, she'd be all sold out!"

In stark juxtaposition to this atmosphere of practical industry, Fran's room was also one of fantasy. Posters, drawings and images of wizards, magic and fairies abounded. Fran "firmly believed" in fairies, she told me, but her reasons were whimsical and romantic. "Little children always believe in magic and they always tell the truth!" she asserted one day, her tone simultaneously archly self-mocking and theatrically naive. On another occasion she told me "*Of course* I believe in fairies and so does my mum."

Grace's room: Smelly Teddies and Violent Femmes

Like Sara, Grace had little physical space to play with and like Fran and many of the other teenagers, she had to attend to many domestic duties. In many ways, I felt Grace became the mother of her family unit. She had a younger brother and had to spend a great deal of her spare time looking after him while her mother was at work. It was a duty she resented, unlike Diane, who when *her* mother had to go into the hospital, was happy to "play mum for a while."[19] Grace also seemed to see herself as emotionally independent of her mother, capable of making all her own decisions, even though at the beginning of the fieldwork period she was still living at home.[20] Unlike Fran, who seemed to see herself as an equal adult to her mother ("My mum is my best friend"), Grace seemed to see herself as *parent* within her family unit.

Perhaps this was the reason that, during my first visit to her home, she made sure that no one else would be present during our discussion. She deliberately arranged our meeting at a time when a friend of her mother would be picking up her younger brother and when her own mother would be at work. My visit became an official business meeting carefully timed and organized. My field notes record how Grace introduced me to her mother's friend as someone who would look after her brother, Matt, for a while. She then kissed Matt good-bye before sitting down, businesslike, at the kitchen table with me to discuss her film.

If Grace seemed to be very much a "parent" outside her room, her room itself revealed the same contrast between child and adult that Fran's had portrayed. One of the first things that Grace decided to record and discuss on video was her collection of toys, housed on her bookcase shelves. Teddy bears, old dolls, and soft furry animals were individually and lovingly introduced to the camera.

> *These are my Smelly Teddies (holding three tiny toys up to the camera). They were given to me by my grandmother for my birthday. They each have a different smell.*

Apart from cataloguing her many toys, Grace also spent a great deal of her footage attempting to video the adhesive stars on her ceiling and the posters and little statues of fairies and wizards. Like

Fran's room and Hilary's Lost Forest, Grace's bedroom was full of such icons of romance and magic. And yet interspersed with these were images of quite brutal violence. Grace was a fan of music that favored quite a nihilistic stance and aggressive or violent lyrics, and consequently a number of her posters depicted relatively gruesome scenes. For example, her poster of one band, called Rage Against the Machine, depicted a graphic photograph of a Buddhist priest passively ablaze after immolating himself as a political protest.

This unexpected juxtaposition of images of romantic childlike innocence and adult aggression was further exaggerated when Grace talked to me on camera about the drug use of her social group. She sat facing the camera chatting knowledgeably about the effects of particular amphetamines or hallucinogenic drugs, carefully selected music of The Violent Femmes (her favorite group) in the background, all the while hugging her favorite large fluffy toy. As an adult observer watching the careful balancing of contradictory worlds without any apparent sense of conflict or irony by the user, I found the whole scene extremely disturbing and profoundly surreal.

So far, I have provided four brief accounts of how four teenagers – Hilary, Sara, Fran and Grace – attempted to create their own private spaces within their domestic worlds. Note that there were both similarities and differences in the ways that they creatively marked out territories of distinction. For example, all the rooms I have described so far incorporated romantic images of fantasy and the teenagers focused primarily on these images when they made their videos or talked about their rooms. These dramatic symbolic images of magic can be considered in three interrelated ways: fantasy as practical nostalgia, fantasy as New Age romanticism and fantasy as serious play and mimetic excess.

Fantasy as practical nostalgia

In one sense, it is obvious that the icons and the particular aesthetic adopted by the girls represented a nostalgic, idealized return to childhood. If we understand that for many of the teenagers the transition into adulthood represented an ambivalent process that was uncertain and in many ways, threatening, then such images can be seen to symbolize a desire for an imagined, idealized past. Such nostalgia may be more than a desire for something that has passed; it is more than sentiment; it is embodied and efficacious. Through her fieldwork observations of the urban Trobrianders who lived in Port Moresby, Debbora Battaglia (1995) noted just such a *practical* use of nostalgia.

> *Nostalgia may in fact be a vehicle of knowledge, rather than only a yearning for something lost. It may be practised in diverse ways, where the issues for users become, on the one hand, attachment of appropriate feelings towards their own histories, products and capabilities, and on the other hand, their detachment from – and active resistance to – disempowering conditions of postcolonial life.* (Battaglia 1995: 77)

Nostalgia, then, in this sense is not simply longing or an imaginary step back to another time and place that seems more "real" or authentic, but an engagement with a different kind of "other" that opens up more possibilities. Because it seems a familiar, comfortable "other," it can reproduce emotions that "open subjects to creative reconfiguration: nostalgic practice invites self-problematisation" (Battaglia 1995: 93). Like mimesis, through which nostalgia is often realized, such revisiting of the past offers the power to reposition the individual to the present. It offers what Taussig (1993) and Bhabha (1987, 1994) have each called "slippage" and ambivalence, a temporary step into the subjunctive in order to reassess the material present.

Fantasy as New Age romanticism

The second, related way that the images of fantasy can be understood is as an aspect of New Age romanticism. As noted previously, stylized, surreal pictures and posters of fairies and magical figures were prominent decorations in many of the girls' bedrooms. The images themselves were quite sophisticated rather than childlike straightforward representations. In their pastel coloring and wispy, indeterminate outlines, the characters in the posters appeared to be very other-worldly and ethereal-looking. They were also minimally gendered and in fact, most often, androgynous in appearance. In my opinion, the figures were very much linked to a highly commercialized New Age romanticism of spirituality, with their flowing hair and medieval-style clothing. For many of the teenagers, especially the ones connected with Cirkidz, such aesthetics and ideals were perfectly in tune with their parents' "grass-roots" socialist and environmentalist values. The New Age movement, like the former Hippie movement of the 1960s, represented a desire to abandon materialism and embrace a new vision of what appeared to be a universal *communitas* (Turner 1967; Handelman 1990; Schechner 1993).

Of course, fairies have long been associated with young teenagers and childhood, but these teenagers aged between 13 and 16 did not see themselves as children but rather as "marginal beings; those left out from the patterning of society" (Douglas 1984: 95) – or in Allison James's terms, "nobodies" – too old to be classified as children and too young to be considered adults (James 1986). One day Claire (15) angrily articulated her perception of the paradoxical predicament when she retorted: "They [her parents] are always telling me to 'grow up' or 'be your age' when they really mean be more adult. But when I want to do something a bit different, they tell me I am too young!"

All of the teenagers in my fieldwork were young women hovering on the brink of adulthood – developing physically and hormonally but emotionally not quite there yet! Their age and personal circumstances meant that some had far more freedom of movement and choices than others. The iconography, symbolism and discourses drawn from the New Age movement and expressed in the posters and drawings decorating the bedrooms of a number of them, seemed to allow a certain symbolic bridging between childhood and adulthood in ways that, I would argue, appeared to permit the teenagers to express and explore this liminoid stage of their lives. In different contexts much of the writing on New Age symbolism has argued that the concept embodies "a self conscious experience of the indeterminate, the decentred and the transitional . . . [it] . . . is a sensibility that deliberately eludes the chains of definition . . . seeks to focus attention on *process rather than product*" (Hall 1994: 13, emphasis added).

In the bedrooms of many of the girls participating in my research project, such symbolism very distinctively lined their walls. The female fairy figures in these posters were all young adults with long flowing blonde hair and waiflike ethereal bodies in the midst of pastoral forests and lush, idyllic greenery. As indicated above, complementing such images were usually colorful candles, music, incense and often tiny fluorescent stars attached to the ceilings.[21] Thus, for these individuals, the magical element of posters appeared to be part of a much larger representation of fantasy in their bedroom space – a semi-mysterious world that often seemed to sit uneasily alongside the newly acquired demands and responsibilities of imminent adulthood, another aspect of the management of uncertain subjectivities.

Fantasy as serious play and mimetic excess

This brings us to the third aspect of fantasy. A closely related way of considering iconography such as that appropriated by a number of girls in the study is to see it as representing a further aspect of mimetic activity and "serious play." The toys, posters, and symbols of fantasy were a practical way of testing out, "feeling out the ambivalent boundaries" of the present – either through the seemingly unchanging aesthetics and representations of a romanticized childhood past or through the fluid, ethereal quality of an idealized (spiritual) future.

Either way, the shifting conceptions of time-space through the use of fantasy-related symbols in their bedrooms imparted to each the necessary ambience of "a space to play." Yet, as indicated above, not every girl in my fieldwork drew upon such romantic "open" imagery. Many had more restrictions placed on them, directly in terms of the decor of their rooms and therefore also in terms of their imagination and their play. Sometimes in those situations the symbolism had to be converted into humor or excess, just as caricature can more freely represent and explore difference than realistic imagery can. Yet for some teenagers, even this oblique symbolic exploration of self through the decor of their rooms was not possible.

Private space? What private space?

For Mary and Janine the concept of "private space" was not the same as that expressed by a number of the other teenagers in my fieldwork: this was not something that they seemed to consider or articulate as a right or even something that was particularly desirable. For Mary, as described in detail earlier in this account, her small housing trust home was certainly her own domestic space for a while as an essential part of the independent living program. Yet at the same time, it was hardly space she could claim as solely her own. She opened her doors to all her friends and acquaintances, many of whom were teenagers who lived on the street or who were escaping the law. The fact that it was her "own" house created a particular status for her in their eyes and she enjoyed that prestige – even though, simultaneously, that also brought her some difficulties:

> *I reckon I'd be the only friend they've got that's got their own house and paying for their own bills and I believe they should have more extra respect [for me] for that. Like they were visiting their own mum each day. Parents think the same way I do.* (Mary)

In many ways, Mary saw her house as offering her a chance to be a mother. As a product of numerous foster homes herself and a recipient of foster parenting, Mary was in many ways demonstrating what she had been taught. She would welcome into her home the young offenders whom she saw as victims of abuse and trauma, who were unwanted in their own homes and who would act out their problems on a more public stage.

> *Sometimes they get physical . . . Most of my friends have got their own problems that they try to deal with. They take it out on my house.* (Mary)

When they "trashed" her house leaving her, in her own words, "with lots of bills and lots of anger" she would shrug and start again.

Mary believed that had she stayed in Papua New Guinea she would have been expected to be married and to have been a mother for many years. She apparently felt ambivalent about this information which she had gleaned from some friends who were expatriates. Transferring this discourse into her world in Australia was far from simple. On the one hand, being in Australia gave her a chance to "run amok," a space to grow up and time to be an adolescent as opposed to being an adult. This granted a degree of freedom and license but brought other problems in its wake. As Barbara Hudson has argued, adolescence is well-documented as a *masculine* construct, so that adolescence, according to these discourses, is antithetical to femininity. That means that "any attempt by teenagers to satisfy themselves *qua* adolescence, are bound to involve them in displaying not only lack of maturity (since adolescence is dichotomised with maturity), but also lack of femininity" (1984: 35).

On the other hand, being too large, aggressive and the "wrong size, shape and colour" to fit comfortably into conventional notions of femininity in her immediate world, meant that Mary had to seek a different kind of self-making. "Mothering" gave her this sense of identity, where currently there was a gap.

This is my place: Janine's room

Like Mary, Janine was officially "in care" and living with a foster family and had been for the past twelve years of her life. Her foster family, like Janine herself, identified as South Australian Aboriginal. It was a warm, close family but run efficiently and strictly by "Auntie Rosa," a diminutive Aboriginal woman. In the small Housing Trust home, Rosa raised four teenagers (one of whom was her own grandchild) and hosted many more children and adults who passed through her doors. The house was always full of family, relatives or other people who could claim and expect hospitality through distant kinship ties. Consequently the home was very strictly, almost austerely run, rather like an institution. I am not suggesting that there was no affection in the home, rather that Rosa's way of maintaining control over the teenagers' behavior was to enforce a very strict regime on the whole household. Each girl shared a bedroom with another but these arrangements were flexible and sleeping arrangements were reorganized regularly, according to the current state of personal friendships (who was feeling particularly compatible with whom at that time) and whether there were any visiting relatives who needed the space.

Partly as a result of this lack of attachment to any particular room, there were very few decorations on the walls or markings of "ownership." In fact the only time I heard Janine refer to a space as *her* room at all was when she announced to me one day that "Nana" was taking her to buy some paint so she could paint her bedroom. The teenagers were all expected to contribute meaningfully to the household in terms of cooking, cleaning and looking after the many small children who stayed at the house. They were also expected to "help Nana" with her various part-time jobs, such as rolling up and delivering local newspapers. Unlike the other homes I had visited, Janine's household had no *mental* space for any clutter in its overall plan. I frequently arrived at Janine's home and found all the teenagers engaged in cleaning, tidying and other house maintenance. Of course Rosa's control of her teenagers' behavior and activities extended to their social world as well. Any outing was strictly controlled, with the teenagers having to seek permission before going. Rosa told me proudly one day that her neighbors had commented on how "good" and quiet her teenagers were, compared to the teenagers of many of her neighbors. It was obviously part of her overall strategy to maintain control over their behavior and therefore their morality.

Nana's firm control was evident in the spaces that Janine introduced to me as her bedrooms over the time of my fieldwork. Although, as did many of the other teenagers, she talked on video in and about her room, it was not a monologue alone to the camera. Her sister, her friends and her tiny cousin were included in that section, often looking extremely formal and uncomfortable. So, unlike the openly playful sections of Diane's or Fran's videos, there were no such lighthearted portrayals of "having fun" in Janine's bedroom. On and off camera, the room always looked immaculate. Carefree play was reserved for the garden or outside the home – in other words, not in "Nana's house."

I am not suggesting that all the Aboriginal homes that I entered during the course of my fieldwork were like Janine's. Some were far less rigidly controlled by an adult and some, like Wanda's, were so overwhelmingly full with family members that there was no way that the teenagers could even conceive of a particular physical or mental space that could be regarded as solely theirs. The teenagers constituted their sense of self, in this situation, by playing a central role in the economic management of the household (as mother, child caregiver or coworker).

Don't be such a child! Claire's room

Claire's room presented as the antithesis of Fran's or Sara's, for it was always when I saw it, on and off the camera, exceptionally tidy and neat. Furthermore, by contrast to Hilary's room, which was also extremely ordered and explicit in its focus on scholarship, Claire's room exuded an old-fashioned, feminine appearance. The dressing table, the bed and the window were all decorated with white and pink lace and flounces, extremely feminine and neo-Victorian or neo-colonial in style. There were no posters of teenage rock or sports stars on Claire's walls. There was a framed picture of James Dean, an old-fashioned framed picture of a little girl and several small toys on a shelf. The only distinctive symbolic indication of Claire's exuberant personality was a colorful poster that spelled out her name.

Claire's parents were immigrants from Zimbabwe. They had come to Australia several years previously but spoke a great deal of the difficulties of migration and the aspects of life that they found problematic or contradictory in Australia, including their view on the "lack of discipline" in the schools and in the family home compared with Rhodesia. They seemed concerned that their two teenagers were not receiving enough structure or direction in their teenage lives.

In contrast to this view of the need for more external control, Claire herself seemed barely able to suppress the excessive animation and exuberance she exuded. Out of the home, where I first met her, she bubbled over in conversation and enthusiasm, each sentence barely being finished before she began the next. At one point in one of our conversations, she told me that she was far more self-controlled at home than at school or with her friends. I laughed and exclaimed that in our talks together I had never seen her *totally* self-controlled or quiet. She grinned at me and replied that I had no idea how *different* she was at school: "Oh my God! [there] I'm a bag of beans!"

Like Kate, Claire also seemed to need to express her personality and love of living through her sheer physicality. However, whereas Kate was permitted to behave in a less adult manner in her home, Claire was not. While Kate could have a conversation with me on her head or hanging upside down from a tire, Claire was very strictly kept in check by her parents about what she wore, how she behaved and what she did. Most of Claire's surplus energy, in fact, was "controlled" by her addiction to sport, particularly hockey. Her father was the school coach and a great deal of her raw footage recorded games where she was playing with her father coaching from the sidelines. Seemingly anxious to achieve his praise and meet her own high standard, Claire was extremely competitive and ambitious. Away from the sports field, her sense of competition and leadership was revealed in her determination to be school captain and to be involved in other committees and youth groups. As the elder of two teenagers, she was also expected to take such responsibility within the home and be a good example to her younger sister. However, in the home, her natural exuberance and vivacity seemed to be read by her parents as excessive. In their eyes, she was expressing inappropriate childishness and irresponsibility.

For the first half of my fieldwork, my conversations with Claire in her home all took place in her family room in front of her family. These were awkward and uncomfortable times because no allowance was made for the fact that we were trying to talk about her film or might want to look at her footage in private. At that stage, because Claire did not want to share her raw footage with her family, we rarely watched her video. Her father would often be working on a computer in the same room. Her sister might be watching television and her mother would be cooking and listening to our conversation in the attached kitchen area. Sometimes our discussion would be interrupted by her mother, who would talk to me about Claire in the third person as though she were not there. Quite understandably, in contrast to my telephone conversations with Claire or in situations outside her home, here the teenager seemed relatively subdued and awkward. The effect, much to my intense frustration, as I indicated above, was to relegate me to the position of a visiting adult or teacher rather than someone who was trying to form a relationship with the teenager herself.

However, one day on the suggestion of Claire's mother, Claire and I started to use her bedroom for our discussions. That week, her mother came to see me at home. Concerned about what she saw as Claire's "developing secrecy" and seeing me as someone who was working with several female teenagers, she asked my advice. She had wanted to see Claire's footage but Claire refused to let her. I pointed out that this was part of the arrangement I had with the teenagers in terms of their own freedom to film when and what they liked. I assured her that it was not that the footage was necessarily sensitive but that Claire wanted to explore ideas by herself so that she could decide what she wanted to keep in the video and what she wanted to remove from her final edit. I pointed out that it was quite difficult for Claire and me to talk meaningfully about her video ideas in the context of the family room with the usual family activities going on around us. "Perhaps you should talk in her room," her mother then suggested. "Then you can find out if she is in trouble or worried about something."

It was clear that Claire's mother saw the video activity as potential surveillance: on the one hand, it was threatening since it could be the family that was being scrutinized. On the other, it was useful in her eyes, as it could be a potential means of keeping a check on her teenage daughter. From that day on, after her mother's suggestion, Claire and I had our discussions in her bedroom and she did some filming there. It could still hardly be regarded as "a private space." If Claire wanted to talk about her social life – even when the content of her discussion seemed totally uncontroversial to my ears – she would turn up her radio in order to mask her voice. On one occasion, when Claire decided to film a direct-to-camera segment, her father began to chop wood outside her window. Her voice was almost drowned out by the constant noise, even though she asked him to stop for a few minutes.

The order and decor of Claire's room then begins to make sense in this familial context. Most of the decor in her room was chosen by her mother. The only item that stood out from the frills and flounces of the furnishings, the dolls, soft toys and neo-Victorian feminine style, was the poster of the 1960s film star, James Dean. I asked about this one day, wondering about Claire's particular fandom of the star. After all, he was not a star who was commonly seen on television or the cinema screen. "No! I'm not a fan," Claire replied with a laugh in answer to my query. "I just found the poster in a shop so I decided to buy it."

I pointed out that there was probably an element of choice in her decision. Were there other posters there? After all, I persisted, there might have been a poster of Madonna in the shop as well, so what made her decide to choose that one? Claire looked at me as though I were insane. "I wouldn't have a picture of a *girl* on my wall," she exclaimed. "People would think I'm a *leso!*"

Such a strident comment brings to the fore the consideration of *habitus.* In the micro-worlds of Fran, Sara and Grace there would be less pressure to conform and less concern that such pictures would imply something about their sexual orientation. In relation to Claire such a possible interpretation of her choice of decor could do just that and would contravene her family values and self-representations. Perhaps here also lies an explanation for Hilary's Lost Forest. With Hilary, and yet in a different way from others such as Diane, the imagination is carefully contained within acceptable limits.

Diane's private space in context

On closer examination we begin to see how Diane's symbolic boundaries were very carefully drawn indeed. Her bedroom was far more than simply an arbitrary reflection of a teenager's personal taste in music, fashion and style. As indicated at the beginning of this chapter, Diane began her video with a close reflexive look at her bedroom, which she called, "My own private space where I can do literally what I want to." As she filmed she talked in voice-over about how her room indicated and reflected her interests and "obsessions" (her own word). She zoomed the camera lens into the name plate on her door and onto some old photos on her dressing table of herself aged three and then at six, "at my mum's second marriage." She focused on the posters of Peter André, Michael Jackson and other male pop stars whose photos covered the entire wall space and then panned the room to show her video and CD collection of their music clips.

As described earlier, her room was quite small, painted and decorated in pink and white. It contained numerous soft fluffy toy animals and pretty china ornaments; she did not, however, comment on these aspects with either the camera or her accompanying verbal observations – they seemed a "natural" part of her world, something she took for granted. Instead, she used the camera to establish herself as "a really big fan" of her favorite musicians. She set up her tape recorder to play their songs as background music as she filmed, turning down the volume at strategic points to enable her to articulate passionately her feelings about their music and the stars themselves.

This very space of the domestic that allows more flexibility of behavior can also constrain. Often, the domestic sphere is an area where domestic obligations and responsibilities, such as household chores and baby-sitting, are carried out mainly by women. Often, also, the home is a place where very specific confining discourses of femininity are articulated and enacted. Thus the maturing female teenager may find herself in a double bind. Out of the home she may be constrained by fear of personal safety. In the home she is constrained by another paradigm of acceptable femininity – domestic obligation and what it means to be a woman and a nurturing female. Her search for a gender-neutral space – if such a place exists – is particularly difficult.

As Diane was not allowed to travel by public transport by herself or even with some of her friends, she spent a great deal of her spare time at home. She loved teenage soap operas like *Neighbours, Home and Away, Heartbreak High, Beverley Hills 90210* and *Melrose Place,* which she usually watched alone in her room on her own television. Her stepfather and brother "benevolently" tolerated but simultaneously verbally derided her media tastes. The gender roles in her family were strictly defined and a very specific form of gendered identity was a constant topic of discussion. Even though finances were difficult, since her father was unemployed, the mother's role as housekeeper was considered paramount. Diane herself was described to me by her parents as outgoing, sensible, domesticated, and hardworking, but perhaps too conscientious as far as schoolwork was concerned. Her academic achievements were recognized and acclaimed – an "A" student, in contrast to the way in which her brother and most of her friends were regarded. Yet it was not considered particularly desirable for Diane to go on to higher education. Rather, Diane modelled herself along very traditional feminine lines, taking over the domestic routine when her mother was ill, "being Mum for a while," or looking after her brother, who was older than she was.

Sharply delineated gender roles were constantly reinforced in family conversations. I was told of her brother's boss, who continually "humiliated" the boys at work by calling them "hopeless girls." There were concerned, anxious family conversations around the kitchen table about teachers or students who were rumored to be homosexual. Diane would frequently be teased by her brother and her father about Peter André, whom they said "looked like a homosexual." She herself was described by her parents through numerous little anecdotes (usually while she was in the room and part of the conversation) as extremely attractive. I was told how she got "special treatment" in shops from boys. On one occasion her mother related to me how she had gone to visit Diane when she was working at the florist's (her part-time job for a while), to bring her some dinner at the shopping center.

> *"I asked for a steak sandwich for Diane at the shop and there was a young boy there," her mother told me. "He said 'I know Diane. I know her brother'." Her mother put on a mock coy voice imitating the boy. "'I'll bring it to her when it's ready.' Then he asked 'Does Diane take mayonnaise on her steak sandwich?' I was having a sandwich too but he didn't ask me if I wanted mayonnaise on my sandwich.'"*

In family discussions the world outside the house was depicted as morally lax, dangerous and violent. Most of Diane's acquaintances and school friends were described as being risk-takers and potentially antisocial because they drank and took drugs. The teenagers were "backstabbers" and their behavior was promiscuous. Her mother frequently talked about Helen, a girl we have already encountered dancing and mimicking in the video taken in Diane's bedroom. Helen, it seemed, was the disreputable daughter of her old friend. She had "stolen" Diane's former boyfriend; she had dropped out of school; she had been before the courts on a dangerous assault charge; they suspected she was pregnant because she had been talking about getting engaged to her current but relatively recent boyfriend. Boyfriends were always represented as difficult conquests that had to be retained like property or possessions. Boyfriends were also the means of cultural capital or status in Diane's world. She complained to me wistfully one day that "It's not fair. Helen seems to get as many boyfriends as she wants."

So in the discursive context of Diane's immediate social world it seems that what the teenager *did* have, in her "own private space," was the freedom to engage in "safe" teenage fantasies *as circumscribed by her familial situation.* Despite Diane's own stated beliefs that this meant she could do "literally what I want to," it was not in fact a *complete* freedom to experiment. Firstly, her room reflected and reinforced her familial values about idealized women and a romanticized femininity: her pink room was overflowing with the traditional trappings of a stereotypical girlhood – soft toys, small pretty ornaments, as well as her many posters of male pop stars. The fact that her room was decorated with only *male* stars was also significant. To constitute herself firmly within female and feminine culture, as it was defined in her immediate world (and similar to Claire's), there could be no hint or suggestion that she identified with female stars or models in case this was interpreted by family or outsiders as a sexual orientation. In Diane's home environment, judging by those intensive conversations around the kitchen table, this would be unthinkable and certainly unsayable.

Moving into the public

I have argued that, for each young woman, the concept of privacy was relative and symbolically bound by what her family and immediate social networks considered appropriate and "normal" in their world. One girl may believe she truly has a "private space" in spite of the fact that she has no desire or expectation of discovering "alternative selves." For each girl, I argue that the "individual" selves reflected in their choice of decor in their rooms, reinforced familial values rather than challenged them.

If serious play was in fact contained by symbolic boundaries inside the home, we are left with the question of what experimenting and playful activity occurred in other kinds of spaces, such as the street, the shopping mall, the school and the dance club. How was privacy conceived of *outside* the home? How were serious play and self-making explored in the spaces that we understand as more "public"? In these (apparently) more inclusive places, the activities of self-making could paradoxically be sometimes more daring and more dramatic, paradoxically, because arenas considered as more "public" also permit greater anonymity – they can enable greater "private" space to play.

Notes

1 Ideas of what constitutes rebellion are of course specific to particular times and places. One of the aspects of contemporary life sardonically satirized in the British television series Absolutely Fabulous is the way not all families share the conventional middle-class moral values and thus, not all share notions of what "teenage rebellion" means. Edina, the mother and former "child of the sixties," longs for her own daughter to be the promiscuous, drug-taking "hippie" that she herself longed to be thirty years earlier. Her daughter, an adolescent in the nineties, is far too conservative for her mother's liking.

2 Self-making of course occurs continuously but the form that it can take at particular times depends greatly on where and when the activities take place. It also important to emphasize that, of course, space does not exist as separate from time. See Urry 1985; Giddens 1985, as well as the specific examples from my fieldwork, detailed below in the main text.

3 Anti-semitism offers a clear example of both the physical and the symbolic boundaries at work. The restrictions on movement on Jewish citizens under various regimes (including Nazi-occupied territories before and during World War II), frequently brought about an internalization and a naturalization of these constraints by the victims and their perpetrators. Their identities became redefined by the system.

4 Ardener (1993) points to the relationship between "ground rules" and what she calls "social maps"; that is, that social structures are reflected by spatial metaphors and that space itself exerts its own influences. In other words, "behaviour and space are mutually dependent" (1993: 2). In my understanding, play is the vehicle for exploring the symbolic boundaries of social maps.

5 Bateson spoke of the necessity of understanding play as a "frame of possibility." It can only occur when the participants acknowledge and recognize that the activity is play and therefore has to be interpreted differently from other actions. Thus, I am suggesting that the political effectivity of play can only take place where it is understood to be allowed to happen.

6 The Lost Forest was the name of an imaginative (and expensive) toy shop in the city, which has since been renamed. The shop specializes in soft toys and in their "serious" attitude toward their potential customers. Any child purchasing a toy has to be assessed by the vendors as to the suitability of their role as a "parent." The point about the name, of course, is that it connotes a return to the idealistic, fantasy realm of childhood rather like Peter Pan's Never Never Land.

7 Mary described herself as a "gift" for she had been given as such to her relatives when she was a young baby. For a fuller account of her story and the significance of this term in Papua New Guinean culture, see Bloustien 1999.

8 The raw footage reveals that this shot was carried out many times by Hilary before the desired effect was satisfactorily obtained.

9 Battaglia (1995) has argued that use of nostalgia in this way can be read as a way of simultaneously representing and constituting the self in a self-affirming past.

10 Angela McRobbie's early discussions about teenage girl "bedroom culture" implied a belief that areas within the house could be separated and marked off as private, "safe" and exclusive in this way (see 1978; see also McRobbie & Garber 1976). Her later work carried the arguments into more "public spaces" where similar discussions about the power of the imagination for symbolic "resistance" were presented (see for example, McRobbie 1991). See below, for a far more detailed critique of this common argument.

11 See for example, Lila Abu-Lughod 1986.

12 As I describe in chapter 4 in relation to one of what must be one of the most supervised of all dance events, the Blue Light discos!

13 Their concerns make sense in their overall concern about "alternative" sexual orientations, which as I explain below was a recurring and seemingly overwhelming issue that was discussed in their family.

14 The violence of the expression suggested to me how much I was expected to be there and accept Janine's terms of contact and time if I wanted to be regarded as a friend of the teenager and of the family rather than an outsider. See chapter 1 for a greater discussion of the complexity of my role in fieldwork and the part that my gender played in access and the relationship. Of course, all of these issues of access and potential exploitation had already been in my mind long before fieldwork as potential ethical problems, simply as a function of my working with quite young participants. For this reason, the parental and caregiver concerns, articulated or implicit, were simply to add another layer to already complex issues and would have practical and ethical implications in terms of my fieldwork.

15 Grace's mother also seemed used to having government agents continually in her home, but in that situation I felt I was not regarded so much with suspicion, but with a sad, powerless kind of resignation.

16 I say "nominally" because Sara's brother stored a great deal of his things in her room and therefore seemed to have access into her space whenever he wished, as indicated below in the main text. There was no lock on Sara's door nor was there actually a handle. A piece of string attached to the top of the door prevented her from becoming "locked inside." This is not to suggest that Sara never demanded to be left alone, but just to suggest that, until the end of our acquaintance, I did not see that side of Sara's personality (see chapter 6).

17 It is important to realize that the limited amount of space did not determine "the lived mess" but rather was translated in the ideology of Sara's home to mean that such clutter was inescapable. Diane's and Janine's homes had even less living space but their houses were almost austere in the way clutter and excess were hidden and controlled.

18 See chapter 6.

19 Of course a major difference was that Diane could see her activity as temporary ("playing" mum for a while) whereas for Grace it was an onerous and ongoing situation until she moved out of the home.

20 For example, she chose her own high school at the age of twelve, arranging all the enrollment and practical details including catching two or three buses across town.

21 I stress again, these particular teenagers – even the ones who attended Cirkidz – did not socialize with each other before we started filming.

Chapter 4

(Public) Space Invaders

> The sense of one's place, as the sense of what one can or cannot "allow oneself" implies a tacit acceptance of one's position, a sense of limits ("that's not meant for us") or – what amounts to the same thing – a sense of distances, to be marked and maintained, respected, and expected of others (Pierre Bourdieu 1991: 235).
>
> *We don't meet there. That's where the townies meet.* (Grace)

Introduction: Public space? Whose public space?

In the previous chapter, I explored the way the young women in my research negotiated "privacy" within their domestic realms. I argued that, for some of the girls, there was very little negotiation of private space for the "serious play" of self-making. Sometimes this was partly because of the limited physical room in their homes, as in the situation of Janine, Sara, or Diane. However, more importantly, this ability to experiment or to negotiate private space could be encouraged or hindered through the symbolic boundaries of the (gendered) familial and familiar value systems of that micro-world. Far more powerful than any physical containment of space, the self-perception and self-surveillance of what was or what was not considered appropriate and acceptable, what was or was not questioned and questionable in their worlds, limited and constrained the form of and the predisposition of "play."

Some "experimental" play was "managed" relatively easily in the home within these often tacit value systems. The constraining framework for many of the young women in my research ironically offered more possibilities of "slippage" in the more public spheres. I say ironically because we usually talk of people being able to "be themselves" and relax their more formal codes of behavior *within* the home space as opposed to the more public arenas; paradoxically also, in that I argue that it is the relative anonymity of the "street" and other areas away from the domestic sphere that gave some teenagers in my research *more* opportunity to "step into the subjunctive" in the process of their continual self-making. The concept of "the street" as I use it is a complex one, since I am not suggesting that the street has an intrinsic meaning separate from the social and cultural meanings that emerge through bodily praxis.

In the context of teenagers as a generic grouping, it is important to realize that, because of their relatively young age and low social status, the appropriation of any "private space" *anywhere* is gained only with difficulty. In this chapter, I look specifically at some of the ways in which that "space to play" was negotiated in the more public locales. I argue that the degree to which the girls felt they *could* "play" in a more public space, their ability and will to do so, were closely aligned to each girl's micro-social grouping. This ability to redefine and negotiate personal space and spatial relationships is "a political power" (Moore 1986: 89) and therefore, as might be expected, it is linked directly to conventional divisions of power and social hierarchies, such as gender, class and ethnicity. I begin by reexamining the nature of public space, in this light, in order to tease out the complexities and contradictions of appropriating private space in more public realms. From there, I will examine more closely the manifestation of this "political power."

The myth of "public" space

On the surface, the concept of "public" space seems far more straight-forward than the notion of the "private." Certain geographical places, like shopping malls, city streets, parks, and public gardens are considered to be accessible to everyone, but in reality, no space is automatically inclusive. Many areas that appear to be welcoming to all, within official discourses, are simultaneously understood by many to be symbolically bounded. To paraphrase George Orwell's famous comment, some *spaces* are, just like people, (perceived as) more "equal" than others. Recognizable categories of social "ordering" and related status, such as age and gender, impose further (symbolic) boundaries on who is welcome in particular places and who is not.[1] Frequently, a number of these symbolic categories apply simultaneous-ly, adding further complexities to the boundaries.

In my research, for example, I quickly perceived that the Aboriginal teenage girls had a very different experience of the city and other public institutions than their more privileged non-Aboriginal peers. While this meant an increased likelihood of being hassled by the police or other authority figures, it could also mean more license. These girls often expressed the view, in passing remarks and disparaging comments, that for the police they represented *Aboriginal youth* rather than (Aboriginal) teenage *girls.*[2] Similarly, Mary from Papua New Guinea seemed to attract the wider observation that she was a troublesome *teenager* rather than a difficult *girl.* Perhaps then, categorized by police or other authority figures as *youth* rather than female, while under more overt surveillance, these girls felt they could be more assertive, more aggressive in public. Perhaps this was also why some of these same female groupings had appropriated, to some extent, the ways that their male friends and relatives took over the city spaces and so in fact had themselves more confidently gained access to more "public" locales.[3]

In the public arenas most of the girls from Anglo–Australian backgrounds behaved quite differently from the Aboriginal girls. They appeared to adhere to the conventional understanding of women's more limited presence in public areas. In most cultures, as part of the social hierarchy of bodies within that particular micro-world, it is widely acknowledged that women tend to be granted less access to public spaces of status, knowledge and power than their male counterparts (Spain 1992; Ardener 1993; Massey 1994). When women *are* present in public life, they tend to be those who "are not yet, or have ceased to be, child-bearing, thus lacking the defining criterion that 'specifies' them as women" (Ardener 1993: 8). In other words, as very young or very old women, they become "generic," being granted temporary status as "men" within that world because they are "non-women" (Hastrup 1978). In many societies and in many eras, the exclusion of women's bodies in what has been designated "men's space" is effected through a number of social practices and discourses that contribute to women's restriction of movement. As Ardener (1993) notes, such means as foot-binding, tight-corseting, and high heels prevented women from being physically active and therefore curtailed their own physical movement as well as making them dependent on more mechanical means of transport. If, at the same time, ideologies or social practices prevent women from having knowledge of or access to these other forms of transport (such as driving a car, or riding bicycles or horses), then their ability to venture into spaces outside the home is severely curtailed.

Restriction is frequently "managed" through a number of less obvious ideologies; for example, women being regarded as being main or sole child-caregivers or having the main responsibilities for the aged in their society; women being regarded as "naturally" emotionally or physically "frail"; women being regarded as particularly at risk and vulnerable to attack or rape if they venture into public domains especially at night; women being required to cover up or enclose their bodies in order to *discourage* a physical or verbal attack. Such practices render women physically or symbolically invisible. In all cases, the overall effect of such control is managed by the power of *symbolic* boundaries that underlie the more overt physical constraints.[4]

Yet, as indicated above, the messages that most young women receive in contemporary Australia are contradictory since, at the same time, *age, ethnicity and class* complicate the issue. On the one hand, in many situations, prepubescence renders a child effectively non-gendered and therefore in some ways grants her more license to "play" within traditionally gendered social practices – little boys can dress up in their mothers' clothes and jewelry and little girls can be "tomboys" and physically active.[5] Both sexes at a young age can wander into areas where, when they are older, their access would be limited or denied.[6]

However, pubescence indicates the arrival at a more clearly and publicly recognized *gendered* status. Appropriate (gendered) behavior is taught and encouraged in most homes, according to what is deemed "right" and appropriate for that particular cultural viewpoint. For most of the young women in my fieldwork that meant, on the one hand, a greater freedom of movement, an awareness of possibilities and expectations – hence the eagerness to embrace the status that comes with advanced age. On the other hand, for many of the teenage girls in my research an imposition of responsibilities and new layers of restrictions came with an increase in years. This was certainly the case with Diane, Grace, Fran and Janine. They, like many other girls their age, were expected to take over a greater proportion of the domestic chores and the childcare of younger siblings (Deem 1989; Henderson 1991). Secondly, in a similar way to the young women in Christine Griffin's 1982 study, all the girls in my research also seemed to see themselves as needing to provide leisure for men "through (hetero)sexual and emotional servicing" (Griffin 1993: 153). Over the time of the fieldwork, Diane frequently talked about "looking after" her current boyfriend, buying or making him clothes, cooking meals, and "nursing" him when he was sick. Even Grace, who was far more independent and eventually shared a flat with one of her boyfriends, took over most of the domestic tasks within that household.

At the same time, more discussion took place in the home about the need for the girls, as they became older, to protect themselves from attack by dressing modestly or taking "other" precautions against such dangers. The paradox inherent in such gendered positioning – that of being simultaneously inside and outside society, and having to take one's place in the public sphere only as a transgressor, has of course been extensively researched from both feminist and post-colonial perspectives.[7] Drawing upon these insights, it is timely to consider what it meant specifically for the young women in my research from both Anglo–Australian and "nonwhite" backgrounds, to negotiate these paradoxes. How did they manage the difficulties of *being* in public spaces in their everyday experiences through their bodily praxis?

Firstly, it is clear that, for all of the girls, advanced age meant that the home was no longer satisfying as a place in which to socialize with friends. This was, of course, also true for their teenage male relatives and the other boys in their familial and social circles. Even in quite straightforward physical terms, an adolescent body takes up far more room, makes more noise and requires more area than does a small child. In addition, lack of physical space, lack of "privacy" and the obvious connection with childhood and protection, renders the domestic sphere far from being a place where the girls could easily experiment with "alternative selves." Yet, their relatively young age and their mainly unemployed or low-paid status meant that they were without independent financial means and therefore had few places where they *could* congregate with friends *outside* the home. At the same time, their (female) pubescent status meant that they were the particular target of overt, circulating discourses and moral panics concerning their sense of, and pleasure in, their developing sexuality. Altogether this was an explosive mix. In this context and in terms of "private space" meaning "negotiating *space to play,"* many of the young people I met through my fieldwork certainly seemed to feel they had "no space of their own" (White 1990; Willis 1990). Of all my experiences during my fieldwork, none seemed to illustrate this more clearly than the Blue Light disco.

No smoking, drinking or fornication!

In previous chapters I described how some of my research time was spent as a volunteer with police at the Blue Light discos. These dances, organized by the police, were promoted as safe places for young people to congregate and spend time together. Their real motive, as quietly stated to me several times by different members of the police force, was to get young people "off the streets and out of trouble." The dances were often held in what normally would be viewed as totally incongruous locations, such as men's Returned Services League halls or bowling club halls. Because the events were held once a month, and to avoid interfering with the decor, the rooms could only be decorated in a perfunctory fashion. To render the room a little more festive a silver rotating ball near the ceiling, some dry ice for special dramatic effect and flashing lights were added on the night by the itinerant disc jockey.[8]

When I first offered my services as a volunteer, I was interviewed by the head of the special unit who was in charge of Blue Light events. A kindly, middle-aged man, he obviously cared about, as he put it, the problem of "juvenile offending," freely giving his own time to help organize these dances. One of his regular volunteers was Bert, a former offender, now in his sixties, who had become a good friend and admirer of this police sergeant. Bert was present at the discos not only to help with the organization and discipline but was also there to provide continual warnings and testimonials to the young people about what could happen to them in prison.

At my first interview, the police sergeant described the expected standards of behavior of the young people attending: once inside the hall the young people had to stay until the end; there were no "pass-outs" as there were in the city dance clubs and raves.[9] There were to be no weapons, no drugs, no smoking and no alcoholic beverages. Bags and pockets of all young people entering the hall would be carefully checked. Girls were the worst offenders, I was warned, as they would use their "feminine wiles" to smuggle in forbidden substances in their bags. My foremost task, as an adult volunteer, was to ensure adherence to these rules. Furthermore, I was to patrol the room to separate any young people "coupling together." Above all, he emphasized, I was to make sure that "there was to be *no fornication!*" I was so amazed at this last stipulation that I asked him to repeat what he'd said. Apparently, the dark corners of the room had to be carefully monitored.[10]

Perhaps because of all of these restrictions, and certainly, after attending several of these discos, I could not honestly understand the attraction for the young people themselves. I thought the dances unbelievably dull and, in spite of the rich ethnographic material they offered, often I found myself counting the minutes until they ended. Normally the dances were held in materially underprivileged areas of high unemployment. While free buses were often provided to encourage children from one area to attend a dance in another, the police frequently complained that far too few children seemed to take up the opportunity of the transport. What I found most surprising was that the young people *queued* up to get into the Blue Light discos. On more than one occasion, I discovered that a number of young men were waiting anxiously in queues outside the discos. These were tough teenagers who had been in trouble with the law, formally reprimanded on more than one occasion for shoplifting, stealing, mugging, or vandalism. As part of their punishment they would be barred from attending a dance for several months. Yet these same young people who had often spent time in the Juvenile Detention Center, would stand outside the hall all night pleading with the police officers staffing the doors, to let them inside.

When I asked the teenagers themselves why they liked to come to the discos, they replied that their friends were there. When I inquired further, the young people would shrug and say "What else is there to do?" Still dissatisfied with the response, I asked one of the younger police officers why the children wanted so desperately to come inside. Surely they would have more enjoyment and could meet their friends somewhere else? The officer shrugged. "Where else *can* they go to meet their friends?" she answered. The two answers prompt closer examination of youth access to, and use of, public spaces.

Youth and access to public space

At a casual glance it would appear that both young men and women are extremely visible in public locations. A visit to any city shopping mall or suburban shopping center reveals large numbers of teenagers wandering fairly aimlessly around, often in groups of two, three or more. However, this apparent freedom of movement appears to be qualified. Firstly, if, as Connell has argued, the street can be understood as an institution, a social milieu like others in society, we can also assume that it is subject to the same boundaries of "gender relations as the family and the state. It has a division of labour, a structure of power and a structure of cathexis" (1987: 134). A great deal of "work" is done in the street – child-care, shopping, policing, selling, driving – work that is also clearly socially hierarchical and gendered. Inevitably then, the street may also be widely perceived as a place where the same power relations are enacted as elsewhere. It can be a scene of a great deal of intimidation for the least powerful, "from low level harassment to physical manhandling and rape" (Connell 1987: 132). In this way, money, power and social status can determine those who feel confident walking openly in the street and those whose legitimacy of presence requires constant negotiation.

Teenagers frequently dress less affluently or less conservatively than most of the older people around them and often wander around in larger groups. These two factors alone are enough to render them both intimidating and suspect to other members of their wider community. Their numbers, their noise and their dress attract attention from people with more authority and the means of surveillance and, as such, are perceived as a threat to order and control. Frequently, for example, even during the day, in the city streets and in the main shopping malls, young people *who are clearly seen to be not purchasing,* are moved on by the police and security guards. At one time in my fieldwork, when I "cruised" one of the larger outer suburban shopping centers with some outreach youth workers, we stopped for a coffee in one of the many cafes. We stayed for a considerable period even though few of us had actually purchased a drink there. One of the youth workers pointed out to me that we could perform a simple action like this because, by our appearances, we were clearly adult. The teenagers doing the same thing would be regarded as suspect and quickly moved on by the security staff.

So much of "public" space is governed by the needs and prerogatives of consumerism: there is the need to make our streets, our parks, our shopping areas and malls appear safe, clean and attractive for potential shoppers, tourists and clients. While this is not an inappropriate goal in itself, it does mean that many people fall outside the "attractive" and acceptable criteria for inclusion into that space. So many areas become understood as spaces where certain kinds of behavior are explicitly and implicitly understood as being *appropriate* for *certain* kinds of people, physical space being thus reflected and constituted by social space. This implicit understanding is (usually) assumed to be shared by the majority of people in that (micro)culture – and enforced, where necessary, by legislation. For example, a "No trespassing" sign or a sign that reads "Private property" is recognized as sanctioned and therefore obeyed by most. It implies not simply exclusion but also indicates economic and social capital to which only certain people have access. The written sign is thus a reminder of the generally held understandings of boundaries and gate keeping. It is understood through circulating discourses that access to specific spaces is only available to particular *kinds* of people. In most cultures it seems, for the young, the marginalized and particularly for women, a particular understanding of access and non-access to particular places and spaces is acquired and reinforced from early childhood.

Similarly, for many young people, male and female, who clearly do not have the *appearance* of being affluent, entering into a shopping mall without the means to purchase can also constitute an implicit trespass. Perhaps this was why Mary insisted on filming a large part of her video as a "fly on the wall" documentary. As noted earlier, I was directed to be her cameraperson on the day she filmed her fortnightly routine of collecting and cashing her social security check. Her confident, leisurely walk through the center of the shopping mall to and from the bank, punctuated by several stops to chat to friends and acquaintances as she went, was captured in her video footage. Was it the camera's presence or her newly acquired financial status that allowed such a confident demeanor? Her teenage male friend, a young male offender who was staying at her house at the time and who accompanied us on that day, did not walk so boldly through the mall. He scurried, keeping close to the walls like a shadow, ducking and weaving his way between the shops trying to make himself as invisible as possible. The video footage of this incident gives no indication that they were together or even acquainted. In the mall sequence, he simply appears as a strangely recurring blurred figure on the edge of the frame.

If we superimpose these preliminary insights on to commonsense understandings of gender relations, then we can see that in the case of young *women*, the combination of both their age and their gender immediately renders them even less "free to play" in spaces designated as public.

> Gender *determines that . . . young women are subject to external surveillance and responsible for internal body management, and it is their gender that makes them feel vulnerable to male sexual threat and assault.* Culture *and* class *determine how; that is the norms of the body and codes of surveillance, management, threat, assault and resistance available to them.* (Fine & Macpherson 1994: 229, emphasis in the original)

In the previous chapter, I examined how body management was particularly a focus of surveillance for women. To these earlier comments and to Fine and McPherson's observations, I would here add that gender, class and culture also determine *where* these various social negotiations are perceived as being "possible," where they are enabled and where they are constrained, and indeed what form they may take. For example, young women, as noted, frequently have far less freedom of movement than young men in spaces usually designated as "public." In some cases, the imposed restraints result from actual negative experiences; others from *fear* of possible danger or harassment, rather than from personal experience. The effect can be the same. Almost from the beginning of urban life, the presence of women in the cities and particularly in city streets, has been questioned, and the controlling and surveillance aspects of city life have always been directed particularly at women (Wilson 1991).[11]

Many researchers (Fiske 1987, 1989; Kaplan 1988; Connell 1987; Lewis 1990), have highlighted that female activity, unlike male activity, does not generally take place in the street. The street is how a girl gets from A to B. She does not loiter and when in the street, she walks quickly and attempts to make herself as invisible as possible by physically shrinking her body. For a girl to take up activities on the street with the boys is to invite gossip amongst the adults and her peers about her sexual availability.[12]

It is still considered neither safe nor wise for a girl to be on the street for any length of time, especially at night. The popular and media discourse that arises after any reported murders or abduction of young women reinforces this notion of illegitimate public space for a woman.[13] The consensual view is that young women can wander around the city streets with relative impunity during the day but the activity has to be seen as purposeful. (Window) shopping or going to the cinema are legitimate activities for young women; hanging around street corners is not.

Yet to speak in general terms of public space and gender is to obfuscate the real-life experiences of the young women in question. As I quickly learned in my own fieldwork, the experience of gender was never separate or separable from each individual girl's perception of, and identification with, her ethnicity, social class, or any other dimension of her life. Such dynamics affected her understanding of "legitimate" use of space. Certain places for nearly all of the girls in my study were regarded automatically as *exclusive,* as being in some way "off limits" to them or being unwelcoming, while others could be used as areas of refuge, safety and play. Other places were more ambiguous, certain ones being regarded as accessible to some of the teenagers and not to others. In other words, how the different girls in my research perceived the city places and how they felt able to negotiate this space depended a great deal on their age, their material/economic circumstances, their ethnicity and their gender – in effect, on their already constituted micro-culture or *habitus.*

Where the teenager came from social networks where her gender was seen as a particularly defining aspect of her identity, she experienced far more external control than those who came from social networks where it was the norm to establish and practise sexual equity (Elley & Inglis 1995; Tsolidis 1995). Because she would usually experience more physical constraint, either directly or through familial expectations, she would also learn to survey and control her own actions, in order to stay within those symbolic boundaries. Although her actions and "freedoms" may seem to be quite severely curtailed to an outsider (for example, Diane's and Claire's upbringing), to the girl herself, these restrictions were often the way things *were* and, more than that, the way things *should be.* What might seem to *others* as confinement or constraint is to the agent herself, naturalized, the way things *are.* Bourdieu (note the epigraph to this chapter) has consistently used *spatial* metaphors in his writings – "the sense of one's place" – to emphasize this point, stressing the symbolic constraints that people place upon themselves.

Thus physical, geographic boundaries are always symbolic boundaries that in turn reinforce material boundaries. This is what Bourdieu means when he speaks of *a space of relations* "which is just as real as a geographical space" (Bourdieu 1991: 232). For example, Diane did not consider that she was at all constrained in her world. Occasionally, she did indicate that she felt uncomfortable when some of her friends articulated *their* sense of her circumscribed life or "overprotectedness," for example, when her friend Helen called Diane "little girl.") On those occasions she would ask me how much "freedom" I allowed my own teenage daughter. But, most of the time for Diane, as for all the girls in my research, the social relations and "moral" values that constituted her personhood as a young woman in her immediate social networks, were how her world *was;* it was "normality" for her as defined by her familial and social micro-cultures. It was indeed "self-evident":

> *Social reality exists, so to speak, twice, in things and in minds, in fields and in habitus, outside and inside of agents.* (Bourdieu & Wacquant 1992: 127)

Within the logic of the micro-culture, such constraints can have clear advantages. As Patricia Jeffrey noted in relation to the Pizada women in India, "*Purdah* may restrict and seclude, but it also shelters and means that secluded women do not seriously have to concern themselves with the harsh economic realities of life in India." None of the young women in my study was in Purdah but their restrictions in space/time, and the constraints on their mobility and on their personal sense of freedom also could render them relatively "silent and invisible" (Jeffrey 1979: 13) in the public sphere.[14]

> *If it is fitting to recall that the dominated always contribute to their own domination, it is necessary at once to be reminded that the dispositions which incline them to this complicity are also the effect, embodied, of domination.* (Bourdieu 1989: 12. Also cited in Bourdieu & Wacquant 1992: 24)

I have already described the more obvious forms of these constraints, such as parental and familial control and surveillance. Also important for discussion are the more complex ways in which the girls themselves internalized control, ways in which they saw themselves belonging or not belonging in public places. The first of these, particularly pertinent in these days of heightened racial rhetoric in Australia, is the way some girls regarded themselves as Australian and others knew that they could not take such an epithet for granted.

Ethnic identity: "I'm an Aussie, really. I'm an Aussie"

> *The assignment of place within a socio-spatial structure indicates distinctive roles, capacities for action, and access to power within the social order.* (Harvey 1990: 419)

Consideration of place is inevitably about a sense of space, about feeling whether one's presence is *appropriate* and welcome within particular material or symbolic boundaries. In a further consideration of a macro-conception of space and place, it is pertinent to consider "national space"; that is, who feels they "belong," who feels comfortable and, in the context of my research, whether they feel they have the right to occupy public space as *Australians.* In Calhoun's words, a sense of nationalism is "the politics of identity writ large" (Calhoun 1995: 231).

> *The discourse of nationalism not only encourages seeing identity as inscribed in and co-terminous with the individual body; it also encourages seeing individuals linked through their memberships in sets of equivalents – classes, races, genders etc. – rather than their participation in interpersonal relationships. It promotes categorical identities over relational ones.* (Calhoun 1995: 256)

My own research demonstrated that most of the girls felt comfortable in their familial and friendship groupings, but when they stepped outside that symbolic "safety zone," some experienced a profound sense of dislocation when it came to their ethnic and national identity. Not all of the teenagers saw themselves as *Australian,* if even though they may have been born in Australia or possessed Australian citizenship. Therefore not all saw themselves as inevitably belonging in the most fundamental way within Australian society. In terms of their everyday experiences, that meant some of the girls clearly felt comfortable and confident *being* in the public places, while others did not. I noted in the previous chapter that Janine and her friends, for example, identified themselves and even more importantly, *described* themselves, as *Nunga.* In contrast, they referred to non-Indigenous people, including certain relatives, friends and acquaintances who were non-*Nunga* or non-*Koori* as *Australians.*[15] If Australians in this discourse are always inevitably "other" and "not me," then this has great significance for how the girls themselves saw their own legitimacy in terms of their presence on the street, in the school and in the youth organizations to which they belonged. This sense of "otherness" was continually reinforced in fact by those very institutions themselves, often through the implementation of well-intentioned proactive policies. If I noted, for example, that Black Image was an exclusively Aboriginal rock group. The girls had specialist ancillary teachers and contact personnel, nearly all of whom were Aboriginal or Torres Strait Islanders, as the girls were seen as requiring a different kind of educational and personal support. Indeed this help was vital if the girls were going to have a chance to succeed educationally, but it also reinforced the notion for all of the students that the girls were somehow outside the mainstream of the school community.

Three other girls in my research – Mary, Sara and Claire – also saw themselves as different from, or outside white "mainstream" Australian society. For Mary and Sara, it was a question of their skin color and cultural differences. For Claire, it was her Rhodesian heritage. In Mary's case her difference – her Papua New Guinean background – was ostensibly a source of pride. She had actually no clear memories of her own of Papua New Guinea, since she had been taken from there as a very small child when she was adopted by her uncle and her Australian aunt.[16] She regularly sought out other people from Papua New Guinea, befriending people in the street, at school, or at dance clubs, people whom she would say "look like me." In other instances she sought connections through skin color, seeking out friends particularly from the Torres Strait Islands or from Aboriginal backgrounds. Mary's most successful relationship with a foster family had been in fact with an Aboriginal family. Apart from their part-icular parenting skills and affection for her, the success was undoubtedly due also to Mary's own sense of belonging through some perceived cultural and physical similarities. When I was with Mary and her Aboriginal friends she would articulate this affinity by immediately sprinkling some appropriate Indigenous words into her conversation, creating a sense of bonding between them and probably simultaneously establishing me as an outsider in that context.

As described in previous chapters, I first got to know Mary while she was living in a small rented house acquired for her under the "independent living" scheme. This was a means by which young people in the care of the state, or who had been in trouble with the law, could live by themselves while still having the support and guidance of social workers. With posters on her walls and artifacts in her rooms and the reggae music that she constantly played on her tape deck, Mary made this house her own. She had few Papua New Guinean artifacts so she made other connections to her perceived cultural heritage by placing huge posters of African American basketball stars (such as Michael Jordan) and singers (such as Bob Marley) on her wall. There were also a few photographs of herself when she was a small child, taken with her biological mother.

Sara too had little direct personal memory of her original cultural background. She had been adopted at the age of three from Nepal and brought to Australia by her Anglo–Australian adoptive parents. Unlike

Mary's early experience of adoption, Sara had been brought up by a family who were very concerned to keep Sara's heritage alive. Both adoptive parents felt great affinity with Buddhist philosophy and both were anxious to maintain links with Nepal through letters, photographs and travel. Sara's adoptive parents frequently attended cultural events that celebrated difference in terms of Buddhism or Nepalese identity. When Sara and her brother were younger, these events were very much a part of their lives. All this had exerted an effect on how Sara saw herself and understood her cultural identity. I thought it particularly significant that she was the only one of the young women in my research who felt it necessary to articulate her sense of being an Australian. Sara was very small and very dark-skinned, both of which attributes seemed to be the bane of her life. "I'm an Aussie, really. I'm an Aussie," she said self-consciously and a little defensively, in direct address to the camera. At the same time Sara talked a great deal during my fieldwork period, about her feeling of difference. Her skin color, her petite stature and her dark features frequently made her feel as though she was an outsider or in some way *exotic*, even within her own social networks.

If nations are *imagined* as Anderson (1983) argues, out of "an immemorial past and glide towards a limitless future" (Sharp 1996: 99), nationality has to be actively created. For Sara, Mary and Janine, artifacts, dress, food and traditional customs allowed them to do just that. Before I enlarge on the relationship between their sense of ethnic difference and "nationality" and the complexities of their particular styles of self-making in different places, I shall discuss a further superimposition and internalization of difference, that of perceived social hierarchies and the role of the "authentic."

A question of trespass

The symbolic division of public arenas considered by the girls either as legitimate spaces for occupation or places of trespass, reflected their incorporation of time-honored cultural divisions of status, conventional social hierarchies and divisions. They indicated the access, legitimation and resources of cultural and symbolic capital. Let us look at some of these divisions more closely.

In its extreme manifestation, such divisions indicate the places where high culture was "legitimated," "protected by their legitimacy against the scientific gaze and against the desacralisation that is presupposed by the scientific study of sacred objects" (Bourdieu 1993: 132). Anyone entering such a "sacred" space usually assumes the appropriate stance, behavior and appearance and possesses the necessary cultural capital to appreciate such knowledge and artifacts. When people behave in ways that differ from this traditional, usually implicit code, their actions are immediately read as inappropriate or deliberately subversive.[17]

The categorizing and "mapping" of space can therefore be understood as a signifier of control and as such, as with all other aspects of social orderings, it is quite clearly gendered (Duncan 1996: 6; Kirby 1996: 46). Kathleen Kirby argues that the concept of the self-contained *male* individual developed from Rationalism. It was this "masculine ego" who mapped out the world around himself and in the process of charting and drawing boundaries designated some areas as not appropriate for marginalized others. The bounded, central areas are separated and discrete. The peripheral spaces become blurred, fluid and porous. This space, Kirby sees as the more "feminine" postmodern space. It is a space of the inclusive rather than the proprietary, the space of "'all enveloping' notions of 'between' and 'around' – spaces that are supportive and enabling in contrast with notions of 'distance and separation'" (Duncan 1996: 6). Another aspect of public space relates to the way it is associated with the persona, the mask that conceals the *real*. Juliet Blair (1993), for example, points out that dramatists have long been fascinated by the role of gender underlying the notion of the "real" (private) beneath the mask (public). The public domain has historically been associated with (male) duty, "role play" and performance. The private, on the other hand, has been perceived as the domain of the real, the domestic and the authentic. Popular magazines and the publicity machines of the media rely on this separation of the "real" person from the star image. Women, on the other hand, as indicated above, frequently have no sense of legitimate "public space." They "are perceived as acquiring *their* social identity and personal individuality solely in the sphere of the private . . . women have functioned as men's private life, secreted in the attic, displayed in the reception room. There is room for her at every level, but not a room of her own." (Blair 1993: 207).[18] If Western men see their private worlds as the place where they can truly "be themselves," women have to dig even deeper into the realms of the private, into their fantasy worlds, "the unknown, unexplored, dark continent – as Freud described it – of women's interiority" (Blair 1993: 209) in order to find an equivalent place of self-identity.

The masculinization of public space meant that any appropriation of space, even temporarily, by the girls in my fieldwork, always seemed precarious and at a cost. It seemed to me less a question of empowerment or resistance and more a question of the degree of trespass. Surprisingly, however, it can also be a place of magic and fantasy in ways that the domestic sphere cannot.

Spaces to play: The street as public stage

If the street is a place of contest and conflict, it also can be seen as a place of display and theater (Connell 1987; Turner 1982; Schechner 1993) and because it is a loosely structured milieu, it can simultaneously be seen as more open to diversity and political challenge. Not only are traditional conceptions of work present in the street but so also are examples of "serious play" and fantasy – displays, advertising, billboards, posters, graffiti, entertainers, and street theater. If the street can be a place of exclusion, as we have seen, it can, at the same time, be one of appropriation and empowerment. As I argued in chapter 4, the combination of place, time and subjectivity can be a powerful mix in the creation of "space to play."

By way of a very obvious example, shopping centers, whether outside or under cover, are used in different ways at different moments throughout the day. Major shopping centers are frequently filled with potential shoppers but also with people seeking to occupy their time with other sorts of activities. They are used for talking, gossiping, eating, watching. On one level, they are designed to be "consecrated to timelessness and stasis, (no clocks, perfect weather . . .) yet lived and celebrated, lived and loathed, in intimately historic terms" (Morris 1988: 206). On another level, the imposed timelessness and uniformity breaks down as performance takes over. For example, often within a mall or outside shops, different areas may be symbolically defined as "stages." Here people such as entertainers create a different kind of space while shoppers temporarily become audiences and spectators, distracted momentarily from their singular purposeful activity of shopping. Relative affluence does not determine *this* form of consumerism. Areas such as these are often the only parts of the public shopping space where young people from less privileged social backgrounds are *not* harassed by police or by store security guards. Here they *can* "hang around," meet friends, just *be,* even if there is still a sense of trespass.

A further relevant issue relates to time, which is crucial in the use and appropriation of public places. During the day the city streets are given over to crowds and seemingly purposeful activity. In the evening, when the malls or the streets are relatively empty of shoppers, and with no gates to close off the area, these young people appear to take over by sheer force of numbers. Most noticeably, it is the teenagers who do *not* have the purchasing power to spend greatly, who appear in the malls then, reappropriating the space and using it loudly, in large groups, for different purposes. As Schechner noted, "unofficial culture worms or bullies its way back into public outdoor spaces" (1993: 48).

Only two of the girls in my research comfortably ventured out into the city streets, especially at night. There was Mary who, as I have already indicated, saw herself as a member of a largely male group. Grace was also prepared to be in the streets at night but normally only in the company of a large group of friends. They both did so usually as part of a mixed large group, almost as surrogate boys, using their numbers, their noise, their dress and their reputation and aggression to occupy the space with some authority and assertion.

For Mary, the area beneath and outside the back of a major department store in the city, was a central gathering place for her and her friends during the day and in the early evening. Indeed, this was a common place for many different groups of young people. Unlike the stores themselves, which attempted to create atmospheres of sophistication and taste, the eating hall areas located in close proximity to the large and elegant department store were unrefined, cheap and noisy – a "back stage" to the store's more fashionable and reputable "front stage" (Goffman 1959). These eating places were always a favorite amongst the young people, and several times during my fieldwork the girls and I would go there for a quick bite and a chat after they had been filming in the city. The peripheries of these food halls were lined with randomly ordered eating stalls of different ethnicities and lifestyle choices. The various food smells and languages all blended to create a multicultural extravaganza of the senses. On weekdays from 3:30 p.m. onwards the food halls were also full of school uniforms and schoolbags as many teenage students from all over the metropolitan area congregated in the city en route to their respective suburbs.

The very strident mix of noise, ethnicity and "taste" suggested a tolerance for difference that, in turn, could allow for boisterous play, exemplifying perhaps the blurred, fluid and porous "peripheral spaces" that I noted above (Kirby 1996). The young people who met here didn't just eat, they laughed, argued, physically fought, loudly and without inhibition, and generally were able to "take over" the area. The food halls were important for another reason too: they connected the "front stage" and "back stage" of the city map. The front entrance of the eating hall led back to the main shopping mall, albeit to the less fashionable section of the mall. That end was closer to the "red light" district – a disreputable area of the city. The back entrance ended with a large escalator leading up to North Terrace, Adelaide's cultural boulevard. At the top of the escalator it was possible to see the row of bus stops located in front of the high walls of Government House. Sandwiched between the rows of bus stops and the high walls of officialdom were narrow strips of grass with benches, shaded by trees and bushes.

From Mary I learned how in this space, between the main street and the walls of Government House, she and her friends would meet and socialize at the end of each day to smoke and drink. Some would venture into the shopping mall adjacent to a large department store at first but many of her group would just wait for the others on the benches. Graffiti scratched on the benches or sprayed on the walls close by in paint, further marked out the territory as appropriated. These were young people who often sat with one eye open for the police or other adult authority figures. Once a large group of young people had congregated, the space was marked as theirs. Disgruntled adults would move on, uncomfortable because of the noise and the language and the spontaneous scuffles that would suddenly erupt.

Grace and her friends would meet at a different time and place. Although occasionally they would assemble in the food hall, they would never meet on the benches where Mary and her friends congregated. "That's where the townies meet," she told me scornfully. Her group would meet at the top end of the main city mall where the shopping precinct met one of the main streets dividing the city. Opposite their meeting place was the street marking the start of the less fashionable, less salubrious area of Adelaide. The "adult" night and dance clubs were mainly in this section of Adelaide so it was perceived as a more exciting and more risqué locale for the young women in my fieldwork.

Space invaders: The art of appropriation

When the reappropriation of space (as described above) does occur, it is where "subversive" or "illegitimate" activity is understood to be *possible* – even if it is purely through imaginative play. This is similar to Bourdieu's concept of counter-legitimacy: "spaces that belong to the dominated classes, haunts or refuges for excluded individuals from which dominant individuals are in fact excluded, *at least symbolically*, and for the accredited holders of the social and linguistic competence which is recognised on these markets" (Bourdieu 1991: 98, my emphasis).[19] So "private space" in this conception becomes arenas where those who feel they usually cannot, do. It appears in the gaps between official and legitimate cultural discourses, even in the most "inappropriate" locales.

> *If there is a tradition (and not only in the West) of constructing grand monuments specifically to present performances – arenas, stadiums and theatres – so there is a long history of unofficial performances "taking place" in (seizing as well as using) locales not architecturally imagined as theatres.* (Schechner 1993: 48–49)

Such play allows the voicing of those usual *silences* of dominant cultural understandings – even if sometimes that voicing occurs just above a whisper or has to take place in the form of distancing humor. So, for example, when Janine and her friends portrayed an alternative view of the city, the girls' excessive play simultaneously implied an acknowledgment and a contesting of those symbolic boundaries of status, even while highlighting their arbitrary nature. It was highly significant that their play took place in the public space occupied by one of the most culturally significant of Adelaide streets, the "front stage" of the city. The reason the teenagers chose to walk down North Terrace rather than the busier main city mall in the first place, was because the main boulevard was perceived as a less restrictive space for them as young Aboriginal women. Like Mary, these girls had often voiced their uncomfortable sense of being in the mall or even in the red light area of Adelaide. "There's too many cops there," Mary had stated emphatically. The *Nunga* girls would agree. The mall was a place filled with shoppers, crowds, security guards, even on that hot summer's day. The greater openness and fewer people of North Terrace meant a greater freedom to walk unhindered and unharassed – and as we saw, then to "play" with possible alternative perspectives.[20]

The *Nunga* girls' descriptions and anecdotes were particularly effective because they were simultaneously acknowledging and debunking the official discourse about the city – that the buildings on the cultural boulevard and the war memorial statue were respected historical and symbolic landmarks. Because their account was enacted *there* and because it differed so strongly from the conventional viewpoints, the teenagers' amusing account crossed over from serious play to mimetic excess, from a "straight" description to parody. As *young Aboriginal women,* they were also highlighting their normal sense of *displacement* from the official dominant discourses relating to "legitimate" use of space on three accounts – age, gender and marginalized ethnicity. In the more crowded city areas, because of their physical appearance, the presence of the *Nunga* teenagers was more conspicuous and more obvious. However, in a less populated, more "open," less obviously commercial area, the girls were afforded greater freedom and greater anonymity. This greater sense of freedom to *be* in the main boulevard, especially with the added status and power of the camera, allowed their mimetic excess full rein. The *content* of their disrespectful play highlighted the arbitrary nature of such legitimations and interpretations of space, while their *parodic stance* pointed to their tacit understanding of the power and status of that discourse.[21]

The act of parody always carries with it a recognition of the way the object of parody is *usually* perceived, while at the same time signalling that such labelling can be challenged. Indeed, the challenge seems so daring and so disturbing *because* it highlights the arbitrary nature of the usually accepted order of things (Douglas 1978, 1984) for "all (institutional) rites tend to consecrate or legitimate an *arbitrary boundary*, by fostering a misrecognition of the arbitrary nature of the limit and encouraging a recognition of it as legitimate" (Bourdieu 1991: 118 emphasis in original). One of the main purposes of the "social magic" is to mark distinctions, boundaries and hierarchies, where inherently there are none.

Yet if the city streets symbolized a place of trespass for most of the girls, one area that seemed accessible to *all* of the girls, without exception, were the public toilets. All of the girls used the toilets as places for gossip, confidences and experimentation.

Toilets are for talking

It is perhaps a fascinating comment on the way women see their own positioning in society, that all of the girls used the public space of the toilets to share private confidences. Hilary's video even wryly acknow-ledged this with her usual self-reflexive humor, as she and her best friend deliberately filmed themselves talking and laughing in front of the mirror in the toilets of a cinema complex. "This is our favorite place to come and talk, isn't it, Sally?"

At the Blue Light discos I was often given "toilet duty," which meant I was to regularly check the girls' toilets for smoking and other recreational drug use. What I discovered more often than transgressions of that kind was the importance of the social role of the toilets. The girls would huddle regularly into the crowded space outside the cubicles to share confidences, ask advice, or talk over problems. Sometimes these could be considered quite serious problems – I often found girls crying and being comforted by their friends – but normally it was a place to discuss the way relationships were developing at the dance itself, or to voice concerns about unwelcome advances. It was in a sense, then, a "time out" – a space away from the noise, the boys, the performance; it was a place to re-assert the "real" by acknowledging the construction of the persona. Here one could redo the makeup and the hair; it was a place to recover, to remove the excess, or to "throw up." It seemed that it was also a place where no one would be denied entry, a truly inclusive space! It was also a space where one could go with a friend without having doubts thrown upon one's (hetero)sexual orientation. Because it was understood that having to wait in a queue was always a distinct possibility, several girls could be absent from the rest of their group for some time without having to explain their absence. Away from more obvious surveillance, the girls in here swore and laughed with less inhibition than I noticed elsewhere. Fantasies and requests for advice were either articulated or expressed in the form of graffiti scrawled on the inside of cubicle walls – often answered by the next interested occupant in the toilet cubicle.

If the quieter blurring of symbolic boundaries described above was hardly noticeable within the larger social context – unofficial culture in the form of a whisper – there were other ways in which the young people declared their presence and their needs as a shout. In other words, they were transformations of space that could not be ignored by the adult authorities. The first was "space invasion" through the holding of raves or massive dance parties. The second was accomplished through an expression of private grief in public places and enacted through the creation of private memorials and shrines. I saw both of these phenomena as examples of a symbolic reclamation of territory while simultaneously exploring "dark play."

Raves: Legitimating space for illicit activities

Pat described herself as a raver, drawing a distinction between her involvement with the techno scene and dance parties and the behavior of pretentious others, who simply were "Try Hards." It was mainly through her accounts and experience that I learned a great deal about the organization of rave parties as well as attending some of the smaller, "tamer" ones myself. The phenomenon of rave grew out of dance clubs. A dance "club" is a constructed and "imagined (youth) community" (Anderson 1991; Straw 1997).

Raves are dance clubs held outside established dance venues and developed partly as an attempt to take the music (and the people) into less conventional and more controversial spaces. Rather than the predictable and familiar locales, raves seem to provide the "forbidden and the unpredictable senses of place" (Thornton 1995: 22). They frequently take place in unconventional settings such as disused warehouses, open fields, aircraft hangars or, as in the case of the particular event caught on Pat's footage, in the old, disused Adelaide Gaol. Unlike the Blue Light discos described above, the physical setting of the raves is organized according to a youth subculture aesthetic such that a great deal of time and money is spent developing the *mise-en-scène* for each event. As the profit motive is the main catalyst, the owners of the venues hire dance organizers (or dance organizers hire venues) and create an atmosphere through music, decor and lighting in order to attract as many young people as they can.[22] Through word of mouth, fliers, telephone, posters, radio promotions, and even now through the Internet, both "conforming" and "rebellious" youth are targeted.

The most important aspect of the rave is the sense of diminished personal space. The dancers have to feel that they are crowded into an enclosed area, the cumulative effect of the throbbing music, the psychedelic lighting, the drugs and the thousands of bodies moving in unison, creating an overwhelming sensation of potent energy. The necessity for an almost claustrophobic lack of space means that the raves are often promoted as being held in a "secret" location – until the organizers know that the numbers of the participants will be sufficient for the venue. Too small a crowd and the rave will be a flop. As a marketing ploy the rave is most successful when the young people feel that they have reappropriated that cultural space for themselves – it becomes, however temporarily, a place that is *theirs.*

Unlike that of pubs or hotels, which the older teenagers can frequent more easily, the ambience of clubs and raves is a far remove from any suggestion of domesticity and the family home. Indeed, dance clubs are *about* escape from the domestic. Through lighting, loud music and interior design they forge an atmosphere that separates the dancers from the everyday pressures and routines of home, school, or work, frequently creating "interior havens with such a presence that the dancers forget local time and place and sometimes even participate in an imaginary global village of dance sounds" (Thornton 1995: 21).

In anticipation of large numbers of attendees, raves are frequently held in huge areas; nevertheless, they practise their own form of exclusivity. Firstly, as indicated above, the entrance fees are extremely high.[23] This fact, together with quite discriminatory gate-keeping practices, produces a sense of elitism and exclusivity. Local councils, for example, frequently demand from the organizers a high level of monitoring of who is admitted entry (Thornton 1995: 24). While the dancers often complain about such restrictions, which they see as a form of surveillance, at the same time they enjoy the fact that they become "protected" members of the "subculture," their admission being proof of their authenticity.[24]

Pat spent a great deal of time and footage recording the preparations for a massive rave at the disused Adelaide Gaol. Her friendship with the organizers meant that she did not have to pay the high entrance fee and also meant that she was directly involved with the transformation of the jail into the rave venue. Recording behind the scenes, her video captured the excitement, the detail and the effort of the organizers as well as the main theatrical event of the dance itself. Through her video, the grim stone walls of the jail gradually became the backdrop for a very different cultural space, a very different social context for ephemeral identities. If a jail in its traditional usage removes offenders from society, this use of the venue, on one level, seemed to turn the panoptic on its head. Here drug experimentation and other illicit activities took place.[25]

Yet none of this was a clear appropriation of public space. While the dancers themselves believed they were "reversing social order" and that their dance and risk-taking was an "authentic" expression of freedom, the basis of their activity was hardly radical and was far from political in intent. I have already noted the gate-keeping, the elitism, the sexism and the other aspects of control characterizing the rave event. These factors alone ensured, as Schechner noted of contemporary festivals and carnivals, that the raves were not "inversions of social order but mirrors of it" (Schechner 1993: 48). The commercial aspect of a rave was paramount; if not enough money could be made from the night, if there were not enough potential supporters, then the event would be cancelled. The dancers themselves did not perform in a frenzy of vortexed, chaotic choreography but danced in machinelike lines. Perhaps a more radical reversal of social order is to be found in a less obvious articulation of appropriation.

Shrines

Not far from where I live a tragic accident occurred. Two young people were killed in a particularly nasty car crash. In many ways these teenagers would have been just another statistic of fatalities, except that their friends erected a memorial shrine to them marking the exact spot where the deaths occurred.

Such a monument is not unique. One of the first pieces of personal information that Mary shared with me was that one of her friends had died a year before in a car accident. She and several other friends would mark the anniversary of the boy's death every year by going to the spot of the accident to sit, talk and *be* there.

Furthermore, such activity is not the province of youth alone. Hundreds of adults placed flowers at the place of Princess Diana's death in Paris. Millions more also marked the place of her London abode after her death. It is, however, a particularly prevalent practice amongst those members of society who are the least powerful and least privileged and have the least status. Since there are a number of significant differences between this practice and the traditional formal rituals marking death, this therefore becomes another example of reappropriation and defining of space. Traditional practice marks the

Fig 14: A memorial shrine

spot where the person was buried or cremated in a church or cemetery. A permanent plaque or stone frequently testifies to the love and respect the mourners bear for the deceased. In many ways traditional memorial monuments are private markers of grief in a place that has been specifically designed and created for such a purpose. In stark contrast, young mourners mark the place of *death*, that is, the place where the young person died, the last place of life.[26] Their actions also demand a particular private interpretation of a place that is very public – a roadside, a lamppost, a bridge. It is as though, in the midst of the normal bustle of life, an ordinary person's moment of passing is being publicly acknowledged. Symbolically too, the testimony that young mourners place on the place of death are usually ephemeral – a cardboard cross, bunches of flowers, written notes.

Undoubtedly, one can argue that young people often do not have the privilege of money to purchase or create a more permanent memorial. It seems to me that their choice of memorial is motivated by something more significant. Their offering in many ways is emblematic of the extreme fragility of life in a way that the stone cross or monument in the graveyard is not. The shrine represents the moment when their friend became something/someone else – the ultimate moment of mimesis! Furthermore, the offering also testifies to friendship, a connection that is also fragile and has less legitimacy in most cultures than traditional ties of kinship.

Notes

1 As a child growing up in Manchester, England in the early sixties, I experienced anti-semitism firsthand. Sometimes, it was relatively subtle. The membership of the tennis club at the end of my street was "known" to be restricted only to Christians. In my Jewish community the information was widely circulated that this club would not admit Jews as members. Far from being something that was openly protested, the adults tutted, shrugged and warned their children not to play there for fear of embarrassment. On the gate of the club was a different sign: "No dogs allowed." In my head quite obviously the two prohibitions, one overt and one tacit, were linked. Even as a teenager when I did "defiantly" play at the club with a non-Jewish friend who was a member, I still felt of course that I was there illegitimately. I played nervously, with my head down and avoided eye contact with any of the older, established members.

2 This is a fascinating observation by the girls, whether supportable by material circumstances or not, since within their own communities, their gender was paramount. As we saw in chapter 2 with Janine's concern over Kena's behavior, any deviance from what was considered appropriate female attitudes and orientations within their own social circles, was decidedly feared and reviled.

3 It was of course, still a different experience again from their Aboriginal brothers or male relatives. From within the wider grouping of Aboriginal *youth*, of course, they were considered, and considered themselves, as less powerful and more vulnerable because they were female.

4 Vulnerability to unwanted sexual attentions or to sexual attack by acquaintances or strangers was a very real concern of all the young women in my research. It was part of the circulating discourses amongst themselves based on real-life experiences, secondhand anecdotes, fictional representations in magazines, television programs and films and on media accounts and warnings.

5 At the same time, little girls are subject to a particular kind of scrutiny and projection in popular media texts in ways that little boys are not. As Valerie Walkerdine argues "there is an erotically coded and ubiquitous gaze at the little girl" (1997: 3).

6 According to Orthodox Jewish practices men and women are strictly segregated in Synagogue so that the women sit upstairs or at least physically separate from the men. Small children up to the age of twelve are free to wander between their parents wherever they are sitting. In a more mundane, "multicultural" example, little boys are often taken into the female toilets or fitting rooms with their

mothers/female caregivers in shopping centers. This is obviously partly for convenience and safety, as again, small children are usually considered primarily the responsibility of a woman. The boys' presence is accepted or tolerated by other women in these spaces until the child reaches pre-pubescence or slightly younger.

7 The list is endless of course but theorists I found particularly pertinent to my study are: Trinh 1989; Moore 1988, 1994; Rosaldo 1974; Ortner 1996; and Ortner & Whitehead 1981.

8 The DJs or disc jockeys were hired by the Blue Light committee according to price and their selection of music. The music was rarely played live by a band. Rather the disc jockey would bring in a selection of records or CDs and play these during the night. This selection would be chosen deliberately to appeal to a broadly based, younger audience so it would be exclusively drawn from a light, non-offensive pop dance music base. Unlike at the raves or the commercial dance clubs that I attended, the disc jockeys at these events were considerably older than their clientele. They did not have the cult following that the rave DJs had. Indeed, at many of the Blue Light discos that I attended the DJ was actually the *mother* of one of the fifteen-year-old boys attending the dance.

9 A pass-out – usually effected by an ultraviolet light-sensitive stamp on the hand – is a license to come and go from the venue during the night after the client has paid her entrance fee. This plays an important socializing function in commercial dance clubs, as indicated below in the main text.

10 I was hopeless at such surveillance I discovered. My heart was not in it. One of the other volunteers was a rather older mother who would intimidatingly patrol the hall representing a caricature of a stage policeman, hands holding a plastic ruler like a baton behind her back. My police supervisor told me one day that this mother "was a natural." I resigned myself to being hopelessly inadequate in the task!

11 See also Boys et al. "House Design And Women's Roles" in Matrix (ed.) 1984. The writers argue that women are disproportionately less mobile than men in urban settings. The design of "ideal" cities assumes that most users of the environment are men. There is thus again a tacit separation between work and leisure. There is an assumption of 100% car ownership and that in these car-owning families, the cars will be used by the male partner and/or by teenage children primarily to get to the place of paid employment. In Boys' study, for example, only 29% of housewives in households owning one car and 69% in households owning two or more cars, knew how to drive. Other pertinent findings were that women were often made to *appear* less mobile, as described in the note below.

12 "Free moving" women were frequently a target for negative comments, danger, or designation (see Boys et al. 1984: 41). In the same publication Cynthia Cockburn showed that the men she interviewed talked about women as pure or sullied according to their location – women were thus mentally contained in the home and were therefore "pure" when they seemed to be in their "rightful" locale. Women in the workplace or outside the home were the opposite. Such gendering of place relies very much on the cognitive and symbolic separation of home and work spheres.

13 With every new atrocity committed on young people, especially young women, the same moral panic emerges. Infamous newspaper accounts of murder victims, such as Shiree Turner (Adelaide *Advertiser* 12 June 1993) emphasize the precarious position of girls in public places. The emphasis in these accounts is always on the innocence, physical attractiveness and the basic "goodness" of the victim. If she does not fit into these categories her murder is not deemed newsworthy.

14 I do not believe it is too extreme to draw on some of Jeffrey's insights concerning Purdah to explore the constraints on the young women in my research in Western

cultural spheres for "Purdah may be seen as an extreme example of a common phenomenon: the dichotomy between the private domestic sphere and the public sphere" (1979: 13).

15 For example, Janelle's aunt was married to a non-Indigenous partner and her foster brother, who was Greek by birth, planned to marry his Italian girlfriend. These close family members were still talked about in their presence as *other* in that they were seen as "white" *Australian* as opposed to *Nunga*. Janine, who had an extremely pale complexion, identified as *Nunga* and talked about herself as "black." She described her very dark-skinned Italian boyfriend as a "white" Australian.

16 In fact she had been given as a "gift" to her aunt and her uncle by the elders of her village. At the time of Mary's birth, her aunt had experienced the sudden loss of her own infant. Mary's own biological mother already had many children. The traditional offering of Mary to her aunt should have been regarded as a sacred bond. Unfortunately, once her relatives came to Australia, Mary's value was not prized. She suffered physical abuse for several years until she was removed from her new family and fostered.

17 The unexpected death and funeral of Diana Princess of Wales is interesting to consider in this light. The extreme outpouring of grief and the untraditional behavior of the thousands of ordinary mourners standing outside the privileged gatherings – the cheering crowds outside Westminster Abbey, for example, who stood and applauded the eulogy by Earl Spencer and even the funeral hearse itself as it went by, were obviously political statements against the Royal Family. They were symbolic markers of subversion. A documentary on the pianist David Helfgott (ABC television 30 August 1998) similarly underscored beliefs about status and place. His public performances, so popular after the success of the film *Shine*, attracted severe criticism from the traditional music critics partly because of David's unorthodox approach to the formality and sacredness of the concert hall. As one critic put it, "David would sing, mutter, grimace and talk to the piano as he played." High art, including piano recitals, is meant to be appreciated in awed silence. When the artist himself adds a "sound track," "sometimes louder than the playing," the effect is regarded as comic or subversive or both.

18 Feminist architects, often drawing upon anthropological insights, have been researching the way domestic buildings reflect and reinforce gender relations for quite some time. See, for example, White 1988.

19 Utilizing the metaphor of economic capital, Bourdieu refers to this phenomenon when he addresses the "economy of linguistic exchanges" (Bourdieu 1991). He asserts that no one can completely ignore the linguistic or cultural law. Every time they enter into an exchange with the holders of the legitimate competence, and especially when they find themselves in a formal situation, dominated individuals are condemned to a practical, corporeal recognition of the laws of price formation that are least favorable to their linguistic productions and that condemn them to a more or less desperate attempt to be correct, or to silence. Counter-legitimacy, he argues, is only possible in the spaces carved out, "only possible within the limits of free markets" (97).

20 Goffman (1959, 1967, 1971) drew our attention to the way space can be designated as not simply public and private but metaphorically as front stage and back stage. That is, certain places connote more status than others and seem to allow for more experimentation and explorative behavior than others. So even within what we would consider to be a "public" arena, some parts are more welcoming or accessible to marginalized groups than others and thus allow a greater sense of "freedom to play.". These areas are not always the ones we would automatically assume would permit such freedoms.

21 The effect of these arbitrary boundaries, these markers of "legitimate" uses of space, is to raise the stakes for the game itself; "everything that makes the field itself, the game, the stakes, all the presuppositions that one tacitly and even unwittingly accepts by the mere act of playing, of entering the game. Those who take part in the struggle help to reproduce the game by helping . . . to produce belief in the value of the stakes" (Bourdieu 1993, 74). I am arguing that in this case, the game itself is the way all the girls in my research project have learned over time to constitute their sense of self within their own specific micro-cultures, in diverse, overlapping social fields. To return to the particularly apt geographical metaphor, it is about the way they have learned very early on, to know their "*place* in the world." It is the basis of their "self-making" that becomes tested, negotiated and ultimately affirmed in the act of playing, and who they are, how they see themselves, is directly linked to how they feel they can use and *be* in different social and geographical spaces.

22 Raves are big business. Admissions to raves are substantially higher than to the cinema, to sporting events, or to ordinary dance venues. A 1993 survey by The Henley Centre for Forcasting, cited in Thornton, revealed that attendance at rave events in Britain was worth nearly two billion pounds a year from admission fees, soft drinks and recreational drugs (Thornton 1995: 15).

23 Although I could have attended some of the larger more exclusive raves through Pat, I contented myself with only going to the smaller, local ones. Partly my reticence was that I felt I would certainly be out of place through my age and I didn't want to call attention to my presence in this way. In the smaller raves I was able to find a niche by bringing the camera myself. The larger raves were more controversial since I knew large amounts of illegal recreational drugs would be present and so the camera and the filming would not be acceptable to the organizers. Pat did some videoing herself of the Adelaide Gaol rave but mainly of the organization behind the scenes.

24 Dancing as a leisure activity is particularly age-specific. Research shows that the most zealous clubbers and ravers are those between the ages of 15 to 19. The younger age group limit occurs because of the practical difficulty that the younger people have in getting out of the parental house and being able to stay out late; having the money for the entrance fees (particularly for raves); and being able to appear to pass for someone of legal drinking age. The activity declines in popularity as the young people move out from home and establish a place of their own with friends or partners. In fact, having a steady partner is the main reason for losing interest in the nightclub/rave scene (Mintel Market Research 1990–92).

25 Of course such activities always occur illicitly and secretly inside a prison. The activity here however seems to highlight that by deliberately juxtaposing symbols of freedom, inhibition and constraint. See the next paragraph. Is this yet another example of mimetic excess?

26 We are accustomed to seeing such recognition of public figures or celebrities such as the place where John Lennon was shot or famous political figures have been assassinated. We are not used to seeing the violent death of ordinary people recognized in this way.

Chapter 5

Learning to Play It "Cool"

> Cliques . . . often function to protect the individual not from persons of other ranks but from persons of his own rank. Thus, while all members of one's clique may be of the same status level, it may be crucial that not all persons of one's status level be allowed into the clique. (Erving Goffman 1969: 73)
>
> *I don't fit in with my group now. I feel like I'm invisible.* (Diane, 16)

Introduction: When is a group not a group . . . ?

In the previous chapters I examined the significance of "private" spaces – the way "space to play" is created and negotiated as a fundamental aspect of "self-making." Chapter 4 examined the way certain spaces can be constituted as private within areas usually designated as public – the inclusive thus becoming exclusive. This chapter develops these ideas further by returning to issues of "best" friendship discussed briefly in chapter 2 and looking at the ways in which symbolic boundaries are drawn around and within particular social groupings. In that chapter I noted how all the girls in my study greatly valued their close female friendships. A "best friend" was as an alter ego or doppelganger. She was the "me" that is "not-me" and frequently she shared food, body and space. In these ways she was central to the representation and simultaneous constitution of the self. I noted the close relationship between Grace and Kate, their bodies seemingly merging in front of the cameras as Grace declared fervently: "she is my best friend, for ever and ever and ever."

Here in this chapter, I am specifically exploring the relationship between the (gendered) self, the close dyadic friendship described earlier, and larger peer groups – for the unit of dyadic friendship, whatever form it takes, does not exist in isolation. While there exists in popular discourse, a romantic notion of friendship as emergent, voluntary and particularistic – the "other" that is a reflection of the self – friendships exist *within* social networks. These networks are created in school, businesses, workplaces and other social institutions and are thus always echoes of, and deeply embedded in, the larger stratifications in society.

Constituting the self through friendship

Friendship is hard work! Earlier I explored the phenomenon of close dyadic friendship (Wolf 1966) and the significance that such intense friendship held in the lives of the teenage girls in my research. In this chapter, I moved out from the arena of the home and the domestic into the domain of the school and other public institutions to explore with the girls themselves, how each of my participants' sense of self was constituted and negotiated in this different context. Earlier, within the familial context, I was examining the phenomenon of selfhood through *difference*, the construction of a distinctive self:

"me" / "not me"

Friendship, on the other hand, offers another and a *paradoxical* perspective, selfhood through *sameness*, for it is the tension between both, the perceived similarity and the perceived distinction between people who call themselves close friends, that is the attraction and purpose of friendship:

"me" = "not me" / "not them"

This immediately presents an interesting paradox because both distinctiveness and sameness in friendships are maintained in this vitally important tension in order to be effective: one has to strive for a sense of individuation while simultaneously belonging to a specific cultural group. *To become friends,* means to construct a bond that is separate and discrete *from* oneself and yet includes oneself. Simultaneously, it is to construct a "symbolic boundary" (Cohen 1986) from others who are not in the exclusive relationship, as a form of cultural "distinction" (Bourdieu 1984).[1]

Teenage friendship groups depend very heavily on the construction of a very particular form of cultural distinction that becomes very clearly demonstrated in the school context. In spite of the fact that most schools attempt to create a sense of homogeneous community, a sense of sameness within often quite large heterogenous populations, the students themselves erect quite rigid symbolic boundaries of inclusion and exclusion, in order to define themselves and each other within wider adolescent groupings. These boundaries are created precisely because the young people themselves are engaged reflexively and earnestly in developing a sense of self-identity. The "serious play" explored earlier in this book now turns its attention to the *other* who is an aspect of the *self.* These alliances frequently form a character and identity of their own, extending far beyond the walls of the school. Whereas dyadic friendships are concerned with closer emotional attachment in areas designated as private, polyadic friendships are often concerned with appropriating public space and marking off boundaries of exclusion.

For the adolescent, these social groups are essential for defining, constructing and elaborating who and what she is, how she sees herself and how she believes others perceive her. One seeks a friend in order to validate one's sense of self, and for adolescents particularly, that sense of self is still very fluid and undetermined. As noted earlier, adolescents themselves acutely feel they are "nobodies" (James 1986), those "marginal beings . . . left out from the patterning of society" (Douglas 1984: 95).

Friendship in modern Western societies has been interpreted as "a non-institutional institution," a relationship founded on premises that are in defiance of bureaucracy (Paine 1974). However, on closer examination, and as I have argued throughout this book, it is possible to see that friendship groupings resonate with the division and segregations of wider society. These social units themselves acquire identities that emanate and evolve from the cultural groupings from which they originated. This, in turn, implies that we can expect to find the same sorts of power relations and thus the same sorts of constraints and difficulties emerging here, particularly for young women.

> *The special form friendship assumes in a given setting is predominantly a function of the role it plays, along with other institutions, in meeting the organisational demands of the society.* (Schwartz 1974: 71)

Groups and cliques: The creation of exclusivity

Friendship or polyadic groupings often require the appropriation of areas designated as private within more generally inclusive space and the marking-off of boundaries of exclusion. This separation is frequently achieved quite overtly and obviously through the body, as when Janine, Janelle, Wanda and their other close friends squeezed under the staircase in the school, separating themselves from others, as described in chapter 2. Or it can be seen in the situation at the Blue Light disco recounted in chapter 4, when small groups of girls huddled into the confined spaces of the toilets. At such times the reduced physical space available can be used to justify the limited numbers of people permitted to be part of the select company. At other times the method of exclusion can be expressed more subtly, indicated by a turn of the body, a distant look, a refusal to smile, or the use of gossip or a secret "language" to block out another person, not considered a privileged member, from the grouping. I shall return to some of these more subtle "tactics" below and in the following chapter.

People, of course, do not function in any everyday sense in terms of *whole* networks but as smaller manageable units, clusters and cliques developing from partial social networks. Epstein (1961) drew a distinction between an individual's effective network and her extended network and this is an important distinction for my analysis here. He argued that when an individual "A" is a member of an elite, then s/he and his/her effective close group of friends construct and maintain a set of norms and values through their gossip. Gossip itself, frequently perceived as a negative form of behavior, can be seen in this way to perform a vitally important function in creating and maintaining significant social groupings through the production and contesting of *symbolic capital.*[2] Bourdieu argued that symbolic capital can be understood as "economic or political capital that is disavowed, misrecognised and thereby recognised, hence legitimate, a 'credit' which under certain circumstances and always in the long run, guarantees 'economic' profits" (Bourdieu cited in Collins 1986: 132).

These values are then disseminated to the wider extended network through "A"'s other friends outside the circle or clique (Barnes 1969). Although superficially simplistic, the framework serves to provide a useful way of looking at school social groupings – as clusters and sometimes as cliques. The term "cluster" has been used to describe a set of people whose links are relatively dense but who do not necessarily constitute a clique. "Cliques," on the other hand, have been defined as a set of people, "each of whom is adjacent to each other," which means they have direct and frequent contact and communication between them (Harary 1959: 391; Barnes 1969). There is almost always a connotation of elitism in a clique; the set sees itself as socially, morally and culturally superior in some regard. The participants of a clique may show considerable interaction and coactivity but they lack the formal organizational qualities of a group and therefore are highly susceptible to changes in personnel (Harries-Jones 1969).

On applying such a construct to the teenager, we can see the ways many friendship groupings of young people develop and function. The construct also underpins the arguments I have been developing so far concerning the way *distinction* and *differance* are vitally important aspects of serious play in the constitution of (gendered) selfhood. These alliances may be fleeting or may be more permanent. They may seem contradictory or even appear to be mutually exclusive, so that an individual who participates in a specific peer group where underage drinking and illicit drug-taking may be the expected "norm" of behavior, may, at the same time, be forced to reconcile that expectation with those of another group. Moreover, the ethical and cultural demands, views, values, expectations of one's family unit may clash with those of one's wider ethnic community, with peer groups at school, or with friendship groups at the disco, youth club, or other regular meeting place. Furthermore, as Cohen (1985) indicated, the way groups understand and utilize the symbolic boundaries that appear to demarcate one social alliance from another is different for those within the grouping from those on the outside.

> *The boundary represents the mask presented by the community to the outside world; it is the community's public face. But the conceptualisation and symbolisation of the boundary from within is far more complex . . . In its public face, internal variety disappears or coalesces into a simple statement. In its private mode, differentiation, variety and complexity proliferate.* (Cohen 1986: 74)

Again, Bourdieu's concept of field is useful here since, the social groupings are both simultaneously predetermined and fluid; the symbolic boundaries are implicitly fixed and continually contested. He argues that "in analytic terms a field may be defined as a network or a configuration, of objective relations between positions" (1993: 97). Positions within each field, the places from which each individual negotiates, are "objectively defined, in their existence and in the determinations they impose upon their occupants, agents or institutions, by their present and potential situation (*situs*) in the structure of the distribution of species of power" (97). Yet, although economics, history and capital determine the overall *shape* that the field takes and the *position* that the players occupy within the field, the *structure* of each field is determined by the *state of play* of the agents who are enmeshed in the struggle for power, authority, control. The analogy with a game that Bourdieu makes is useful since, although as in any sport or game, the rules are set and understood, the players are able to work, "strategize," and negotiate within their positions in order to gain power and control.

As before, and in keeping with Bourdieu's insights, I am not using the word "strategize" in the traditional sense, "strongly associated with the intellectualist and subjectivist tradition" but rather to indicate a different theoretical orientation, "to designate the objectively orientated lines of action which social agents continually construct in and through practice" (Bourdieu 1993: 129). In other words, I am returning to Bourdieu's notion of the "feel for the game." The analogy is also particularly useful for my purposes since the term "play" usually implies an activity not taken seriously by outsiders, yet for the players themselves, those engaged in the game, the state of play is a very serious undertaking indeed. It reminds us again why friendships are so vitally important to teenagers.

The value of understanding adolescent friendship groups in this way is that such a framework foregrounds the wider social context of the groupings and thus the social network from which they emerge and to which they are connected. It enables us to see that, while the behaviors of young people might seem rebellious and alternative, their actions can be interpreted as attempts to gain social capital or status in ways that actually cohere with their parent or familial groupings. Thus, unlike so much earlier research on adolescent social groups, this paradigm places the friendship units firmly within the parent cultures and not as separate *subcultural* expressions of youth culture. The metaphor also serves as a reminder of the important role that forms of play, language, and gossip serve in the maintenance and exclusivity of such social groupings.

School groups can have a particularly important effect on teenage girls' sense of self because of this powerful, built-in, concept of exclusion. High school is a time of constant readjustment and conflicting needs for female adolescents. As indicated earlier, many studies indicate that teenage girls place a higher value than boys do on how others see them and on interpersonal relationships, particularly at a time when they are likely to be in situations least favorable for such concerns:

> *Girls might be placed in increased jeopardy both because they value peer opinion more ("the reflected self"), especially at the point of transition to secondary school and also because they value body image more at a time when their body is changing dramatically and social comparisons along this dimension become more problematic.* (Hendry et al. 1993: 17–18)

Once into the secondary sector, school becomes a place where notions of gender and gendering are both implicit and pervasive. Stanworth's (1981) study revealed that:

> *Girls may follow the same curriculum as boys – may sit side by side with boys in classes taught by the same teachers – and yet emerge from*

> *school with the implicit understanding that the world is a man's world, in which women can and should take second place.* (Stanworth 1981: 58)[3]

By examining these social groupings closely, within and outside school, we can see why, in spite of affirmative action strategies and policies that aim to rectify issues of gender bias and inequity, girls can still "emerge from school with [this] implicit understanding" as indicated above. To do this we need to explore the *unwritten* or *hidden* curriculum, that is, the social values and networks that form and evolve in the classrooms, and school yard, on the sports field and in the activities that then take place out of school.[4] Acceptance into the desirable friendship school groups is dependent upon the individual recognizing, adopting, and sometimes internalizing the rules and criteria of membership. Most of these rules for the girls in my fieldwork related to dominant notions of femininity, particularly in relation to conventional Western notions of gender relations, because the micro-social friendship grouping had *already* appropriated and incorporated these dominant value systems of the adult world. Concerns about appropriate appearance, leisure activities, musical and fashion taste, style, general demeanor and sexual relations underpinned the most coveted social groups within each school. This did not mean that the young people appropriated these criteria unquestioningly; rather, I suggest that their understanding of these "rules" was reflexive and their adherence was contradictory, an understanding indicative of the power relationships that experienced young women have and that permeate every aspect of their lives. As Valerie Walkerdine, in discussing teenage girls' use of romantic comics, similarly argued:

> *This does not mean that the girls simply accept and adapt to these models but that their adoption of femininity is at best shaky and partial . . . That the girl appears willing to accept the position to which she is classically fitted does not . . . tell us something basic about the nature of the female body, nor the female mind, but rather tells us of the power of those practices through which a particular resolution to the struggle is produced.* (Walkerdine 1984: 163).

Consequently it is important to consider the phenomenon of relatedness from two interconnected perspectives. Firstly, I develop further the relationship between (self) identity, space and symbolic boundaries by exemplifying the process of social closure. This is the means by which groups and individuals include and exclude others, denying all but those selected access to resources and status (Parkin 1979. Also cited in Nilan 1992). A considerable amount of the process of social closure for girls in this context involves learning, appropriating, adopting and negotiating the required "feminine behaviors." Secondly, I begin to explore the relationship between the friendship groups that form and evolve within schools and the larger, often more spectacular, youth subcultures that are so highly visible in other institutions. It is my contention that, far from being a separate cultural phenomenon, youth styles and groupings are clearly tied in complex ways to the everyday lived experiences of the young people. Furthermore, the role and style of young women in different youth groupings tend to be defined and constrained in very similar ways across all social boundaries, for it is here that, as Gilligan (1990) argues, girls "seriously confront the disadvantages of their gender and suffer from a lack of confidence and a confused sense of self" (cited in Hendry et al. 1993: 17).

The fluid formation of groups

What are the different teenage groupings and how are they formed? The most significant place for friendships during the teenage years is the school. All of the girls in my study, although attending different types of institutions, talked about the various "groups" within their own schools. These groups were seen as important and distinctive. Membership and acceptance within a particular grouping indicated to others that the individual in question possessed the ability to relate well, be popular and feel secure inside her own school. Exclusion from a particular group could mean that the individual could feel and be seen as an outsider to the school community as a whole. In other words, membership in a particular group signified social acceptance and acceptability in a far wider context than just that particular selection of friends.

The most frequently mentioned groupings identified across a number of different types of schools – government, private, single-sex, coeducational, conservative and progressive – were defined as the Trendies or the Cool Group, the Druggies or Alternative Group, the Try Hards and the Dags, Nerds or the Square Group. I have referred to some of these terms in earlier chapters, recorded either in casual conversations or as more forceful condemnations of others by the various participants in the research. Highly significantly, none of the girls in my study would define their *own* groups in these terms: these were the names they gave to *other* groups, not the group they belonged to. Most of the girls in my fieldwork defined themselves as ordinary or *Normals*. Nevertheless, as outsiders, they could identify and define various groups with confidence. After some discussion, a few of the girls would admit rather reticently, that they supposed their group would have been considered the most popular group but they saw themselves on the margins of these groups, adding "*I'm not really trendy.*"

In South Australian schools, which are my primary focus here, the perceived sharp boundaries between groupings were particularly pronounced in the middle and senior school, for students aged from 13 to 16 years. Although there were friendship groupings in the junior school, the girls themselves perceived the boundaries, the invisible borders that separated groupings, to be far more fixed and divisive once the students reached secondary school. This may have been due to the more formal structure of the larger institution resulting from the transition from primary school to secondary school. The student groups were divided and separated according to subject choice and often academic standard, even in schools which advocated non-streaming. Furthermore, in high school, children who were considered slow learners were understandably placed into smaller groups so that they could be taught more effectively. Alternatively, students identified as gifted or talented were channelled into other special programs. Children perceived as having special talents in music or sport, were also singled out. This is not to suggest that such differentiation was necessarily educationally wrong but to signal that segregation of some form always took place. Unlike elementary schools, where a student may be with the same group of over twenty children all year for most subjects, in most secondary schools students move from class to class, from group to group every forty or fifty minutes. It was only in their home-class group that they met regularly every morning and evening for attendance records and messages. This effectively meant that a child could be associated with six or seven peer groups, potentially mixing with 80 different children or more every day.

The context of a large group of seemingly undifferentiated people demands that the students impose some sort of controllable order, some sort of differentiation on the mass. That is, they applied their own sense of order and stratification based on these larger groupings to create their own smaller exclusive social units. In fact, it could be interpreted as the students unconsciously clarifying and exposing the inherent contradiction in school policy. As indicated above, while most schools espoused the desirability of equality and uniformity, they simultaneously advocated competition rather than cooperation, through marking systems, examinations, streaming, grading procedures, prizes, and awards. In other words, the school ideals simultaneously promoted egalitarianism and yet worked within a hierarchical structure. Even the student representative councils or prefect systems, supposedly designed to teach and promote leadership skills *and* democratic representation, operated on a system of differentiation; the most ostensibly able students in terms of cooperation, reliability, communication skills – and often the most academically talented – were deemed by the staff to be the best student leaders.[5] Such was the formal structure of most schools, and underpinning it, despite a lauded policy of equally sanctioned diversity, there was a tacit curriculum of hierarchy, a ranking of students, of which the pupils were well aware.

Out of the classroom, in the playground or schoolyard, a parallel structure of hierarchy in the friendship groupings emerged from the social networks of the school, one far more important to the student body than any meritocracy based on academic achievement. As I noted earlier, academic research has frequently interpreted student styles and demeanor as antiestablishment, a manifestation of counter-school resistance, a micro or subculture. However, a closer examination of these groups within the wider context of the students' everyday experiences, reveals a very different interpretation. Far from expressing a rejection and contestation of dominant adult values, the student behavior and style was actually very closely aligned to meaningful familial, and what were perceived as local community, values and practices, as I shall demonstrate below.[6] Because these groupings impacted on how the students saw themselves, how individuals understood their self-worth and the way they perceived and constituted themselves, they had a far greater weight in the young people's perspectives than did their academic progress and success.

From the outside, these friendship groupings seemed quite open and flexible. After all, within the classroom, in different subject classes, different students seemed to sit and chat together easily. However, the invisible boundaries formed between the social groupings were perceived by the students themselves as quite rigid and bounded, firmly controlled in terms of inclusivity and thus also exclusivity. For example, I often asked the teenage participants in my fieldwork, most of whom, as I noted earlier, regarded themselves as belonging to an average or "normal" group, what would happen if they decided to go and sit with the most popular group. Each time, there would be a snort of derision and amused disbelief that I had asked the question. "You just wouldn't!" came the answer. On several occasions different students would then try to elaborate the reasons but it was always a variation of the same answer:

Steven *You see the Cool Group can go and talk to other groups because they think they are superior, better than everyone else. But you just can't go and sit with them.*

Jane *You'd look a total idiot.*

Helen *You'd just get "paid out" out so much.*[7]

One boy assured me that he would get physically attacked if he tried it. Sometimes the criteria for inclusion were overt and sometimes tacit, but the terms of inclusion were well understood by all students. They incorporated what emerged as an often contradictory moral, economic and social hierarchy. Scott, one of Diane's friends, explained to me in some detail the social networks operating in the school:

Scott *It's like a ladder, you see. At the top there is the Cool Group, the real hard-core group. Then there are the Druggies (the Cool Group do drugs too but the Druggies, that's all they do). At the bottom there are the Nerds, the complete losers. In the middle have the Normals, like us – the people who don't really fit into a group.*
Gerry *What about the Try Hards? Where do they fit in?*
Scott *Well, they sort of attach themselves to the Cool Group. You know how little fish attach themselves to whales? Well that's what the Try Hards do. They think if they hang around long enough they'll become the Cool Group.*

Like the word "cool" discussed in chapter 2, the epithet "hard core" again implied an authenticity, a seemingly solid reality underneath the shifting, transient image. Hence the Try Hards could never become members of the Cool Group because they only managed to acquire the external trappings but not the inner core. As with places, as I noted in the previous chapter, all groups were not *created* equal, it seemed; some are more equal than others!

Hilary identified about nine recognizable, acknowledged and self-defined groups in her school at each year level, as well as a few "floating" individuals who were not seen as forming a separate group. To an outside observer visiting the school, the first apparent aspect of the phenomenon of the social groupings was that they *did* exist in a patently concrete form. The groups manifested themselves by forming a physical unit in particular places during lunch and recess times.[8] In other words, a particular group could nearly always be found in a specific area. Most students would know where to find another student during lunchtime because of the group to which that student was known to belong. At Hilary's school in her year, the group designated as the Cool Group could always be found on the oval in a particular spot, except when it was raining, in which case they would be found under the balcony in an area designated theirs; the Alternative Group regularly sat under the stairs. In Beverley's school the Cool Group would always sit by the school canteen, near a number of long benches enabling them to place their schoolbags along the wall of the building, symbolically marking off their territory. Thus, around the school grounds at every school, during recess or lunch breaks the students could be seen sitting in large circles or huddles in specific places. *Where* they sat was as significant as *who* they were, because it was another expression of their cultural identity and their social capital within the school community.

The group that was acknowledged as the most popular needed space in order to accommodate their large numbers, for although membership was limited and monitored, it was not small. As public acknowledgment was a vital aspect of this identity, the Cool Group also had to be *seen* to be in a large group in an easily accessible, conspicuous area.[9] Fran told me that, in her school, the Cool Group was always on the school oval, which meant that the younger children in the school community could easily notice and recognize them as being members of the select crowd.

The alternative group, usually called the Druggie or Rebel Group – those who tended to be known by the others as being more frequent users of illicit drugs – would frequently and understandably inhabit the further recesses of the oval or less accessible corners of the school building. This group wanted to be less conspicuous as it did not want to attract the attention of teachers and other authority figures while smoking cigarettes or marijuana or taking other drugs on campus.

The art of being cool!

Every girl in my project talked about social group formation and its importance in the school and in noninstitutionalized leisure activities. Although, in effect, the groupings could have been regarded as relatively fluid *networks*, in that the students did communicate with individuals across groups especially outside school, the students saw the most popular and highly regarded groupings as relatively closed and exclusive. While the groups were thus formed *inside* school, the criteria of membership were based on leisure activities *outside* school, for what one *did* defined who one *was*. The groups were not regarded as equal and *différance* was strictly constructed and rigidly maintained. As indicated previously, the most popular clique, the group with the most numbers and the one held in the highest regard, that was frequently talked about – albeit often ambivalently – was the Cool Group.

Every girl in my research project could nominate a group from her own school experience as equivalent to the Cool Group, the most popular and desirable group. Although this group has different names in different schools, such as the "Trendies" or sometimes by the names or surnames of "core" members, the constituency of this group was remarkably similar across public and private schools. Pam Nilan's (1992) research also identified a number of self-differentiated peer groups in the Sydney schools she investigated. The groups defined as the most privileged by her informants were also seen as the most affluent and they were dubbed The DBTs (The Double Bay Trendies) regardless of where they actually lived. In that research, the girls who were not DBTs identified the privileged group members as girls who bought clothes from Country Road and Sportsgirl (both high-quality women's clothing shops). As I suggested previously, expensive clothes indicated a particular aesthetic style. The overall image here was one of classic conformity and superiority, an image of effortless high social status. During a discussion about Cool Groups, two different girls in my research, on two separate occasions, asked me if I'd seen the film *Heathers.* This is a commercially released film about a group of girls in a school in America who, believing themselves superior to the other girls in the school, exerted a powerful, and ultimately deadly, influence over other students. The fictional group *Heathers* was thus known collectively by the same given name (Heather) of each of its members. "It's just like that in my school," said each of these participants quite independently and seriously.

What exactly did being "cool" mean in the context of my female participants? Firstly, it always connoted an image of superiority which, although supposedly authentic and innate, was also paradoxically understood to be mainly constituted through style and demeanor. Secondly, it always retained the characteristics of the adult cultures *from which it emerged;* that is, "coolness" held a variety of connotations for adolescents from different cultural and social backgrounds. To illustrate this further, I will look at three different examples of schools situated in different socioeconomic areas and, having different ideologies and discourses surrounding them, I will demonstrate their respective understandings of "coolness."

"Cool" equals self-possession

Firstly, the students who were excluded from the Cool Group saw the inside members as superior and privileged. They usually expressed an ambivalence about whether they really wanted to be part of this group. Membership for this group was understood by all, both inside and outside the group, as indicative of a "natural" ability, an authenticity, an inherent quality of superiority. As noted in chapter 2, an individual considered to be socially mature is one who possesses complete control over his/her body. An acknowledged member of a Cool Group was assumed to personify these qualities of self-containment and wholeness.[10]

In all of the schools, related to this notion of authenticity and inherent qualities, was the tacit understanding that membership meant physical attractiveness, especially for girls. Outsiders often commented that female members of Cool Groups were attractive. The criterion for this attractiveness was usually only vaguely articulated as it was assumed to be implicit. It was indeed only articulated when some dispute arose about whether a person genuinely qualified for membership. Diane and her friends noted that the Cool Group in her school consisted of all the "beautiful girls and hunky guys." At Beverley's school, she and her friends seemed to spend a great deal of their recess and lunch times "on the outside, looking in." They commented that they had noticed that all the female members of the Cool Group in *their* school, from which they felt they were automatically excluded through their own physiques, had blonde hair and were "beautifully skinny."[11] When they occasionally noticed that someone did not quite meet these aesthetic criteria, they pondered this phenomenon endlessly among themselves, trying to account for what appeared to be an anomaly in their eyes. They tried desperately to understand what attributes the particular girl *did* have that gained her entry into the desired circle.

Yet physical attractiveness alone, while present and commented upon, was not seen as the *key* attribute. Self-possession and a self-confident demeanor certainly were key qualities: Janine, who identified as *Nunga,* told me that the Cool Group in her school was comprised of the "tough, popular girls." Her school was a single-sex government school in an industrial materially disadvantaged area. The use of the epithet "tough" in this context did not necessarily mean violent or aggressive but had more to do with being streetwise, having self-control, confidence, and easy social skills. Significantly, no one in that school's Cool Group was *Nunga.* What was important in *that* Cool Group was to appear self-contained, at ease with oneself, nonchalantly unselfconscious, a strong independent individual. As the sense of self for a girl identifying as *Nunga* was far more strongly connected with her sense of familial relatedness, her roles and obligations, it was hardly surprising that the female Aboriginal teenagers did not see themselves, or behave as, members of the Cool Group, in spite of their frequent posturing and bravado.

From the outside, the Cool Group frequently seemed to be an ideal place. One girl noted that the people in the Trendy Group always had friends. This was because in each school the Cool Group appeared to move around as a unit. They were all close friends. In more affluent areas, they held parties at one another's houses. The qualities that *coolness* implied then were confidence and self-control, and because group membership seemed effortless, these were seen to be natural abilities. Because of these attributes, they were simultaneously admired, envied and resented by outsiders. Beverley told me that, at the end of the year, some of the school leavers (a number of the final year students who had *not* been members of the select group) had turned a garden hose on a group of Year 11 Trendies, the incumbent Cool Group, who were sitting on a bench one lunchtime. "Everyone around clapped!" she said, in great delight. While outsiders would like to have the apparent cohesion and social status of the Cool Group, they simultaneously seemed to detest and resent the effortless control and self-possession that this group appeared to have. Spraying them with water demolished the image of superiority for a moment and made them look foolish, flustered and out of control. Their solidarity and containment had "dissolved" for a few moments!

Getting the look

If "coolness" meant different things in different social networks, this left the young people in rather a dilemma. How does one acquire the necessary authentic look if it is implied rather than stated? In fact, if anyone had to *ask* about the look, or articulated anything that suggested its construction rather than its natural development, obviously the person enquiring didn't possess it naturally. Clothes were therefore a key and immediate way of suggesting knowledge, status, and group membership. Outward appearance, the total image, attempted to reinforce and reflect the self-contained demeanor. In all of the discussions about "coolness" – whether I was participating and listening or just overhearing discussions, boys and girls noted that the choice of clothes of the Cool Group indicated their sophistication, their cultural knowledge, their self-possession. In most cases during the time of my fieldwork, this meant that the members wore what were, for most teenagers, clothes with brand names, labels or designs that prominently indicated affluence. So for that particular group of girls, brand names such as Nike, Country Road, Sportsgirl, Adidas Equipment, or Mosimo were most commonly worn. For other girls in different schools, as illustrated below, "coolness" meant displaying a very different appearance. For example, sometimes it meant the deliberate choice of "retro" fashions from Op shops or sporting nose or navel rings. In all cases, the portrayal of the body through clothes, style and image was an important aspect of the performed right to authentic membership.

In all cases, too, the main image sought was one of individual choice, the implication being that the clothes and/or physical appearance were making a statement about the wearer's cultural knowledge and status that the individual *chose* to emphasize. Even in schools where the students were obliged to wear uniforms, outsiders of the group could identify group members just by looking at them. "They are still Trendies, even in their school uniform," noted Belinda. The group set the tone of what was supposed to be worn by others if they wanted to appear knowledgable and culturally aware. They did this by wearing the clothes or accessories themselves and making derogatory remarks about other styles of clothes and appearance. Again, these clothes, the style and the demeanor not only suggested group identity, but often hinted at a wider musical fandom and also leisure activities. So, Techno or Hip Hop music fans tended to wear Adidas tops and Nike shoes. Students wearing a great deal of black, with dyed black hair or heavy black makeup were often expressing an allegiance to the Goths, Gothic styles and music. Scott, a boy at Diane's school, commented that the Cool Group set the fashion trends; the other people wanted to wear what the Cool Group wore and "They 'gave you heaps' [harassed or embarrassed you] if you were wearing other types of clothes." But for many young people acquiring the clothes simply emphasized the gap between themselves and the high-status Cool Group they were attempting to emulate.

As indicated in chapter 2, clothing and appearance were important for group membership and acceptance. Getting the appearance, "the look" right was of course very important. To make a mistake or to appear as if the style were *not* "innate" ran the risk of being perceived as a Try Hard. I overheard a number of young people talking about fashionable clothes amongst themselves, and discussing what look made people appear cool or trendy. On joining the conversation, I pointed out that I had seen a number of *Nunga* girls wearing exactly the same clothes as they were describing. Did this make the *Nunga* girls cool or trendy? "No," came the reply. "They would still be *Nunga*."

In a different context, I was talking with Grace about some young people in the city, a group of people she disparagingly called townies. Many of them, like her friends with whom she spent so much time and like Pat's group of friends, the ravers, wore Adidas tops and baggy trousers. To my uninitiated eye, the appearance of these three groups was the same. Grace insisted that these *other* people in the city were *different*. "They are Try Hards," she said firmly. As I said I was still confused, she tried to explain further: "Try Hards means someone might wear the same clothes and even the way they wear their *hats* – but you know it's not really *them*. Townies (these Try Hards) always hang around outside Myers [the large department store] and just talk. They don't *do* anything."

What one *did*, combined with what one *wore*, created the core of authenticity necessary to *become* a particular kind of person. A slight deviation and one was branded as a Try Hard. The search for the right look and demeanor was important since it affected whom one was allowed to be, where one could go and with whom one could be seen. This leads us on to consider the difficulties some young people had fitting in with their particular groupings. A more detailed look at the schools of four different girls from my fieldwork – Hilary, Diane, Sara and Fran – will serve by way of example of this phenomenon. What will become clear is that the rules and tacit criteria of membership of the girls' groupings, and therefore the role these play in their particular self-making are incomprehensible, unless the wider social context of their school's local community is explored.

Hilary's school groups

Hilary's school was a large government coeducational institution on an attractive campus. Sandwiched between two main roads in the more affluent Eastern suburbs of the city, the school comprised a number of older heritage buildings as well as a number of more attractive, modern buildings. The more recent brick-and-glass buildings, facing onto one of the main roads, were surrounded by large grassed areas through which a stream meandered, imparting an almost park-like appearance to the school grounds. The school provided good sports facilities for soccer, Australian rules football and tennis. Despite its excellent academic reputation, location and popularity, comparatively few of the students at the school came from extremely affluent backgrounds, a phenomenon attributable perhaps to the number of private high schools in the area able to attract the more affluent students. Hilary's own family's financial situation was not particularly good; she lived in a small house not far from the school with her mother and younger brother and was a recipient of AusStudy, a means-tested, federally funded financial support system for students. Although the school was zoned, it attracted many students from further afield because of its specialist music programs. Indeed, several children from less-privileged backgrounds were able to gain access to the school and its facilities through music scholarships.[12]

Yet, it also had a reputation for affectation among the student population, within and outside its community: it was known as the "Clayton's" or "pseudo" private school[13] because many students felt that the tacit ideology of the school was an elitist, exclusive one – it wanted to be perceived as a private school. Concern about public image, uniforms and overtly disciplined behavior, academic results, awards and formal prizes was a vital part of the overt structure and the circulated discourse within the school. Certainly, the school community consisted of many students whose parents would have preferred their children to attend a private school for reasons of status, or because they believed the children would gain an academic advantage there, but who couldn't afford the high fees this would entail. In spite of these reservations, or maybe because of them, Hilary enjoyed her school, was a high achiever, and had always been an active, prominent member of the student representative council. In her final year, as stated earlier, she became school captain (head girl), a prestigious and highly sought-after position of responsibility and leadership. In order to be eligible for such a position a student had to be selected by her peers and have her election approved by the staff, who behind the closed doors of the staff room undoubtedly had the ultimate power of veto.

Hilary identified the Cool Group in her school by the surnames of two of the core members: that was how that group identified itself and was nicknamed by others. Despite the fact that she defensively described herself as belonging to the margins of this group, acknowledging perhaps the potential derogatory connotation of such membership ("I'm not *really* part of the group"), it was, nevertheless, the social group in which she spent most of her leisure time. The fact that the members were known in this instance by their family names rather than their given names was significant. Because the members of the Cool Group spent a great deal of time together at one another's houses, the parents of the group members were very aware of who was in the group and who was not. Parents were also aware that the group was highly regarded within the student body and often by the school staff themselves – after all, many leaders from the student body were group members. I was told of parental approval of the group, encouragement for the young people to stay as an exclusive unit with parents on occasion deciding who should or should not be in the group. This was not difficult since parties and other social occasions took place at the students' family homes and so parents would strongly discourage access to particular students through their own children. In return, parents were often tolerant of alcohol, cigarettes and marijuana being consumed at these parties, the rationale being that they were present at the house and could "supervise." Little formal supervision would actually take place – students were frequently drunk or similarly affected by drugs – as the parents tended to believe that, because the activities took place within the domestic sphere, they were allowing the adolescents the necessary freedom to experiment safely with drugs. Thus individuals in this group received a great deal of emotional support and encouragement to remain as a closed unit – from their families, from the school authority figures and therefore also from each other – and thus was their sense of status and superiority sustained.

Some students who were excluded from this popular group referred to its members in a derogatory fashion as the 90210 Group after the popular American teenage soap opera *Beverley Hills 90210*. Why they were described in this way deserves closer examination since it highlights the ambivalence the outsiders felt toward the group. Just as audiences of the soap opera itself speak of their viewing as an almost furtive pleasure, in such terms as, "I know it's stupid but . . ." so these girls talked about the Cool Group from which they were barred, with admiration mixed with disdain. The ambivalence arose because firstly, within the context of this particular school, the Cool Group contained the members of the student body who were seen as the most confident and the most sophisticated. They were notably at ease with their own bodies, their peers and with most adults and therefore had acquired an admirable level of communication skills. Usually the group contained several people who were school prefects or members of the student representative council, and therefore were regarded by the adult authorities as responsible members of the school community. They knew how to balance the demands of the adult world and the student world – innocuously "naughty," they experimented with social drugs, such as marijuana and alcohol. In this way the group could socialize and experiment with "alternative selves" without becoming a threat to the adult world and contesting authority and middle-class values. To appropriate adult values too much was to become a Square or a Nerd. To flout adult values too much was to be considered a rebel – to belong to an alternative, perhaps a Druggie Group. The popular Cool Group knew how to play the system just right.

Like the characters in the fictional teenage soap opera, to the outside "audience," the group members, particularly the girls, appeared exceptionally and "naturally" physically attractive. Moreover, the Cool Group itself, by its possession of these coveted qualities, qualities seen as inherent rather than acquired, thus automatically excluded non-members, designating them as clearly "other." The supposed authenticity of the clique members is a vital clue to understanding their power. If individuals are members of a closed group through qualities acquired from birth not through hard work or virtue, it therefore establishes their membership and status as inalienable and non-contestable. Hence, the outsiders simultaneously both desired and rejected the Cool Group in order to preserve their own sense of self. They would have liked to belong to the popular clique, but, being rejected had to justify their non-acceptance by scorning it. In this particular case, the nickname, 90210, implied that the group was pretentious (not authentic!), theatrical, insular and *inordinately* preoccupied with their relationships, a real-life version of a teenage television melodrama.

The invisible boundaries of the groups were tightly maintained. It was not possible to just join a group: approval had to be sought, criteria met and an invitation issued. Of course by definition, not all people can be deemed eligible for membership because then the cultural capital necessary for membership would be devalued. In a coeducational school the Cool Group always comprised fairly equal numbers of boys and girls. The prerequisite for a girl being fully integrated into the group was that she had a boyfriend (usually from within the group) and that she was prepared to accept the social norms of the group. In Hilary's school, as already indicated, this meant sharing social drugs such as alcohol, cigarettes and marijuana and being involved with some level of sexual activity with one's boyfriend. A girl could enter the group though her boyfriend; a boy from the group could introduce her to the group and if she was deemed acceptable to the group she could gain and retain membership even after the demise of the initial relationship.

The group members talked about the group which was viewed from the outside, as unified and possessing cohesive values, but from the inside not all members felt so secure about their status. As indicated earlier, Hilary told me she often felt on the margins of the group, because she did not take any drugs at all. When her friendship with two "central" members disintegrated she felt even less secure within the group. It was only after she and a male group member started to date as boyfriend and girlfriend that she felt she was accepted more into the group. Sandy, one of her former friends, began to behave more warmly and affectionately towards her. She told Hilary that now that they both had boyfriends, they could be friends again. She was told that now their friendship would be "more sophisticated" rather than childish.

Diane's school groups

Diane's school was located in a far less affluent area than was Hilary's – in one of the newer northeastern suburbs. In many ways appearing as an institution of glaring contradictions, the school sat uneasily in an economically deprived, high-unemployment area on the edge of newly established housing estates. Drawing on both working-class and lower middle-class areas, the school appeared to comprise an uneasy mix of established small group communities (mainly from British backgrounds), an unskilled and semiskilled workforce and the unemployed. Also part of the school community were newer families struggling with large mortgages and upwardly mobile aspirations.[14] The school believed it had a more affluent population than it actually had[15] but in fact during 1995, 30 percent of the school population were welfare card holders.[16]

When the school had been built twenty years earlier, the area was known locally as the "New Large Mortgage Belt," indicating that quite a few new large houses had been built by small business holders primarily interested in material acquisitions. Since the recession of 1986, many of the small businesses had failed or were struggling. Families still saw the school as holding the potential for material advancement for their children but the parents themselves had little previous history or experience of education beyond secondary school. Education was seen as a commodity: children were encouraged to stay on at school by their parents to "get Year 12" qualifications but there was little understanding about the education system, how it worked and what was necessary at home to help their children succeed. Nor was there much expectation that the children would proceed to institutions of higher education other than for strictly short-term vocational training. At Diane's house I had noticed a vast quantity of material goods – three television sets, a computer, a video recorder and a mobile phone. This was typical of the pattern of procuring possessions for their children, whether they could afford the goods or not.[17] Many of the students grew up expecting a higher standard of living, including expensive, designer-label clothes because it was seen locally as a sign of prestige and outward success.

Almost the entire school population had Anglo–Celtic backgrounds. I was told proudly (and unwittingly, hilariously) by one of the school counsellors that there was "half an Aboriginal child" attending the school. As mentioned in chapter 1, the school had suffered a severe blow to its reputation the year before I commenced my fieldwork, as a result of an unpleasant and dangerous incident whereby a student had held teachers and pupils at bay for several hours with a loaded shotgun. Although no one was badly injured, at the time of my research the school still smarted from the sensational headlines plastered across the tabloids and in the electronic media, with, according to both present students and children from other schools, a reputation for violence and drugs. Violence was a very real issue for many of the pupils, as I noted in earlier chapters, since domestic violence (as parental discipline) was a common way of handling disputes and discipline problems at home.

Another idiosyncratic aspect of the school was its sense of territory and isolation. Because of the large local shopping center and other community facilities such as the swimming and leisure center, many families did not venture out of the area. Children had grown up there, gone to various primary schools in the vicinity and then on to the high school. The pupils of the high school retained fierce loyalty to their friends from primary school, and friendship groups were formed on that basis. Outside school they would meet up again with their original primary school friends even when those friends were now at a different high school. Friendship groupings were very much defined according to a theory "protecting one's turf," sharing the common childhood experience of location and perceived sense of community.

The recorded academic outcomes of the school, in terms of which students went on to higher education, were not high, but a relatively high proportion of students did stay on to complete their Year 12 certificate.[18] Diane told me several times that the school was an "academic school." Parents expected that the children would gain white-collar employment as a result of the education system. In other words, the purpose of school for the parent population, was the "good job" the students should gain at the end of the time spent there, even though the area itself was one of high unemployment. This very utilitarian view of school and education in general reflected the desire for material goods in the home. Material goods were a sign of success. Professionalism was not an outcome that was particularly sought after. Success for girls meant employment in hospitality or service industries or other white-collar jobs, until they were married and had children.

The school had been built in 1975, the two-storied glass-and-cement buildings reflecting the basic and fairly austere design. Diane was in a large, all-female group at school when I first met her. "We like being in an all girls' group," she told me, "because we can talk and the boys aren't really mature enough."[19] However, as she moved up through the school, she discovered that acceptable and desirable femininity in her world meant regular and publicly acknowledged relationships with the opposite sex. To be accepted and viewed as "normal," one was assumed either to have a boyfriend or be seeking a boyfriend. Gaps between relationships seemed to cause great apprehension and concern: Diane anxiously described these times as being "single again." Without a boyfriend Diane would spend a great deal of her time looking for a suitable candidate, as did most of her friends. To be without a male partner could leave one open for concerns about one's sexual preference or orientation, as I noted earlier.

Gradually over the following year she moved into a larger mixed group. At first, this group sat near the administration block, and over a period of time, moved their territory to the grassed oval, a move that symbolically stressed a more confident progression out into the public arena. It was in this group that Diane acquired her "first serious boyfriend." He was at another school but was close friends with members of Diane's group and so she got to know him through them. This also meant she was automatically included in their activities outside school as well as gaining status in their eyes. It certainly wasn't designated as the Trendy Group and neither was it the hardworking Nerd Group, so it was comfortably acceptable. At first, she felt comfortable in their company because she had known several members for a long time.

Later, however, two different incidents concerning prospective boyfriends greatly affected how comfortable she felt with her other friends and affected her membership of the group as a whole. Anna and Diane were discussing Diane's current infatuation with a boy at school. He had been informed about her interest through some mutual friends but had said that their relationship "wouldn't work." Anna explained why. "The groups are too different," she said. "His group do different things [from Diane's group]. He's in a 'bad' group." This meant he was into drug-taking, antiauthority activities inside and outside school. Diane didn't say anything. I was reminded of an earlier comment of hers when, sighing over her relationship with Helen, she had told me plaintively that "bad girls seem to have more fun and get the exciting guys." Diane resigned herself to knowing that she would not be welcome in his group and that he would not fit into hers.

The second incident involved Diane's attraction for a younger boy in the school. "He seemed nice and a gentleman," said Diane when she first got to know him. They eventually arranged to go to the cinema together and although they seemed to have a good time as far as she was concerned, he suddenly told her at the end of the date, that he didn't "like her like *that*" (that is, romantically). She was mortified, especially since she felt she had clearly indicated to him that she was really attracted to him. The next week the situation became worse as the boy attached himself to Diane's group. Because he was physically attractive and confident, he made the transition smoothly, easily accepted into her circle of friends despite his younger age. Yet notwithstanding their earlier friendship, he now ignored her. From her comments to me I understood she felt extremely embarrassed and compromised. Her friends turned their attention to him, obviously enjoying his company. Diane felt totally humiliated. She had already been embarrassed by an unrequited relationship, felt he regarded her as a "slut" because she was too easy to attract, and now she was being ignored within her own group. Suddenly she did not "fit" into her own circle of friends. She was the stranger. "I feel like I'm invisible," she said.

Sara's school groups: A search for belonging

Sara had attended a more academic government school in the northeastern section of the city. The school was actually created through an amalgamation of two very different schools in distinctly discrete social locations. For example, one area was characterized by significant cultural diversity, the school population being constituted from a considerable range of ethnic backgrounds. Sara had been reasonably happy at her junior high school because it was smaller, friendlier and less academic and the students were able to communicate easily with the staff. "We called many of them by their first names – and we certainly knew what their first names were," she said. However, on her progression to the high school campus she became extremely unhappy.

The senior high school was far larger and more competitive. She said they met a great deal of "school prejudice." The students from the second school had apparently publicly protested against the amalgamation as they felt the first school would lower its academic reputation. The headmaster, who had apparently condoned the protest, subsequently became the principal of the new amalgamated school, so it was obvious, Sara felt, that there would be prejudice there. The second school was large and impersonal, and school groups were quite rigid and exclusive. "It saw itself as a private college (academic, exclusive, elitist) without really having the money," Sara commented, "and felt *we* were not good enough for it."[20]

Although there were probably as many Indian and Vietnamese students at her new campus as at her former one, there were far greater numbers of pupils joining cliques and a far greater informal division of students into friendship groupings along ethnic and perceived social lines. Among the most predominant groups, there was again the Cool Group: "Rich kids," said Sara, "who have the money to look good and spend on the latest fashions. They have all the cute guys and girls." Several of the student representative council members were in this school group. She identified several other groups including the Druggies, which was seen as the exciting alternative group. This group in Sara's school, unlike its counterpart in Hilary's school, did not have the sanction of the adult world. The group identified by all as losers were the Dags or the Nerdy Group. Students who belonged to this group worked conscientiously to achieve academic success.

Although the school body seemed to see itself as a high-achieving, academic school, the most overtly hardworking students were not the most popular. Again "coolness" invoked notions of natural qualities and authenticity rather than acquired skills; the most popular students were those who achieved seemingly without effort and who appeared to be generally at ease in their social networks. This is probably why students who are successful sports people are nearly always included in the Cool Group.

Sara felt she had very few friends in her new campus and saw herself as the victim of racial slurs and prejudice, on occasion from both teachers and students. "The teachers are into discipline," she said, "and you have to call the male teachers, *Sir.*" Apart from the color of her skin, she said, she also felt different because she had different values and indulged in leisure activities different from most of the students at this school. At first she joined the Druggies Group at the high school because this was the group several of her former friends had joined. "I just went along with them." But soon she felt an outsider to all groups. "I'm not into drugs or fashion, so what else is there?" she asked me rhetorically. On another occasion she noted plaintively, "they're into parties and I'm into performing (Cirkidz)."

Into Fran's school group

Finally, in her last year of school Sara decided to transfer to Fran's school, a school very different from Hilary's and from Diane's. It was a single-sex government girls' high school, one of the few remaining in South Australia, founded on feminist principles with the aim of empowering girls.[21] Its information brochure asserted that it was a school that "encouraged academic excellence at all levels and developed an awareness of the changing choices available to women in our society." Most of the students were there because their parents decided that, educationally and ideologically, it was the place for them to be. This was indicated by the fact that, despite its less-than-salubrious location, it attracted many children of college-educated parents. A relatively small school on the edge of the more leafy affluent suburbs, the campus sat on a busy main road near the local railway station. The school seemed hemmed in by the busy, dusty street along which trucks and buses thundered throughout the day. It was plainly a commercial area as opposed to the quieter residential area where Hilary's school was positioned, and contrasted markedly with that school's immediately pleasing aesthetic presence. Apart from a modern double-storied brick-and-glass block, there were several older low brick buildings and quite a number of transportable classrooms, rectangular, prefabricated wooden and tin-roofed structures huddled against one end of the small sports oval.

Its stated aim, as implied above, was to teach its students to actively challenge and question traditional societal values, particularly those effectively subordinating or curtailing women's opportunities and advancement. Thus the curriculum stressed nontraditional subjects for girls and the school ethos emphasized cooperation rather than competition. Children traveled from all over the metropolitan area and beyond to attend the school.[22] The potential was there for girls from many different backgrounds to take advantage of the more progressive curriculum.

Yet there seemed to be still a predominance of Anglo–Australian children. I saw very few non-European faces amongst the students, although the school did have specialist facilities and programs to teach children from non-English-speaking backgrounds. It could have been that many parents, especially from migrant backgrounds, still sought a far more traditional curriculum, a more disciplined and less liberal approach, or one with a more overtly religious basis.

Despite the stress on cooperation, the emphasis on egalitarianism, negotiation and tolerance, hierarchical school groupings still existed at Fran's school. But the quality of "coolness," the attribute of the most popular group, as one might expect, was very different in style, values and behavior from that of Hilary's school or Sara's former school. For the individuals in this school, to be *cool* meant to be not simply nontraditional but actively *antitraditional* in terms of codes of femininity; that is, to be unsophisticated, although still greatly interested in and aware of the opposite sex; to talk freely and openly about sex and sexual encounters; to be scathing about what they perceived as usual female preoccupations with fashion and weight. It would seem, just as in Hilary's school, that the Cool Group had absorbed and were reproducing the same value systems and ideals of their parents. What would have been seen as oppositional in other schools was seen here as the acceptable, even desirable norm. Again membership of the most popular and coveted group in this school was constituted by some of the most able and confident students – seemingly at ease with both peers and adults.

Fran took the video camera to the school one day to film her friends. Most of this section of her video comprises her group sitting on their favored position on the oval. What is immediately striking to the casual observer is the body and verbal language of the girls. The film provided many examples of totally uninhibited use of sexual innuendo and swearing. One of her friends was filmed telling a joke to the rest of the girls, urged on by the others and, no doubt, by the presence of the camera itself. "How do you know when someone has had oral sex with a chicken?" she asked. Then she coughed out of her mouth bits of torn yellow paper to the great delight and amusement of her classmates. Someone asked her who had told her the joke. "My mother," she replied, to more squeals of mirth. Whatever they were talking about, the girls used "fuck" or "fucking" as the most frequent and regular epithet and their general conversation centered on their sexual relationships outside school.

Into Fran's reasonably established group came Sara, the move occurring during the last part of my fieldwork after I had already known both girls for over a year. She had heard a great deal about the school from Fran and Hannah at Cirkidz and felt, with these friends there already, she would have a happier and an easier social time there. At first, there followed a very easy transference into this social group of high status in the school; she seemed accepted and felt quite at ease. Not completely at ease, though. Sara was aware that in general, she should stay respectfully in the margins, not assuming that every joke or every activity included her.[23]

She had thought she had understood the banter, the sexual innuendos of the group, and what was and what was not appropriate behavior in this circle of friends. However, one day when I telephoned her, about four months after her starting in the school, she indicated she was feeling quite mixed-up and upset. She said she was feeling very confused about who she was and her sense of identity. I immediately assumed this was about her being adopted from Nepal, as this had intermittently been a source of confusion and uncertainty for her. She would talk to me about her background, and her occasional feelings of difference and the emotional insecurity that she felt flowed from this. However, when she did talk in detail to me about this particular incident, its source was far more complex. In her attempt to get closer to her new friends, she had given some flowers to another girl in the group. The flowers had been growing wild around Sara's house so she picked them as she left home in an impulsive gesture. The girl had mentioned the day before that she liked flowers. When Sara arrived at school that day and presented them, the recipient was taken aback. "Why are you giving these to me?" she asked, apparently shocked and embarrassed. Sara guilelessly replied, "because you said you liked flowers."

After that Sara suddenly found herself ostracized from the group – people didn't speak to her and wouldn't sit with her. Too marginalized to ask why, she accepted her rejection stoically, at first simply feeling confused and alone. Finally, another girl from the group explained Sara's mistake. The present of the flowers had been taken, together with other facetious comments Sara had made, or remarks that had been interpreted out of context, to suggest that she was "coming on to the other girl."[24] In other words, she was being accused of being a lesbian. What Sara found difficult was not the inappropriate interpretation of her gesture but rather the complex and contradictory reaction to this; it was as if the social rules had suddenly been changed, or more accurately, that she had misinterpreted the "rules" that she believed she had understood and mastered. Her comments and actions had branded her as an outsider to the group again.

In its shared conversations and attitudes, the group had seemingly prided itself, in being *cool* about alternative sexualities, preferences and orientations. The school, as indicated earlier, encouraged tolerance and openness in all aspects of identity, and several girls in the school, even at that relatively early age, identified openly as lesbians, two even pairing off as partners. What had been discussed, gossiped about and expressed about *other* girls in terms of interesting speculation and acceptance of difference, was suddenly not deemed appropriate behavior for their own circle. Sara had unwittingly exposed a raw nerve – the assumed shared values and feelings of the group were suddenly not quite as fixed and immutable as they had believed.

Discussion: "Coolness" revisited

A number of aspects emerge from this overview of four girls in four different school groupings. Belonging to a friendship group deemed desirable meant accepting and striving toward specific goals and group norms. Remember that, in Hilary's school, the most coveted group reflected the middle-class adult values, with the friendships sanctioned and encouraged by significant adults, leisure activities taking place within the homes, and acceptance and tolerance of "soft" social drug-taking. The clothes worn by this group were of such a quality that the purchase required independent income or parental contribution. The group was perceived by outsiders as being physically attractive, judged according to a fashionable, commodified yardstick – the girls being skinny, blonde and confident and stylish in dress. Many of the parents were professional, two-income families, although not necessarily comprising two biological parents: many of the families were blended. While the female role models were professional women, to be accepted into the desirable social circles, to be regarded as sophisticated and mature, the girls had to be seen with a boyfriend.

Diane's world espoused different values and consequently, it was characterized by a different discourse of adolescence and femininity. Few of the significant adults in her world were professional. Most – when they *were* employed – were skilled or semiskilled work people. The women largely saw their role of mother, housewife and home-keeper as paramount. Youth unemployment and juvenile crime were prevalent; violence in and out of the home was openly talked about. The Cool Group in Diane's world were the Surfies – again, physically attractive young people whose worlds revolved around leisure rather than work. Establishing oneself as a young female adult again involved being "attached" to a male.

And what of Fran and Sara's group? Even in this feminist, more progressive and all-female world, femininity, particularly in relation to masculinity, was clearly circumscribed and defined. How is it these norms were so powerful and narrowly defined? What was the *process* that enabled the friendship groups to work and control so effectively? The first step to understanding this process is to reject the analytical frameworks that attempt to see adolescent lifestyles as totally separate entities from their familial backgrounds and values.

Critiquing subcultural theory

> *There has been a tendency in the most influential approaches to youth culture to concentrate on the youth cultural practices at the expense of the cultural context out of which the young people have come.* (Stratton 1993: 88)

To perceive that a connection exists between young people's social, class and cultural backgrounds and the particular friendship and youth subcultures they belong to, is not new. In earlier explorations of youth culture, Stanley Cohen (1980) noted that "these youth cultures, although located in forms of spectacular consumption are nevertheless not independent totalities but have a basis in traditional social practices" (cited in Stratton 1992: 21), a useful insight that has tended to be subsumed by subsequent studies and analyses of what are now understood as youth subcultures.

Observations and analyses of friendships and friendship groupings in previous studies of young people in Western industrialized countries are usually framed within subcultural theory. Within this paradigm, young people are seen to be self-consciously and symbolically expressing the difficulties and struggles of a dominant parent culture: in the academy in particular, this was seen in terms of a working-class struggle against the dominant culture that has marginalized and subordinated them. Patently and obviously failing at middle-class standards of steady employment, education and economic security, the young people were seen as expressing their discontent with the social injustice by embracing values and aesthetics clearly antithetical to middle-class mores. Such discontent was expressed frequently in riots (such as the notorious fights between Mods and Rockers on British beaches in the 1960s), aggression, risk-taking behavior, including sexual promiscuity, and other antisocial acts against the establishment, all of which were designed to create moral panics.

The problem of style

A great deal of the earlier research into youth was modelled on the Marxist ideology of alienation and class struggle. Style, image and violence were often seen as techniques of resistance to the dominant ideologies of the day. In this neo-Marxist paradigm, sample groups of "problem" young people, usually working-class and predominantly male, such as those in street gangs, were defined as a subculture, a discrete group adopting particular cultural codes, such as appearance, music and language, culturally separate and distinctive from the wider parent culture. In this framework too, the young people were analyzed separately from their familial backgrounds, often in quite simplistic ways.

> *Through this logic, a diverse group of individuals are transformed into and positioned as, a discrete identity, seemingly with specific codes of behaviour and ways of relating to the outside world.* (Tait 1993: 1)

Earlier insights, such as Stanley Cohen's (1980) as noted above, had pointed to the inherent links of youth culture and style to parent cultures:

> *... a given life style is actually made up of a number of symbolic subsystems, and it is the way in which these are articulated in the total life style that constitutes its distinctiveness.* (Cohen 1980: 83. Also cited in Stratton 1992)

However, this perception was overtaken by a focus on the so-called *spectacular* youth subcultures and their associated symbolic systems of meaning. Because these were seen as particularly working-class youth subcultures, researchers began to interpret youth subcultures as strategies of resistance, separate symbolic manifestations of class struggle (Hall & Jefferson 1976; Brake 1980; Hebdige 1979, 1988). As Jon Stratton comments about the research undertaken on youth culture at the Centre for Contemporary Cultural Studies: "the Birmingham Centre's work has recognised the working-class origins of most British youth cultures but has tended to ignore the cultural influences on those youth cultures which come from that working class background" (1993: 89). The high level of visibility of the groups, largely due to their particular style, whereby specific commodities, clothing, fashion, gait and argot were appropriated, led to their being termed "spectacular."

Because of the explosion of cheap commercial fashion outlets from the 1960s onwards, style rapidly became a particularly effective symbol for expressing perceived cultural distinctiveness. Fashion had taken to the streets in a way not experienced before. New technologies, new cheaper fabrics, new marketing strategies all opened up the possibilities of differently perceived demographics for the fashion market. The blossoming of the small boutique created the outlets that were controlled and run by the same age market as those who bought the clothes. Style was interpreted as image, which embraced appearance, clothes, accessories and hairstyle; demeanor, which involved physical deportment, gait, posture, and expression; and "argot" – a particular vocabulary and the way it is expressed (Brake 1980, 1985). These elements served to reinforce allegiances while also serving to distinguish one subculture from another, to differentiate the symbolic boundaries of one social group from another.

Finally, youth style has also been perceived to appropriate images, artifacts, and items from older contexts, recontextualizing them to symbolize something *other* (Hebdige 1979; Brake 1980, 1985). These new ways of meaning are forged through use of "bricolage" (Clarke 1976), a form of cultural collage that reinvents meaning by displacing or juxtaposing items and contexts. Thus the use of safety pins for body piercing by some groupings, elaborate tattoos, or the use of heavy industrial boots by some middle-class groups, not only recreates group identity and reinforces mutual recognition of members, but implies a connection between appearance and behavior. Within the context of this study, style is concerned with "posing," the self-conscious, reflexive appropriation of a new set of images blended with the usual everyday aspects of the individual's micro-culture. In Fran's video, one of her friends held a card up to the camera. "Fuck Fashion. *This is Style!*" read the postcard.

Thus, according to most of the traditional cultural studies literature relating to youth, those participating in a youth subculture were seen as resolutely rejecting middle-class mores and values. Teenage behavior, and especially adolescent group behavior, is perceived in this way, especially in popular discourse, a perception reinforced in tabloid media descriptions of "problem" teenagers.[25] Youth in Western culture is considered a time of rebellion, a period for challenging established adult values and seeking new identities that contest the standards and even traditional moral codes of the older generation. The analytical structure that underpins academic studies of youth frequently makes a number of assumptions from this older model. Firstly, there is the belief that generational consciousness is equivalent to, and also an expression of, class consciousness (Tait 1993). It follows in this argument that what young people appear to express through apparently alternative (life) styles, music and appearance (Hebdige 1976), is a dissatisfaction with and resistance to their social positioning in the subordinate class. Because young people are seen as lacking the means and the power to change their lot, they are understood in this framework to be expressing their discontent symbolically through the creation of an alternative, frequently disturbing culture that unsettles the complacency of the adult authorities.

While not disagreeing that social injustices are clearly evidenced by youth unemployment and youth patterns of behavior, and while the cultural studies model has provided some valuable insights, I would argue that this framework with its simplistic vision of power and social control also obscures a number of significant issues.

Adolescence as problem

Another undoubtedly related reason for the emergence of a distinctive set of behaviors during the teenage years may be attributable to adolescence becoming *defined* in the West as a period of biological change and disturbance, a period previously highlighted through the observance of significant cultural rituals. In other words, the argument itself was circular, self-prophesying and self-perpetuating. Because all cultures appear to symbolically acknowledge the transference from child to adult and sexual responsibilities, the teenage years in our society have been understood to be a time of rebellion, challenge and resistance against wider adult norms. Recent Australian studies have also drawn on this theoretical framework (Cunneen et al. 1989; Carrington 1989; Stratton 1992).

Yet, in practice, can this understanding of adolescence be applied hegemonically to experiences of youth across differently nuanced social and ethnic groups?[26] Further, is its application to girls' experiences appropriate? As indicated in previous chapters, Barbara Hudson (1984) argued that teenage girls have to contend with and negotiate two contradictory public discourses – one of femininity and one of adolescence. These two discourses provide the framework through which the behavior of teenage girls is judged and articulated in both professional and public forms. Hudson's main contention is that the discourse of femininity and that of adolescence are antithetical and subvert one another.

Adolescence is well documented as a "masculine" construct (the spectacular subcultures noted above have been described as being concerned with masculine identities). The dominant image in literature and the media – scientific/academic as well as popular/fictional accounts – describes a restless youth, one who is immature, a trouble-maker, a searcher for identity and one who is struggling to test his new physical powers and emotional awareness.

> *If adolescence is characterised by male constructs, then any attempt by girls to satisfy themselves* qua *adolescence, are bound to involve them in displaying not only lack of maturity (since adolescence is dichotomised with maturity), but also lack of femininity. Thus the girl playing a lot of sport is doing something which is still conceived of as essentially masculine.*

> *Girls playing football, for instance are often afforded headlines in the popular press such as "playing the boys at their own game"; girls displaying competitiveness, or "adolescent" aggression, will be displaying qualities thought of as masculine.* (Hudson 1984: 35)

Hudson contends that the discourses of both adolescence and femininity have a professional form (articulated through teachers, social workers, doctors and other adults in authority), and that these versions then become available to the girls in their public form as sets of stereotypical images of adolescence and femininity through the media, for example, teenage magazines. The result is a barrage of generalized statements from adult society directed toward female teenage appearance and behavior.

> *They experience the fact of being judged by two, incongruent sets of expectations as the feeling that whatever they do, it is always wrong.* (Hudson 1984: 53)

A more complex way of understanding circulating discourses of gender and class has been explored in the work of Beverley Skeggs. She points out that "difference is usually theorised through historical descriptions and 'read off' categories already constituted. It is rarely understood through theoretical categories which analyse *processes* of differentiation" (Skeggs 1997: 20). In other words, neither femininity, masculinity, ethnicity nor class can be taken as given categories. The terms are constantly being renegotiated as aspects of cultural capital.

> *Femininity, for instance, can be seen as a form of cultural capital. It is the discursive position available through gender relations that women are encouraged to inhabit and use. Its use will be informed by the network of social positions of class, gender, sexuality, region, age and race which ensure that it will be taken up (and resisted) in different ways.* (Skeggs 1997: 10)

Friendship groups

The discourses of femininity and adolescence therefore can be seen to circulate in a very particular way through the teenage friendship groups themselves. It is only because youth groupings are viewed as separate units and, in their most extreme forms, as spectacular youth subcultures, that the continuous link between youth behaviour, styles, and values and their parent cultures, has been overlooked.

In the context of this study, the subcultural model of teenage groups is particularly flawed when applied to young women's experiences, a fact long and extensively argued by feminist writers. This critique originally concentrated on the lack of awareness of gender issues in the studies of youth subcultures, arguing that the romanticization of masculine style and image that celebrated working-class "resistance" concealed the problem of the ongoing subordination of the young women in the groups and in the families of the boys. Firstly, and most importantly, it was noted that it was not necessarily logical to assume a separation between the cultures of the parents and the cultures of the teenagers; indeed, there is an inbuilt contradiction in talking about a youth working-class *sub*culture. The term assumes that the young people are challenging parental values while simultaneously being embedded within them.

Thus, in spite of what appears at first sight to be a unifying, distinctive style, youth social groupings were not – and are not – discrete units. It goes without saying that the clothes, the hairstyles, the music are sourced and appropriated from the wider community and often from international markets. Furthermore, teenagers who are part of a street gang or what has been defined as a subculture, also have homes or are affiliated with a family/adult unit. They have simultaneous life experiences in a number of intersecting social spheres, not just one. I argue here, then, that it is not a simple matter of the young person absorbing or contesting the dominant values of their society. Rather, within each (experiential) community, the significant adults value and stress some aspects of the larger culture and downplay others – their values influenced perhaps, by the interplay of ethnicity, social background, economics and religion.

Affiliation and identification occur within and through a number of social contexts simultaneously, and in fact it is far more helpful to consider individuals as *continuously* negotiating allegiances in ways that render emotional investment far more complex than theories of class and ethnicity normally imply. Subjectivity operates dialogically; that is, it constantly shifts between reflection, recognition and production through *representations* of self and other. In describing the young women in her study, Skeggs also points out that: "their subjectivity is not part of the discourse of individualism; rather, it is part of a discourse of dialogism and connection" (1997: 164).

The growing child, and certainly the teenager, accept, challenge and negotiate these aspects of culture as they meet other facets, views and ideologies in the wider world outside the home and as they become more widely enculturated. However, enculturation is an ongoing process, where the individual readjusts her cognitive map *to fit in* with the familial and local community background. One way to understand this is to see friendship groups and groupings as part of a much wider social network and not as a separate phenomenon.

Finally, in linking the moral and social hierarchies in the teenage friendship groups to the wider familial and social networks, I argue that such an approach challenges our understanding of teenage subcultures and sees the groupings more constructively as partial networks. Analytical frameworks, which generalize in terms of class or gender, are inevitably limited because they cannot adequately demonstrate the diversity *within* groups that are frequently perceived, even by the participants, to be convergent. Rather, it is important to see that subjectivity is constituted through a constant ongoing dialogical process. In the next chapter, I will discuss some of the ways the constitution of those subjectivities within experiential communities were effected. I will demonstrate more fully how meaning assumed to be shared, was negotiated and contested, particularly through the argots of music, language, and gossip. Ultimately these aspects of symbolic capital, tied into local parent cultures and international/global markets, formed the foundations of the serious play of the teenage girls in my fieldwork. It is these paradoxical layers of the micro/macro, local/global (gendered) self that I now explore.

Notes

1 This has interesting parallels with observations in Schneider's work on American family and kinship (1968), particularly his discussions on individuals who are not biological family members but who are treated as one within the family unit.

2 This is of course one of the reasons why toilets are particularly important in female social groupings. It is a place for gossip – a place that allows and encourages intimacy and confidences to be shared.

3 This is not to say in contemporary Australia, at least on the surface, that girls are necessarily underachieving academically. Over the last few years girls are achieving higher grades at matriculation level than boys – leading to renewed concerns about boys' academic achievements. However, a closer look at the choice of subjects and future careers the girls select indicates they are still tending to choose areas that emphasize "traditional" female skills of communication and nurturing over more prestigious future paths.

4 The term "hidden" or "unwritten" curriculum was an extremely common expression in circulation when I undertook my teacher training over twenty years ago. It referred to the often subliminal or subconscious messages students learned that had nothing to do with the official content of the lesson. Some of these "lessons" were acquired through the teaching styles of the teacher but far more were gained through the interactions and the power struggles of the students themselves. The term of course is applicable not only to formal education. It can refer to many social situations where the participants learned the tacit social rules as opposed to the formal structural rules that are articulated. My interest and application here is in exploring why and how these social rules or understandings

underpin the social groupings formed within a school and how they relate to wider social contexts.

5 As indicated in earlier chapters, Hilary was clearly an undisputed choice for school captain. She was reliable, hardworking, bright and suitably conformist. Claire also became school captain in her school but hers was a less straightforward choice as far as the teaching staff were concerned. Although she showed determination, ambition and public spirit, she had proved herself less clearly academically able. It was probably her undisputable prowess in the arena of sport that allowed her to be granted the most prestigious title in the student community.

6 See Bott 1971 for her distinction between personal values and perceived local community values. This distinction helps to clarify how "shared meanings" come to seem more uniform than they are and also points to the processes of negotiated meanings.

7 At the time of my fieldwork "paid out" meant, at one end of the spectrum, to be teased. At its most extreme it meant to be totally derided and humiliated. Usually, unless they were giving me a particularly devastating example, the girls were suggesting something in between.

8 When I first started to teach at a girls' high school in Adelaide I was struck by the way the girls in that particular school sat in closed "neat" circles dotted over the school concreted areas. It was rather like seeing a particular pattern of a ritual that hadn't been explained to me yet.

9 This is an interesting aspect of the phenomenon of the social groupings that is often overlooked. It is very important for the Cool Group to simultaneously stress its superiority and its normality. Therefore it has to be large enough to appear to portray the yardstick for "normal" and desirable behavior, but small enough to indicate that the membership is still exclusive.

10 See earlier discussions of the epithet "cool" in chapter 2.

11 Again it is important to keep in mind that the criteria of membership to the Cool Group differed from institution to institution according to the most valued attributes and values of the parent cultures of that school.

12 Because of its great popularity, students had to live within the zoned area in order to gain entry. Others could also apply for a music scholarship or could sometimes enter by direct appeal to the principal.

13 An old advertisement for a nonalcoholic beverage was popular some years ago. The slogan ran "Clayton's, the drink for when you're not a having a drink." The epithet "Clayton's" then started to mean pretence or surrogacy in popular discourse.

14 During conversations with administrators and teachers from this school, the staff spoke about the school population as though a large number of the children in the school were from affluent homes. This was in stark contrast to the statistical information available on the school area provided by the local council.

15 Several teachers told me the families of children who came from that area had "too much money." See below for a further explanation of this.

16 Information provided by the school counsellor.

17 One of the school counsellors told me that on "civvies" day (days when the children could come to school out of school uniform usually for a small fee donated to charity) some children came to school wearing shoes known to cost over two hundred dollars. I learned that other children, shamed by their inability to compete, stayed away, their parents conceding it was better to stay at home on such occasions.

18 The number was 134 children out of a total school population of 923 in 1994.

19 This is an interesting insight about the role of talk or gossip in female culture – not as something that is trivial but something that indicates maturity.

20 Note how she sees herself here right on the margins of this senior high school campus. The dominant value system of the school doesn't seem to apply to her.

21 At the start of my fieldwork there were three such government high schools in South Australia but during the time of my project one was closed by the state government, due to lack of numbers. This school was certainly the only one that attracted a more educated and middle-class clientele.

22 The information booklet informs prospective parents that it "caters for *all* girls wishing to have single-sex education. Students travel from as far away as Gawler and Strathalbyn. Many students travel by privately chartered buses from the southern suburbs; others travel from the hills and surrounding suburbs by train or bus" (emphasis in the original).

23 This belief about appropriate behavior and the following story were related to me by Sara a few months later when she started to talk about her experience in the group.

24 For example, on one occasion when one girl made a comment about sexual orientation meant to be a joke, which was common in the group, Sara added a further remark thinking she was compounding the humor. Inadvertently she stepped over an invisible boundary about who can say what to whom within the group.

25 Many print media articles still depict young people in this way. See "Children the Cause of Many Family Splits," Adelaide *Advertiser* 10 December 1994 p. 9; "Lost Generation" *The Weekend Australian* 2–3 September 1995, p. 28. When not depicted as victims, teenagers are frequently represented in the print and electronic media as trouble and disturbance.

26 In fact, there has been a great deal of recent work exploring the experiences of youth from a variety of cultural backgrounds. See for example, Griffin 1993; Amit-Talai & Wulff 1995; Stokes 1994.21. The effect of these arbitrary boundaries, these markers of "legitimate" uses of space, is to raise the stakes for the game itself; "everything that makes the field itself, the game, the stakes, all the presuppositions that one tacitly and even unwittingly accepts by the mere act of playing, of entering the game. Those who take part in the struggle help to reproduce the game by helping . . . to produce belief in the value of the stakes" (Bourdieu 1993, 74). I am arguing that in this case, the game itself is the way all the girls in my research project have learned over time to constitute their sense of self within their own specific micro-cultures, in diverse, overlapping social fields. To return to the particularly apt geographical metaphor, it is about the way they have learned very early on, to know their "*place* in the world." It is the basis of their "self-making" that becomes tested, negotiated and ultimately affirmed in the act of playing, and who they are, how they see themselves, is directly linked to how they feel they can use and *be* in different social and geographical spaces.

Chapter 6

"Music is in My Soul"

> It follows that an identity is always already an ideal, what we would like to be, not what we are . . . And what makes music special in this familiar cultural process is that musical identity is both fantastic – idealising not just oneself but also the social world one inhabits – and real; it is enacted in activity . . . music gives us a real experience of what the ideal could be. (Simon Frith 1996: 274)

Gerry	*Is music important to you when you are not playing in the band?*
Wanda	*Yeah. I always listen to music because music is in my soul.*

Introduction: Why music matters

In the previous chapter I argued that the girls' school social groupings were linked to their extramural leisure activities and their wider social networks. Further, each teenager, while engaged in the serious play of self-making, struggled to maintain the quite rigid symbolic boundaries between one social grouping and another. The necessary "art of being cool" was extremely hard work! This chapter is concerned with the nexus between those social groupings and networks, self-making and a particular cultural form. By uniting the thematic threads of play and mimesis described in the previous chapters, this chapter highlights the significance of popular music in the everyday lives of the young women in my research. Wanda's passionate comment, recorded above, points to this significance. This reply was given so seriously and unselfconsciously that I was taken aback. I wasn't prepared for the way this worldly, vivacious and somewhat self-mocking Aboriginal teenager spoke about her love of music in such personal and spiritual terms. It confirmed for me, yet again, how much music is bound up in the way cultural identities are constituted and represented.

From the earliest period of my fieldwork to the final postproduction edits of the teenagers' composite documentary, I became aware of how vital popular music was to the girls' rhetoric of "self-making.". The participants in my project revealed the centrality of popular music in their lives – through their first discussions with me, in their casual conversations with their friends, in the way they dressed and decorated their rooms, in the ways in which they "carved out" and appropriated private spaces, in their music-making and in their music consumption and indeed, in *all* their social activities. As Simon Frith suggests in the citation that heads this chapter, music, because it is an effective vehicle for establishing and sustaining an idealized identity, is profoundly important in their lives. Moreover, that identity, which depends upon shades of difference within the similarities to express a sense of individuality, is perfectly expressed through music. These were girls of approximately the same age, living in the same city, sometimes attending the same school and undertaking similar leisure activities, but they were not from exactly the same social and ethnic backgrounds. Significantly, their musical "tastes" and musical activities highlighted and maintained these differences, to emphasize both distinction (Bourdieu 1984) and *différance* (Derrida 1978).

Previously, I have drawn attention to the powerful and serious role of play in the lives of the young women in my fieldwork. I argued that play is hard work because it is the basis for the constitution and representation of the "real me" or the "authentic" self, that shadowy, slippery concept that eludes definition and closure. On the surface, especially in the late 1990s in postindustrial societies, the authentic "self" seems even harder to pin down since it has become impossibly fragmented. Former social categories and symbolic boundaries through which we attempted to define ourselves to ourselves and to others, have become suspect; ethnicity, gender and class all seem less stable in a world where communications, customs and allegiances are constantly shifting.[1] In the midst of this sea change, one of the ways people attempt to demonstrate who they are is through their loyalty to particular social groupings, through their clothes, their demeanor, their argot, their activities, their music, and their style. Polhemus suggests that: "we are, as our most distant ancestors were, dependent on style – in our dress and our dance – as the definitive means by which we can crystallize our social experiences into cultural realities" (Polhemus 1993: 14). Yet, perhaps inevitably, the symbols themselves, appropriated to express those social realities, have also become fragmented. Indeed, it has been argued that today's youth, frequently "jumbling geography as well as history" in fashion, dance and music, often attempt to express that idealized self, in a "supermarket of style" (Polhemus 1997: 150).

However, that resulting mosaic or *bricolage* of style and symbol does not mean that the search is any less serious. In fact, despite the association with trivia, with "a sort of street-style theme park" (Polhemus 1997: 149), young people's expressions of cultural identities through fashion, style, dress and dance could be considered particularly important and serious *because* they represent attempts to embody a stable, "authentic" sense of self *despite* the shifting, segmented cultural contexts. Again to cite Paul Willis, "symbolic creativity is not only part of everyday human activity, but also a . . . part of *necessary work*" (1990: 9, emphasis in the original). Willis identifies three interrelated elements of "necessary symbolic work" – language, bodily praxis and drama – that underlie symbolic creativity. These aspects of self-making are discussed in this chapter in relation to the young girls' engagement with popular music, for "it is symbolic work and creativity which realise the structured collectivity of individuals as well as their differences, which realise the materiality of context as well as the symbolism of self" (Willis 1990: 12).

The magic of music

Music is a fundamental element of all cultures. Making and using music are essential components of human life (Storr 1992). In relation to my own research, Belinda expressed a parallel insight, declaring dramatically that "Music is *everything*." Her words point to the need to explore ways in which music is so vitally important to cultural identities, indeed why it *seems* that "Music is *everything*." During this process, many of the dichotomies often assumed about popular music's "essential nature" and significance will be overturned: this investigation will demonstrate from the outset that particular forms of pop and rock music are neither potentially progressive nor exploitative; that they are neither simply trivial nor politically potent; that they are neither solely a vehicle for resistance nor appropriation. Furthermore, music is not simply something that does little more than "fill a silence left by something else" (Stokes 1994: 2). The musical allegiances and expressions of fandom of my teenage participants were further manifestations of the hard work of play: music informed their sense of space, their relationship to their idealized selves and, by its very plasticity, allowed for a dialogic engagement with others. It was indeed the major vehicle for serious play, mimetic exploration and mimetic excess in their everyday lives.

In his writings on music and trance Gilbert Rouget has defined music "in its most empirical and broadest sense" as "any sonic event . . . that cannot be reduced to language . . . since we then have to speak of words, not music – and that [which] displays a certain degree of rhythmic or melodic organisation . . . not treated here as an art but as a practice displaying the greatest possible variety of aspects" (Rouget 1985: 63).[2] Rouget discusses the use of music in non-Western religious rituals in relation to trance-like or ecstasy-induced states. Yet, many of his insights and observations can just as readily be applied to the young women in my research project in their engagement with popular Western musical forms and genres. They also used music as an essential part of their bodily praxis to establish symbolic boundaries between self and other. Music clearly plays as central a part of modern, (post)industrialized 1990s life in Australia, as it did in the societies and cultures that Rouget investigated.

It is important to realize that much of the pleasure and power of music is that it produces emotions and affective states of mind. In other words, music seems to have the ability to affect the body at an unconscious level before any other, more intellectual awareness has been reached (Levi-Strauss 1972; Willis 1990). Furthermore, recent research suggests that the affective qualities of music are universal. That is, despite commonsense and academic assumptions that musical aesthetics are culturally specific, one of the most interesting aspects of current musicological research has been to point to the way certain pieces of music can arouse similar kinds of emotional states in the listeners without the listeners knowing a great deal about the context of the music or its original purpose (Storr 1992: 24). Indeed, there are aspects of music that seem to be common to all cultures, even when they are not familiar with the type of music and its usual social context (Storr 1992; Blacking 1976, 1987). Of course, not all states of arousal by music are equally pleasant: they can be disturbing emotions such as intense grief, fear, rage, or sexual excitement or they can be gentler emotions that induce peace, sleep or relaxation. The point is that *all* music invokes some emotional reaction in the listener and this emotional arousal manifests itself in various physiological changes (Harrer & Harrer 1977).

Certainly for younger people in contemporary Australian society, existing simultaneously in a local and a global cultural postindustrial context, music permeates and shapes everyday experiences. It is, in fact, *the* defining social context and often the "social *glue*" through which teenagers in particular, study, shop, relax, communicate and socialize. Particular music is used to define specific experiential cultures and social groupings, even when to an outsider, of course, the same music seems common to several groupings. In fact it is the arbitrary nature of the symbolism of a particular piece of music, the connection between the signifier and its particular referent, that points to another vitally important aspect of music; that is, its ability to blur cultural boundaries and move beyond historical time and space. Storr points out the ironic ease with which the same tune, "God Save the Queen" – the British national anthem, is used in the Unites States for "My Country, 'tis of Thee." Similarly, the Christian hymn "Abide With Me" is often played at football matches for its emotional and spiritual power without the singers feeling that they have to subscribe to Christian beliefs or even perhaps knowing that the music originally indicated such values (Storr 1992: 22). It is now common practice for advertisers to appropriate particular songs associated with original ideologies of rock music – freedom, rebellion, youthful exuberance, antimaterialism – and to reassociate them with commodities from multinationals, such as denim jeans, Coca Cola and cigarettes. This is only possible because of the arbitrary nature of the sign, underscoring my observations that, despite the insistence on identifiable differences and distinctions between the diverse teenage social groupings by insiders, the same music was often appropriated by different groups for their own use.

The fluid nature of music lends itself to easy appropriation by different groups for diverse purposes. The way the teenagers in my project talked about and demonstrated their allegiances to "their" kind of music points to the way specific music genres and styles become commonly associated with groupings, whether these are teenage subcultures, sporting affiliations, or wider national cultures.

> *Particular pieces of music continue to be associated with particular societies and come to represent them in the same way as a national flag. "They are playing our tune" is a phrase which can have a much wider significance than our habitual reference of it to the courtship memories of a mated couple.* (Storr 1992: 22)

Storr's words remind us here of the mnemonic power of music, still very much used in contemporary societies. The rhymes and the repeated rhythms are an invaluable aid to memory and could explain another aspect of musical pleasure, its nostalgic quality. Birthdays, anniversaries, and ritual events are almost always associated with particular pieces or forms of music. It habitually accompanies religious ceremonies and other rituals and has a collective importance in many cultures, underpinning and linking so many disparate activities so that sometimes, as in ancient Greece: "there is no separate word for music as such" (Storr 1992: 17; see also, Middleton 1990; Shepherd & Wicke 1997).

In the context of the teenagers I met in my fieldwork, their definition of self was often informed by their music allegiances, allegiances expressed in the way they spoke about their favorite musicians, singers and bands, how and where they danced or listened to these musical styles and the activities they engaged in while listening to their favorite music. From all of these aspects of their engagement with music emerged their idealized selves, seemingly temporally "crystallized" at that moment, simultaneously both "fantastic" and "real" – "a real experience of what the ideal could be" (Frith 1996: 274).

Music and cultural identity

Music is central to both the materiality of social context and the symbolism of the self for a number of related reasons. Firstly, music is universally tied tightly into concepts of cultural identity and community. Musical appreciation, the critical and aesthetic response, is one part of the whole experience of music for "music gives us a way of being in the world . . . music doesn't represent values but lives them" (Frith 1996: 272). These values, however, are broader than those of the immediate social groupings, being integral components of much larger aspects of culture. For example, although rock and pop are commonly perceived as being particularly *teenage* music, for the young people themselves this music enables a particular pathway to enable them to link into broader *adult* cultural activities. It allows them "to situate themselves historically, culturally and politically in a much more complex system of symbolic meaning than is available locally" (Frith 1992: 77). So, rather than seeing such associations as *sub*cultural and by definition, *oppositional* to adult values, I argue that youth affiliations are very much *micro*cultural, simply aged, gendered and ethnically nuanced perspectives and distillations of their larger parent cultures.

Secondly, and perhaps by way of contradiction, music is an intensely personal bodily experience, "a subjective sense of being sociable." As our senses engage in song, dance, and performance "we absorb songs into our own lives and rhythm into our own bodies"

(Frith 1996: 273). Music is powerful because it brings together both the experience of the intensely subjective and personal with the external, cultural and collective.

> *Music is concerned with feelings which are primarily individual and rooted in the body, its structural and sensuous elements resonate more with individuals' cognitive and emotional sets than with their cultural sentiments, although its external manner and expression are rooted in historical circumstances.* (Blacking 1987: 129)

The physicality that can be expressed through music is not simply through dance, although that is clearly one of its most common manifestations.[3] In the processes of musical production and consumption – listening, singing, instrument playing or dance – the body becomes not only a way of experiencing but also a way of *knowing,* a "site of somatic knowledge" (Willis 1990: 11). A similar concept is developed in Bourdieu's notion of *cultural* and *symbolic* capital. He argues that what is manifested as "taste" is also, in fact, *physical* capital; not just an intellectual way of asserting who one is, but also a way of asserting *authenticity,* constituting and "proving" who one is or who one would like to be, through bodily praxis. So for example, the guests at a Greek wedding I attended, who took to the dance floor to perform a solemn rendition of a stylizsed national dance, seemed to be saying to others around them through their dance – "see I can do this. I am authentically Greek."[4] Similarly, as discussed in an earlier chapter, Diane and Bekk asserted *their* particular differences and distinctions from the boys and from each other by the way they moved and behaved and by their physical manner. Mary's demeanor, assertiveness, dress, and hairstyle indicated to others that she was strong, tough, streetwise and proudly from Papua New Guinea. Her preferred choice of music – Reggae – like that of the Aboriginal girls, indicated her affinity with a proud, assertive transcultural "black culture."

Referring to the indigenous South African band Ladysmith Black Mambazo (particularly popularized overseas after their musical collaboration with Paul Simon on *The Graceland* album), Timothy Taylor (1997) also perceives the same creation of experiential and affective cultural communities. He argues that "wider spread commodification of musical forms allows distant solidarities to be fashioned, even 'across the ocean'" (76). Similarly, examples in Philip Hayward's collection of essays in *Sound Alliances* point to the cultural complexities of musical appropriation. For example, John Castles writes of the Australian indigenous band No Fixed Address, "embracing Reggae as an expression of solidarity with black people everywhere" (1998: 16) and Stuart Ewings argues "Reggae doesn't sound like rock, it's not usually laced with country and western sentiment, nor does it sound like rockabilly – CS (Coloured Stone) do" (1989: 12, cited in Castles 1998: 15–16).

But if music is concerned with the boundaries of the local, material body, it is also concerned with the "out of body," the blurring of historical and geographical boundaries. Music transcends the local to be in several places at the same time, simultaneously *transforming* physical and social space; it becomes a way of appropriating and distinguishing space. Undoubtedly, on one level, that is why music is so central to most religious rituals in all cultures. It explains the ways the music of one culture can be appropriated by another to express a powerful political affinity. On another level, it explains the ubiquitous popularity of radios, the Walkman and personal radio, tape and CD players in contemporary life (Hosokawa 1984; Thornton 1995). As each new technology develops, new ways of producing, consuming and marketing music produce marked effects on the *meanings* understood to emanate from all of its forms, one of the first issues to emerge being the authenticity of the particular style and its attendant cultural forms and meanings.

The technologized self

The advent of electronic media and new technologies has other implications for concepts of musical authenticity and therefore also the perceived "authenticity" of the performer and consumer of that music. It means that the performance and consumption of music can be undertaken far from the original place of origin and endlessly repeated. As Jody Berland reminds us: "Music is now heard mainly in technologically communicated form, not live, and its circulation through these spaces (in connection with that of its listeners), along with its assimilation to and appropriation of previous contexts for musical performance, is part of the elaboration of its forms and meanings" (Berland 1992: 39; also see Rosing 1984: 119–49). Music, in other words, has become completely mobile, moving with us from room to room, country to country, from work to leisure. It can also move us emotionally, as from depression to elation.

In these ways, contemporary practices of engaging with music particularly through new technologies, through ever-evolving "mimetic machinery" (Taussig 1993: 20), can blur our sense of time and space. Music connects the private experience with the public. It blurs the self and other; the song I listen to expresses *my* feelings even though I did not write it. When I perform someone else's music, I express their feelings although I am a different person. So music is indeed a powerful, "magical" vehicle of mimesis.[5]

In Sarah Thornton's (1995) study of British club cultures she states that "the cultural form closest to the lives of the majority of British youth is in fact music. Youth subcultures tend to be music subcultures" (19). In my own research, I discovered a similarly perceived centrality of music. Obviously, while Belinda's declaration, cited above, is an exaggeration (for music cannot *literally* be everything), yet such a comment does signal the ways the perceived ubiquitous nature of music is used by many people as a metaphor. It takes the form of symbolic capital in a variety of arenas to represent different aspects of everyday practice, knowledge and experience. It is a way, for young people particularly, of situating themselves within wider cultural contexts.

However, these cultural contexts have become even more complex with the advent of new ways of performing, producing and listening to music. New technologies, for example have brought about particular changes in the way we *engage* with music. The music we hear is affected by the choices we make on the turntable, the dial, or the mixer. In the dance clubs and rave scenes, the DJ and MC who skillfully mix and sample the pre-recorded sounds to create new music have become the revered artists of the 1990s. As the advent of the VCR affected television watching, so also have the CD players and burners, the Walkman and the computer terminals affected music audiences. Consumers can now produce, rearrange and recreate the kind of music they listen to. The lines between consumption and production, between the original and the copy, become blurred. In other words, like those ephemeral self-identities that we struggle to "fix," music itself has become a *process* of becoming, something we now experience as fragmented and unstable (Hosokawa 1990; Berland 1992).[6]

Such examples point to the connection between ongoing, popular concepts of "self" and musical authenticity, the nexus between the "real" and representation in the enormity (some would say the impossibility) of the search for "the real me." Walter Benjamin (1969) had believed that in "the age of mechanical reproduction" uniqueness or "aura" would cease to be considered the most important quality of a work of art. New technologies, he hoped, would bring about a new democratization of cultural goods. Yet, as he suspected, the desire for uniqueness would be difficult to dismiss and indeed, the magical "aura" has not disappeared with the diffusing of what was previously thought of as high culture. It hasn't even been demystified but has disseminated and dispersed into other cultural forms (Thornton 1995). Now the "authentic" has switched from the original to the copy. For example, the new technological methods of producing music from the 1970s meant that original music was created in the studio not on the stage: the authentic was the recorded. Furthermore, more importantly for my purposes and as discussed in earlier chapters, Benjamin also saw the advent of technology bringing about the rebirth of the mimetic faculty. As Taussig described this: "the nature that culture uses to create a second nature, the faculty to copy, imitate, make models, explore difference, yield into and become Other" (Taussig 1993: xiii).

These two related notions, the power of the mimetic faculty and the dissemination of "the aura," lead us to an explication of the concept of musical authenticity, perhaps the most fundamental aspect of musical meaning with its embeddedness in the rhetorics of self-making. This highly debated and complex concept is probably the most important issue emerging from the discourses of popular music. It permeates discussions of Western popular music, fandom, fanzines and dance clubs because, ultimately it is concerned with the expression of the individual vision, the individual self, the "real me" that is seen simultaneously to be part of a particular cultural perspective.[7] Indeed, popular music for most of the young women in my research project seemed to be valued above everything else for its capacity to underpin the concept of musical authenticity and the individual self.[8]

I argue of course, as I have throughout this book, that experimentation in self-making, the search for authenticity, occurs through play. Further, that the aim of play is to find the comfortable degree of "fit" and accommodation, a pushing of the symbolic boundaries of "otherness" while still allowing "a sense of the game" (Bourdieu 1977, 1990). In following sections we will see again the close connection between the teenagers' self-making, the musical styles and forms they employed and their wider social networks. Here again we will see how the girls negotiated "space to play" both within and outside the domestic realm but with an emphasis on the role of music in that process.

Desperately seeking authenticity: Music and bodily praxis

> *Music constructs our sense of identity through the direct experiences it offers of the body, time and sociability, experiences which enable us to place ourselves in imaginary cultural narratives.* (Frith 1996: 124)

The occasion I am about to describe was one of the clearest demonstrations I had witnessed of the sheer potential power of dance and music to place the individual in an "imaginary cultural narrative."

The episode took place during my fieldwork spent at the Blue Light discos. Wendy, one of the young police constables on duty that night, pointed out a young girl whom she said had been "acting strangely." Addressed by adults and teenagers alike as JD, this young teenager, probably aged thirteen, was also identified by the police as a "troublemaker." I looked carefully and with a new respect at this petite, young woman who, at first sight, seemed far too small and insipid to have such an awesome reputation. Wendy soon discovered that JD was "*illicitly* attending the dance" that night, in that she had absconded from a correctional services' halfway house just to attend the disco.[9] By the time the police realized who she was, they felt it was too late to send her back and allowed her to stay until the end of the evening. When not on the dance floor or chatting in the toilets, JD and her friends stood just outside the main door talking to the young *male* offenders who had not been permitted to attend that week. Apparently, they hadn't been as wily as JD to get in unidentified.

What JD lacked in physical size, she apparently made up for in personality and sheer dynamism: she seemed to be a tiny bottle of energy just waiting to explode, rarely standing still, even in the confined space of the women's toilets. Even when Wendy challenged her about her attendance at the disco, JD stood swaying slightly, eyes half-closed, as though her energy was just simmering under the surface of a temporarily quiescent body. After the brief discussion with JD and dismissing her with an impatient shrug, the policewoman turned to me. "Did you see how she was swaying?" she asked crossly. I nodded. "She wasn't *really* drunk or stoned," she said, both in frustration and with a resigned smile. "She does it for attention. It's all for attention."

However, JD's behavior was not designed to attract the attention of the police or other authority figures, but rather that of the boys at the dance through a very dramatic display of self. At one point she appeared by my side while I was talking to her friend Emma. Without ceremony and ignoring me, she grabbed Emma's arm. "Quick come in," she urged, "Jessica's getting all the heap cool guys. There'll be no heap cool guys for us to get off with." She then dragged Emma back into the dance area.[10] It was there that she suddenly executed a most astounding display of dancing.

The song being played was "The Time Warp," a popular track from *The Rocky Horror Picture Show.* It was a dance that people usually conducted in unison, most participants knowing the steps. However, in the middle of this formality, JD danced flamboyantly and idiosyncratically. A space cleared around her as others stopped to stare and admire. JD's dance was an exaggerated parody of the usual steps and movements but here was also something splendid! This tiny figure suddenly became an extravagant expression of uninhibited movement, the epitome of mimetic excess! JD was presenting her admirers with an extraordinary performance in which she made explicit her sense of her own freedom, despite (or perhaps because of) the fact that she would shortly be returned to the juvenile detention center. This hardly represented an attempt to escape the notice of the authorities. The underlying paradox was that her expression of authenticity and individual personhood was expressed through a particularly self-conscious and stylized *representation* of freedom. The movement had to indicate to all around her that *this* was freedom! *This* was uninhibited movement. Its deliberate self-consciousness rendered it a particularly fine example of mimetic excess.

Music and other bodies

JD's display offers an extreme example, in the way Bekk's performance, described in chapter 2, had also been excessive. Yet it brings to mind many other examples throughout my fieldwork of the way music was used by the teenagers to explore, to underpin, and to experiment with the very physicality of their self-making. I noted in chapter 2, how Bekk had made links between her own behavior and "Madonna's great body" and how she had argued that Madonna "stood up for what she believed in." I described elsewhere how Grace had danced silently and alone in front of the video camera, watching and recording herself dancing to her favorite band; how Diane and her friends exaggeratedly mimicked the movements of the models and dancers on the Peter André video as they danced and postured in front of Diane's television set. While it is easy to overlook the significance and the wider implications of such play, behind the obvious fun and pleasure lie very purposeful reflections, explorations and (self) creativity: "The imaginative is self-validating!" (Willis 1990: 10).

In terms of musical taste, the "imaginative," expressed through creativity and "distinctions" (Bourdieu 1984), points to more than intellectual and conscious choice. It points to the way claims to cultural and symbolic capital are necessarily embodied. In his influential article on the power of music, Barthes described the direct communication between singer or musician and listener by describing it in terms of the "grain of the voice" (1977: 179–89). That is, the evocation of pleasure and desire through music is not purely a conscious intellectual practice but involves the unconscious grittiness of physicality. In spite of his apparent reluctance to talk about music, when pressed, Bourdieu described it as follows:

> *Music is a "bodily thing". It ravishes, moves, stirs, carries away: it is not so much beyond words as below them, in movements of the limbs and body, rhythms, excitements and slowings, tensions and releases. The most "mystical", the most "spiritual" of the arts is perhaps simply the most corporeal.* (1993: 103)

Through their bodies individuals experience and claim as their own, a sensation of being (appropriately) other. "Appropriately" because such a claim and adherence must reflect and help constitute the self within a framework that one already accepts for oneself. Diane, for example, in her attachment to Peter André or to New Kids on the Block ("I'm a *really* big fan of theirs") is creating the sensation of bathing in the glow of a romantic (heterosexual) ideal. In her situation, with her particular style of music, the romantic lyrics and the overt "maleness" of the stars are particularly important. In her video footage, for example, she suddenly interrupted her own flow of direct address to the camera to listen more closely to the music she had been playing in the background.

> *I'll leave you with this song* Dream a Little *by Peter André* (eyes closed for a moment in an extravagant gesture of immense pleasure). *It is such a beautiful, beautiful song.* (Diane, direct to camera)

In the same way she had previously indicated that her choice of popular brand-named clothes pointed to her knowledge of fashion and taste ("I can hold my head up"), so her selection of music here indicates her knowledge of and embeddedness in discourses of romance and heterosexual love. In contrast, Fran's declared choice of popular music allowed her a different kind of knowledge. *Her* exaggerated dance movements and her accompanying raunchy language ("Hey, everyone, look at M! She's fucking a pole") described in chapter 2, indicated her worldliness and her casual sexual knowledge. In terms of her sound track, she was the only one of the girls to use original music from the guitar of her boyfriend of the time, rather than commercial music. The sound track of her video footage serves as a backdrop to scenes of partying, intimacy and hilarity in the company of her friends. It also serves to point to her non-conventionality, her separation from the usual, more normal representations of passive, objectified femininity. Just as Fran's film stresses her claims to be "an individual," her refusal to be easily categorized ("I don't fit into any category. I've got a bit of this, and a bit of this and a bit of this"), similarly her music choices underpin this desire to express nonconformity and *différance*. Particularly aware of the importance of narrative in her footage, she framed her section significantly and dramatically, not with music but with a *verbal* introduction from a Small Faces album over a black screen, "Are you all sitting comfortably two square on your botty? Then I'll begin."

Footage of small children watching her performance at Cirkidz together with the startling original music followed this introduction.

Fig 15, 16: Video stills – Fran performs before her audience

As stated in the epigraph to this chapter, Wanda affirmed that "music was in her soul." Her friend Janelle seemed to echo these sentiments in her own way, and again this was captured on video and included in Janine's edited video footage. She did not verbally articulate her love of a particular style/type of music on camera but she demonstrated her embodiment of knowledgeable "authentic" musician as she played the drum in her band practice. As she played she suddenly closed her eyes, slowly moving her head from side to side as though immensely moved by the music. It was a wonderful moment of "striking a pose," a simultaneous representation and constitution of the "real-me-as-musician."

In these ways, the teenagers in my research project used their musical taste to express and constitute a self that was associated with a particular musical style, genre or star. It was vitally important to them that this sense of belonging was seen as "real," part of their whole being, even if sometimes, as with Janelle, I also caught their self-conscious reflexive gaze in *my* camera lens.

The musical style selected was not simply an expression of what they *liked* but who they *were*. Not simply who they *were* but also who they *would like to be*. It was a dialectic exploration of "being" and "becoming" at the same moment, identity as process. Janelle, Janine and their friends practising their dance steps in front of the long hall mirrors at school also demonstrated this phenomenon.

Figures 17 &18: Janelle drums for Black Image

Polhemus, in fact, argues from a different perspective. He suggests that today young people are far less committed to a particular style or musical taste. He states: "back in 1964 you *were* a Mod or a Rocker. Today you are *into* Techno, Reggae or Acid Jazz. It's the difference between swimming and sticking your foot in the pool to check out the temperature – an exploratory dalliance versus immersion and commitment" (1997: 149 emphasis in the original). My experience and observations were very different. For the young people who participated in my research, how they dressed, moved, and danced were particularly clear pointers to their "authentic" selves, even if today those selves are perhaps even more difficult to "fix" than those of people in the 1960s. It separated the "real" from the "fake," from the Try Hard.

Questions of authenticity revisited: On not dancing like a Try Hard

The distinctions between the authentic and the Try Hard find resonance in Pat's claim to being a raver. As both a producer and a consumer of techno music, she spoke with scorn of the townies who, by dressing in similar clothes and attending the same venues, attempted to appropriate her cultural identity. She expressed this clearly to me one evening when I was invited to attend one of the raves with her. I was holding the camera because Pat hadn't wanted herself to be seen filming on that night but she wanted the event to be recorded on video. While we were standing on the edge of the main dancing "circle," Pat drew my attention to a girl dancing flamboyantly in the middle of the area. Her white luminous blouse was catching the lights from the lasers and her movements were large and exaggerated. "She's not a raver," hissed Pat in my ear, "She's a Try Hard." I asked how she knew. "Look at the way she's moving her arms. And look at the clothes. She's not here to dance. She's here to pick up guys."

The "authentic" is what distinguishes the "real" from the "Try Hards" although what exactly constitutes the "real" differs from group to group, girl to girl, even within one cultural activity. Association with a particular musical style, grouping or fashion is an attempt to "prove" one's established authenticity. But that authenticity is founded on wider cultural links than the music alone. Once again the link is provided by the concept of *habitus*.

> *What is called "creation" is the encounter between a socially constituted* habitus *and a particular position that is already instituted or* possible *in the division of the labour of cultural production.* (Bourdieu 1993: 141, emphasis in the original)

As Bourdieu points out, to analyze cultural tastes, including those of popular music, in sociological terms, "means understanding, on the one hand, the conditions in which the products on offer are produced, and on the other hand, the conditions in which the 'consumers produce themselves'" (1993: 112). In other words, musical tastes and the underpinning relationship created between musical and personal authenticity, depens upon the emotional investments that the individual has already established. Moreover, as argued elsewhere in this book, Bourdieu defines "investment" as "the propensity to act that is born of the relation between a field and a system of dispositions adjusted to the game it proposes, a sense of the game and of its stakes that implies at once an *inclination* and an *ability* to play the game, both of which are socially and historically constituted rather than universally given" (Bourdieu & Wacquant 1992: 118).

In other words, understanding the differences in musical preferences between the young women in my fieldwork requires searching beyond the teenager's immediate perspective and examining into their established familial and social networks. The allegiances are not separate nor, more importantly, are they trying to be. So, for example, Pat's sense of self through her participation in raves and techno music in her "dance club scenes," Diane's fandom of New Kids on the Block and Peter André, Fran's attraction to New Age music, Sara's passion for World Music, Grace's love of Violent Femmes, Janine's playing and Mary's enjoyment of reggae were significant *precisely* because they expressed an aspect of each girl's sense of an idealized, individualized self while *simultaneously* being intrinsic to each girl's wider social allegiances.

Most research carried out on youth cultures does not incorporate the whole of the teenagers' worlds – their home and their extramural activities. It is only on closer everyday contact across these different contexts, by means of a thoroughly ethnographic approach and by engaging with the participants in their different social "fields" (Bourdieu 1977, 1990, 1993), that it becomes apparent that the concept of the "authentic" that seems to be idiosyncratically linked to a particular music taste and youth microculture, was in fact firmly embedded in each girl's parent culture. For example, if we look again and more closely at Pat's representation of her love of rave culture, on and off the camera, we can see beyond the obvious. She tells the viewer:

> *I wanted to show the nightclub scene and the part it plays in my life. Some people resort to drugs and alcohol – but me, I just like to dance.*

In fact, she is offering far more information than simply that she enjoys that particular activity. Implicit in her comment is a whole social "scene" of which she feels she is an established, confident member. Indeed her words express a personal affinity with the nightclub (in this case, rave) scene, implying a particular youth subculture. It may also be that she believes her words to imply that a "scene" is a class-based micro-world and her involvement in it an aspect of her own distinctive, immutable identity. In fact, however, what she is articulating, through words and performance, is the *process* of her strategically "safe" engagement with a particular social world through the medium of music. Her account of her involvement with what she calls "the rave scene" portrays the negotiation of her (self) (gendered) identity-making through musical taste, where both the identity and the micro-world itself are in flux. The cultural activities and social practices which express this aesthetic taste and cultural identity highlight the everyday blurring of what are often considered conventionally "fixed" class and ethnic groupings. In other words, they *constitute* and *justify* a particular kind of idealized, experiential (musical) community that is still able to be accommodated within a wider cultural and social identity.[11]

Pat was from an Anglo–Australian family living in what would be identified as a middle-class neighborhood of Adelaide. The people she met at the raves and dance clubs she attended in the city were often from far less affluent areas and many were from non-Anglo–Australian backgrounds, such as Vietnamese, Italian and Greek. In her research in England, Thornton (1995) describes this behavior as a "pursuit of classlessness" common amongst middle-class youth, pursuit that is more romantic than "real." The music, and the scene that it underpinned, enabled and seemed to encourage just such social blurring (and sometimes social juxtapositionings) to occur. Yet Pat's identifications and forays into this *other* social world stopped short of their becoming too threatening and too disturbing for her usual, "habituated" sense of self. She would dress up, as described in chapter 2, she would look the part of an "authentic" raver. As an established member of the cultural grouping she was affiliated with, she would even be involved in the backstage setting-up of some of the raves in abandoned warehouses or in some of the more exotic places, like the Old Adelaide Gaol. Occasionally she would date boys from the other side of town whom she met through the rave scene, boys of whom her parents inevitably disapproved. She would vehemently point out the distinction between ravers and Try Hards through their actions, their dance, their dress and their activities, as we saw above. Her adherence to the group's implicit code of membership justified her legitimate and idealized belonging to a privileged group. However, as she said herself, she did not become too involved in the drug-taking scene nor did she drink excessively. Rather, she asserted she: "just liked to dance" for it was the dance and the music that safely gave her this "aura" of authenticity.

One of New York's star dancers, Willi Ninja, gives an account of the DJ culture that seems to echo Pat's words:

> *How the* DJ *clips the music – certain combinations – can totally inspire you. Sometimes people think I'm on major drugs because when a song clicks, I am gone. I mean I don't see, hear, smell or taste no one. I get such a high from dancing.* (cited in Haslam 1997: 178)

In other words, on the one hand, Pat's *play* with this lifestyle and this *otherness* only went so far: she could explore the excitement of this otherness, and then return to her middle-class, Anglo–Australian life after each event. On the other hand, she could justify her nonindulgence of drugs and alcohol because those things were not part of her concept of an "authentic" raver.[12] She attended rave parties and nightclubs where techno music was played on a regular basis. Her friends were all part of the same scene, so dancing, attending rave parties and assisting at the community radio techno station were established parts of the set routine of her social life. In these ways, Pat's play was symbolically bounded by the constraining discourses of the parent world where she had a deep emotional "investment" (Holloway 1984). She was demonstrating, yet again, her knowledge of the "rules of the game" (Bourdieu 1977, 1990) within this particular field of cultural activity.

Even such a relatively straightforward example as Pat's highlights the complex involvement of music in social ordering and serious play. Firstly, such paradoxical involvement and investment, the simultaneous belonging and not belonging to a social grouping unsettles conventional notions of what are usually conceived of as subcultures (Brake 1985; Hebdige 1979; White 1993) or adolescent cliques (Denholm 1993; Polk 1993). Recent writings on youth have certainly challenged earlier, narrower definitions of teenage social groupings as subcultures and yet often the common assumptions about such groupings being a manifestation of "youth alienation" and "struggle" and "resistance" against adult values still remain (see Tait 1993 and Taylor 1993). These assumptions tend to overlook the complex way whereby distinctions in style of music, fashion and style are used *simultaneously* by youth to explore, negotiate and *form* social identities. The resultant social identities are always in some aspects extensions of the *parent* cultures and wider social networks. In the words of Simon Frith:

> *Pop tastes do not just derive from our socially constructed identities: they also help to shape them . . . What music does (all music) is put into play a sense of identity* that may or may not fit *the way we are placed by other social forces.* (1996: 276–77, my emphasis)

"May or may not" because music encourages and permits the play that blurs those symbolic boundaries.

Music production and the search for the "real me"

The search for distinction between the real and the inauthentic and the struggle to manifest the difference, are also tacitly behind the respective bodily praxes, the (playful) "practices" of styles of dance and movement of the teenagers in front of mirrors or cameras, detailed earlier. This also helps to explain the different forms of music *production* that the girls were engaged in. Apart from involvement with music as consumers, several of the teenagers were also actively engaged in making or producing music. Kate played a trombone and electronic keyboard, Sara played the violin, Diane played a guitar, Janine played guitar and some keyboard within her rock band, andPat worked in a voluntary capacity at a techno radio station and learned how to MC at raves. In light of their familial contexts and "investments," their choice of instrument and style of musical production were not as arbitrary as appears at first sight. Firstly, the kind of instrument selected was largely determined partly by finances and educational opportunity and access, for all of the teenagers who played an instrument were taught through an educational institution. Pat's abilities in her techno production skills were the result of a special training course, the fee for which she had saved herself.

Secondly, even within these constraints were other factors. Janine's choice of instrument and style of music is perfectly in keeping with a paradigm acceptable to her Aboriginal family and wider social network. During my fieldwork I attended several of Black Image's concerts and performances where Janine's band would play alongside Indigenous musicians, even sometimes including those who have become very widely appreciated, such as Archie Roach or the members of Trochus. During WOMADELAIDE, a biennial World Music event held in the city parklands, I often saw Janine and her friends wandering the grounds, enjoying the music and attending some of the Aboriginal performances. In other words, they could attend not only as consumers of the music, but also knowing they could be part of the "scene" as Indigenous musicians in their own right.

In a similar way, Kate's trombone was used to express a sense of self that fitted within *her* familial schema for an idealized self. I have described how Kate was brought up to see herself as an independent, nonconformist, feminist young woman. I have also given several examples of the way Kate demonstrated her chosen persona through her clothes, her activities and her ebullient physicality. She took great delight in showing me her musical ability on the trombone, delighting, of course, in its size, its awkwardness, its loud noise, and its unconventional image for a fifteen-year-old girl. The loud farting noise that she could produce from it also added to her sense of fun and incongruity. Like Kate herself, her brass instrument and its sound in the house were physically excessive, appropriating space and deliberately unsettling domesticity through its noise and sheer presence. This leads us on to consider another aspect of the relationship between musical and personal authenticity, the appropriation of physical and symbolic space. In terms of constituting the real me, music is frequently used as a way of creating the *mise-en-scène,* placing that real me into an appropriate, material context.

Music and the *mise-en-scène*

It seems to me, as I occasionally review the girls' footage, that music continually served as a cultural thread and an effective link between the worlds that we would popularly designate as private and public. For example, within the domestic arenas, it highlighted the centrality of the home in the girls' videos and the various ways in which it was depicted, indicating both the "investment" (Holloway 1984) and the ambivalence that the participants felt toward this "private" aspect and locus of their lives. Although the participants sometimes videoed their rooms without verbal commentary, music was frequently played in the background to provide a particular ambience. In cases where it became a vitally significant component of the *mise-en-scène,* the music was chosen deliberately to match a particular mood or to tie in with a specific cultural style. As in all drama and film, the music served to integrate the characterization and themes of the scene. At other times, if the participant were in front of the camera, talking about herself, she often had some appropriate music playing softly – and sometimes not so softly – in the background. In those situations, the music was often selected to underscore an aspect of her sense of group identity. For example, Grace intentionally selected music from The Violent Femmes, which she described to me as "a kind of 90s folk punk." Mary, from Papua New Guinea, played reggae songs while she was taking the imaginary "visitor" on a video tour of her house. As I witnessed such "performances" I became aware that the teenagers were utilizing the music as another symbolic aspect of their sense of self along with the posters and other cultural icons in their rooms and their homes.

Even when the music was not being played, the importance of its wider status as an essential commodity was evident through the presence of the record sleeves, CD covers, posters, and T-shirts frequently decorating the wall spaces. It was not simply the obvious significance of fan-group membership that the music implied, but the wider meaning imparted by such an icon. In the bedrooms of Janine and her Aboriginal friends, for example, were posters of Bob Marley and, sometimes, Aboriginal musicians. Mary's walls also contained photos of Bob Marley and many posters of Jamaican and African–American basketball stars. For these teenagers, obviously the color of the stars and their personalities were significant. What their choice implied was not simply their own fandom of these cultural groups but that it cohered with their immediate familial and community values and expectations (see Hayward 1998 for comparative examples). Their choices suggested an awareness of the constraints in their performed subjectivity and of their "investments" in these chosen positions.[13]

Music and symbolic boundaries

Many theorists have pointed to the special role performed by music when a culture is under stress or threat – a significant finding in the context of my research. In preliterate societies music was consciously used to ward off the power of evil spirits; in modern societies such actions are rationalized by using music to unite the nation and the troops, civilians and the military, especially in times of war, to create a bond amongst the "we" as opposed to the "them." Yet ironically, the same vehicle can be used against conformity, to express dissent and rebellion, creating a different "us" against a different "them." For example, Schechner describes the way the young people in Tiananmen Square responded to the ominous threat of the rigidly conformist lines of the Communist military by dancing expansively and idiosyncratically to Western pop music (1993: 51–63). In a less serious context, but equally partisan, supporters at football matches sing their own team's "anthem" as they symbolically mark out their space and identity against the threat of the other, both sides competing, of course, within the same territory. Similarly, in my fieldwork, when Sara played her tape deck loudly from her bedroom or when Kate turned up the volume of her radio to mask our "private" discussion from her parents, territory is being marked out and appropriated.

If we consider the transformation of places necessary to accommodate large-scale music and dance events, we are given another insight into this phenomenon. I have already described the perfunctory transformation of the Returned Services League halls for Blue Light discos. I was to witness far more dramatic transformations through Pat's affiliation with the rave scene in Adelaide, and through my own attendance at several rock concerts.

The rave at Old Adelaide Gaol

During my fieldwork I attended several raves and dance clubs with Pat, sometimes being "official" cameraperson for her when she didn't want to film herself but wanted the event recorded, and sometimes merely as a participant attempting to be part of the scene as unobtrusively as possible. Aware that my age and appearance could not easily render my presence invisible or unnoticed amongst the usual patrons, I experienced some anxiety when attending these functions. On one occasion I became aware that there were fewer young people at the event that night than usual: the presence of the camera and an older person were assumed to represent some sort of legal authority. I relied on Pat's comments and camera footage for information on major rave events. One such event filmed by her, as I noted earlier, was held at the Old Adelaide Gaol. The jail had been closed as a correctional institution for some years but was still used as a museum and could be hired as a function center. Several successful raves had been held there previously, probably because of its romantic and dark past.

Since she was particularly excited about this rave, being one of the voluntary assistants to the organizers, Pat videoed the different stages of setting up the event and then explained each section to me as we watched the footage together. As we watched the workers erect scaffolds, lights and lasers, and witnessed the prison space filling with young people and music, the prison was transformed into a totally different space. Of course such a transformation is particularly fascinating in terms of the building's original function – a place of incarceration, surveillance and control. Raves held outside club venues have several added advantages: firstly, they are often not subjected to the same kinds of legal controls, especially if the venue is a secret one. Secondly, they have the potential to accommodate far more bodies. Thirdly, the unusual setting, especially if it offers "forbidden and unpredictable senses of place" (Thornton 1995: 22) can add to the excitement of the event. In fact, as Thornton points out, although the rave scene often sees itself as an "outlaw culture," their main antagonists are not the police (who threaten, arrest, and confine) but the media "who continually threaten to *release* its cultural knowledge to other social groups" (1995: 90, emphasis in the original).

On the evening of Pat's rave at the Old Adelaide Gaol, the strident electronic sounds of the techno music and the mechanical and almost synchronized movement of the young people as they danced, ironically reappropriated that control for new purposes. It would be incorrect to claim that the people who attended raves as a leisure activity belonged to the same class or ethnic background. Clearly, a mix of different populations and cultural groupings attended different dances at different times and places, depending on the particular genres and practices that were popular at any time. However, the clothing, style, music and gatekeeping strategies gave an overall impression of homogeneity. As the camera presented it – as I subsequently witnessed the event – dance, image and movement appeared not as potentially anarchic and individualistic but as a seething, homogeneous mass of similarly clad bodies moving in relative unison to insistent, repetitive beats. Indeed, the composition of the crowd itself at each rave can appear remarkably similar, since the gatekeeping controls, whether overt or tacit, are extremely effective. Furthermore, under the influence of the techno beat, narcotics and alcohol, a sense of idealized unity and "communitas" (Turner 1977) is experienced. Under the influence of Ecstasy or other designer drugs, in particular, the ordinary seems remarkably clever, turning "banal thoughts into epiphanies" (Thornton 1995: 91). Similarly, the differences and distinctions between the ravers appeared to blend into one unified vision. The individual loses a sense of self within the larger pulsating whole.

At the Adelaide Gaol music demonstrated its transformative capacity; at a rock or pop concert – more public arenas – it demonstrates this same power but on a different level. During my fieldwork I attended several concerts I knew the girls would also be attending. Madonna's concert, *The Girlie Show*, where Peter André was a supporting act, was particularly memorable and took place not long after my discussion about the star with Bekk and Diane at school. Both vehemently admired Madonna because "she stands up for what she believes in," and of course Diane had long been an ardent fan of Peter André. I felt sure she would try to obtain a ticket somehow but in fact I did not see either girl at the concert. The ticket prices certainly were prohibitive. Hilary told me later that she did attend but sat outside on the grass. She couldn't afford a ticket but wanted to hear the music. I did however see a few of the other teenagers from my research project there, such as Grace and some of her close friends. I went with my own teenage daughter and two of her friends.[14] The concert was held in the immense football stadium where regular sporting events and some of the larger, prestigious rock concerts take place. I soon realized a fascinating aspect of Madonna's clever marketing strategy: that the massive size of the venue, together with Madonna's persona of excessive and transgressive sexuality, was a deliberate ploy to lay the groundwork for a media-dispersed moral panic with its potential for disturbance and concern. It also highlighted, for her fans, a potential for symbolic play. As Skeggs points out: "Madonna (like Bowie and Prince) has always played with multiple subjectivities that vacillate between gender categories. Whilst her continual change of image is an effective marketing strategy, it also demonstrates . . . that femininity is a masquerade and performance" (Skeggs 1993: 71). I will return to this point below but firstly, I make use of my detailed field notes to describe Madonna's concert.

Madonna concert—1 December 1993

The first thing I became aware of, as we approached the external gate, was the row of yellow-shirted bouncers. They stood by the trestle tables to search everyone's bags to check for all the "forbiddens" –

alcohol, cameras, umbrellas, cans, food and drink, weapons, drugs. Their searching appeared not to be as thorough as that of the bouncers at U2, another heavily promoted concert I had attended in this same venue a few weeks earlier. I questioned why they weren't searching the binocular case I was carrying. The gatekeeper looked a bit sheepish. "Aren't they just binoculars?" he asked. They were, but they easily could have concealed something else.

As we climbed up into the oval area, away from the food and toilets, the sight was amazing: row upon row of neatly arranged chairs on the flat oval in front of the grandstands giving the appearance of a huge prayer meeting, an unusual arrangement for a rock concert. The audience space for rock concerts normally included a large general admission area – a space clear of seats that enabled the audience to be close enough to the stage to dance to the music. This stage had crash barriers around it and immediately behind this, the $200 seats. The regular ticketed seats of $62.50 were quite a way from the front.

The age group of the audience appeared to be very varied. Gender seemed to be quite evenly divided, which surprised me at first since I had expected more women; however, many of the young men could be accompanying their female partners or relatives, rather than being fans of the pop star.

The stage was relatively bare and the teenagers I was accompanying commented on the absence of large video screens, which we had heard would be there, and the lack of a catwalk into the audience. The stage was framed by the words *The Girlie Show* in huge lights with a red, scalloped curtain framing a proscenium arch. On either side of the stage were two massive speakers, but that was it. It all looked remarkably drab.

I saw Grace and after saying "hello," commented that I hadn't realized she would be there. Grace informed me that the boyfriend of her friend's mother had passed on some free tickets to them. They had to stay in the general admission area. I hadn't realized there *was* a general admission area, which turned out to be behind the rows of seats but to the left of the stage. Apart from Grace I didn't recognize anyone else, but my daughter and her friends did seem to expect to know many people there and went off to find them. There was a sense that one *could* wander through the crowd that was building up now without fear of getting lost or separated. The seats were clearly marked so geographical areas were easily identified. The careful marking of the auditorium was echoed by the attempts at control via the loudspeaker: an unidentified male voice, presumably from the stage area, continuously and seemingly unnecessarily ordered the crowd to: "Move to your seats. Move out of the aisle and into your seats. Keep out of the aisles and keep off [don't stand on] your seats." The crowd seemed incredibly sedate and obedient. We were even warned about how to behave *after* the show. Fifteen minutes before the performance started, the audience was told: "After the show the crash barriers will be down. Get out quickly after the show."

At eight o'clock Peter André's act was announced. The audience began screaming and in front of us everyone stood up. We could hear the music but there was absolutely no visual sense of the stage or the performers. I decided to move right to the back of the grandstand, an area elevated with stone steps.

The huge spotlights were not completely on since it wasn't quite dark. Peter André's act was applauded by the audience – especially his better-known songs like "Give Me a Sign." However, there appeared to be no real sense of engagement with the audience. Perhaps his contract stated that his performance should not compete with that of Madonna.

Very few signs or advertisements were displayed around the oval. There was a West End tent that sold Coke, two tents selling Madonna memorabilia at either end of the oval and one large tent selling programs and T-shirts in front of the stands, identified by a flashing red light. The lack of commercial activity combined with the constant public warnings and announcements served to make the audience docile and rather subdued.

After Peter André left the stage the technicians began to prepare a different set of lights, during which time the public commands continued: "Don't jump the barriers! Remember, some people queued up for days to get the front tickets so do not go into that area unless you have the correct ticket. They deserve to get to their seats at the front."

This constant reminder concerning security was interesting since the actual police presence, as indicated earlier, was minimal. The yellow T-shirted bouncers, called "the yellow walls" by the voice on the loudspeaker, provided the only evidence of a security presence. As the time for Madonna's entrance came closer – marked down by the voice: "Five minutes to show time" – the background music, which was fairly muted, changed to a repetitive drumbeat. Two large cloth screens were unrolled on either side of the stage revealing large video screens. Diagrams and occasionally shadows appeared on the screens, suggesting Madonna's fingers or body – just for a moment, like a tease. At the sight of these shadows on the screens loud screams would emanate from the crowd.

The two older teenage girls in front of us suddenly turned round and asked if any of us in the vicinity had any cigarette papers. A woman in the seat next to me said: "No" but then asked if they had any "dope." The girls laughed and produced a small packet of marijuana. The woman then showed them how to remove the tobacco from one of her cigarettes and fill the paper with the marijuana leaves. They then borrowed another cigarette of hers to repeat the activity. As they all lit up another young woman in front of them looked back and smiled. I probably missed the interchange but she too was smoking dope within the next quarter of an hour. I got the impression that she borrowed either dope or cigarette papers or the light from the girls in front of us. One of these two girls extracted a full flask of whisky from its hiding place in the waistband of her jeans. I remembered the yellow T-shirted bouncers outside and my earlier impression that they were rather relaxed about their searching. I also pondered on the combination of the dope and the straight whisky – the girls finished off the flask before the end of the show.

While waiting for the technicians to finish and the act to begin, the crowd became restless. Suddenly people below us in the oval began to point excitedly to their right. I wondered if Madonna were suddenly going to appear from there, but it turned out to be a "Mexican Wave." It was the first time that evening that the crowd started to behave like a cohesive group, perhaps a spontaneous reaction to the boredom. The wave of hands moved through the entire area beginning along the stands near the oval. It was fun to watch, and interestingly appeared to contradict the carefully constructed sense of order and control that had been developed during the evening. The wave wasn't permitted to continue for long – the lighting changed, the oval went darker, the lights on the stage area became more dramatic, and the music became more insistent. *The Girlie Show* lights in blue and green were illuminated as circus music began and the red scalloped curtain descended to form an old-fashioned formal stage setting. The dancing lights made balloon patterns on the curtain and the crowd started to scream.

The overall impression of the show was one of extreme burlesque and carnival. The lights were glaringly bright and the curtains, sets and costumes frequently gold and silver glitter. The emphasis was on dance and movement more than on the music itself. On occasion there were sections of pure modern ballet, no lyrics at all – especially in sections where all male performers danced in what was meant to be a mildly erotic routine.

Clothing, style and movement were exaggerated, with a great deal of erotic posturing taking place throughout the show, either by Madonna herself or by the other dancers, frequently deliberately blurring conventional gender lines. Madonna appeared as Marlene Dietrich in her famous drag outfit of a dinner suit, white shirt, and cropped hair and cane during several numbers like "Bye Bye Baby" and "Like a Virgin," emphasizing the blurring of gender and representation. Madonna then danced with female dancers so she was male to their female characters. At other times, she would appear as female but was partnered by another female, as in the overtly erotic "Justify My Love."

At the end of the concert the chaos that had been carefully controlled and contained within the concert areas erupted as thousands of cars attempted to leave the parking area at once. Cars were everywhere and facing all directions. We all sat in our cars, some people patiently and some not so patiently, and all the cars had their radios blaring and Madonna's voice was everywhere to be heard!

So what is meaningful about concerts such as Madonna's for the young women in my research? Madonna clearly made connections between her music, her body and freedom from sexual inhibition. As I noted earlier, the concert served to reinforce in the audience, aspects of cultural identity and identity as process: firstly, Madonna's manipulation of style and gender through carnival, posturing and excess reinforces the sense of shifting identities, the "striking of poses" discussed throughout this book. The pop star highlights and exploits the normal binary definition of young women – as good girl/bad girl (Summers 1994). She also holds up sexual identity and orientation for scrutiny by playing with different gender roles even within one song. Again to quote Beverley Skeggs:

> *Popular culture, especially music, is a prime site for challenges. Bricolage, appropriation and pastiche enable the popular to remain popular . . . By playing popular culture so well Madonna is able to use its spaces to make challenges. They may not be perfect, sometimes even problematic, but . . . they contribute to a shifting of the discursive boundaries.* (Skeggs 1993: 72)

Barbara Ehrenreich and associates observed a similar use of cultural commodities through their study of the way Beatlemania in the 1960s permitted recognition and vocal expression of female sexuality by the young female fans for the first time.

> *To abandon control – to scream, faint, dash about in mobs – was in form if not in conscious intent, to protest the sexual repressiveness, the rigid double standard of female teen culture. It was the first and most dramatic uprising of women's sexual revolution.* (Ehrenreich 1992: 90)

None of this is to suggest a simple relationship between popular music and empowerment; rather, it hints again at the complexity of young people's engagement with popular culture in all its forms and its integration into their lives through bodily praxis. Acts of rebellion and illicit behaviors emerge in this forum – hence the exchange of marijuana and secret (and excessive!) drinking of alcohol. Lawrence Grossberg, writing specifically about young audiences, called this phenomenon "the affective sensibility of fandom":

> *There is the satisfaction of doing what others would have you do, the enjoyment of doing what you want, the fun of breaking the rules, the fulfilment – however temporary and artificial – of desires, the catharsis, the comfort of escaping from negative situations, the reinforcement of identifying with a character, and the thrill of sharing another's emotional life.* (Grossberg 1992: 55)

Such insights bring us back again to notions of play and its role in shifting boundaries and testing symbolic barriers.

Conclusion

In this chapter I have examined the ways in which serious play and its more extreme, theatrical manifestation of mimetic excess enabled explorations of each girl's sense of self to be constituted and performed, both materially and symbolically. Through their bodily behaviors, gestures, dress and food preferences, the girls tested out their "being" in the world within preconceived boundaries, as gendered, classed, ethnic and aged subjects. I identified the subsequent tension created between this serious, sometimes "desperate play" and the girls' "sense of the game" through their creative appropriation of cultural symbols within domestic and public spaces. All of these aspects of self-making, the physical, the emotional, the sexual, the material, and the symbolic, are, of course, intricately linked. The sense of our "place" in the world is concerned with how we "relocate" ourselves and about how our social identities are established within discursive contexts and within moral and political hierarchies. In Giddens' phraseology, it is also how we "re-embed" ourselves, as spaces become "phantasmagorically" separated from place (Giddens 1990: 88). As a consequence of modernity, places become "thoroughly penetrated by and shaped in terms of social influences quite distant from them" (18). These influences, expressed through diverse activities and practices, highlight the way they both reflect and *create* social groupings.

On one hand it is clear that popular cultural activities emerge as an expression of particular values from social groupings – clearly, they have a material, social origin. On the other hand, and perhaps more importantly, the social groupings themselves are *created* and shaped through the shared aesthetic expression of specific cultural activities. These activities and social performances have to be understood as practices "in which meanings are generated, manipulated and even ironised, within certain limitations" (Stokes 1994: 4). In the case of most young people, the practices are underpinned by, and expressed through, popular music.

But, as suggested earlier, the musical tastes and distinctions of my teenage participants both were derived from their familial and social backgrounds and simultaneously helped to form them. So, for example, rather than music and musical taste *reflecting* aspects of a preconceived sexuality or conventional gendered or "classed" behavior, we need to see that the forms and aesthetics of popular music are signifying *practices* through which discourses of sexuality, gender, ethnicity and "class" are negotiated (Frith 1985).

As indicated throughout this book, music played a central role in the everyday lives of the young participants of my research, its paramount place reflected in the video footage taken by all of the teenagers as they recorded and mused upon these experiences. In fact, their insistence on the inclusion of the music and on its importance caused problems when we later completed the documentary and considered where and how the film could be distributed since we potentially had a great deal of music copyright to pay for!

Notes

1 Paul Patton refers to this as "authentic inauthenticity" for "it is not that postmodern lives lack meaning, but rather that the meanings are multiple, temporary and unstable . . . They involve investment in the image or the idea of the moment, insecure in the knowledge that it is only of the moment" (Patton 1988: 91).

2 There seem to be very few appropriate all-encompassing definitions of music available in the literature as concise as this one. I am concerned with the cultural significance of the various forms of popular music in the processes of self-making in the lives of the young women in my research project. For this purpose, although perhaps limited as an overall account of musical forms, Rouget's definition is an excellent springboard.

3 Several essays in Helen Thomas's collection *Dance, Gender, Culture* make this point, that "there is evidence to suggest that dancing not only plays an important role in the life of a number of pre-industrial societies, but it also performs a significant function in the process of gender construction and identification" (Thomas 1993: 71).

4 I have seen the same phenomenon of course at many other cultural celebrations – Jewish, Italian, Scottish and Aboriginal celebrations amongst many others – where dance is performed dramatically and self-consciously to indicate a cultural pride, an ethnic consciousness and a possession of cultural capital.

5 Which is again why it is so powerful a tool in advertising. It is another parallel between this concept and Raymond Williams' analysis of the transformation and "sympathetic magic" in advertising.

6 That is, although in common usage and in the writing of music critics,

distinctions and definitions are made between different types of musical genres, on the ground, young people are very aware that such distinctions as, for example, between techno, hip hop, and dance music are not so finely drawn.

7 So Billy Bragg's music is seen to represent a particular neo-Marxist, working-class stance while Ani Di Franco's music portrays a young feminist vision. It is these wider cultural and collective affinities their fans can hold on to and appropriate as their own.

8 But not quite the same way for the Aboriginal girls or for Mary, as indicated earlier. The sense of self for each of these girls seemed to be one of relatedness and kinship rather than a Western sense of independent individualism. It is important to realize that the concept of "the real me" is enabled through either the production or consumption of the music or indeed through being able to engage in both practices.

9 These were assessment centers where young offenders were placed for a short period of time while the assessment team, youth workers, psychologists, and legal representatives decided between them where the young person should be sent – to a remand home or back into the community.

10 In spite of the concern about competition for "guys," I noticed that JD, Jessica and Emma stayed around each other for most of the night, only occasionally talking to a small group of boys. Only Jessica seemed to be actually moving away from the girls to dance romantically with any of the boys.

11 The word "scene" tends to indicate the experiential community beyond the immediate physical and geographic environment. See Cohen, 1997: 17–36.

12 Similarly, as we saw in an earlier chapter, Fran and her friend Cindy would adamantly declare that smoking was abhorrent to them because it was "unnatural" while willingly indulging in marijuana. This drug fitted more closely into their idealized selves drawn from each girl's familial background.

13 As noted in earlier chapters, Wendy Holloway (1984) argues that particular subject positions are taken up over other possible conflicting ones at different times according to the amount of "investment" that the person perceives therein. "Investment" is conceived here as both emotional commitment and vested interest. I would argue further that that investment stems from the familial and community framework within which the individual develops her sense of self and thus her range of possible subjectivities.

14 All of these teenagers had saved up their money from part-time jobs for quite a while for this event. They spent considerable time after the event discussing the length of time it took them to be able to purchase the tickets and the consequent (perceived) entertainment value of the concert itself.

Chapter 7

Global Girl-Making: 10+6

> We participate simultaneously in a number of areas, groups, and dimensions of social and cultural life; we are consumers, we use services, we participate to varying extents in social and cultural life, we are members of associations, parties, groups and clans of various kinds. In each of these settings we live a part of ourselves, certain dimensions of our personalities and experience . . . futures [are] so much more open to a range of possible and unforeseeable factors than ever before in the past. (Alberto Melucci 1992: 54)

> *My vision of the future seems to change constantly [but] I keep these thoughts to myself, trying them on for size for a while. I tuck them away when they don't seem to fit, perhaps coming back for a second round . . . but I am willing to keep trying them on until one fits perfectly. (Hannah, 22, Chicago, US)*

Widening the circle of inquiry

I am heading this final chapter with two apt quotations. The first is from Alberto Melucci, which highlights again the importance of change and reflexivity in the ways in which identity is both represented and constituted at the same time. Hannah's words that follow, underscore this notion, as this young woman, also, contemplates how she makes conscious choices about the many ways in which she engages in her "self-making." The paradox that underlies such a claim – that identity is both a "thing" and a "process," a thing that we are and a way of being in the world – has been a continuing theme throughout this work. In this concluding chapter, I am elaborating upon this discussion by transferring the fieldwork to another time and place. In 2001 and early 2002, I traveled on study leave to the United States and then on to Britain, thereby extending my original research into girlhood and self-making into other cultures and into other social arenas. Just as I had already discovered in the Australian context, I found again, that to presume homogeneity of class, ethnicity, or even gender regimes within particular social groupings, was misleading and indeed often obfuscating. For, within each new cluster of young women, I found the same ongoing struggle to create and maintain that same refracted sense of distinction (Bourdieu 1984) and *différance* (Derrida 1981) – the business of constituting the self from overlapping, sometimes contradictory possibilities within a range of social fields (Bourdieu 1993) as I had observed earlier. At certain times, for example, a group of girls might work hard to present themselves as female as opposed to male. At other times it was their youth or adolescence they stressed as opposed to their potential adult selves. Others emphasized their identities as producers of music or popular culture rather than their being consumers. For others it was the fact that they belonged to a black, ethnic, or religious minority not part of a white dominant, secular social grouping that they highlighted at that moment and time. Not one of these identities precluded another, of course, but they were frequently presented like the layers of plastic transparencies: one or two being particularly visible at any one moment but hinting at the other aspects of self, slightly less in focus, at that moment. As Melucci's words above remind us, these are possibilities, which change emphasis according to the particular needs of the moment. Equally, however, the possibilities are always dependent for their anchor on a particular set of core familial values, highlighting the continual negotiation of constituting a (gendered) self within a particular microworld.[1]

As before, the descriptions and analyses from my later fieldwork are not intended to provide a wide, definitive sample of young people's behaviors and desires, suggesting that this is the way all Australian, US, or British girls *are.* Rather my study points to the parallels and similar *processes* of self-making. The small but intense focus should be seen as providing a rich perspective, the anthropological "jeweler's-eye" (Marcus & Fischer 1986: 15) to heighten our awareness of the role of young people's music-making and consumption in the complex process of self-making.[2] These new examples also offer the opportunity to place the concept of girl-making in a global context. As we shall see, all young women, white and black, affluent and underprivileged, were clearly experiencing the same process of self-making in a very uncertain and rapidly changing world. While some of the young women are at a later stage of development than were the Australian girls when I first met them, all place the same reliance on "serious play" within their familiar and familial symbolic boundaries to constitute that often ephemeral sense of self.

To launch us on this new exploration, I begin with a few snapshots – moments from my later fieldwork. Then I will elaborate on the significance of these findings, deepening my exploration of what it means to "become female" from a variety of transnational perspectives.

Snapshot 1: February 2001, Notre Dame, Indiana

Following my undergraduate seminar at their university in the United States, three of the final-year students, Hannah, Meryl, and Susan, took it upon themselves to "host" the visiting "Australian professor." After attending my talk on my previous ethnographic work in Australia, they graciously invited me to lunch. The following night I was invited to dinner at their student apartment with their extended group of friends so I could see how they lived and so that we could continue to share insights about cultural differences. It was a very special evening, stretching far into the night as our conversation ranged across many topics – the intricacies of growing up female in different cultures and societies, our dreams and ambitions, world problems and how they could be solved and the various merits of favorite foods, books and movies. Many other friends drifted in and out of the room and conversations. At the end of the night we agreed to continue the conversations across time and space by email and letter. Some of the material, described in more detail below, developed from those long-term discussions over the Internet.

Snapshot 2: April 2001, London

Several months later, in London, UK, I began my research at the Weekend Arts College (WAC),[3] a community-based youth arts center. I was invited through two of the Black–British girls, Trea and Cara, to come to a UK Garage[4] party in a sports pub in the city council of Mornington Crescent, London. I went, thinking I was about to hear Hip Hop and then realized that the scene was very different. The small pub was intensely noisy, smoky and crowded. Because the function room shared a connecting bar to the main part of the pub, the manager entered this space frequently to complain about the pulsating Garage music, the crowd and what, to many customers, would have sounded like raucous noise. Most of the young people there at the gig were Black–British, many from African–Caribbean backgrounds. The majority of them were male – the girls who *were* present, even the organizers, like Trea and her friends, occupied the edges of the room, talking in small groups and occasionally moving quietly and unobtrusively a little nearer to the center to dance. They danced either alone or in small female groups, their movements understated, their eyes focused on the floor or in the mid-distance, suggesting an intense personal involvement with the beat rather than a connection with anyone around them. This was in clear contrast to the effervescent group of MCs,[5] the vast majority of whom were young men surrounding the male DJ at the far end of the room and waiting their turn to rap or "chat."[6] The DJ, managing and linking the music flows of one track to the next, was situated on a raised platform and behind a temporary mixing desk. The MCs circled the platform, craning over the desk and watching his movements closely as they performed their songs. This first group of five or six MCs (there were to be several during the evening) was particularly boisterous, ebullient and theatrical. Only one girl occupied a space there amongst them. She "chatted" her lyrics assertively with the rest of them, making her presence felt. As a group, the MCs freestyled their lyrics over the music, taking it in turns to improvise with noise and sound, competing with each other to claim their five minutes of sonic and physical space in chat and gesture. They all faced inwards towards the DJ, reminding me of old-time singers huddled around a piano, rarely acknowledging their audience on the dance floor. Occasionally the audience responded to a particularly clever phrase or sentence in the lyrics by calling out or applauding, but on the whole, the MCs seemed to be performing for themselves and each other.

Snapshot 3: January 2002, London

When I returned to London for another six weeks' fieldwork at WAC and at other music centers, I caught up with some of the young people from the previous year's fieldwork while making new contacts and friendships. One young woman, who was interested in being involved in this new stage of the project and was eager to teach me more about her micro-world, was Bernie. Bernie was short, and on first meeting, deceptively quiet, being softly spoken in her broad cockney accent. She was, I quickly discovered, also self-possessed, old and wise beyond her 16 years. I soon learned that, having been brought up in a single-parent family of all boys, she had learned to claim her space and take control where necessary. At WAC where, in contrast to her own cultural background, most of her classmates were black as well as male, this was no mean feat. However, she quickly seemed to gain their respect and friendship. "Grow up!" she once called across the room to a particularly belligerent, large classmate. Surprised, he stopped in the middle of his verbal abuse, sat down again and accepted her admonishment. Part of that respect came from her music skills: Bernie was a budding DJ, performing under her professional pseudonym of DJ Lady Lick. She had already produced one CD (on a privately funded independent label) and individual tracks for other artists. She told me that she was following her uncle's and her father's interests and in their professional footsteps, as they too were musicians. Her father had played with the well-known musician Sting, she told me several times. She said that she would like to be a DJ full-time. She also commented that she was realistic. She would probably train to be a primary school teacher, she thought. In the meantime, for at least two or three hours every night, she practiced her mixing and turntabling skills in her crowded bedroom in the family council apartment – despite the thin walls and confined space – until family members or neighbors would tell her to stop.

The meanings of distinction and *différance*

Who are these very different young women, described here both within and outside their homes and their cultural leisure "scenes"? What relationship does their behavior, their needs, desires, and sense of self have to the earlier portraits of teenage girls growing up in Australia? What sorts of differences will we find several years hence for those original Australian girls and for these others who grew up in a different time and place? Let us return to the insights of Bourdieu (1992), Derrida (1981), Handelman (1990) and Taussig (1993). Here I demonstrate again how the seriousness of play, social fields, and mimesis can explain the variety of complex ways in which young women across the globe learn to understand and make sense of growing up female.

For example, in these later fieldwork periods in the United States, I was particularly struck by the ways in which one particular cluster of young women developed their sense of personhood through the prism of a materially and socially advantaged framework of family and close relatives. The sense of self of these girls had inevitably developed through a highly spiritual, Christian sensibility that found expression through their own personal contribution to applied social justice and service in a wider, less affluent community than their own. A few months later, somewhat ironically, I was to learn more about a cluster of young people in Britain, the majority of whom were both proud and limited by their African–Caribbean identities. Many of these young people were also practising Christians, but in their world they were struggling to gain recognition and personal affirmation within an often equally underprivileged *white* British world.

In all cases, I stress again, the personal identity being represented and simultaneously (re)constituted was a shifting sense of self within overlapping and often contradictory social, cultural and ethnic cultural fields, since, in today's world of rapid change, cultural identities are clearly in flux, projects continually and impossibly in the process of completion. Increasingly, too, as we shall see, the camera, the video, music and the computer and their related technologies, prove to be central in the simultaneous representation and constitution of this sense of self. For in Homi Bhabha's words:

> *What is transformed in the postmodern perspective, is not simply the "image" of the person, but an interrogation of the discursive and disciplinary place from which questions of identity are strategically and institutionally posed.* (1987: 5)

The interrogated self that emerges and is continually renegotiated is the product of "*the relation between two realizations of historical action*, in bodies and in things" (Bourdieu 1993: 126, emphasis in the original). Kate's self-conscious posing in her photograph and her related discussions about image and representation, which began this study, point toward the same thought:

> *Even while the notion of the individual is assailed on all sides, it is a necessary fiction for the reproduction of the kind of society we live in.* (Dyer 1987: 10)

From my more recent fieldwork, in the United States and United Kingdom, I was to find many more examples of young people struggling with the same issues of selfhood. From many similar stories, I will outline just six more accounts of self-making by referring to two clusters of young women–the first group whom I originally met in Indiana, in the US, and the second cluster from London, England. While these stories tell of different kinds of lives, different kinds of opportunities, the next section will introduce the more overt differences between the two clusters.

US stories: Meeting Hannah, Meryl, and Susan

The first cluster of young women in my later fieldwork were all studying for their undergraduate degree in Humanities in South

Bend, a university town in Indiana, although all had grown up in large cities elsewhere in the USA. During my stay there, I was privileged to make the closer acquaintance of Hannah and her two friends Meryl and Susan. At the end of their first degree in higher education, these young women were very bright, articulate, gracious, self-assured and eager to reflect on their secure backgrounds, their social opportunities, and their self-acknowledged, relatively privileged lives.[7] Their education, both at home and at the university, had prepared them to be remarkably self-confident, equally relaxed, it seemed, talking to adults and to their peers. As noted above, over dinner at Hannah's student apartment, the three friends shared their memories of childhood and their hopes for their futures with me and, to the present day, continue to keep up a lively correspondence of writing and photos by email.

I learned that all had come to that particular city because of the university's high academic reputation and for the important social networks they would make there. Even more significantly perhaps, it was the continuation of the familial ties and social networks that had already been established there by parents and relatives who had attended the college before them. Understanding that their attendance at the college could not be gained by monetary privilege or social status alone, but was more dependent upon their own high examination scores, these young women were very aware of their own contributions to the process.[8] They recognized the challenge of following a family tradition as being an essential part of their overall marking-out of whom they felt they were and whom they could become. As Susan explained:

> *I started to realise that maybe my dream of going to this college was not really my dream at all, but rather something that I did to see that fulfillment in my parents' eyes. I wanted to make my dad proud, I wanted my family to see that I had done it. I started to think how I fulfilled everyone's fantasy for me, without filling my own.*

At the same time as she gained that insight – that her ambitions were deeply embedded in her familial past – Susan was also quite clear that she never felt an overt sense of coercion, for her parents "were *never, ever,* pushy. They were actually very quiet and let me pick and choose the things I wanted to do" (emphasis in original email). I found in her words, in her understanding of her own sense of freedom and choice, an echo of the Australian girls' perceptions of their world, described in earlier chapters. For example, just as Diane's understanding of "her own private space" reflected the established, though often subconscious values of her family, so we see this also in the case of this American girl. It was the same need to constitute the self within the established familial values and immediate social networks. Here again the taken-for-granted ways in which embodied (gendered) subjectivity and (micro)culture intertwine become apparent; the ways in which each individual is enmeshed in her own social world and how she perceived and interpreted these enmeshments.

In other words, we are reminded of the ways in which the perceived frameworks for understanding and interpreting one's world are inevitably symbolic boundaries, erected, internalized and naturalized. For to return to Bourdieu's conception of "habitus," "the individual, whether he likes it or not is trapped . . . within the system of categories he owes to his upbringing and training" (Bourdieu & Wacquant 1992: 126). Furthermore, the everyday experience of being in this world where habitus and social fields correspond, is like being a "fish in water" for "it does not feel the weight of the water, and takes the world about itself for granted" (Bourdieu & Wacquant 1992: 127). During 2002, I learned that, to a large extent, these girls were already fulfilling their immediate goals: all three are now engaged in full-time professional employment and are actively involved in service to the wider community.

Other (British) ways of being: Cluster 2

The second cluster, from London, had very different backgrounds, appearances and communicational skills from the American young women. At the beginning of this chapter, I described a UK Garage event organized and attended by some of the British girls. Among this grouping of young people, through their social networking and their connection with WAC, the community college they all attended, I was to get to know several young women particularly well: Trea, Shona, Karen and Bernie. Trea (18), introduced in the earlier extract, was from an African–Caribbean background. She became pregnant during the period of my fieldwork and consequently as a single parent, was supporting her young child while she worked part-time. When I first met her, she lived at home, but subsequently was struggling to maintain some independence in her own small apartment with her current boyfriend. She was deeply involved in the R&B (contemporary electric-based genre of rhythm and blues) and UK Garage scene, explaining that it was the fun and the lack of politics in the music that she enjoyed. "I don't like the politics and I'm not into the technical side," she explained. Like Trea, Shona (aged 17 and also of Jamaican heritage) lived in a suburb of South London where the many immigrant families from the West Indies and Africa had settled, joining friends and families who had emigrated before them. Like many of the Black–British girls that I was to meet in the UK, Shona seemed to have developed a carefully calculated air of defensive aloofness. One overt manifestation of this was her attachment to a thick white fluffy coat that she wore with a huge hood dramatically framing her head even in the height of an English summer. While her friends dressed in the usual strapped tops and short skirts, Shona often used her thick winter coat with its large fur hood to envelop her slight body and her head in a coy air of mystique. She would only take the coat off when she was ordered to by the teacher to enable her to perform in a drama or singing class. It became her trademark when she studied at WAC, earning her immediate, though good-humored notoriety for eccentricity. Undoubtedly, on some level, it also covered up some insecurity, since when she talked to me on a more individual basis away from the college and without the coat, she seemed far more shy and self-conscious than I had anticipated. By 2002, she had gained a place to study drama part-time at a public college while she worked for her uncle as a graphic designer. One day she would make a full-time career from her acting, she told me.

Karen and Bernie, both 17, were from Anglo–Celtic backgrounds. Yet they not only came from very different kinds of familial backgrounds from the American girls, but also grew up in different areas of London from each other. Karen's home address in northwest London would have been perceived as far more affluent, being situated at the edge of an upwardly mobile, middle-class suburb of the city. Many of the houses in this district were privately owned although surrounded by large council housing estates. While it was previously known for its heritage-listed buildings, past affluence and gentility, the locality was currently undergoing considerable demographic change. Part of that change was reflected in the large number of Asian families who had moved into the area. The rich tapestry of their influence was reflected in the brightly colored saris far more commonplace on the high street, and the increasing number of grocery shops and restaurants that offered *hallal* meat or displayed oriental spices and exotic-looking fruits and vegetables. Hindi and Bhangra music more usually emanated from the shops, clamoring for sonic space alongside the top ten pop tunes or the strident cries of the street sellers, and on the streets a rich cacophony of spoken languages blended with the more usual English words or north London dialect.

This rich cultural mix had long been present in Bernie's locale. She lived in an inner-city council, a densely populated area, with many of the houses being clearly far older and more dilapidated than in Karen's local district. Closer to the central business district and therefore lively and richly diverse in its ethnic variety, her area boasted local stores, street markets, stalls and cafés offering African, Jamaican, Chinese, Italian, Greek, Asian as well as the more traditional Anglo–Celtic foods and artifacts. The atmosphere was saturated with the sounds and smells of these many cultures – of spices and herbs and loud, pulsating music. It had become an area particularly popular with itinerant workers and tourists, the students and the younger unemployed, since the food, clothing and lodging were known to be cheap. Exotic and exciting to an outsider, for a longer stay, the sensory mix could become overwhelming as overt signs of poverty suddenly became more visible as did the large amount of discarded garbage on the streets, the overwhelming amount of unattractive and sometimes racist graffiti, the broken and boarded windows, the oppressive sense of litter and waste food and papers in the gutter, and the people begging or sleeping rough on the street. Altogether, undoubtedly due to the greater population in this area, there seemed to be an unpleasant tension here – a sense of imminent violence or rumbling social frustrations waiting to erupt.[9]

The common link between the four London teenagers – and the notable difference between them and their American counterparts – was that they had all been identified as low achievers by youth workers and outreach educational advisors. When I first met them, they had all left formal schooling without gaining any formal qualifications and had no real plans for the future. Because all had been identified by the educational authorities as "at risk" due to their lack of direction and formal skills, they had been offered the opportunity, through their local councils and outreach youth workers, to attend a special six-month program for unemployed youth. The course was held at the Weekend Arts College, more commonly known as WAC. This institution, not only open on the weekend, offered many courses for disadvantaged or marginalized young people, their innovative curricula particularly focusing on music, performance, and digital arts. It was there, where I was attached as a voluntary worker, that I made the girls' acquaintance and over time learned about their particular talents, concerns, and interests.

While they shared a lack of educational qualifications in common, not unexpectedly, their ambitions and their plans for their futures as young women were largely different from each other's and from those of the Australian girls of the previous chapters.

Future pathways

Let's return to the girls whom I met in Indiana. The first thing the three young women were keen to stress, as they reflected on their personal journeys, was their idealism and their concern to reach beyond their own lives to others. Susan, for example, told me that one of her dreams was of:

> *going to some remote town in Honduras to serve the poor. I just had this vision of myself wearing sandals and shorts and hugging little orphan children or teaching them and just living this simple lifestyle.*

Yet, just as she acknowledged that her original desire to attend her family's "alma mater" university had not been completely her own, Susan realized here also that her dream accorded perfectly with her religious upbringing and her parents' idealism and social activism. That she was able to consider such a move with any seriousness was also because she knew that she had been given the "space to play," to push the symbolic boundaries – although in her case, they were boundaries of self-sacrifice and altruism. Knowing that her parents were not "too keen on the Honduras thing," Susan also knew that they would support her decisions, and that the key element of her dream, perfectly in keeping with their ideals, was to work with others less fortunate than herself. Thus she compromised, deciding instead to work for two years within a community service program closer to home:

> *I gave up my vision of going to a third world country to serve, and was sent to Montgomery, Alabama to teach in an all African–American high school there. I am one of two white people in the school and am teaching Spanish and Religion. The school is poor, poor, poor, and the kids are almost entirely Baptist.*

Fig 19: Susan with her students

Hannah also sought self-fulfillment through her job and her commitment to others. Finding her first secure job as an accountant in an advertising firm in Chicago, her first big step was to pay back student loans and to become financially independent. Her ultimate goal, however, was threefold. On the one hand, she wanted to move into graduate school, for learning was her "first love" and she had been "toying with the idea of getting a degree (perhaps an MBA) in non-profit administration." Her emphasis on a charity or nonprofit organization was important, for working in a strictly commercially based venture did not sit well within Hannah's oft-stated idealism and altruism. Hannah's second goal related to her personal life. As was the case with her two friends, romance and love were central to her concept of self for she wanted to be "married by the time I am 30." She was also very clear about the kind of relationship she wanted in the future married life, for she was "looking for a husband who shares my love for children and family."[10] This taken-for-granted goal of finding a suitable marriage partner was not voiced (or even overtly considered) by most of the Australian or even the British girls. None of the groupings of British girls who participated in this research project discussed marriage as one of their primary goals, although having a steady relationship with a boy was certainly desirable and valued. Just as Beverly Skeggs (1997) demonstrated in her earlier study of young women, the British teenage girls in my research also clearly felt that their romantic (heterosexual) relationships were an essential aspect of creating the "respectable" gendered self.

The third aspect of Hannah's sense of self-making, which is important for our discussion here, was her need to be of service to others. Like her friends, and despite her demanding work schedule, Hannah was also active in the community outside her paid work. "I have been volunteering one night a week at a domestic violence shelter," she told me.

I found the way that the American girls interpreted the meaning of service to the wider community and their participation in active social justice, in this way, was both impressive and admirable. As I indicated in earlier chapters, most sociological studies that have been carried out with young people have concentrated on the disadvantaged, the marginalised and the disaffected. It is relatively commonplace to hear studies of failure or of spectacular resistance to the system (see Carrington 1993, for example). In the face of these recurring paradigms, it is easy to dismiss the voluntary community work by young women who come from relatively privileged social positions, as a sort of neocolonialism or postcolonial patronage. Yet I would argue that their activity points instead to our own theoretical "blind spots." What we should realize is that these young women were clearly creating for themselves effective pathways for future success and happiness that made complete sense within their own social and cultural networks.

In fact, the girls' altruism, observed from within the framework of their own world values, can also be understood as "successful" and "resilient" behavior. For example, drawing from their own recent studies of adolescents in Australia, Howard and Johnson (2000, 2002) argue that the ability to survive and succeed in all aspects of life should be seen as an acquired amalgam of five particularly effective, multifaceted behaviors. Firstly, in all successful or resilient individuals it is possible to discern the development of the person's own strong sense of agency and ability; that is, the young people who demonstrate resilience have a clear sense of belief in their own ability to succeed and take action. Secondly, the successful adolescents have possession of strong social support networks. They know they can enlist support from key people around them, including nuclear and extended family members and peers. Thirdly, the young people possess good interpersonal skills, attributes that attract others to them because of their openness and warmth. Next, the successful adolescents have a strong sense of pride in their own achievement and competence even when the skills they possess may not be what are recognized as valuable within their more traditional educational institutions.[11] Finally, the researchers point to the importance of the opportunity to show leadership in the community and to serve others.[12] To their arguments, I would add that all of these interrelated factors are dependent on the ways in which these behaviors are modeled, explicitly or tacitly at home, and therefore any ways of exploring the various life options are seen as safe and acceptable from the young person's perspective.

A clear example of this can be seen if we return to the situation of Hannah. Voluntary community service was clearly deeply embedded in Hannah's life, as it was for her friends Meryl and Susan. It was a taken-for-granted, confident stepping into risk and otherness, which none of the girls considered remarkable in any way. All of their families were actively engaged in their own local and church communities, so it was perfectly acceptable for the girls that they should and could do this as they moved towards adulthood. While such community work for young people is not common, the underlying motivations to successfully explore boundaries, which sometimes means stepping out of one's comfort zone, were echoed in very different circumstances by the British young people as I shall demonstrate below.

Beats, babies and boyfriends

For the two British girls of Anglo–Celtic origin, Bernie and Karen, personal fulfillment lay in gaining recognition and work in the field of arts. More specifically, this meant developing their skills as musicians and singers. As a DJ (she also performed as an MC occasionally), Bernie usually had the opportunity to perform publicly about once a month. Her most regular job was in a pub in Camden because the owner knew her uncle. However, it was not a venue she enjoyed. The equipment was often broken and the crowd openly took various forms of illicit drugs, usually right in front of her mixing desk. "It's a horrible place," she warned me several times in preparation for my visit to watch her perform, "but at least it ain't violent because most of 'em are too stoned." Her uncle regularly accompanied her to these gigs to help with the technical side, speedily soldering broken cables where necessary, and clearly also to ensure there was "no trouble" from the clientele.

On another occasion, Bernie invited me to video her as she practised her skills at her home. She carefully explained the intricacies of turntabling and mixing to me as she demonstrated her art. To achieve what she has, Bernie has had to be determined and focused:

> *I practice and practice and practice until I get that mix perfect. If it takes me three hours or it takes me three days I still practice and practice until I get that mix perfect.*

The space in her flat was not large, so her family had to be particularly understanding and supportive. Again, I was struck with Bernie's conception of her "own private space" within the confines and limitations of what was available to her. I was reminded constantly of Diane's room in Australia, for Bernie's bedroom was also predominantly pink, tidy and equally a "femininized space." Like the Australian teenager's room, this bedroom still housed the many teddy bears and soft toys from childhood, nestling somewhat incongruously, it seemed to me, with the (adult) (masculinized) music technology with which she now played. This hardware – the decks, turntabling equipment, electronic mixing desk – located along one wall in her small bedroom had all been given to her by her male relatives and family friends. Her father, grandfather and uncle had also given her the mini-disc player and the large speakers attached to her wall. However, she had purchased the records herself, she told me proudly, spending about £50 a week, which was a huge percentage out of her part-time job earnings.

Bernie's choice of music was eclectic and taken from genres of contemporary R&B, UK Garage, Hip Hop and Drum and Base genres and styles, but some, she explained were far more rewarding and more challenging to mix and blend than others. To my untutored ears, much of the music sounded very similar, but she was finely attuned to the different tempos and pitches. Sometimes, she improvised, freestyling and pounding out her own rapid vocals to blend with the music, telling me that she drew her inspiration from "what's going on in the world, really. It's basically about what's going on. People used to have fun but now everyone – well not everyone – has turned to drugs. That's what it's all about really."

I recorded some of her lyrics which she then "translated" for me:

Back in the day it was all about Cotchin'.[13]
Have a little smoke to live' up the scene[14]
Now people turn to the other side
All that stuff that plays with their mind.[15]
It's a sad sound so far[16]
Till the bad vibe . . .
Dropping E's every other night
And sniffin' up through the nose . . .

Her ambition, not easily verbalized in everyday conversations with me, as was Hannah and Susan's, was instead written into her lyrics:

I was born to reach to the top of the box
Climb the highest mountain and never drop
(in the music industry, you know?)
I'm not lying in the shadows anymore
Where I can't be seen . . .
Check it out. It's Lady Lick!

Fig 20: Bernie in her room

Karen too was determined to "make it big" in the British music industry and was the lead vocalist of a Grunge rock cover band.[17] I went to watch and video one of their gigs at a pub in North London. It was described to me by Karen as "a rough working man's pub." I found it crowded and noisy, with pool tables, poker machines and the stage act all competing for attention. Burly security guards stood grimly at each of the three doors to the pub. I asked the guards if there was a particular concern warranting such security, but they shrugged, confirming that it was just a normal evening. In her jeans, braids and black net T-shirt, Karen's stage persona was a strange juxtaposition of toughness and "girliness" – her strong, strident voice competing with the guitar chords and the heavy drumbeats while her physical stance was slightly understated and deferential.

Figure 21: Karen in performance

Like the girls from Cirkidz or even Bekk's mannerisms, described earlier, Karen's demeanor seemed to offer an attempt to find a femininity that was both challenging and yet not too alternative within her micro-world. It was one that suggested sexual equality but one that retained a crucial gender difference. Her dynamic performance as a musician leads into the next area of self-making considered here – the self-conscious marking of distinction and difference with the body. I want to return briefly to aspects of embodiment and ownership, to examine what was particularly noticeable about the ways in which the girls from these three locales, Australia, the United States and London, understood and explored their sense of (gendered) embodiment.

Bodies, style, and cultural identities

In my earlier fieldwork, I found inevitable similarities between the ways in which each girl presented and "performed" her femininity (Butler 1990) and between the cultural understandings of who "owned" the body (Bordo 1993; Bloustien 2001). The girls studied in this later period were no different. It was clear, for example, that for the American girls, romantic relationships and particularly marriage and children, were central aspects of their sense of self. So while on one level, these girls saw themselves as needing to be independent and self-possessed, they all clearly felt incomplete and unfulfilled as "single women." Indeed, the fact that the term "single" itself has changed meaning amongst young people is significant. It is now used to mean not having a boyfriend or girlfriend (for however short a period) as opposed to not being in a long-term committed relationship (or marriage), as was previously the case. Being single, then, often implies for many (young) women failure, as indicating that something is lacking in their lives. So as Hannah, aged 22, explained to me:

> *Sometimes I get down about my singleton status, but generally I try to work through my feelings of loneliness and concentrate on improving myself and dealing with being my own keeper. It really isn't so bad at all.*

By contrast, none of the British girls talked about their romantic plans for the future, although several of them did have boyfriends. Marriage was not a topic that was often raised or voiced. For some, this was because they saw themselves as young and free to make life decisions for a long time to come. This seemed to be particularly the case for Bernie and Karen. For them, the subject of long-term relationships or marriage and children was something far off into the future, the timing of which they felt they could control and determine. The babies would occur, they seemed to feel, when they and their partners were ready for the event, and it certainly was not desirable for the pregnancies to occur before that time. This was a different perspective on relationships and pregnancy from that of some of the other girls from African or African–Carribean backgrounds. For Trea for example, while unexpected and difficult, the unplanned motherhood was accepted stoically and in some ways, positively. In her world, single motherhood was more acceptable and possibly even seen as inevitable. This was partly because, for many of the African–Caribbean girls, untimely pregnancy and the resulting babies, were part of a broader understanding of gender relations and particularly of being a woman. Perhaps even more significantly, the status of being a mother was an important step into the status of adulthood that could enhance one's standing in the eyes of the local community rather than diminish it. While the girls talked positively about pregnancy and early motherhood, almost all saw abortion as totally unacceptable. Thus decisions about pregnancy and termination were clearly central to the ways the girls understood the key values within their micro-world and expressed through their own gendered bodies.[18]

Because a sense of ownership and control over one's body underpins self-making, even simple routines of deportment, style, dress and body maintenance or otherwise have deeper cultural significance than might first appear. For example, as with the Aboriginal teenagers in Australia, I found that the girls from African and African-Caribbean backgrounds did not see themselves as separate individual entities totally independent from their parents and wider familial connections. Their role and positioning within their extended family relationships, as daughter, niece, or girlfriend, was a vitally important way of understanding who they were in their worlds. Many talked about having particularly close relationships with their mothers and their aunts, a phenomenon which was reflected in the ways they walked, the clothes they wore, and their hairstyles. These intimate familial bonds were also expressed through the girls' sense of pride and confidence in the way they dressed. It seemed as though, in their dress and deportment, they were making clear statements about who they were as women and how they saw themselves as part of a contemporary pan-African heritage.[19]

For example, while many of the Anglo–Celtic girls dressed in comfortable unisex baggy T-shirts and tops for classes at WAC, most of the girls from African and African– Caribbean backgrounds chose their clothes more carefully. These girls would arrive looking perfectly groomed as if they wanted to emphasize their developing self-consciousness as black British women. Although many of the youth at WAC had been born in the UK, their parents and relatives constantly talked of the West Indies as "home." These young people were encouraged to return to the West Indies as often as the family could afford, for holidays and to make connections with relatives and traditional family values. Conversations about "home," "identity" and the practical nostalgia (Battaglia 1995) for the West Indian culture was quite clearly defined in the ways the speakers coped with their everyday feelings of exclusion and other problems in British society. As many previous studies have also shown, the participants in my research indicated that they felt they coped better with most problems if they relied "on community spirit and spirituality, with regular group meetings and discussions . . . from family, friends, religious and cultural networks and prayer" (Hylton 1997). For many families of African and African–Caribbean heritage, the West Indies was the source of strength through a sense of shared history and cultural identity. As one respondent in a previous study put it:

> *I am West Indian because of my philosophy and historical sense of being; and we relate to the Caribbean as home. Even though my sisters and my brother were born here, they're very much Caribbean.*[20]

This sense of cultural identity was echoed many times in my own discussions with the British youth. Apart from the many stories by the young women as they talked about their previous or planned trips back "home," their strong sense of cultural identity was maintained through their involvement in religious practices and festivals, traditional food and cooking, their language and dialects and, as indicated above, through their appearance. Many of the girls, for example, paid great attention to their hair, taking pains to create a different elaborate hairstyle every day. Their elegant and intricate interwoven hair, composed of minute, tightly braided strands, which must have taken them several hours to perfect, was "reminiscent of the patternings of African cloth and the decorative designs of African ceramics, architecture and embroidery" (Mercer 1995: 127; see also Sagay 1983).

It was quite clear that these elaborate creations spoke of personal control and of a deliberately heightened African aesthetic. Even more importantly, it seemed that here was a use of bodily style where artifice itself took center stage. It was an aesthetic valued not just for its own sake – a playing with image and self in a way that was powerfully unique – but it also seemed a statement of important and valued difference, "fronting out oppression by the artful manipulation of appearances" (Mercer 1995: 132). The complex hairstyles were clearly ways of marking out a positive sense of difference, one way in which the body could be used to make personal and political statements of ownership and control in a world where opportunities for such statements in other ways are severely limited.

I would argue that in the deliberate stress on artifice of the style is yet another example of mimetic excess. For this is not simply an overt political stance through the body, but rather, in its very artifice, it is an ironic drawing of attention to the anxieties and difficulties of difference through "dialogic interventions of diasporean, creolizing cultures" (Mercer 1995: 135).

In contrast to the ways in which the British youth took control of their lives through the bodily style, I found that the American girls used a more traditional paradigm of health to assume control. For example, I learned that concerns about health issues and maintaining a healthy lifestyle were foremost in the minds and conversations of the girls from Indiana. This was true both for their personal lifestyles and in the topics chosen for their studies. Susan's final year university research project had centered on issues of anorexia and bulimia and she was keen to investigate the relationship between these food disorders and material disadvantage. During her community service she had found that, contrary to popular medical belief, bulimia was just as common amongst the residents of a South American orphanage as in the affluent suburbs where she lived. More importantly, she found that her findings clashed with the accepted wisdom of the institution, so that she had great difficulty having her concerns and report taken seriously. Hannah underwent a similar journey of discovery about health. In this instance it related to her own body. She had become seriously ill after she had left her university, about one month after she graduated, and had to be hospitalized for three weeks. She had developed complications from an earlier abdominal surgery.

> *After I got out of the hospital, it was such a frustrating feeling, to know that I was 22 years old, but did not have the same stamina or strength of everyone else my age.*

However, her reaction was to fight her way back to health – overcoming the illness by grim determination and resolution. She determined to improve her health bit by bit, firstly by walking a block at a time and then by jogging. I will let Hannah explain her developing sense of pride and self-control in her own eloquent manner:

> *Well, to be perfectly honest, the jogging did not start for quite a while. When I got out of the hospital, I could hardly walk the seven houses down to the end of the block without sitting down. I knew it was going to be a long time before I would be able to jog or run, but I was determined to get myself there. So I began taking a couple of walks per day, steadily increasing the distance and building my endurance. By the time I moved out of my house and into my apartment at the end of September, my jogs averaged a very slow two miles – but I was proud of my progress.*
>
> *Over last year, I started running four to six times a week, maxing out at five miles on a good day – by the picturesque lakefront or through the neighborhoods of Chicago. Much to my surprise, I have become one of those people who doesn't feel right without my daily run (or some form of exercise). My runs give me a chance to think and clear my mind . . . as the stressors of work and my personal life seem to fade away with the pounding of my feet and the sound of my heavy breathing. I zone out and focus on how my body feels as I can tell I am getting stronger and increasing my stamina. Running also allows me to be outside which is so nice after a day inside at work. I especially love running by the lake because I am reminded of how much I love Chicago and how proud of myself I am for being able to support myself and live on my own.*

Not all of the girls in this study had the capacity or the inclination to literally appropriate time and space in this way to underpin their self-making. And yet if we look more closely at Hannah's description, we can see that her actions do echo those of the other girls in more ways than we might have observed at first glance. She describes the power of her jogging as a "zoning out" through "the pounding of [her] feet and the sound of [her] heavy breathing" – her own body making the necessary music for her to clear her mind and focus upon her ongoing process of reflexive self-making.

Her words return us to so many of the narratives recounted in these pages. They are all tales of ways in which self-making is negotiated, explored and effected through bodily praxis. They remind us too, of the ways in which all of the participants drew upon music to do this, either as producers or consumers, or sometimes both. Music experienced through the body, was the central means by which they all carved out specific moments of time and space to create and manage their cultural selves.

As I have stressed throughout this book, music is a perfect vehicle for self-making, largely because of its links to specific cultural values and its significance to the wider social networks from which the values emerged. This was quite clearly seen in the involvement of many of the black British youth in gospel choirs: most sang regularly in their churches or in social groups with relatives and friends. Being part of a church community was not such an important factor in the musical lives of the white British youth, but the musical forms they chose gave them their own opportunity to step into and try out different forms of a gendered adulthood. The fact that Karen could perform as a singer in a grunge band and Bernie could be a DJ provides ample example of the ways in which particular musical forms facilitated this transition to occur within their own social fields.

The incompletable self?

And so we come full circle. We have seen accounts of young women struggling, achieving and negotiating how they are and who they can be in their worlds.

At the start of this book, I offered a description of two very different young women in Australia, Kate and Hilary, who occupied very different social fields. Through the following chapters, I demonstrated how, despite clear differences, they and all the participants in the study were desperately engaged in the serious, embodied play of self-making. I argued that, for all of us, such self-making is a universal, delicate process that tests possibilities while simultaneously heeding the material and symbolic boundaries that circumscribe the whole of our social and cultural life. It is this that underlies Bourdieu's concept of "habitus" (1977) and that can only take its meaning from within the various overlapping, sometimes contradictory social fields in which it is embedded. Every thought and action, which we feel to be so much a mark of our individuality and personhood, is in fact an articulation and negotiation of the intense emotional investments and values in which our lives are enmeshed.

The specific focus throughout the stories and vignettes in this book has been on the notion of the ways in which habitus informs identity-as-process. That is, I have demonstrated through the girls' own stories and perceptions that identity is not fixed or even fixable, but rather more like a problem constantly in search of a solution. By centering my analytic lens on the process of "self-making" of a number of teenage girls, from different social and cultural backgrounds in Australia, I revealed that several other facets of personhood – age, gender, class and ethnicity – come more sharply into focus. But these represent just some of the many layers of refraction, aspects of one's embodied personhood or "habitus" that profoundly influence, but do not totally determine, the ways in which all people negotiate the social fields of everyday life.[21] They are separate facets of identity that are often assumed to be self-fulfilling and determining constituents of human behavior on their own. However, when placed within the broader context of everyday experience, they are shown to be overlapping nuances or shades of possibilities. All of the young women in these stories have been carefully exploring and negotiating their own sense of personhood – stretching their possibilities to the limit but always trying to maintain their sense of balance.

As we watched the different young women in my fieldwork perceive, survey and articulate their sense of self, the sheer enormity of their task, their project of self-making has become clearer. Indeed, it is only through the various forms of fantasy, serious play and occasionally "dark play" that the constitution of the embodied self can be negotiated, although never completely achieved. It can never be a completed project. An army of consumer and cultural icons, accessories and cultural expectations standing in the wings consolidates this assumption, that this ephemeral self can never be finally managed, never finally be complete.

Notes

1 This is not to suggest that self-identifications in terms of class, race and ethnicity do not exist, but to stress again that they are part of the ongoing process by which each individual marks out an ongoing cluster of attributes that define the self.

2 The observations and analysis here, part of a much larger cross-cultural longitudinal study entitled "Playing for life," is ongoing. Funded largely by the Australian Research Council, this project explores the everyday lives of marginalized youth across four geographical sites, Adelaide, SA and Newcastle, NSW in Australia and London, UK and Boston, USA, particularly focusing on the impact of their involvement in a variety of musical cultures and activities. The work discussed here stems from the pilot work for this project and therefore heralds the broader studies to come. Some of this later work will appear in 2003.

3 WAC is the name of a highly successful London-based performing and media arts project established in 1978 for young people from low-income families that aims to provide a route into performing arts careers and build confidence, self-esteem and wider creative skills through the arts. It is supported mainly by local arts and charitable organizations with a small amount of its additional funding gained from the local council through strategically designed collaborative programs with local schools and colleges. Through the development of reflective and inclusive pedagogic practices, WAC has had a number of notable achievements, including a significant proportion of students progressing to formal full-time training at institutions such as the Old Vic, Rambert School and the Northern School of Contemporary Dance. Their students also demonstrate marked development in confidence, communication and team skills, realized in other learning environments.

4 Garage is a fast British genre of contemporary dance music which evolved from Hip Hop.

5 The MC (master of ceremonies) is the lyricist who sings or chants the words over the music.

6 To "chat" means to rap particularly rapidly for Garage music, which is a much faster beat than Hip Hop. Often the words sung or spoken are nonsense words, linked onomatopoeically or through rhyme, seemingly for the pure joy of the sound rather than for any overt political purpose as in rap.

7 None of these girls would have described themselves as wealthy, but according to their own accounts, each had benefited from very stable home backgrounds, with a reasonable degree of material comfort tempered with practical activism for others in their communities. All the parents of these American girls were college-educated and therefore access to higher education for their children was considered appropriate and desirable. Even more significantly for this discussion, from their observations of their own family life, the girls saw marriage as desirable and watched their parents successfully negotiating equal working partnerships both within and outside the home.

8 Clearly, while each young person had to obtain the necessary grades, the fact that they could even contemplate going to this college and had the opportunity, the resources and the cultural capital to obtain scholarships or other monetary support to study there, is a major factor in their success. See below for a further discussion of this aspect in understanding the nature of resilient behaviors.

9 This was the area where several "race" riots had notoriously erupted over the past few years instigated and inflamed by social injustices, poverty and high unemployment.

10 At time of writing, at 23 Meryl is already married and Susan plans to be engaged next year. Hannah was in a steady relationship from her middle teenage years but

now "is single." Her immediate goal, she says, is "improving myself and dealing with being my own keeper."

11 A good example of this is detailed below, where several of the young people in Britain were regarded as highly skilled turntablists or rappers in their musical cultures.

12 See S Howard & B J Johnson 2000, "Resilient and non-resilient behavior in adolescents," *Trends and Issues in Crime and Criminal Justice*, no. 183; S Howard & B J Johnson 2002, "Participation and involvement: Resiliencing factors for young adolescents" in M Gollop & J McCormack (eds.), *Children and Young People's Environments*, Dunedin, New Zealand, Children's Issues Centre, pp.110–38.

13 Having fun, hanging around the neighborhood.

14 Smoking marijuana, seen as a far more acceptable and innocuous recreational drug.

15 Hard drugs such as heroin, cocaine, amphetamines, Ecstasy.

16 In the argot of the time, words mean the opposite of what they seem so the adjectives "sad," "bad," or "wicked" mean particularly good.

17 They had not performed any original material as yet, preferring to "cover" material from established musicians.

18 See Tabberer, S, Hall, C, Prendergast, S, & Webster, A 2000, *Teenage pregnancy and choice: Abortion or motherhood: Influences on the decision,* November, UK, Rowntree Foundation, YPS, http://www.jrf.org.uk/ knowledge/findings/socialpolicy/n50.asp [accessed online 11 August 2000].

19 For more information see Hylton, C, 1997, "Moyenda: Black families talking – family survival strategies," *Social Policy Research,* 135, November, http://www.jrf.org.uk/knowledge/findings/socialpolicy/sp135.asp [accessed online 12 August 2002].

20 Respondent cited in Hylton, C 1997.

21 Again this is because so often contemporary researchers drawing upon Bourdieu's work tend to forget that the concept of "habitus" cannot be understood without considering the variety of overlapping social fields in which one's habitus is embedded and through which it is forever negotiating and justifying its existence. See again the Introduction in this volume.

Bibliography

Abu-Lughod, Lila. 1986. *Veiled Sentiments.* California: University of California Press.

Amit-Talai, Vered. and Helena Wulff, eds. 1995. *Youth Cultures: A Cross Cultural Perspective.* London: Routledge.

Anderson, Benedict. 1991 [1983]. *Imagined Communities: Reflections on the Origins and Spread of Nationalism.* 2nd ed. London: Verso.

Ardener, Edwin. 1975. "Belief and the Problem of Women." In *Perceiving Women,* ed. Shirley Ardener. London: Malaby; 1–27.

Ardener, Shirley, ed. 1993. *Women and Space: Ground Rules and Social Maps.* Oxford: Berg Publishers.

Bakhtin, Michel. 1968 [1965]. *Rabelais and His World.* Cambridge, Mass.: MIT Press.

Barnes, John Arundel. 1969. "Networks and Political Process." In *Social Networks in Urban Situations,* ed. James Clyde-Mitchell. Manchester: Manchester University Press: 51–76.

Barthes, Roland. 1977. *Image - Music - Text.* London: Fontana.

_____ 1981. *Camera Lucida.* New York: The Noonday Press.

Bataille, Georges. 1962. *Death and Sensuality: A Study of Eroticism and Taboo.* New York: Walker and Co.

Bateson, Gregory. 1982 [1972]. "A Theory of Play and Fantasy." In *Steps to an Ecology of Mind.* New York: Ballantine: 177–193.

Battaglia, Deborah, ed. 1995. *Rhetorics of Self-Making.* Berkeley, L.A.: University of California Press.

_____ 1995. "On Practical Nostalgia: Self-Prospecting among Urban Trobrianders." In *Rhetorics of Self-Making,* ed. Deborah Battaglia. Berkeley, L.A.: University of California Press.

Baudrillard, Jean. 1983. *Simulations.* New York: Semiotext(e).

Baudry, Jean-Louis. 1986. "Ideological effects of the basic cinematic apparatus." In *Narrative Apparatus and Ideology: A Film Theory Reader,* ed. Philip Rosen. New York: Columbia University Press: 286–298.

Becker, Anne E. 1994. "Nurturing and Negligence: Working on other's bodies in Fiji." In *Embodiment and Experience: The Existential Ground for Culture and Self,* ed. Thomas J. Csordas. Cambridge: Cambridge University Press: 100–115.

Benjamin, Walter. 1969 [1935]. *Illuminations.* New York: Schocken Books.

Benston, Margaret Lowe. 1988. "Women's voices/men's voices: technology as language." In *Technology and Women's Voices: Keeping in Touch,* ed. Cheris Kramarae. New York: Routledge and Kegan Paul:15–28.

Berger, John. 1977 [1972], *Ways of Seeing.* Harmondsworth: Pelican.

Berland, Jody. 1992. "Angels Dancing: Cultural Technologies and the Production of Space." In *Cultural Studies,* eds. Lawrence Grossberg, Carey Nelson. and Paula Treichler. New York: Routledge: 38–50.

Bhabha, Homi. 1987. "Interrogating Identity." In *The Real Me: Post Modernism and the Question of Identity,* ed. Lisa Appignanesi. ICA Documents 6. London: Institute of Contemporary Arts: 5–12.

_____ 1994. "Of Mimicry and Man: The Ambivalence of Colonial Discourse." *In The Location of Culture*, ed. Homi Bhabha. London: Routledge.

Blacking, John. 1976. *How Musical Is Man?* London: Faber and Faber.

_____ (ed.) 1977. *The Anthropology of the Body.* London: Academic Press.

_____ 1987. *A Common-Sense View of All Music.* Cambridge: Cambridge University Press.

Blair, Juliet. 1993. "Private Parts in Public Places: The Case of the Actresses." In *Women and Space,* ed. Shirley Ardener. Oxford: Berg: 200–221.

Bloustien, Geraldine. 1999. "The Consequences of Being a Gift." *The Australian Journal of Anthropology* (TAJA), 10: 1: 77–93.

_____ 2001. "Far From Sugar and Spice." In *Gender in Interaction*, eds. Bettina Baron and Helga Kotthoff. Benjamin Press: The Hague: 99–136.

Bordo, Susan. 1988. "Anorexia Nervosa: Psychopathology as the Crystallization of Nature." In *Feminism and Foucault: Reflections on Resistance,* eds. Irene Diamond and Lee Quinby. Boston: Northeastern University Press: 87–118.

_____ 1993. *Unbearable Weight: Feminism, Western Culture and The Body.* Berkeley: University of California Press.

Bott, Elizabeth. 1971. *Family and Social Networks.* London: Tavistock Publications.

Bourdieu, Pierre. 1977. *Outline of A Theory of Practice.* Cambridge: Cambridge University Press.

_____ 1986 [1977a]. "The Production of Belief: Contribution to an Economy of Symbolic Goods." In *Media Culture and Society,* eds. Richard Collins. et al. London: Sage: 131–165.

_____ 1982. *Ce que parler veut dire: L'économie des échanges linguistiques*. Paris: Artheme Fayard.

_____ 1984. *Distinction: A Social Critique of the Judgement of Taste.* Cambridge. Mass: Harvard University Press. London: Routledge and Kegan Paul.

_____ 1989. "Social Space and Symbolic Power." *Sociological Theory.* 7: 14–24.

_____ 1990. *In Other Words*. Cambridge: Polity Press.

_____ 1991. *Language and Symbolic Power.* Cambridge: Polity Press.

_____ 1993. *Sociology in Question*. London: Sage Publications.

_____ 1998. *Practical Reason: On the Theory of Action.* Cambridge: Polity Press.

Bourdieu, Pierre, and Loic J.D. Wacquant. 1992. *An Invitation to Reflexive Sociology.* Chicago: University of Chicago Press.

Boys, Jos. Francis Bradshaw. Jane Darke. Benedicte Foo. Sue Francis. Barbara McFarlane. Marion Roberts, and Susan Wilkes. 1984. "House Design and Women's Roles." in *Making Space: Women and The Male Environment*, eds. Matrix. London: Pluto Press :55–80.

Brake, Mike. 1980. *The Sociology of Youth Culture and Youth Subcultures: Sex and Drugs and Rock 'n' Roll?* London: Routledge and Kegan Paul.

_____ 1985. *Comparative Youth Culture: The Sociology of Youth Cultures and Youth Subcultures.* London: Routledge and Kegan Paul.

Brown, Michael F. 1996."On Resisting Resistance." *American Anthropologist*, 98: 4: 729–749.

Butler, Judith. 1990. *Gender Trouble.* New York: Routledge.

Bynum Walker, Caroline. 1987. *Holy Feast and Holy Fast: The Religious Significance of Food to Medieval Women.* Berkeley: University of California Press.

Caillois, Roger. 1959. *Man and The Sacred.* Glencoe: The Free Press.

Calhoun, Craig. 1995. *Critical Social Theory : Culture, History and The Challenge of Difference.* Oxford: Blackwell.

Caputo, Virginia. 1995. "Anthropology's Silent Others." In *Youth Cultures, A Cross Cultural Perspective*, eds. Helena Wulff and Vered Amit-Talai. London: Routledge: 19–42.

Carrington, Kerrie. 1989. "Girls and Graffiti." *Cultural Studies*: 3: 1: 89–100.

_____ 1993. *Offending Girls: Sex, Youth and Justice.* Australia: Allen and Unwin.

Castells, Manuel. 1996. "The Net and The Self: Working Notes for a Critical Theory of the Informational Society." *Critique of Anthropology*, 16: 1: 9–38.

Castles, John. 1998. "Tjungaringanyi: Aboriginal Rock (1971–91)." In *Sound Alliances: Indigenous Peoples, Cultural Politics and Popular Music in the Pacific*, ed. Philip Hayward. London: Cassell: 11–25.

Cixous, Helena. 1981. "The Laugh of Medusa." (transl. Keith and Paula Cohen). In *New French Feminisms: An Anthology*, eds. Elaine Marks and Isabelle de Courtivron. Brighton: Harvester: 245–264.

Clarke, John. 1976 [1975]. "Style." In *Resistance through Rituals*, eds. Stuart Hall and Tony Jefferson. London: Hutchinson.

Cohen, Anthony P. 1985. *The Symbolic Construction of Community.* London: Tavistock Publications.

_____ ed. 1986. *Symbolising Boundaries: Identity and Diversity in British Cultures.* Manchester: Manchester University Press.

Cohen, Sarah. 1997. "Men Making a Scene: Rock Music and the Production of Gender." In *Sexing The Groove*, ed. Sheila Whiteley. London: Routledge: 17–36.

Cohen, Stanley. 1972. "Subcultural Conflict and Working Class Community." *Working Papers in Cultural Studies:* no 2: CCCS: 5–52.

_____ 1980. "Symbols of Trouble." In *Folk Devils and Moral Panics.* Oxford: Moutin Robertson.

Collins, Richard et al., eds. 1986. *Media Culture and Society.* London: Sage.

Connell, Robert W. 1987. *Gender and Power.* Oxford: Polity.

Coward, Rosalind. 1984. *Female Desire: Women's Sexuality Today.* London: Paladin Grafton Books.

Cranny-Francis, Anne. 1995. *The Body in the Text.* Melbourne: Melbourne University Press.

Crapanzano, Vincent. 1986. "Hermes' Dilemma: The Masking of Subversion in Ethnographic Description." In *Writing Culture*, eds. James Clifford and George E. Marcus. Berkeley: University of California Press: 51–76

Csordas, Thomas. 1990. "Embodiment as a Paradigm for Anthropology." *Ethos*, 18: 5–47.

Csordas, Thomas ed. 1994. *Embodiment and Experience The Existential Ground for Culture and Self.* Cambridge: Cambridge University Press.

Cunneen, Chris, Rob Lynch, Vernon Tupper. and Mark Findlay. 1989. *The Dynamics of Collective Conflict.* Sydney: Law Book Co.

De Certeau, Michel. 1988. *The Practice of Everyday Life.* Berkeley: University of California Press.

Deem, Rosemary. 1989. "Feminism and Leisure Studies: opening up new directions." In *Relative Freedoms*, eds. Erica Wimbush and Margaret Talbot. Milton Keynes: Open University Press: 1–4.

Denholm, Carey. 1993. "In: Red Hot Chilli Peppers, Out: Jason Donavon: The Current ins and outs of Tasmanian Adolescent Peer Groups." In *Youth Subcultures: Theory, History and The Australian Experience*, ed. Rob White. Hobart Tasmania: National Clearing House for Youth Studies: 136–143.

Derrida, Jacques. 1973. *'Différance' in Speech and Phenomena.* Illinois: Northwest University Press.

_____ 1976. *Of Grammatology* (transl. Gayatri Chakravorty Spivak) Baltimore: John Hopkins University Press.

_____ 1978. "Structure, Sign and Play in the Discourse of Human Sciences." In *Writing and Difference*. Chicago: University of Chicago Press: 278–294.

_____ 1978. *Writing and Difference.* (transl. Alan Bass) London: Routledge: 278–294.

_____ 1981. *Positions*. Chicago: University of Chicago Press.

Deutsch, Eliot. 1993. "The concept of the body." In *Self as Body in Asian Theory and Practice*, ed. Thomas P. Kasulis. New York: State University of New York.

Dorn, Nicholas, and Nigel South. 1989. "Drugs and Leisure, Prohibition and Pleasure: from Subculture to the Drugalogue." In *Leisure for Leisure: Critical Essays*, ed. Chris Rojek. London: Macmillan.

Douglas, Mary. 1973. *Rules and Meaning: The Anthropology of Everyday Knowledge.* Harmondsworth: Penguin.

_____ 1978 [1970]. *Natural Symbols.* Harmondsworth: Penguin.

_____ 1982. *In The Active Voice.* London: Routledge and Kegan Paul.

_____ 1984 [1966]. *Purity and Danger: An analysis of the concepts of pollution and taboo.* London: Routledge and Kegan Paul.

_____ 1986. *Risk Acceptability According to the Social Sciences*. London: Kegan Paul.

Dragadze, Tamara. 1993. "The Sexual Division of Space among Two Soviet Minorities: The Georgians and Tadjiks." In *Women and Space*, ed. Shirley Ardener. Oxford: Berg: 156–164.

Drotner, Kristen. 1994. "Ethnographic Enigmas: The Everyday in Recent Media Studies." *Cultural Studies*, 8: 2: 341–57.

Duncan, Nancy, ed. 1996. *BodySpace: Destabilizing Geographies of Gender and Sexuality*. London: Routledge.

Dwyer, Kevin. 1982. *Moroccan Dialogues*. Prospect Heights, Ill: Waveland Press.

Dyer, Richard. 1987. *Heavenly Bodies*. New York: St. Martins Press.

Eckermann, Liz. 1994. "Self Starvation and Binge-Purging: Embodied Selfhood/ Sainthood." In *Bodies: Australian Cultural History*: 13: 82–99.

Ehrenreich, Barbara, Elizabeth Hess and Gloria Jacobs. 1992. "Beatlemania: 'Girls Just Wanna Have Fun'." In *The Adoring Audience*, ed. Lisa A. Lewis. London: Routledge: 84–106.

Elias, Norbert. 1978 [1939]. *The Civilizing Process Vol 1: The History of Manners*. Oxford: Basil Blackwell.

_____ 1982 [1939]. *The Civilizing Process Vol 2: State Formation and Civilization*. Oxford: Basil Blackwell.

Elley, Joy. and Christine Inglis. 1995. "Ethnicity and Gender: The Two Worlds of Australian Turkish Youth." In *Ethnic Minority Youth in Australia*, eds. Carmel Guerra and Rob White Hobart. NCYS: 193–202.

Epstein, Arnold Leonard. 1961. "The Network and Urban Social Organisation." *Rhodes-Livingstone Institute Journal*: 29: 29–62.

Ewings, S. 1989. "Koori Beat" (review) *Ots (On the Street)*. 18 October: Sydney.

Falk, Pasi. 1994. *The Consuming Body*. London: Sage.

Featherstone, Mike, Mike Hepworth, and Brian Turner, eds. 1991. *The Body: Social Process and Cultural Theory*. London: Sage.

Feher, Michel, Romona Naddaff and Nadia Tazi. 1989. *Fragments for the History of the Human Body*. New York: *Zone*, special issues 3, 4, and 5.

Fergie, Deane. 1995. "Whose Sacred Sites? Privilege in the Hindmarsh Island Bridge Debate." *Current Affairs Bulletin*, 72: 2: Aug/Sept: 14–22.

_____ 1998. "Unsettled." In *The Space Between: Australian Women Writing Fictocriticism*, eds. Heather Kerr and Amanda Bettlebeck. Nedlands: University of Western Australia: 173–200.

Figes, Eva. 1978. Patriarchal Attitudes, London: Virgo.

Fine, Michelle. and Pat Macpherson. 1994. "Over Dinner: Feminism and Adolescent Bodies." In *Power/Gender: Social Relations in Theory and Practice*, eds. Lorraine H. Radtke and Henderickus J. Stam. London: Sage: 219–246.

Fiske, John. 1987. "British Cultural Studies and Television." In *Channels of Discourse: Television and Contemporary Criticism*, ed. Robert C. Allen. Chapel Hill: University of North Carolina Press: 284–326.

_____ 1989. *Understanding Popular Culture*. Boston: Unwin Hyman.

_____ 1992. "Cultural Studies and the Culture of Everyday Life." In Lawrence Grossberg,*Cultural Studies*. London: Routledge: 154–165.

Forrester, John. 1987. "A Brief History of The Subject." In *Identity: The Real Me*, ed. Lisa Appignanesi, ICA Documents: 6.

Foucault, Michel. 1976. *The History of Sexuality*. (vol 1.) London: Penguin Books.

_____ 1979 [1977]. *Discipline and Punish: The Birth of the Prison*. Harmondsworth: Penguin.

_____ 1981. "Questions of Method: an interview with Michel Foucault." *IandC* 3–14.

Freud, Sigmund. 1961. *Beyond the Pleasure Principle.* (transl. James Strachey.) London: The Hogarth Press.

Frith, Simon. 1978. *The Sociology of Rock.* London: Constable.

_____ 1990 [1985]. "Afterthoughts." In *On Record: Rock, Pop and The Written Word,* eds. Simon Frith and Andrew Goodwin. London: Routledge: 419–424.

_____ 1992. "The Cultural Study of Popular Music." In *Cultural Studies,* ed. Lawrence Grossberg. London: Routledge.

_____ 1996. *Performing Rites.* Cambridge, Mass: Harvard University Press.

Frith Simon. and Angela Mc Robbie. 1990 [1978]. "Rock and Sexuality." In *On Record: Rock, Pop and The Written Word,* eds. Simon Frith and Andrew Goodwin. London: Routledge: 371–389.

Geertz, Clifford. 1975 [1973]. "Deep Play: Notes on the Balinese Cockfight." In Clifford Geertz, *The Interpretation of Cultures.* New York: Basic Books: 412–53.

Gebauer, Gunter and Christopher Wulf. 1992. *Mimesis.* Berkeley: University of California Press.

Gerth, Hans H., and Charles Wright-Mills. 1974 [1948]. *From Max Weber: Essays in Sociology.* London: Routledge and Kegan Paul.

Giddens, Anthony. 1985. "Time, Space and Regionalisation." In *Social Relations and Spatial Structures,* eds. Derek Gregory and John Urry. London: Macmillan.

_____ 1990. *The Consequences of Modernity.* Cambridge: Polity Press.

_____ 1991. *Modernity and Self Identity.* Oxford: Polity Press.

Gilbert, Pamela, and Sandra Taylor. 1991. *Fashioning the Feminine: Girls, Popular Culture and Schooling.* North Sydney: Allen and Unwin.

Gilligan, Carol. 1982. *In A Different Voice: Psychological Theory and Women's Development.* Cambridge, Mass: Harvard University Press.

_____ 1990. "Teaching Shakespeare's Sister: Notes from the Underground of Female Adolescence." Preface to *Making Connections: The Relational Worlds of Adolescent Girls at Emma Willard School,* eds. Carol Gilligan, Nona P. Lyons and Trudy J. Hammer. Cambridge, Mass: Harvard University Press: 6-29.

Ginsberg, Fay. 1995. "Production Values: Indigenous Media and The Rhetoric of Self-Determination." In *Rhetorics of Self-Making,* ed. Deborah Battaglia. Berkeley: University of California Press: 121–138.

Goffman, Erving. 1956. "The Nature of Deference and Demeanour." *American Anthropologist:* 58: June: 473–502.

_____ 1959. *The Presentation of Self in Everyday Life.* London: The Penguin Press.

_____ 1967. *Behaviour in Public Places: Notes on the Social Organisation of Gatherings.* New York: The Free Press.

_____ 1970. *Strategic Interaction.* Oxford: Blackwell.

_____ 1971. *Relations in Public: Microstudies of the Public Order.* London: Allen Lane/The Penguin Press.

Goldstein, Laurence, ed. 1991. *The Female Body: Figures, Styles, Speculations.* University of Michigan.

Good, Byron. 1992. "The Body in Pain." In *Pain as Human Experience: An Anthropological Perspective,* eds. Mary J. Good, Byron Good, Paul E. Brodwin and Arthur Kleinman. Berkeley: University of California Press: 29–48.

Goodman, Lizbeth. 1992. "Comic subversions: comedy as strategy in feminist theatre." In *Imagining Women: Cultural Representations and Gender*, ed. Frances Bonner. Milton Keynes: Polity Press, in association with The Open University. 301–320.

Greer Germaine. 1991. "The Changing Woman." *The Age* (Saturday Extra): November 2nd: 1991: 1 and 6.

Gregory, Derek. and John Urry. 1985. *Social Relations and Spatial Structures.* London: Macmillan.

Gregory, Derek. 1986. "Spatial Structure." In *The Dictionary of Human Geography,* eds. Ron J. Johnston. et al. 2nd ed: Oxford: Blackwell: 451.

Griffin, Christine. 1993. *Representations of Youth.* Cambridge: Polity Press.

Griffin, Susan. 1978. *Women and Nature: The Roaring Inside Her.* New York: Harper and Row.

Grossberg, Lawrence, ed. 1992. *Cultural Studies.* New York: Routledge.

Grosz, Elizabeth. 1990. "A Note on Essentialism and Difference." In *Feminist Knowledge: Critique and Construct*, ed. Sneja Gunew. London: Routledge: 332–344.

Grove-Hall, Susan. 1994. "New Age Music: an analysis of ecstasy," *Popular Music and Society,* Summer: Vol. 18: 2: 23–34.

Hall, Donald. 1994. "New Age Music: a voice of liminality in postmodern popular culture." *Popular Music and Society*, Summer: Vol. 18: 2: 13–22.

Hall, Edward T., and William F. Whyte. 1960. "Intercultural Communication: A Guide to Men of Action." *Human Organisation*: 19: 1: Spring: 5–12.

Hall, Stuart, and Tony Jefferson, eds. 1976 [1975]. *Resistance through Rituals.* London: Hutchinson.

Hall, Stuart. 1995. "Fantasy Identity and Politics." In *Cultural Remix: Theories of Politics and The Popular,* eds. Erica Carter, James Donald and Judith Squires. London: Lawrence and Wishart: 63–72.

_____ 1996. "Music and Identity." In *Questions of Cultural Identity*, Stuart Hall and Paul du Gay: London: Sage: 108–127.

Handelman, Don. 1977. "Play and ritual: complementary frames of metacommunication." In *It's a Funny Thing: Humour,* Anthony J. Chapman and Hugh Foot. London: Pergamon: 185–192.

_____ 1990. *Models and Mirrors: Towards an Anthropology of Public Events.* Cambridge University Press.

Handelman, Don. and Shulman, David Dean. 1977. *God Inside Out: Siva's Game of Dice,* Oxford: Oxford University Press.

Harary Frank. 1969 [1959]. "Graph Theoretical Models in The Management Services." In *Social Networks in Urban Situations*, ed. James Clyde Mitchell. Manchester: Manchester University Press.

Hardman, Charlotte. 1973. "Can there be an anthropology of children?" *Journal of Anthropological Society of Oxford,* 4: 1: 85–99.

Harraway, Donna. 1990. "Investment Strategies for the Evolving Portfolio of Primate Females." In *Body/Politics: Women and the Discourses of Science,* eds. Mary Jacobus, Evelyn Fox Keller, and Sally Shuttleworth. New York: Routledge: 139–62.

_____ 1991. *Simians, Cyborgs and Women: The Reinvention of Nature.* New York: Routledge.

Harré, Rom. 1981. "Philosphical aspects of the micro-macro problem." In *Advances in Social Theory and Methodology: Towards an integration of micro and Macro-sociologies,* eds. Karen Knorr-Cetina and Aaron V. Cicourel. Boston: Routledge: 139–160.

Harrer, Gerhart and Hildegund Harrer. 1977. "Music Emotion and Automatic Function." In *Music and the Brain,* eds. Macdonald Critchley and R.A. Henson. London: William Heinemann Medical Books: 202–216.

Harries-Jones, Peter. 1969. "'Home-Boy' Ties and Political Organisation in a Copperbelt Township." In *Social Networks in Urban Situations,* James Clyde Mitchell. Manchester: Manchester University Press: 297–342.

Harvey, David. 1990. "Between Space and Time: reflections on the geographical imagination." *Annals of the Association of American Geographers,* 80: 418–434.

Haslam, David. 1997. "DJ Culture." In *The Club Cultures Reader,* ed. Steve Redhead. Oxford: Blackwell Publishers: 168–179.

Hastrup, Kirsten. 1978. "The Semantics of Biology: Virginity." In *Defining Females,* ed. Shirley Ardener. London: Croom Helm: 49–65 (1993: 2nd. ed'n.: 34–50).

Hayward, Philip, ed. 1998. *Sound Alliances: Indigenous Peoples, Cultural Politics and Popular Music in the Pacific.* London: Cassell.

Hebdige, Dick. 1976. "Reggae, Rastas and Rudies." In *Resistance through Rituals: Youth Subcultures in Post war Britain,* eds. Stuart Hall and Tony Jefferson. London: Hutchinson: 135–54.

_____ 1979. *Subcultures: The Meaning of Style.* London: Methuen.

_____ 1988. *Hiding in the Light.* Comedia Series. London: Routledge.

Henderson, Karla. A. 1991. "The contribution of feminism to an understanding of leisure constraints." *Journal of Leisure Research:* 23: 4: 363–77.

Hendry, Leo. Janet Shucksmith. John G. Love. and Anthony Glendinning. 1993. *Young People's Leisure and Lifestyles.* London: Routledge.

Henriques, Julian. Wendy Hollway. Cathy Urwin. Couze Venn. and Valerie Walkerdine. 1984. *Changing the Subject.* London: Methuen.

Hirschon, Renee. 1983. "Under One Roof: Marriage, Dowry and Family Relations in Piraeus." In *Urban Life in Mediterranean Europe,* eds. Michael Kenny and David Kertzer. Urbana: University of Illinois Press: 299–323.

_____ 1993. *Essential Objects and The Sacred: Interior and Exterior Space in an Urban Greek Locality.* In *Women and Space,* ed. Shirley Ardener. Oxford: Berg: 70–86.

Holloway, Wendy. 1984. "Gender Difference and the production of Subjectivity." In *Changing the Subject,* eds. Julian Henriques, Wendy Hollway, Cathy Urwin, Couze Venn and Valerie Walkerdine. London: Methuen.

hooks, belle. 1991. *Yearning: Race, Gender and Cultural Politics.* London: Turnaround Press.

Hosokawa, Shuhei. 1984. "The Walkman Effect." *Popular Music:* IV: 165–180.

_____ 1990. *The Aesthetics of Recorded Sound.* Tokyo: Keisó Shobó.

Hudson, Barbara. 1984. "Femininity and Adolescence." In *Gender and Generation,* eds. Angela McRobbie and Mica Nava. Basingstoke: Macmillan: 31–53.

Hylton, Carl. *Family Survival Strategies: Moyenda Black Families Talking, An exploring parenthood project,* Joseph Rowntree Foundation.

Iso-Aholas, Seppo E., and Edward D. Crowley. 1991. "Adolescent substance abuse and leisure boredom." *Journal of Leisure Research*: 23: 3: 260–271.

Jackall, Robert. 1994. "Re-Enchanting the World: Some Reflections on Post Modernism." *International Journal of Politics, Culture and Society:* 8: 183–192.

Jackson, Jean E. 1992. "'After a While No One Believes You': Real and Unreal Chronic Pain." In *Pain as Human Experience: An Anthropological Perspective,* eds. Mary-Jo Good et al. Berkeley: University of California Press: 138–168.

Jaggar, Alison M., and Susan R. Bordo, eds. 1989. *Gender/ Body/ Knowledge: Feminist Reconstructions of Being and Knowing.* New Brunswick: Rutgers University Press.

James, Alison. 1986. "Learning to Belong: the Boundaries of Adolescence." In *Symbolising Boundaries: Identity and Diversity in British Cultures,* ed. Anthony P. Cohen. Manchester University Press: 155–170.

Jeffrey, Patricia. 1979. *Frogs in a Well: Indian Women in Purdah.* London: Zed Press.

Kamuf, Peggy. 1991. *Derrida Reader.* Hemel Hemstead: Harvester.

Kaplan, Anne E. 1988. *Rocking Around the Clock: Music Television, Postmodernism and Consumer Culture.* New York: Routledge.

Kirby, Kathleen. M. 1996. "Remapping Subjectivity: Cartographic Vision and the Limits of Politics." In *BodySpace,* ed. Nancy Duncan. London: Routledge: 45–55.

Kozicki, Z. A. 1986. "Why do adolescents use substances (drugs/alcohol)?" *Journal of Alcohol and Drug Education,* 31: 1: 1–7.

Kramarae, Cheris, ed. 1988. *Technology and Women's Voices.* New York: Routledge and Kegan Paul.

Lees, Sue. 1993. *Sugar and Spice: Sexuality and Adolescent Girls.* Harmondsworth: Penguin.

Lefebvre, Henri. 1991. *The Production of Space.* Oxford: Blackwell.

Le Roy, Margaret. 1993. "Why women will always hate their bodies." *The Weekend Australian,* October 16th:,10–11. Extracted from *The Truth about Female Sexuality*. London: Harper Collins.

Lesko, Nancy. 1988. "The Curriculum of the Body: Lessons from a Catholic High School." In *Becoming Feminine: The Politics of Popular Culture,* eds. Leslie G. Roman, Linda K. Christian Smith, and Elizabeth Ellsworth. Lewes: Falmer Press.

Levi-Strauss, Claude. 1972 [1966]. *The Savage Mind.* London: Weidenfeld and Nicholson.

Lewis, Lisa. 1990. *Gender Politics and MTV.* Philadelphia: Temple University Press.

_____, ed. 1992. *The Adoring Audience: Fan Culture and Popular Media.* London: Routledge.

Lifton, Robert J. 1993. *The Protean Self: Human Resilience in an Age of Fragmentation.* New York: Basic Books.

Lock, Margaret. 1993. "Cultivating the Body: Anthropology and Epistemologies of Bodily Practice and Knowledge." *Annual Review of Anthropology,* 22: 133–155.

Lupton, Deborah. 1996. *Food, the Body and the Self.* London: Sage.

MacCormack, Carol P., and Marylin Strathern, eds. 1980. *Nature, Culture and Gender.* Cambridge: Cambridge University Press.

Marcus, George E., and Michael M. J. Fisher. 1986. "Ethnography and Interpretive Anthropology." In *Anthropology as Cultural Critique: An Experimental Moment in the Human Sciences,* eds. George E. Marcus and Michael M. J. Fisher. Chicago: University of Chicago Press: 17–44.

Marcus, George. and Michael M. J. Fischer. 1986. *Anthropology as Cultural Critque: An Experimental Moment in the Human Sciences.* Chicago: University of Chicago Press.

Massey, Doreen B. 1994. *Space Place and Gender.* Cambridge: Polity Press.

Mathieu, Nicole-Claude. 1978. "Man-culture and women-nature?" *Women's Studies,* 1: 55–65.

Matrix, eds. 1984. *Making Space: Women and the Male Environment.* London: Pluto Press.

McEachern, Charmaine. 1998. "A Mutual Interest? Ethnography in Anthropology and Cultural Studies." In *The Australian Journal of Anthropology,* 9: 3: 251–264. (Special Issue 10, ed. Ade Peace)

McRobbie, Angela. 1978. "Working Class Girls and the Culture of Femininity." In *Women Take Issue,* ed. Women's Studies Group London: Hutchinson: 96–108.

_____ 1980. "Settling Accounts with Subcultures. A Feminist Critique." *Screen Education,* 34: 37–49.

_____ 1984. "Dance and Social Fantasy." In *Gender and Generation,* eds. Angela McRobbie and Mica Nava. London: Macmillan Educational Publications: 130–161.

_____ 1991. *Feminism and Youth Culture.* London: Macmillan.

_____ 1994. *Post Modernism and Popular Culture.* London: Routledge.

McRobbie, Angela, and Jenny Garber. 1976. "Girls and Subcultures." In *Resistance through Rituals,* eds. Stuart Hall and Tony Jefferson. London: Hutchinson: 209–229.

McRobbie, Angela and Mica Nava, eds. 1984. *Gender and Generation.* London: Macmillan Educational Publications.

Melucci, Alberto. 1989. *Nomads of the Present: Social Movements and Individual Needs in Contemporary Society* Philadelphia: Temple University Press.

Mercer, Kobena. 1995 [1987]. "Black Hair/Style Politics." In *Cultural Remix: Theories of Politics and the Popular,* eds. Erica Carter, James Donald and Judith Squires. London: Lawrence and Wishart: 115–140.

Middleton, Richard. 1990. *Studying Popular Music.* Milton Keynes: Open University Press.

Mintel Market Research. 1990–1992.

Modleski, Tania. 1988. *Loving With a Vengeance: Mass produced fantasies for Women.* New York: Routledge.

Moore, Henrietta L. 1986. *Space Text and Gender: An Anthropological Study of the Marakwet of Kenya.* Cambridge: Cambridge University Press.

_____ 1988. *Feminism and Anthropology.* Minneapolis: University of Minnesota Press.

_____ 1994. *A Passion for Difference.* Cambridge: Polity Press.

Morley, David. 1981. "'The "Nationwide" Audience' – A Critical Postscript." *Screen Education,* 39 (Summer): 3–14.

_____ 1992. *Television, Audiences and Cultural Studies.* London: Routledge.

Morris, Meaghan. 1988. "Things to do with shopping centres." In *Grafts: Feminist Cultural Criticism,* ed. Susan Sheridan. London: Verso: 193–226.

Myerhoff, Barbara, and Jay Ruby. 1982. "Introduction." *A Crack in the Mirror: Reflexive Perspectives in Anthropology.* Philadelphia: University of Pennsylvania Press: 1–38.

Neustadter, Roger. 1994. "Back to the Future: childhood as utopia." *Extrapolation,* 35: 2 (Summer): 145–155.

_____ 1994a. "The Obvious Child: the symbolic use of childhood in contemporary popular music." *Popular Music and Society,* 18: 1 (Spring): 51–68.

Nightingale, Virginia. 1993. "What is ethnographic about ethnographic audience research?" In *Australian Cultural Studies,* eds. John Frow and Meaghan Morris. NSW: Allen and Unwin: 149–161.

Nilan, Pamela. 1992. "Kazzies, DBTs and Tryhards: categorisations of style in adolescent girls' talk." *British Journal of Education,* 13: 2: 201–214.

Nixon, Helen. 1996. "GP and the X files." *Metro Magazine,* no. 106: June: 50–57.

Ortner, Sherry B. 1974. "Is Female to Male as Nature is to Culture?" In *Woman, Culture and Society,* eds. Michelle Rosaldo and Louise Lamphere. Standford: Standford University Press: 67–88.

Ortner, Sherry B., and Harriet Whitehead eds. 1986 [1981]. *Sexual Meanings: The Cultural Construction of Gender and Sexuality.* Cambridge: Cambridge University Press.

Ortner, Sherry B. 1996. *Making Gender: The Politics and Erotics of Culture.* Boston: Beacon Press.

Paine, Robert. 1974. "Anthropological Approaches to Friendship." In *The Compact: Selected Dimensions of Friendship,* ed. Elliott Leyton. Newfoundland Social and Economic Papers, No. 3: Canada: Memorial University of Newfoundland: 1–14.

Parkin, Frank. 1979. *Marxism and Class Theory.* London: Tavistock.

Patton, Paul. 1988. "Giving Up the Ghost: Postmodernism and Anti-nihilism." In *It's a Sin: Essays on Postmodernism, Politics and Culture,* ed. Lawrence Grossberg. Sydney: Power Publications: 88–95.

Peace, Ade. 1991. *The Family Album.* Unpublished seminar paper to Department of Anthropology. University of Adelaide.

Penley, Constance. 1989. *The Future of An Illusion.* Minneapolis: University of Minnesota Press.

Polhemus, Ted. 1993. "Dance Gender and Culture." In *Dance Gender and Culture,* ed. Helen Thomas. London: Macmillan: 3–15.

_____ 1997. "In the Supermarket of Style." In *The Club Cultures Reader,* ed. Steve Redhead. Cambridge: Blackwell: 148–151.

Polk, Kenneth. 1993. "Reflections on Youth Subcultures." In *Youth Subcultures: Theory, History and The Australian Experience*, ed. Rob White. Hobart Tasmania: National Clearing House for Youth Studies: 99–106.

Poole, Marylin J. 1986. "Choices and Constraints: The Education of Girls." In *Australian Women: New Feminist Perspectives*, eds. Norma Grieve and Ailsa Burns. Melbourne: Oxford University Press: 105–121.

Rabinow, Paul. 1988. "Beyond Ethnography: anthropology as nominalism." *Cultural Anthropology*, 3: 4: 355–64.

Radtke, H. Lorraine, and Henderickus J. Stam. eds. 1994. *Power / Gender: Social Relations in Theory and Practice*. London: Sage.

Redhead, Steve, ed. 1993. *Rave Off: Politics and Deviance in Contemporary Youth Culture*. Avebury: Aldershot.

_____ 1995. *Unpopular Cultures: The Birth of Law and Popular Culture*. Manchester: Manchester University Press.

_____ ed. 1997. *The Club Cultures Reader.* Oxford: Blackwell.

Rodin, Judith. 1992. "Body Mania." *Psychology Today*, 25: 1 (Jan/Feb): 56–60.

Rojek, Chris, ed. 1989. *Leisure for Leisure: Critical Essays*. London: Macmillan.

Roman, Linda, and Linda Christian-Smith. 1988. *Becoming Feminine: the Politics of Popular Culture*. London: Falmer Press.

Rosaldo, Michelle Z. 1974. "Women, Culture and Society: A theoretical Overview." In *Women, Culture and Society*, eds. Michelle Z. Rosaldo and Louise Lamphere. Stanford: Stanford University Press: 17–42.

Rosing, Helmut. 1984. "Listening behaviour and musical preferences in the age of 'transmitted music'." *Popular Music*, 5 *(Continuity and Change)*: 119–149.

Rouget, Gilbert. 1985. *Music and Trance: A Theory of Relations between Music and Possession*. Chicago: The University of Chicago Press.

Rubin, Jerry. 1970. *Do It!* New York: Simon and Schuster.

Ruby, Jay ed. 1982. *A Crack in the Mirror: Reflexive Perspectives in Anthropology*. Philadelphia: University of Pennsylvania Press.

Sacks, Oliver. 1984. *A Leg To Stand On*. New York: Harper and Row.

Sagay, Esi. 1983. *African Hairstyles: Styles of Yesterday and Today*. London and Nairobi: Heinemann.

Sahlins, Marshall. 1993. *Waiting for Foucault*. Cambridge: Prickly Pear Press.

Said, Edward. 1989. "Representing The Colonised: Anthropology's Interlocutors." *Critical Inquiry*, 15: 2 (Winter): 205–25.

Schechner, Richard. 1982. "Collective Reflexivity: Restoration of Behaviour." In *A Crack in The Mirror: Reflexive Perspectives in Anthropology*, ed. Jay Ruby. Philadelphia: University of Pennsylvania Press: 39–82.

_____ 1983. *Performative Circumstances from the Avant Garde to Ramilila*. Calcutta: Seagull Books.

_____ 1985. *Between Theatre and Anthropology*. Philadelphia: University of Pennsylvania Press.

_____ 1993. *The Future of Ritual*. London: Routledge.

Schilling, Christopher. 1993. *The Body and Social Theory*. London: Sage.

Schneider, David M. 1968. *American Kinship: A Cultural Account*. New Jersey: Prentice-Hall.

Schwartz, Ronald. 1974. "The Crowd: Friendship Groups in a Newfoundland Outport." In *The Compact: selected dimensions of friendship;* Newfoundland social and economic papers, ed. Elliot Leyton. No 3: Canada: Memorial University of New Foundland: 71–92.

Sciama, Lidia. 1993. "The Problem of Privacy in Mediterranean Anthropology." In *Women and Space,* ed. Shirley Ardener. Oxford: Berg: 87–111.

Scott, Jody. 1997. "New Wave of Rockers Take on the World." *The Weekend Australian,* April 19–20: 3.

Seaman, William. 1992. "Active Audience Theory: Pointless Popularism." In *Media, Culture and Society,* 14, 2.

Sharp, Joanne P. 1996. "Gendering Nationhood: a feminist engagement with national identity." In *BodySpace,* ed. Nancy Duncan. London: Routledge: 97–108.

Shaviro, Steve. 1993. *The Cinematic Body.* Minneapolis: University of Minnesota Press.

Shepherd, John. and Peter Wicke. 1997. *Music and Cultural Theory.* Cambridge: Polity Press.

Shwartz, Deborah. 1959. "The Heavy Bear." In *Selected Poems: Summer Knowledge.* USA: New Directions Publishing Corp.

Simmons, Roberta G., Florence Rosenberg, and Morris Rosenberg. 1973. "Disturbance in the self image at adolescence." *American Sociological Review,* 38: 553–68.

Skeggs, Beverly. 1993. "For Women Only." In *Madonna,* ed. Fran Lloyd. London: Batsford Press: 271–81.

_____ 1997. *Formations of Class and Gender: Becoming Respectable.* London: Sage.

Smith, Dorothy. 1988. "Femininity as Discourse." In *Becoming Feminine: The Politics of Popular Culture,* eds. Leslie G. Roman and Linda Christian-Smith. London: Falmer Press: 37–59.

_____ 1990. *Texts, Facts and Femininity.* London: Routledge.

Soja, Edward W. 1989. *Postmodern Geographies: the Reassertion of Space in Critical Social Theory.* Verso: London.

_____ 1996. *Thirdspace: Journeys to Los Angeles and Other Real-and-Imagined Places.* Cambridge, Mass.: Blackwell Publishers.

Sontag, Susan. 1977. *On Photography.* New York: New York Dell Publishing.

_____ 1979. *Illness as Metaphor.* New York: Vintage.

Spain, Daphne. 1992. *Gendered Spaces.* Chapel Hill: University of North Carolina Press.

Spender, Dale. 1980. *Man Made Language.* London: Routledge and Kegan Paul.

Stanislavski, Constantin. 1980 [1936]. *An Actor Prepares* (rev. ed, translated by Elizabeth Reynolds Hapgood). London: Methuen Drama.

Stanworth, Michelle. 1981. *Gender and Schooling: A Study of Gender Divisions in the Classroom.* London: WRRC.

Stewart, Susan. 1984. *On Longing.* Baltimore: John Hopkins University Press.

Stokes, Martin, ed. 1994. *Ethnicity, Identity and Music: The Musical Construction of Place.* Oxford: Berg.

Storr, Anthony. 1992. *Music and the Mind.* London: Harper Collins Publishers.

Strathern, Marilyn. 1987. "The limits of auto-anthropology." In *Anthropology at Home,* ed. Anthony Jackson. ASA Monographs 25, London: Tavistock Publications: 16–37.

Stratton, Jon. 1992. *The Young Ones: Working Class Culture, Consumption and the Category of Youth.* Perth: Black Swan Press, Curtin University of Technology.

_____ 1993. "Bodgies and Widgies: Just Working Class Kids Doing Working Class Things." In *Youth Subcultures: Theory, History and The Australian Experience,* ed. Rob White. Hobart Tasmania: National Clearing House for Youth Studies: 87–91.

Straw, Will. 1997. "Organised Disorder: The Changing Space of the Record Shop." In *The Club Cultures Reader,* ed. Steve Redhead. Oxford: Blackwell: 57–65.

Suleiman, Susan Rubin. 1986. "(Re)writing the Body: The Politics and Poetics of Female Eroticism." In *The Female Body in Western Culture,* ed. Susan Rubin Suleiman. Cambridge: Harvard University Press 7–29.

_____ 1986. ed. *The Female Body in Western Culture.* Cambridge: Harvard University Press.

Summers, Anne. 1994. *Damned Whores and God's Police.* Harmondsworth: Penguin Books.

Suransky, Valerie Polakow. 1982. *The Erosion of Childhood.* Chicago, Ill: University of Chicago Press.

Tait, Gordon. 1993. "Reassessing Street Kids: A critique of subcultural theory." In *Youth Subcultures, Theory, History and The Australian Experience,* ed. Rob White. Hobart Tasmania: National Clearing House for Youth Studies: 1–6.

Taussig, Michael. 1987. *Shamanism, Colonialism and The Wild Man.* Chicago: University of Chicago Press.

_____ 1993. *Mimesis and Alterity.* New York: Routledge.

Taylor, Sandra 1993. "Subversions: Feminist Perspectives on Youth Subcultures." In *Youth Subcultures: Theory, History and The Australian Experience,* ed. Rob White. Hobart Tasmania: National Clearing House for Youth Studies: 19–26.

Taylor, Tim. 1997. *Global Pop: World Music. World Markets.* London: Routledge.

Thomas, Helen, ed. 1993. *Dance, Gender and Culture.* London: Macmillan.

Thornton, Sarah. 1995. *Club Cultures: Music, Media and Subcultural Capital.* Cambridge: Polity Press.

Trinh, Minh-ha. 1989. *Woman, Native Other: Writing Postcoloniality and Feminism.* Bloomington: Indiana University Press.

Tsolidis, Georgina. 1995. "Cultural Difference and Australian Feminism." In *Ethnic Minority Youth in Australia,* eds. Carmel Guerra and Rob White. Hobart Tasmania: National Clearing House for Youth Studies: 71–84.

Turkle, Sherry. 1995. *Life on the Screen: Identity in the Age of the Internet.* New York: Simon and Schuster.

Turner, Bryan S. 1984. *The Body and Society.* Oxford: Basil Blackwell.

_____ 1992. *Regulating Bodies: Essays in Medical Sociology.* London: Routledge.

_____ 1994. "Theoretical Developments in the Sociology of the Body." In *Bodies. Australian Cultural History*, 13: 13–30.

Turner, Victor. 1967. *The Forest of Symbols.* Ithaca, NY: Cornell University Press.

_____ 1977. "Variations on the Theme of Liminality." In *Secular Ritual*, eds. Sally Moore and Barbara G. Myerhoff. Amsterdam: Van Gorcum, Assen: 36–52.

_____ 1982. *From Ritual to Theatre: The Human Seriousness of Play*. New York City: Performing Arts Journal Publications.

_____ 1982a. "Dramatic Ritual /Ritual Drama: Performative and Reflexive Anthropology." In *A Crack in The Mirror: Reflexive Perspectives in Anthropology*, ed. Jay Ruby. Philadelphia: University of Pennsylvania Press: 83–97.

Urry, John. 1985. "Social Relations, Space and Time." In *Social Relations and Spatial Structures*, eds. Derek Gregory and John Urry. London: Macmillan: 20–48.

Wagner, Roy. 1975. *The Invention of Culture.* Chicago: University of Chicago Press.

Walkerdine, Valerie. 1984. "Some Day My Prince Will Come: Young Girls and the Preparation for Sexuality." In *Gender and Generation*, eds. Angela McRobbie and Mica Nava. London: Macmillan Educational Publications: 162–184.

_____ 1997. *Daddy's Girl: Young Girls and Popular Culture.* Houndsmills: Macmillan Press.

Walters, Suzanna Danuta. 1995. *Material Girls: Making Sense of Feminist Cultural Theory.* Berkeley: University of California Press.

Weiner, James. 1996. "On Televisualist Anthropology." *Current Anthropology*, 38: 2 (April): 197–236.

Weldon, Fay. 1992. *Growing Rich.* London: Harper Collins.

Wexler, Philip. 1983. "Movement Class and Education." In *Race Class and Education*, eds. Leon Barton and Stephen Walker. London: Croom Helm:17–39.

White, Deborah. 1988. "Half the Sky but no Room of her Own: Women in the Built Environment." *Transitions* 25: 23–32.

White, Rob. 1990. *No Space of their Own: Young People and Social Control in Australia.* Melbourne: Cambridge University Press.

--- ed. 1993. *Youth Subcultures: Theory, History and The Australian Experience.* Hobart Tasmania: National Clearing House for Youth Studies.

Whiteley, Sheila. ed. 1997. *Sexing The Groove: Popular Music and Gender.* London: Routledge.

Willett, John. ed. and transl. 1964 [1957]. *Brecht on Theatre: The development of an aesthetic;* rev. ed. London: Methuen.

Williams, Linda, 1983. "When a Woman Looks." In *Re-Vision: Essays in Feminist Film Criticism*, eds. Mary Doane et al. Frederick, Md: University Publications of America: 83–99.

_____ 1989. *Hard Core: Power, Pleasure and Frenzy of the Visible.* Berkeley: University of California Press.

Williamson, Judith. 1986. *Consuming Passions: The Dynamics of Popular Culture.* London: Marion Boyars.

Willis, Paul. 1977. *Learning to Labour.* Farnborough: Saxon House.

_____ 1990. *Common Culture.* Buckingham: Open University Press.

Willis, Roy. 1994. "New Shaminism." *Anthropology Today,* 10: 6 (Dec): 16–18.

Wilson, Elizabeth. *The Sphinx in the City: Urban Life, the Control of Disorder and Women.* London: Virago.

Wimbush, Erica, and Margaret Talbot, eds. 1988. *Relative Freedoms: Women and Leisure.* Milton Keynes: Open University Press.

Winnicott, Donald W. 1971. *Playing and Reality.* London: Tavistock.

Wolf, Eric R. 1966. "Kinship, Friendship and Patron-Client Relations in Complex Societies." In *The Social Anthropology of Complex Societies,* ed. Michael Batton. ASA Monograph, no. 4. London: Tavistock Publications.

Wolf, Naomi. 1990. *The Beauty Myth: How Images of Beauty are used against Women.* London: Chatto and Windus.

Woolf, Virginia. 1977. *A Room of One's Own.* London: Penguin.

Wulff, Helena. 1988. *Twenty Girls.* Stockholm Studies in Social Anthropology, no. 21: Stockholm: Department of Social Anthropology, University of Stockholm.

_____ 1995. "Introducing Youth Culture in Its Own Right: the state of the art and new possibilities." In *Youth Cultures: a cross cultural perspective,* eds. Helena Wulff and Vered Amit-Talai. London: Routledge: 1–18.

Wulff, Helena. and Vered Amit-Talai. eds. 1995. *Youth Cultures, a cross cultural perspective.* London: Routledge.

Yeatman, Anna. ed. 1984. "Gender and Social Life." *Social Analysis: Journal of Cultural and Social Practice,* Special Issue Series: no. 15, August.

Yeatman, Anna, 1990. "A Feminist Theory of Social Differentiation." In *Feminism and Post-modernism,* ed. Linda J. Nicolson. New York: Routledge: 281–299.

Young, Jock. 1971. *The Drugtakers.* Harmondsworth: Penguin.

Index

D

E

F